高职高专物业管理专业系列教材

物业管理英语

全国房地产行业培训中心组织编写
王 娜 主 编
王亚男 副主编
王世庆 主 审

中国建筑工业出版社

图书在版编目(CIP)数据

物业管理英语/全国房地产行业培训中心组织编写.
北京：中国建筑工业出版社，2004
（高职高专物业管理专业系列教材）
ISBN 978-7-112-06619-3

Ⅰ.物… Ⅱ.全… Ⅲ.物业管理—英语—高等
学校：技术学校—教材 Ⅳ.H31

中国版本图书馆 CIP 数据核字(2004)第 071683 号

高职高专物业管理专业系列教材
物 业 管 理 英 语
全国房地产行业培训中心组织编写
王　娜　主　编
王亚男　副主编
王世庆　主　审

*

中国建筑工业出版社出版、发行（北京西郊百万庄）
各地新华书店、建筑书店经销
北京市密东印刷有限公司印刷

*

开本：787×1092 毫米　1/16　印张：21½　字数：520 千字
2004 年 9 月第一版　　2009 年 7 月第四次印刷
定价：29.00 元
ISBN 978-7-112-06619-3
(12573)

版权所有　翻印必究
如有印装质量问题，可寄本社退换
（邮政编码 100037）

本书共 10 个单元,每个单元包括课文、对话、补充阅读和写作练习四大部分。课文主要选自澳大利亚、英美物业管理和房地产专著及杂志,内容包括物业管理概述、物业管理相关合同、维修管理、能源管理、成本管理等,文后附有词汇表、注释、练习等内容;对话部分针对物业管理公司日常用语及专业服务语言流程规范而编写,分为经典短句和情景对话两部分,对话后配有相关练习;补充阅读部分内容主要为英美背景知识介绍,文后附有练习。第五单元后配有期中练习,第十单元后配有期末练习。书后附录包括练习答案、词汇表、不规则动词表、物业管理从业人员日常用语、物业管理常用的信函、文本与合同等内容。

　　本书可作为高职高专物业管理专业、房地产专业及相关专业学生使用教材,对学员传授一些基础英语知识,训练他们的基本语言技能,使之能够初步运用英语进行物业管理会话,同时能巩固他们的物业管理专业知识。也可作为正在从事和有志于从事物业管理工作人员的专业英语进修课本。

* * *

责任编辑　　吉万旺
责任设计　　崔兰萍
责任校对　　李志瑛　　王金珠

《高职高专物业管理专业系列教材》编委会名单

(以姓氏笔画为序)

主　　任：肖　云

副 主 任：王　钊　杨德恩　张弘武　陶建民

委　　员：王　娜　刘　力　刘喜英　杨亦乔　吴锦群

　　　　　佟颖春　汪　军　张莉祥　张秀萍　段莉秋

参编单位：全国房地产行业培训中心

　　　　　天津工商职业技术学院

　　　　　天津市房管局职工大学

前　言

作为《物业管理系列教材》之一的《物业管理英语》一书的问世，主要源于物业管理从业人员的实际需求。经过调研我们认为物业管理从业人员掌握一定的物业管理专业英语知识及具备一定的英语会话能力是非常必要的。

本书编写力求实用性强、翻译流畅、内容全面。为了便于教师讲授和学生学习，准备了补充对话、补充阅读、词汇知识等许多内容，以便把物业管理专业知识与英语语言技能有机地结合在一起。

本书由天津外国语学院英语学院副院长、副教授王世庆同志主审；天津市物业管理招投标服务中心主任刘喜英同志和澳大利亚新南威尔士房协为本书的编写提供了大量资料，特此致谢。

由于编者水平有限，书中缺点错误在所难免，恳请广大读者不吝指正。

编者
2004 年 3 月

Contents 目 录

Unit 1. Property Management ········· 1
  Part 1. Text   An Introduction to Property Management ········· 1
  Part 2. Dialogue   Welcome! New Owners ········· 11
  Part 3. Supplementary Reading: ········· 15
          Passage A United States of America——A Melting Pot ········· 15
          Passage B American Festivals ········· 17
  Part 4. Practical Writing ········· 18

Unit 2. Building Maintenance ········· 19
  Part 1. Text   An Introduction to Building Maintenance ········· 19
  Part 2. Dialogue   Move Into the New House ········· 32
  Part 3. Supplementary Reading:
          How To Be True To You Give wisely and carry a big stick ········· 36
  Part 4. Practical Writing ········· 40

Unit 3. Performance of Building Services ········· 41
  Part 1. Text   Performance of Building Services ········· 41
  Part 2. Dialogue   Room Decoration ········· 55
  Part 3. Supplementary Reading: British Pub Customs ········· 59
  Part 4. Practical Writing   个人简历写作参考 ········· 62

Unit 4. Security ········· 64
  Part 1. Text   Security ········· 64
  Part 2. Dialogue   Parking Car in the Community I ········· 77
  Part 3. Supplementary Reading: Tips on Tipping ········· 82
  Part 4. Practical Writing   求职信(Position Application) ········· 85

Unit 5. Comprehensive Contract Maintennace ········· 87
  Part 1. Text   Comprehensive Contract Maintennace ········· 87
  Part 2. Dialogue   Parking in the Community II ········· 99
  Part 3. Supplementary Reading: If Only ········· 103
  Part 4. Pratical Writing   求职信范例 ········· 106

期中测试 ·· 108
    Part 1. 专业练习 ·· 108
    Part 2. 能力练习 ·· 115

Unit 6. Reducing Cost ·· 124
    Part 1. Text　Reducing Cost ·· 124
    Part 2. Dialogue　Welcoming the Visitors ··· 136
    Part 3. Supplementary Reading： ··· 140
        Passage A　China to Improve Community Health Service System ·········· 140
        Passage B　President George W. Bush ··· 141
    Part 4. Practical Writing 常用句首短语及句式
        (Phrases and Sentences used to Start an Essay) ··· 144

Unit 7. Maintenance ··· 146
    Part 1. Text　Maintenance ·· 146
    Part 2. Dialogue　Pets Management ·· 162
    Part 3. Supplementary Reading： ··· 166
        Passage A　Country & Town ··· 166
        Passage B　Thanks and Apologies ··· 168
    Part 4. Practical Writing 常用句尾短语及句式
        (Phrases and Sentences Used to End and Essay) ··· 170

Unit 8. Monitoring The Cleaning Contract ·· 171
    Part 1. Text　Monitoring The Cleaning Contract ··· 171
    Part 2. Dialogue　Cleaning Service in Community I ··· 184
    Part 3. Supplementary Reading：
        Passage A　The Standard of Living ·· 189
        Passage B　What does an astronaut look like? ·· 191
    Part 4. Practical Writing 有关抱怨函的回复(Reply) ··· 193

Unit 9. Emergency Evacuation ·· 195
    Part 1. Text　Introduction ·· 195
    Part 2. Dialogue　Cleaning Service in Community II ·· 207
    Part 3. Reading Activity：A boy with a Mission ··· 211
    Part 4. Practical Writing 海报启事范例 ··· 215

Unit 10. Improvements in Efficiency ··· 217
    Part 1. Text　Improvements in Efficiency ··· 217
    Part 2. Dialogue Maintenance Service ·· 236

  Part 3. Supplementary Reading: Don't Sweat the Small Stuff ················ 241
  Part 4. Practical Writing 演讲致辞 ·· 246

期末测试 ·· 247
  Part 1. 专业练习 ··· 247
  Part 2. 能力练习 ··· 257
附录一 本书练习答案 Keys ··· 266
附录二 物业管理从事人员日常用语 ·· 299
附录三 物业管理常用的信函、文本与合同（中文参考） ···························· 308
附录四 本书生词表 Word List ·· 315
附录五 不规则动词 ·· 326
参考文献 ·· 333

Unit 1. Property Management

Part 1. Text

An Introduction to Property Management

What is property management? First of all, you have to know what property is. In simple terms[1], property means what one owns. Your books, your cash and your savings in the banks all can be called your personal property.

However, property can mean something else. Consider the following example.

Suppose a company pays the local government a large sum of money for 100 acres of land usage[2]. Then this company builds several dozens of residential houses, houses for people to live in. In addition, it sets up a bank, a post office, a school and other public services. Undoubtedly, the above-mentioned are all property. As a matter of fact[3], this is what the word property means in Property Management: land and its buildings. Therefore, property management is the process of overseeing the operation and maintenance of real property to achieve the objectives of the property owner.

Property management has long been an underrated function in the real estate industry. The need for professional management did not become apparent until the depression of the 1930s[4], when numerous foreclosures revealed a pattern of management deficiencies. This oversight might seem strange, since running a large commercial or residential project in which hundreds or thousands of people reside or work is a highly challenging task, calling for training, good judgment, and a variety of technical skills. Traditionally, however, the emphasis in the real estate industry has been on the so-called permanent elements of the investment.—— good location, sound construction, and resonable long-term financing——rather than on the day-to-day operation of the property. It has sometimes seemed as if a property owner, having made a very large investment in the permanent structure, assumed that the property would run itself with a minimum amount of supervision.

This concept of property management has changed substantially in the past decade. In an era of rising costs, it has dawned on owners that good property management is the major controllable influence on residual cash flow (i. e., the number of dollars that end up in the owner's pocket). It is true that both rent rates and operating expenses are largely shaped by market forces beyond the control of any one property owner[5] (witness the very sharp rise in energy costs in the 1970s). But it is also true that comparable properties within the same geographic area often show significant variances in rental income and operating costs. Why? Close inspection often shows that "above-average" operating expenses and lower than average rent levels result from inadequate property management. The classic mistake of the stock and bond investor moving into real estate involves underestimating the importance of management. Some investors have the feeling that real estate manages itself. There is a story about the importance of property management. A San Francisco real estate broker recently noticed a project that was on the market for $1 million. He knew how the property had been managed in the past and that the million dollar valuation was based on a capitalization of historic income figure. He borrowed money to buy the property, renegotiated certain leases, and established more efficient operating procedures. In six months he sold the property for $1.4 million based on the capitalized value of the new, higher net income. His contribution was management expertise.

参考译文：

对物业管理的介绍

什么是物业管理？首先，你得明白什么是财产。简单地说，财产就是一个人所拥有的东西。你的书本，你的现金和你在银行的存款都是你的私人财产。

可是，property 这个词还可以指别的东西。请看下面的例子：

比如，某公司付给地方政府一大笔钱，获得了使用 100 英亩土地的权力。然后公司修建了数十栋住宅楼，它还设立了银行、邮局、学校和其他公共设施。毫无疑问，上面提到的这些都是财产。实际上，上述东西正是 Property Management 这个词语中 property 所指：土地和建筑。因此，物业管理是监督物业运行和维护以实现业主目标的过程。

长期以来，物业管理在地产业中的作用被低估了。直到 20 世纪 30 年代的大萧条时期，对专业化物业管理的需要才显现出来。当时大量的取消赎回权反映了一系列的管理缺陷。这一疏忽，看似奇怪，但对于一个大型商用或居住物业来说，由于成百上千或成千上万的人居住或工作在其中，要对其实施管理，是一项非常具有挑战性的任务。该任务要求管理者受过培训，并具有良好的判断力和各种技能。但是，传统意义上的地产业重点是放在所谓的投资永久性因素上——好地点、好建筑和合理的长期财务收支——而不是日复一日的物业运作。好像只要业主在永久性因素上投了巨资，物业自身就能在最少的监督管理下自我运作。

近十年来物业管理的概念已在本质上发生了变化。业主已明白：如果费用上涨，良好的物业管理是剩余现金流量的主要可控制性影响因素（即业主口袋里最终拥有的现金数）。租金和运行开支很大程度上由市场力量决定，而不由任何业主控制（如 20 世纪 70 年代的能源费用暴涨），这是事实。而在同一地理位置上的类似物业在租金收入和运作开支上时常表现出很大的差异，这也是事实。这是什么原因呢？仔细分析便可发现：高于平均水平的运作开支和低于平均水平的租金收入都是由于管理不善而引发的。购买地产股票和债券的投资者所犯的典型错误,就包括了低估管理的重要性。一些投资者有物业可自行运作的想法。有一个关于物业管理重要性的故事。一位旧金山的地产经纪人近来注意到有一个100万的物业在市场上出售。他知道该物业过去的管理状况,并清楚100万美元的估价是基于其过去的现金流量所给出的。于是,他借钱买下了该物业,并重新制订了某些租赁条款,建立了更为有效的运作机制。6个月后,他以140万美元价格卖掉这幢物业,该价格是以新的更高的净收入的投资价值为基础制订的。他的贡献就在于专业化管理。

Vocabulary
单词表:

1.	property	['prɔpəti]	n.	财产,所有物,所有权,性质,特性,(小)道具
2.	management	['mænidʒmənt]	n.	经营,管理,处理,操纵,驾驶,手段
3.	residential	[ˌrezi'denʃəl]	adj.	住宅的,与居住有关的
4.	undoubtedly	[ʌn'dautidli]	adv	无庸置疑地,的确地
5.	process	['prəses]	n.	过程,作用,方法,程序,步骤,进行,推移
			vt.	加工,处理
6.	oversee	['əuvə'si:]	v.	俯瞰,监视,检查,视察
7.	maintenance	['meintinəns]	n.	维护,保持,生活费用,抚养
8.	underrate	[ˌʌndə'reit]	vt.	低估,看轻
9.	professional	[prə'feʃnl]	n.	自由职业者,专业人员,职业运动员,职业艺人
			adj.	专业的,职业的
10.	apparent	[ə'pærənt]	adj.	显然的,外观上的
11.	depression	[di'preʃn]	n.	沮丧,消沉,低气压,低压
12.	foreclosures	[fɔ:'kləuʒə(r)]	n.	丧失抵押品赎回权,排斥
13.	deficiency	[di'fiʃnsi]	n.	缺乏,不足
14.	oversight	['əuvəsait]	n.	勘漏,失察,疏忽,失败,小心照顾
15.	commercial	[kə'mə:ʃəl]	adj.	商业的,贸易的
16.	challenging	['tʃælindʒiŋ]	adj.	引起挑战性兴趣的,挑逗的
17.	investment	[in'vestmənt]	n.	投资,可获利的东西
18.	permanent	['pə:mənənt]	adj.	永久的,持久的
19.	supervision	[ˌsju:pə'viʒən]	n.	监督,管理
20.	substantially	[səb'stænʃ(ə)li]	adv.	充分地
			n.	黎明,拂晓,破晓
21.	dawn	[dɔ:n]	vi.	破晓,开始出现,变得(为人所)明白
			v.	破晓
22.	flow	[fləu]	n.	流程,流动,(河水)泛滥,洋溢
			vi.	流动,涌流,川流不息,飘扬
			vt.	溢过,淹没

23. expense	[ik'spens]	n.	费用，代价，损失，开支，费钱之物
24. comparable	['kɔmpərəbl]	adj.	可比较的，比得上的
25. inspection	[in'spekʃən]	n.	检查，视察
26. valuation	[vælju'eiʃən]	n.	估价，评价，计算
27. capitalization	[kəpitəlai'zeiʃən]	n.	资本化，股本，资本总额，大写
28. negotiate	[ni'gənʃieit]	v.	（与某人）商议，谈判，磋商，买卖，让渡（支票、债券等），通过，越过
renegotiate	['ri:ni'gəuʃieit]	vt.	重新谈判
29. contribution	[ˌkɔntri'bju:ʃən]	n.	捐献，贡献，投稿
30. expertise	[ˌekspə'ti:z]	n.	专家的意见，专门技术

Useful Expressions

first of all	首先，第一
in addition	此外，加上，并且
set up	提出意见，排版，建立，创立，开办，竖立，振作精神
not…until…	直到……时候才……
as if	好像
in the past decade	在过去十年中

Notes
备注：

1. "In simple terms"的意思是简而言之。其中"term"一词既有"学期，期限，期间"又有"术语，条件，表达方式"的意思。在此处其意为"表达方式"。

2. "Suppose a company pays the local government a large sum of money for…"的意思是："比如，某公司付给地方政府一大笔钱，获得了使用100英亩土地的权力。"其中，"pay…for…"为短语，意为："为……而花费……". 例如，"I paid 3 yuan for this pen"："我花3元钱买了这支钢笔。"

3. "As a matter of fact…"："实际上……". 在这个短语中"fact"的意思是"事实"；"as a matter of fact"意为"实际上……". 类似意思的短语还有："in fact"，"as the case stands"；类似的词语有："actually"，"practically"和"virtually"。

4. "The need for professional management did not become apparent until the depression of the 1930s,…"意为："直到20世纪30年代的大萧条时期，专业化管理的需要才显现出来". 在此句中隐含着一个句型"…not…until…"："直到……才……"，例如，"I didn't get up until 10 o'clock."："我直到10点才起床。"

5. "It is true that both rent rates and operating expenses are largely shaped by market forces beyond the control of any one property owner"：意为："租金和运行开支很大程度上由市场力量决定，而不由任何业主控制，这是事实。"其中，大家应当掌握的句型是"It is…that…"，此句中的"It"没有任何意思，只是起到代词的作用，代词"that"引导的从句中的内容。例如，"It is well known that nobody is allowed to smoke in the public place."："众所周知，公共场合不准吸烟。"

Ⅰ. Exercises for the text(课文练习)

(Ⅰ) Decide whether the following sentences are True or False according to the content of the text.

1. Property means what one owns.
2. In Property Management, the word property means land and its buildings.
3. Property management is the process of overseeing the owners' personal money.
4. The need for professional management is always apparent in the history.
5. The traditional emphasis in the real estate industry has been on the permanent elements of the investment.
6. The traditional concept of property management has never changed and last to nowadays.
7. Both rent rates and operating expenses are largely affected by market forces instead of the control of any one-property owner.
8. It is a belief of some investors that real estate needs no management at all.
9. The story from San Francisco tells us about the importance of property management.
10. The San Francisco estate broker's success is contributed by the professional management.

(Ⅱ) Match the words in column A with their corresponding explanation in column B with a bar.

Column A	Column B
1. undoubtedly	a. cost
2. flow	b. fully
3. oversee	c. lasting
4. professional	d. expert
5. expense	e. certainly
6. dawn	f. evident
7. substantially	g. monitor
8. supervision	h. currency
9. permanent	i. inspect
10. apparent	j. daybreak

(Ⅲ) Choose the best answer(选择最佳答案):

1. "The teacher can't be in the office now, _____ she?" "Yes, I think, she _____ be there."
   a. mustn't...can't   b. can't...mustn't   c. must...can   d. can...must
2. That company will not take anyone _____ eyesight is weak or hearing is bad.
   a. of whom   b. who   c. that   d. whose
3. Our teacher often had us _____ our homework before the class began.
   a. hand in   b. handing in   c. handed in   d. to be handed in

5

4. They decided _____ at once _____ on our match till next Wednesday because of the snow.
   a. delay...go b. to delay...to go
   c. to delay...going d. delaying...going
5. "Listen, Wang Ling is crying in the next room." "That _____ be Wang Ling, she is at school."
   a. shouldn't b. can't c. may not d. wouldn't
6. The poor man stopped in the doorway and _____ a final look before he went out.
   a. took b. take c. takes d. will take
7. Wang Ling said she _____ love to come and see you again, but could not.
   a. had b. would c. should d. could
8. Zhang Hong _____ last month, so he had to go out every day to look for work.
   a. is fired b. was fired c. has fired d. would fire
9. _____ do you make in your job every month?
   a. How many b. How often c. How much d. How long
10. I have not got the book at hand, but I _____ it to you later.
    a. show b. showed c. would show d. will show

(Ⅳ) Translation

Translate the following Chinese into English

1. 简单地说,财产就是一个人所拥有的东西。
2. 长期以来,物业管理在地产业中的作用被低估了。
3. 该任务要求管理者受过培训,并具有良好的判断力和各种技能。
4. 良好的物业管理是剩余现金流最主要的可控制性影响因素。
5. 一些投资者有物业可自行运作的想法。
6. 物业管理是监督物业运行和维护以实现业主目标的过程。
7. 那是一项非常具有挑战性的任务。
8. 但是,传统意义上的地产业重点是放在投资的所谓永久性因素上。
9. 租金和运行开支很大程度上由市场力量决定。
10. 他的贡献就在于专业化管理。

(Ⅴ) Extra Reading Activity

Extra reading: read the following passage and choose the best answer to complete each of the statements that follow.

PROPERTY MANAGEMENT

The asset management role is completely compatible with the more detailed property management role discussed elsewhere in this semester.

The property management functions contribute to asset management in many ways. Stewardship, that is insurance and risk management, will be very much day to day issues important to asset management.

The Property Manager will, in broad terms, be seeking to maximise income and minimise expenditure, within reasonable limits, in operational terms.

It could be viewed that property management is an operational function related very much to the existing investment format. It may reflect a relatively short to medium term outlook, e.g. 3~5 years.

The Property Manager's operating plan should have been developed in conjunction with the asset manager. The latter is likely to have prepared longer term strategic plans including capital expenditure plans.

WHAT IS ASSET MANAGEMENT?

Asset management has been previously described as the role of maximising the value of the investment to the investor.

The need for, and development of, the asset management role has come about largely through the development of large investment portfolios, both public and private, where a structured management approach was needed and subsequently evolved. Asset management describes the role which could be fulfilled by a person known as the asset manager.

In such institutional portfolios there may also be substantial investment in cash, bonds, equities and/or operating assets as well as property.

The asset manager is the specialist who directs and accepts ultimate responsibility for investment decisions leading to achievement of the overall objective(s) of the ownership of these assets.

Equally an asset manager might be referred to as a portfolio manager or investment manager.

1. The asset management role is _____.
   a. to contribute to property management in many ways
   b. completely compatible with the more detailed property management role discussed elsewhere in this semester
   c. insurance and risk management
   d. very much day to day issues important
2. Which of the following statements is not true?
   a. The property management functions contribute to asset management in many ways.
   b. The Property Manager will, in broad terms, be seeking to maximise income and minimize expenditure, within reasonable limits, in operational terms.
   c. The property management is not an operational function related very much to the existing investment format.
   d. The property management may reflect a relatively short to medium term outlook.
3. The Property Manager's operating plan should have been developed in conjunction with _____.
   a. the asset manager   b. the owner
   c. the contracter   d. other manager
4. _____ role has come about largely through the development of large investment

portfolios, both public and private, where a structured management approach was needed and subsequently evolved.

    a. The property management   b. The building management
    c. The maintenance management   d. The asset management

5. The asset manager is not _____.
    a. the specialist who directs and accepts ultimate responsibility for investment decisions leading to achievement of the overall objective(s) of the ownership of these assets
    b. might be referred to as a portfolio manager
    c. might be referred to as a investment manager
    d. seeking to maximise income and minimize expenditure, within reasonable limits, in operational terms

Ⅱ. Language Ability Drill(语言能力练习)

(Ⅰ) Vocabulary Exercise

Study the following words. Then choose proper words for the sentences below.

Verbs	Nouns	Adjectives(形容词)	Adverbs(副词)
care	care	careful	carefully
	carelessness	careless	carelessly
add	addition	additional	
use	use	useful	
		useless	
		used	
mean	meaning	meaningful	
		meaningless	
comfort	comfort	comfortable	comfortably
	probability	probable	probably

1. carelessness, careful, careless, carefully, carelessly, care(v.), care(n.)

  1) You should be very _____, and not to say anything to Paul.
  2) Xiao Hong _____ for the old man as if he were her own father.
  3) A _____ driver is a danger not only to us but also to himself or herself.
  4) All the students in this school are taken good _____ of.
  5) If Jane drove much more _____ she wouldn't have made so many accidents.
  6) He is not a diligent(勤奋) student. He shows great _____ in everything he does.
  7) Spend more time on your study, Tom. You really did your homework very _____.
  8) You should be more _____ in future about your saying.

2. add, addition, additional

  1) In _____ to English, Wang Hai speaks another foreign language.
  2) He should attend to an _____ class for this examination.

3) Please _____ more salt to make it more tasty.

4) This is an _____ of (证据) of his carelessness.

3. use (v.), use (n.), useful, useless, used

1) Students should make good _____ of their free time after class.

2) I want to buy a new bicycle since this one is broken (坏了) and is completely _____.

3) May I _____ your pen for an hour or two?

4) This is a very _____ guidebook for travelers.

5) I don't have much money, so I want to buy a _____ car instead of a new one.

6) What's the _____ of complaining?

4. mean, meaning, meaningful, meaningless

1) Could you explain what is the _____ of this sentence?

2) The more you read the poem, the more _____ you will find from it.

3) Stopping making improvement _____ moving backwards.

4) It's a waste of time playing such a _____ game.

5) To some young men, marriage _____ losing freedom.

5. comfort (v.), comfort (n.), comfortable, comfortably

1) You need to find a place that both of you can sit _____.

2) I'm trying to _____ her, but it doesn't work at all.

3) Be seated, please, and make yourself _____.

4) Young people should not seek _____ and enjoyment and shirk (逃避) hardship.

5) Taking a _____ travel is the selection of many families for their vocation.

6. probability, probable, probably

1) If you go to the park early in the morning, you will _____ taking a walk there.

2) In all _____ she will go to U.S for further study.

3) It is _____ that the interest of the loan will increase.

4) Mary is _____ the worst teacher in this primary school.

(Ⅱ) Cloze

Some thirty years ago, I was studying in a public school in New York. One day, Mrs. Nanette O'Neill gave an arithmetic 1 to our class. When the papers were 2 she discovered that twelve boys had made exactly the 3 mistakes throughout the test. There is nothing really new about 4 in exams. Perhaps that was why Mrs. O'Neill 5 even say a word about it. She only asked the twelve boys to 6 after class. I was one of the twelve. Mrs. O'Neill asked 7 questions, and she didn't 8 us either. Instead, she wrote on the blackboard the 9 words by Thomas Macaulay. She then ordered us to 10 these words into our exercise-books one hundred times. I don't 11 about the other eleven boys. Speaking for 12 I can say: it was the most important single 13 of my life. Thirty years after being 14 to Macaulay's words, they 15 seem to me the best yardstick(准绳), because they give us a 16 to measure ourselves rather than oth-

9

ers.   17   of us are asked to make   18   decisions about nations going to war or armies going to battle. But all of us are called   19   daily to make a great many personal decisions.   20   the wallet, found in the street, be put into a pocket   21   mined over to the policeman? Should the   22   change received at the store be forgotten or   23 ? Nobody will know except   24 . But you have to live with yourself, and it is always   25   to live with someone you respect.

1. A. test   B. problem   C. paper   D. lesson
2. A. examined   B. completed   C. marked   D. answered
3. A. easy   B. funny   C. same   D. serious
4. A. lying   B. cheating   C. guessing   D. discussing
5. A. didn't   B. did   C. would   D. wouldn't
6. A. come   B. leave   C. remain   D. apologize
7. A. no   B. certain   C. many   D. more
8. A. excuse   B. reject   C. help   D. scold
9. A. above   B. common   C. following   D. unusual
10. A. repeat   B. get   C. put   D. copy
11. A. worry   B. know   C. hear   D. talk
12. A. myself   B. ourselves   C. themselves   D. herself
13. A. chance   B. incident   C. lesson   D. memory
14. A. referred   B. shown   C. brought   D. introduced
15. A. even   B. still   C. always   D. almost
16. A. way   B. sentence   C. choice   D. reason
17. A. All   B. Few   C. Some   D. None
18. A. quick   B. wise   C. great   D. personal
19. A. out   B. for   C. up   D. upon
20. A. Should   B. Must   C. Would   D. Need
21. A. and   B. or   C. then   D. but
22. A. extra   B. small   C. some   D. necessary
23. A. paid   B. remembered   C. shared   D. returned
24. A. me   B. you   C. us   D. them
25. A. easier   B. more natural   C. better   D. more peaceful

(Ⅲ) **Fulfill sentences according to the Chinese given in the bracket**(按照括号中的中文完成句子)：

1. I took an English book with me (以便有空可以读一下).
2. He posted the letter early in the morning (为的是让她下午能收到).
3. Would you speak a little louder (好让每个人都听得见)?
4. We'd better get some milk, some bread, (再弄一些鸡蛋).
5. He is a versatile (多才多艺) writer. He writes poems, novels, (还有剧本).
6. Last year he visited Japan, Canada, (还有美国).

7. He plays basketball and football,（他还游泳、滑冰(skate)）.

8. You should （尽早给他们一个答复）.

9. （请尽快把这本书看完）. I have to return it to the library tomorrow afternoon.

10. When he left his parents he promised them that he would （尽量多写家信）.

Part 2. Dialogue

Welcome! New Owners
（欢迎您的到来，新业主）

Ⅰ. **Typical Sentences**（经典短句）

（Ⅰ）**Daily Conversations**（日常用语）

欢迎语：Welcome to our habitation community.
　　　　欢迎来到我们的居住小区。
　　　　Welcome to become one of members in this habitation community.
　　　　欢迎您成为这里的一员。

问候语：How are you!（Hi! Hello!）
　　　　你好！（回答为：Fine, thank you!）
　　　　Good morning! Good afternoon! Good evening!
　　　　早晨好！　　　下午好！　　　晚上好！

见面语：Come in , please!
　　　　请进！
　　　　Take a seat , please!
　　　　请坐！
　　　　Have some tea , please.
　　　　请用茶！

（Ⅱ）**Professional Conversation**（专业会话）

1. The residential fees includes charges for cleaning rubbish, using elevator, the deposit for room decoration and one-year property management toll.
   入住费用包括垃圾清运费、电梯使用费、装修押金及一年物业费。

2. The property management toll is charged on the building proportion.
   物业费按建筑面积计算。

3. The property management toll should include the Integrated Service Charge proved by OPS (Office Price Stabilization) and the cost from running the water pump in the building.
   物业费包括物价局批的综合管理费和楼内水泵运行发生的费用。

4. After you finish registering for the residence, people from engineering division will help you with building test.
   办完入住后由工程部人员跟您去验房。

5. You are required to fill in the application form before starting your decoration work.
   装修前必须填写装修申请表。

11

Ⅱ. Conversation Passages

(Ⅰ) Passage 1.

A: Good morning, sir. Can I help you?
早上好,先生。有什么我可以为您效劳的吗?

B: Yes, I would like to know the price of the houses here.
嗯,我想了解一下这里的房价。

A: We have many patterns for you to choose. Some of them are our special offer.
我们有许多式样供您选择。有一些特价房。

B: Oh, really? But I have no idea about what kind of patterns should I choose.
哦,是吗?可是我真的不知道该看些什么样式的。

A: It's O. K. What price range do you prefer?
没关系。您的预算在多少的价格范围之内?

B: Well, something between 400000 to 450000.
在40万到45万之间吧。

A: You can take a look at these patterns. They are all in your range.
您可以看一下这几款,价格都在您所要求的范围内。

B: Thank you very much.
非常感谢。

(Ⅱ) Passage 2.

A: May I come in?
我可以进来吗?

B: Sure, come in, please. Can I help you?
当然了,请进。您有什么事吗?

A: I want to consult you about the business of inhabitation and decoration.
我想向您咨询一下有关入住和装修的事。

B: I see. Sit down, please and have some tea.
我知道了。坐吧,请喝茶。

A: Is there any fee should I pay for?
我需要付些什么费用?

B: The residential fees, I think, which includes charges for cleaning rubbish, using elevator, the deposit for room decoration and one-year property management toll.
我想您需要办理入住费用,它包括垃圾清运费、电梯使用费、装修押金及一年物业费。

A: How is the property management toll measured?
物业管理费怎么计算?

B: The property management toll is charged on the building proportion. It includes the Integrated Service Charge proved by OPS (Office Price Stabilization) and the cost from running the water pump in the building.

物业费按建筑面积计算。包括物价局批的综合管理费和楼内水泵运行发生的费用。

A：And how about the decoration?

那装修怎么办呢？

B：After you finish registering for the residence, people from engineering division will help you with building test. Then you can make your decoration plan. Anyway, you are required to fill in the application form before starting your decoration work.

办完入住后由工程部人员跟您去验房。之后您就可以开始设计装修了。可是在正式动工前您必须填写装修申请表。

A：Thank for your help.

感谢您的帮助。

B：It's my pleasure!

这是我的荣幸！

Ⅲ. Exercises for Dialogue in text.

(Ⅰ) Fill in the following blanks while observing the conversational manner（按照日常会话习惯完成以下填空）

A：How are you!

B：_____!

A：_____?

B：Yes, please tell me how to get to the engineering division?

A：It is just behind this building. You can find it right beside the fountain.

B：_____.

A：_____.

(Ⅱ) Make a conversation with your partner about asking the price of the house. (there should be at least 3 turn-taking in the dialogue)

Ⅳ. Spoken Language Drill (fill in the blanks according to the Chinese translation)

Dialogue 1.

A：Excuse me. Could you please tell me how to _____ to the station?

劳驾,请问到火车站去怎么走？

B：Turn left at the first light. You can't _____ it.

到第1排红绿灯处往左拐。你肯定会找到的。

A：Will it take me _____ to get there?

到那里要花很长的时间吗？

B：No. It's not far at all.

不用。很近的。

A：Thank you.

谢谢你了。

B：You are welcome.

13

不用谢。

Dialogue 2.

A：Excuse me. Can you tell me where Main Street is?
　　劳驾,你能告诉我正街在哪里吗?

B：Turn left at the second light and then go _____ for two blocks.
　　到第 2 排红绿灯处往左拐,然后一直往前走,过两个街区。

A：Is it far?
　　远吗?

B：No. It's only a _____ walk.
　　不远。只需走 5 分钟。

A：Thanks a lot.
　　多谢。

B：You're welcome.
　　别客气。

Dialogue 3.

A：Pardon me. I _____ if you could tell me how to get to Mott Street?
　　对不起,不知道你能否告诉我到莫特街怎么走?

B：Keep going straight for two blocks, then turn right on Elm street and you'll run right into it.
　　一直走,过两个街区,然后往右拐是埃尔姆街,再往前走,迎面就是莫特街。

A：Is it too far to walk?
　　走着去很远吗?

B：No. It's only _____ way.
　　不远,只有一小段路。

A：Thanks.
　　谢谢。

B：Sure. Have a good day.
　　应该的。祝你度过愉快的一天。

Dialogue 4.

A：Can you help me out? I'm trying to find a post office.
　　你能帮我个忙吗? 我想找个邮局。

B：Go three _____ and make a right turn. It's _____ there.
　　过 3 个街区,然后往右拐。那里就有个邮局。

A：Should I take the bus?
　　要乘公共汽车吗?

B：No. It's only _____ about five minutes to walk.
　　不用。只需走 5 分钟左右就到了。

A：Thank you very much.
　　太谢谢你了。

14

B: Any time.
随时都愿意效劳。

Part 3. Supplementary Reading:

Passage A
United States of America——A Melting Pot

A look at the history of the United States indicates that this country has often been called "a melting pot", where various immigrant and ethnic groups have learned to work together to build a unique nation. Even those "original" Americans, the Indians, probably walked a land bridge from Asia to North America some thousands of years ago. So, who are the real Americans? The answer is that any and all of them are! And you, no matter where you come from, could also become an American should you want to. Then you would become another addition to America's wonderfully rich "nation of immigrants". The United States is currently shifting from being a nation of immigrants of mainly European descent to one of immigrants from other parts of the world, such as Asia and Latin America. The number of recent immigrants has skyrocketed. They desire to escape economic hardship and political oppression in their native countries as well as the desire to seek a better education and a more prosperous life in America, "the land of opportunity". Although there are frequent conflicts between the cultures they have brought with them from the "old country" and those found in America, most immigrants learn to adjust to and love their adopted land. Americans have also learned much from the customs and ideas of the immigrants and are often influenced by them in subtle and interesting ways. Immigrants bring their native cultural, political, and social patterns and attitudes, varied academic and religious backgrounds, as well as their ethnic arts, sports, holidays, festivals, and foods. They have greatly enriched American life. For immigrants from all parts of the would, the United States has been a "melting pot" in which the foreigners have sometimes remained culturally and linguistically what they were in their native lands even as they move toward becoming citizens of the United States, a country whose people share a common cultural outlook and set of values. The melting pot does not melt away all recollections of another way of life in another place——nor should it. On the contrary, immigrants should maintain the languages, skills, religions, customs and arts of their own heritage, even while they are working towards entering the mainstream of American culture.

参考译文：

美国——一个熔炉

纵观美国历史，这个国家经常被称为"一个熔炉"，在此，各种移民和种族团体学会了共同建设一个独特的民族。甚至那些"本土的"美国人——印第安人,可能是几千年以前,从亚洲走过大陆桥来到北美洲的。所以,谁是真正的美国人?答案是他们中的任何一个人都是!无论你来自何处,如果你想成为美国人,就会成为美国人;你就会变成这个极其富有的"移民之国"的一个新分子。美国现在正由主要是欧洲血统移民的国家变为世界上其他各洲,如亚洲、拉丁美洲移民的国家。最近移民的数字急剧增长。他们希望摆脱在本国的经济困难、政治压迫,并在美国这片"充满机遇的土地上"寻找更好的教育和更富裕的生活。尽管他们从"故国"带来的文化与美国文化之间往往会产生冲突,但是多数移民还是学会了适应并热爱他们所归化的土地。美国人从移民的风俗和观念中也学到了很多东西,并且在极其细微和有趣的方面受到了它们的影响。移民们带来了他们本族的文化、政治以及社会模式和态度,不同的学术和宗教背景,以及他们种族的艺术、体育、节日和饮食。这些极大地丰富了美国人的生活。对于世界各地的移民而言,美国已经是一个"熔炉",在这个熔炉中,甚至当外国人快要成为美国(一个其人民有着共同的一套文化观和价值观的国家)公民时,他们从文化和语言上仍然是在他们本国的样子。这个熔炉没有、也不应该熔掉对另一个地方的另一种生活方式的记忆。相反,即使移民们努力地要进入美国文化主流之中,他们也应保存自己原有的语言、技能、宗教、习惯和艺术。

Exercise for Reading(阅读练习)

1. Who are the real Americans?
   A. The local Indian people
   B. Asian people
   C. European people
   D. All the people who live in U.S

2. The word "skyrocket" here means:
   A. To fly a rocket in the sky
   B. A rocket flying in the sky
   C. To increase rapidly
   D. To decrease rapidly

3. Why more and more people want to live in America?
   A. They want to escape economic hardship and political oppression in their native countries.
   B. They are attracted by the American culture.
   C. They want to seek a better education and a more prosperous life in America.
   D. Both A and C

4. Which of the following is not brought by the immigrants to America?
   A. Firing cracker(爆竹)
   B. Eating Pizza
   C. Eating turkey(火鸡)
   D. Eating curry food(咖喱食品)

5. "The melting pot" means to
   A. Melt away all recollections of another way of life in another place
   B. Keep all recollections of another way of life in another place
   C. maintain all of the immigrants' heritage while they are working towards entering the mainstream of American culture
   D. abandon all of the immigrants' heritage while they are working towards entering the mainstream of American culture

Passage B
American Festivals
美国节日

January
1 New Year's Day（新年）
15 Martin Luther King Jr.'s Birthday
19 Martin Luther King Jr.'s Birthday Observed

February
12 Lincoln's Birthday
14 Valentine's Day（情人节）
16 President's Day
22 Washington's Birthday
25 Ash Wednesday

March
8 International Women's Day（国际妇女节）
17 St. Patrick's Day

April
1 Fools Day（愚人节）
5 Palm Sunday
10 Good Friday Arbor Day（植树节）
11 Passover
12 Easter（复活节）
17 Orthodox Holy Friday
19 Orthodox Easter
22 Secretaries Day 22 Earth Day

May
6 Nurses' Day
7 National Day of Prayer
10 Mother's Day（母亲节）
16 Armed Forces Day
25 Memorial Day Observed
30 Memorial Day

June
14 Flag Day（美国国旗纪念日）
21 Father's Day

July
4 Independence Day（美国独立日）

August
2 Friendship Day

September
7 Labor Day Grandparents Day
17 Citizenship Day
21 Rosh Hashanah
30 Yom Kippur

October
11 National Children's Day
12 Columbus Day
16 National Boss Day
17 Sweetest Day
24 United Nations Day
31 Halloween（万圣节前夜）

November
3 Election Day
11 Veterans Day（退伍军人节）
26 Thanksgiving

December
14 First Day of Hanukkah
25 Christmas（圣诞节）
26 First Day of Kwanzaa

Part 4. Practical Writing

Form of envelope: Make the address on your envelope identical to the inside address. In the upper left corner, type your address as it appears in the heading, type the receiver's address on the lower area as shown in sample1.

Your own address : Kevin Oppenheimer 2264 N. Cruger Avenue Milwaukee, Wl 53211

The receiver's address: Mr. Robert F. Stone Customer Relations Kaiser Appliances, Inc. 834 La Salle Street Chicago, IL 60632

Sample1.

```
┌─────────────────────────────────────────────────┐
│   Kevin Oppenheimer                             │
│   2264 N, Cruger Avenue                         │
│   Milwaukee. WI 53211                           │
│                                                 │
│                                                 │
│                         Mr, Robert F Stone      │
│                         Customer Reletions      │
│                         Kalser Appliances, Inc  │
│                         834 La Salle Slreet     │
│                         Chinago, IL 60632       │
│                                                 │
└─────────────────────────────────────────────────┘
```

Try to write your own envelope downside while observing the rule:

```
┌─────────────────────────────────────────────────┐
│                                                 │
│                                                 │
│                                                 │
│                    Envelope                     │
│                                                 │
│                                                 │
└─────────────────────────────────────────────────┘
```

Unit 2. Building Maintenance

Part 1. Text

An Introduction to Building Maintenance

The maintenance of buildings is an activity that often takes place in an ad hoc manner in response to breakdowns or a sudden awareness of deterioration.[1] Very few buildings have a documented record of maintenance activity going back for any length of time and not infrequently, expenses are allocated to a general account and soon lost track of. This paucity of information has a number of implications, all of them negative. It is difficult at best to estimate future expenditure if past maintenance work and associated costs are not known. A lack of identification of those areas of the buildings, which require high levels of maintenance, makes it difficult to direct design activity to improve those areas. Planning by those responsible to ensure ongoing optimum levels of service from a building facility, and corresponding user satisfaction, is therefore unlikely or not possible at all.

The above situation contrasts with the levels of planning, both technical and financial, which are undertaken in creating a new building in the first instance. Detailed feasibility studies provide financial profiles, both before and during construction, and later enduring occupancy, and form a framework in which to evaluate alternative designs, proposals and construction methods.[2] The finance for a building is assembled from a variety of sources, all of which require substantiation of the particular estimates or cost plans.

Much greater attention is now being paid to building and maintenance issues, partly because many buildings are now reaching an age when the owners need to decide whether to refurbish or rebuild, but also because many buildings are deteriorating faster than was anticipated. More attention is being paid to preventative maintenance in an attempt to defer the high costs of replacement and to ensure increased user satisfaction with the quality of the working environment and facilities provided, and thus rental provided. In many circumstances buildings contain more than just the usual plant and mechanical equipment in these cases and especially detailed records are required for such buildings.

MAINTENANCE MANAGEMENT
Fundamentals

For a maintenance plan to be truly effective, it should or must prevent a failure. That is firstly a particular item of equipment must demonstrate an identifiable "wear out" characteristic, and there must be available a defined maintenance action which prevents, or delays, this wear out. Maintenance work which achieves little in terms of improved reliability, improved performance, or does not prevent or delay, failure is necessary.

A maintenance plan must also be cost effective having regard to the total cost of likely failures.

The principal objectives of any maintenance plan should be:

To ensure the safe and reliable operation of plant or facilities.

The compliance, where necessary, with local regulations e. g. mandatory inspection of lifts, fire alarms, etc.

To ensure the plant continues to meet specified minimum acceptable performance requirements.

To maintain an "acceptable level of risk", having regard to the probability and the consequences of a failure.

BUILDING SERVICES MAINTENANCE

One of the major concerns of Building Owners and Managers is the poor quality of maintenance, primarily on air-conditioning and lifts. Poor service generally results in increased operation costs and, in some cases, heavy expenses due to failure of plant.[3] A minimum expectation should be the "upkeep" of facilities and equipment to initial design standards.

Inspections of buildings have revealed alarming trends including:

Room thermostats incorrectly calibrated resulting in the simultaneous operation of heating and cooling cycles.

Economy cycle damper motors operating in a reverse manner which, due to the air-conditioning system operating on ambient air, results in high energy costs.

Time clocks incorrectly operating the plant on holidays or in one case 24 hours per day.

All of these buildings in which these problems were observed had maintenance policies in place and were supposedly being maintained by skilled technicians.

With air-conditioning systems consuming approximately 45% of the energy required in office buildings and combined with the current high energy costs, maintenance operating budgets are becoming more and more significant to building owners and managers.

Tenants also are demanding higher standards of comfort and to achieve this end air-conditioning system controls are becoming increasingly more complex.

Building owners and managers are also now required to provide a minimum standard of maintenance with respect to the control of microorganisms. The most logical step to ensure indoor comfort, health standards and efficient running costs is a well structured maintenance program carried out by skilled and experienced personnel. The normal procedure taken by building owners to establish a maintenance program has been simply to obtain quotations from maintenance companies.

Unfortunately this results in a wide range of costs.

Maintenance service schedules need to be provided for each item of equipment.[4] Report sheets should assess the number of services required, checking procedures and any pro-active comments on those items of equipment that need attention.

On the completion of the service visit these schedules should be forwarded to the building owner or his engineer.

Continuity of service provided by the specialist maintenance contractor should be addressed with the nomination of a skilled technician who is responsible for the project and one other technician as his replacement.

Service Records play a vital role in preventive maintenance. Too often project logbooks waste away in the corners of plant rooms with no indication noted in them that any service visits have been carried out.

To this end, the maintenance specification should require that logbook records are updated and copies are forwarded with associated invoices for breakdown maintenance visits.

Automatic control systems are the most important single item in any building air-conditioning system.

They generally determine the level of comfort and system energy consumption.

Maintenance contractors generally do not have specialist control technicians, so the maintenance specification must ensure the control systems are checked and tested by the original control manufacturer. These should be carried out at quarterly or monthly intervals, depending on the size and nature of the project.

Service assurance is essential to the effectiveness of the maintenance program. Building owners and managers must be certain that the maintenance contractor has inspected the items listed and not simply ticked them off as has sometimes been the case.[5]

With increasing tenant expectations and rising energy costs, building owners and managers are realizing the importance of adhering to a well-structured maintenance program.

A correctly structured maintenance program will provide a return on investment as high as 30%, while also enhancing equipment life as well as tenant comfort and satisfaction!

参考译文：

建筑物维护介绍

房屋的维护经常是在注意到设施破损之后以特别方式进行的行为。很少有房屋会有以前任何一段时期的经常性的维护记录，当初为此所拨的各款项在一段时间后便失去了踪迹，这是司空见惯的。仅从这少量的记录中，我们发现境况是不容乐观的。如果不了解以前的维护状况和维护开支，也就无法预测未来的维护费用将会是多少。如果不知道房屋的哪些部位需要特别修护,也就很难在维护工作中改善它们的状况。于是,要使得房屋管理部门专门负责此事的人员制订出相应的维护方案,或是要满足住户的要求也就都是不可能的事了。

以上所提到的情况与当初建造房屋时在技术和财政上所制订的计划的情况形成了鲜明对比。在工程施工前、施工中以及之后的入户期间,对可行性的具体研究工作为整个工程提供了财政参考,并形成了一个系统,它可以对辅助方案,计划和施工方式进行评价。建造房屋的的资金是由许多各单项汇总得来的,而这各个单项都需要分别进行预测和计划。

现今,房屋维护越来越受重视。部分是由于许多房屋状况已到了要求房主决定是重新修护还是重建的地步;而更重要的是,许多房屋状况劣化的速度要比预期的快。更加重视对房屋的维护与保养是为了能够降低修换房体所带来的高额开销,也是为了提高用户对房屋管理部门和房主的满意度。许多情况下,对屋内设施的要求固然必要,房屋的维护记录也是不可或缺的。

维护管理
基本原理

维护计划要达到真正的有效,就要能避免一切失败的可能性。首先,特定的部件必须显示出明显的老化现象;而且,必须有一个明确的维护措施来阻止或延缓这种老化。如果维护工作在增强可靠性、增强功用方面收效甚微或无法阻止延缓老化,那失败是必然的。

考虑那些由于可能的失败所带来的成本浪费,一个维护计划也必须是能获得收益的。

任何维护计划的根本目的应该是:

确保机械或设施的安全和可靠运转。

必须遵守当地的法规。例如,对于电梯和火灾警报器的法定检查,等等

确保机械能够满足可以接受的最低功能要求。

让风险应保持在一个可以接受的水平上,尤其在考虑到失败所带来的可能性和后果时。

建筑物维护

建筑物所有者和经理们所关心的一个重要问题是:维护工作的质量偏低,特别是空调和电梯。不好的服务常常导致操作费用的增加,而且有时,机械的损坏会带来巨额的损失。最低的期望应该是使设施设备保持在最初的设计标准水平上。对于房屋的检查已经为人们敲响了警钟:

错误读取室内恒温器的刻度导致了冷热循环系统的同时操作。

由于空调系统对周围空气的调节,使得经济循环节气闸倒转造成很大的能源浪费。

计时表在节假日中错误地操作机器,或是一天二十四小时只重复做一件事。

存在这些问题的所有大楼都有适当的维护守则,而且应该是由有经验的技术员来完成的。

由于空调系统要消耗大约办公楼所需能量的45%,再加上现在能源的高额费用,维护操作预算对于房屋所有者和经理们变得越来越重要了。

同时,业主在要求更高的舒适标准,为了达到这个目的,对于空调系统的控制变得越来越复杂了。

现在,房屋所有者和经理们的维护工作还必须达到一个有关微生物控制的最低标准。

一个兼顾保证室内舒适程度、健康标准以及运营资本行之有效的最合理的方法就是做一份完善的维护计划书,并由熟练而且有经验的人员实施完成。

房屋所有者所起草的维护计划书通常只是简单重复维护公司的话。不幸的是,这样做

只会花费巨额开支。

需要为每种设备制定维护服务计划表。报告单应该估计需要提供的服务种类的数量，检查程序，以及判断任何有关值得注意的设备情况的评价。

完成服务设施巡回检查之后，这些计划表应当交予房屋所有者或他们的工程师。

专业维护承包者所提供的连贯服务应该有明确的一名负责此项工程的熟练技师，以及另外一名技师作为他的替补。

服务记录在可预防的维护工作中起着至关重要的作用。工程记录册被扔在机械室角落里，册子里对于以往进行的巡回检查没有丝毫记载，这种现象十分常见。

因此，维护工作细则应当要求记录手册中的内容每日更新，而且副本连同有关故障维修费用的单据一并上缴。

自动控制系统是任何大楼空调系统中最重要的一个环节。

通常，它决定了舒适程度和系统能量消耗的水平。

维护承包者一般没有专业控制技术人员，因此维护工作细则中必须确保由原控制系统的制造者来检查、测试控制系统。

这些工作应该每月或每季度进行一次，这要根据工程的份量和性质而定。

服务保险对于维护计划的有效实施十分重要。

房屋所有者和管理者必须清楚的是维护承包者已经仔细研究合同上的条款，而非像有些时候只是一扫而过。

随着业主期望值的增高和能量开支的增长，房屋所有者和管理者已经意识到有一个完善的维护计划是多么的重要。

一份设计良好的维护计划书能取得高达 30% 的投资回报，同时还能延长设备的寿命以及让业主得到舒适和满意。

Vocabulary

单词表：

31. maintenance	['meintinəns]	n.	维护，保持，生活费用，抚养
32. breakdown	['breikdaun]	n.	崩溃，衰弱，细目分类
33. deterioration	[di͵tiəriə'reiʃən]	n.	变坏，退化，堕落
34. allocate	['æləukeit]	vt.	分派，分配
35. paucity	['pɔːsiti]	n.	极小量
36. expenditure	[iks'penditʃə]	n.	支出，花费
37. identification	[ai͵dentifi'keiʃən]	n.	辨认，鉴定，证明，视为同一
38. ongoing	['ɔngəuiŋ]	adj.	正在进行的
39. optimum	['ɔptiməm]	n.	最适宜
		adj.	最适宜的
40. facility	[fə'siliti]	n.	容易，简易，灵巧，熟练，便利，敏捷，设备，工具
41. feasibility	[͵fiːzə'biliti]	n.	可行性，可能性
42. profile	['prəufail]	n.	剖面，侧面，外形，轮廓
43. occupancy	['ɔkjupənsi]	n.	占有

44. alternative	[ɔːlˈtɜːnətiv]	n.	二中择一，可供选择的办法，事物
		adj.	选择性的，二中择一的
45. fundamental	[ˌfʌndəˈmentl]	adj.	基础的，基本的
		n.	基本原则，基本原理
46. demonstrate	[ˈdemənstreit]	vt.	示范，证明，论证
		vi.	示威
47. characteristic	[ˌkæriktəˈristik]	adj.	特有的，表示特性的，典型的
		n.	特性，特征
48. define	[diˈfain]	vt.	定义，详细说明
49. compliance	[kəmˈplaiəns]	n.	依从，顺从
50. mandatory	[ˈmændətəri]	adj.	命令的，强制的，托管的
51. alarm	[əˈlɑːm]	n.	警报，惊慌，警告器
		vt.	恐吓，警告
52. minimum	[ˈminiməm]	adj.	最小的，最低的
		n.	最小值，最小化
53. booster	[ˈbuːstə]	n.	＜美俚＞热心的拥护者，后推的人，支持者，后援者，调压器
54. optimize	[ˈɔptimaiz]	vt.	使最优化
55. expectation	[ˌekspekˈteiʃən]	n.	期待，预料，指望，展望，[数]期望（值）
56. inspection	[inˈspekʃən]	n.	检查，视察
57. damper	[ˈdæmpə]	n.	起抑制作用的因素，节气闸，消声器
58. approximately	[əˈprɔksiˈmətli]	adv.	近似地，大约
59. tenant	[ˈtenənt]	n.	承租人，房客，租客
		v.	出租
60. enhance	[inˈhɑːns]	vt.	提高，增强
		v.	提高

Useful Expressions

take place　发生，产生，举行（会议）
not at all　不客气，不用谢，一点也不
pay attention to　注意，关心
in terms of　用……的话说，从……的角度
result in　结果，形成，导致，引起……的结果
due to　由于，归于，起因于
with respect to　关于，就……而论，在……方面
be responsible for　对……负责

Notes
备注：

1. The maintenance of buildings is an activity that often takes place in an ad hoc man-

ner in response to breakdowns or a sudden awareness of deterioration. that 所引导的是个定语从句。定语从句用来充当句中定语的主谓结构；它主要用于修饰句子中的名词、代词。而定语从句的位置常常是紧跟在被修饰的名词、代词的后面。在被修饰的名词、代词与定语从句之间往往有一个关系词将其前后两部分联系成一个整体，或是构成一个名词短语，或是构成一个代词短语。但从结构上说，关系词与从句是一个整体。排除句子的其他各部分，这种带有定语从句的名词短语或是代词短语的构成可演示如下：

1) three signs that indicate a person is suffering from a panic attack rather than a heart attack

"三种意味着一个人是患有惊恐症而不是心脏病的迹象"，在这个带有定语从句的名词短语中：

signs 是被修饰的名词；

that 是关系词；

that indicate a person is suffering from a panic attack rather than a heart attack 是定语从句。

2) those who drink a lot 那些大量饮酒的人，在这个带有定语从句的代词短语中：

those 是被修饰的名词；

who 是关系词；

who drink a lot 是定语从句

通过上面的演示，我们可以归纳出定语从句在句子中的位置、结构如下：

被修饰的名词/代词＋关系词＋句子（其中，"被修饰的名词/代词"在语法中叫作"先行词"。）

3) 关于关系代词：

关系代词有 who，whom，whose，which，that 等。

who 用于代替"表示人的意义"的先行词，并且在从句中作主语；在现代英语里，也可取代 whom 在从句中作动词的宾语。例如：

I have no idea about the man who wrote the article．

我不认识写这篇文章的那个人。

whom 用于代替"表示人的意义"的先行词，并且在从句中作动词或介词的宾语。在现代英语里，如果 whom 在从句中作动词的宾语，它与 who 可以通用；但是如果 whom 在从句中作介词的宾语，那么就只能用 whom 而不能与 who 通用了。当然，如果在口语或非正式文体中，介词没有提前，也就没有这点要求了。例如：

Who is the girl whom (who) you talked to just now ?

刚才和你说话的那个女孩子是谁？

whose 用于代替"表示人或物意义"的先行词，在从句中作定语，往往与它所修饰的名词一起构成一个名词短语在从句中担当成分。whose 常表达"某人的、某物的"之意。例如：

Do you know the name of that girl whose brother is your roommate ?

你知道她的哥哥与你同寝室的那位女孩的名字吗？

that 既用于代替"表示人的意义"的先行词，也用于代替"表示事物意义"的先行词；在从句中既可以作主语，也可以作谓语动词的宾语，但是不能作介词的宾语。在一定范围内，

that=who/whom/which。例如：

Views that (which) are entirely new or foreign may also be hard to accept.
那些全新的或是来自国外的观点或许也很难被接受。

2. Detailed feasibility studies provide financial profiles, both before and during construction, and later enduring occupancy, and form a framework in which to evaluate alternative designs, proposals and construction methods. 对可行性的具体研究工作为整个工程提供了财政参考，并形成了一个系统，它可以对辅助方案，计划和施工方式进行评价。provide 一词还可与介词 with 或 to 组成

(1) provide ... with ... 或

(2) provide ... to ... 的搭配表达相同意思："为……提供……"

在此句中使用的是第二种搭配，以上两种搭配的区别在于：在第一种中 provide 接的是提供的对象，with 接的是提供的物。而在第二种情况中则截然相反。是比较以下两个表意一样的句子：

a. Nature provides human beings with food and water.

b. Nature provides food and water to human beings.

3. "Poor service generally results in increased operation costs and, in some cases, heavy expenses due to failure of plant."："不好的服务常常导致操作费用的增加，而且有时，机械的损坏会带来巨额的损失。"一句中"result in ..."为短语，意为："导致……"与其构成相似但语义截然相反的一个搭配是："result from ..."意为："由……原因造成的"。

例句：

a. Waste gas from mobiles may results in air pollution.
汽车排放的尾气会造成空气污染。

b. Success necessarily results from diligence.
成功必然源于勤奋。

4. "Maintenance service schedules need to be provided for each item of equipment."：
"需要为每种设备制定维护服务计划表。"一句中的"need"不是情态动词，所以可以接不定式。译为："需要"。

5. "Building owners and managers must be certain that the maintenance contractor has inspected the items listed and not simply ticked them off as has sometimes been the case."："房屋所有者和经理们必须清楚的是维护承包者已经仔细研究合同上的条款，而非像有些时候只是一扫而过。"中的"certain"相当于"sure"的意思，译为"确定"。

Ⅰ. Exercises for the text(课文练习)

(Ⅰ) Decide whether the following sentences are True or False according to the content of the text.

1. Most buildings have documented records of maintenance activity.

2. Detailed feasibility studies can provide financial profiles only before and during construction.

3. It is not the only reason for much greater attention now being paid to building and ma-

intenance issues that many buildings are now reaching an age when the owners need to decide whether to refurbish or rebuild.

4. In many circumstances buildings contain just the usual plant and mechanical equipment.
5. The poor quality of maintenance of air-conditioning and lifts is one of the major concerns of Building Owners and Managers.
6. Time clocks incorrect operation will cause the plant work wrongly.
7. Building owners and managers neednt bother providing a minimum standard of maintenance with respect to the control of microorganisms.
8. Continuity of service should be the charge of a skilled technician who is responsible for the project and one other technician as his replacement.
9. Logbook records are required to be updated.
10. Service assurance is useless to the effectiveness of the maintenance program.

(Ⅱ) **Match the words in column A with their corresponding explanation in column B with a bar.**

Column A	Column B
1. optimum	a. cost
2. paucity	b. becoming worse
3. expenditure	c. a side view
4. ongoing	d. tiny
5. fundamental	e. keep
6. minimum	f. what is happening
7. characteristic	g. best, most favourable
8. maintenance	h. basic
9. deterioration	i. the smallest
10. profile	j. feature

(Ⅲ) **Choose the best answer**（选择最佳答案）

1. Wang Ling is _____ in her class, and she is _____.
   a. the prettiest... the most diligent   b. prettier... more diligent
   c. pretty... diligent   d. prettiest... most diligent
2. It is _____ than all the other river in China. It is _____ in China.
   a. long... longest   b. longer... the longest
   c. longer... longer   d. longest... longest
3. I got a letter from my friend, _____ me that she would visit us next week.
   a. to tell   b. tells   c. telling   d. told
4. _____ what the situation would be like, we decided to keep silent.
   a. Not knowing   b. Knowing not
   c. Not know   d. Having not known
5. They won _____ many gold medals _____ they did at the last National Games.
   a. as twice... as   b. as... as twice

    c. twice as... as   d. twice... than

6. Our teeth _____ once a year or more often.
    a. should examine   b. should be examined
    c. examine   d. will be examined

7. My elder sister is a kind woman. she _____ always _____ of others before of herself.
    a. has... thought   b. is... thinking
    c. was... thinking   d. had... thought

8. We _____ be there by half past six at the least, or we will _____ go on foot.
    a. have to... have to   b. must... must
    c. must... have to   d. have to... must

9. After thinking it over the old man came to a decision _____ up smoking.
    a. give   b. to give   c. giving   d. gives

10. I praised the naughty children for _____ his English in a very short time.
    a. improved   b. has improved
    c. improving   d. having improved

(Ⅳ) Translation

Translate the following Chinese into English:

1. 仅从这少量的记录中,我们发现境况是不容乐观的。
2. 现今,房屋维护越来越受重视。
3. 维护计划要达到真正的有效,就要能避免一切失败的可能性。
4. 现在,房屋所有者和经理们的维护工作还必须达到一个有关微生物控制的最低标准。
5. 服务记录在可预防的维护工作中起着至关重要的作用。
6. 许多房屋状况已到了要求房主决定是重新修护还是重建的地步。
7. 更加重视对房屋的维护与保养是为了能够降低修换房体所带来的高额开销。
8. 不幸的是,这样做只会花费巨额开支。
9. 需要为每种设备制定维护服务计划表。
10. 自动控制系统是任何大楼空调系统中最重要的一个环节。

(Ⅴ) Extra Reading Activity

Extra reading: read the following passage and choose the best answer to complete each of the statements that follow.

The Maintenance Management System

    There is a complex interaction between the many factors which lead to the development of a maintenance plan. This plan may be operated either along manual lines or with the assistance of a computer. The key components in the formulation of the system are the staff training requirements, facility resources, spares analysis, the publishing of the maintenance plan and the review function (incorporating the feedback loop from workforce).

Developing the Plan

    The key component of the maintenance system is the preventive maintenance plan.

When planning workforce resources it should be remembered that sufficient resources must be available to also cope with the unplanned (breakdown) maintenance function.

The key steps are:
1. Divide the facility into major systems.
2. Subdivide major systems into minor systems and component sub-systems.
3. Define and classify each critical item in the sub-system.
4. Establish its likely failure mode.
5. Examine the consequences of failure in the following terms:
    safety criticality
    functional criticality
6. Explore the means of predicting failure.
7. Define the maintenance which will prevent failure.
8. Assess the maintenance period.
9. Prepare the worksheet.

A key factor underlining this process is the concept of 'condition monitoring'.

Conditioning monitoring is the science of detecting without dismantling the condition of key components in the equipment. The detection of symptoms leading to early failure of equipment is a fertile field for substantial savings in the area of life-cycle cost.

TYPES OF MAINTENANCE CONTRACTS

Generally the two major types of maintenance contracts are:—
1. Preventative Maintenance
2. The building owner/manager arranges for a contractor to perform regular service at prescribed intervals for a period usually ranging from one to ten years. In addition to a tendered contract price, an hourly rate is quoted for equipment breakdown work, plus an amount for overheads such as travel, overtime etc. The building owner would normally have to take out a Machinery Breakdown Insurance Policy to cover against major and costly breakdowns.

    Comprehensive Maintenance

The building owner arranges for a contractor to take full responsibility for maintnenace and performance of the building services included in the contract. Regular service is performed and any plant failure is covered by the contractor. This form of contract is more "expensive" but has the benefit of peace of mind for the building owner/manager who is then able to budget for maintenance costs and resources more accurately.

1. Which of the following statements about "the maintenance plan" is not true?
    a. There is a complex interaction between the many factors which lead to the development of a maintenance plan.
    b. This maintenance plan may be operated either along manual lines or with the assistance of a computer.
    c. The key components in the formulation of the maintenance management system are

the stafftraining requirements, facility resources, spares analysis, the publishing of the maintenance plan and the review function (incorporating the feedback loop from workforce).

  d. The building owner arranges for a contractor to take full responsibility for maintnenace plan and performance of the building services included in the contract.

2. The key component of the maintenance system is _____.
  a. the Comprehensive Maintenance plan
  b. the preventive maintenance plan
  c. the building maintenance plan
  d. the machine maintenance plan

3. Conditioning monitoring is _____.
  a. the science of detecting without dismantling ? the condition of key components in the equipment
  b. the science of detecting with dismantling the condition of key components in the equipment
  c. the science of detecting without dismantling the condition of components in the equipment
  d. the science of detecting with dismanfiing the condition of components in the equipment

4. _____ leading to early failure of equipment is a fertile field for substantial savings in the area of life-cycle cost.
  a. The functional criticality   b. The safety criticality
  c. The detection of symptoms   d. The component sub-systems

5. Generally the two major types of maintenance contracts are _____.
  a. Preventative Maintenance and building maintenance
  b. Comprehensive Maintenance and building maintenance
  c. Preventative Maintenance and machine maintenance
  d. Preventative Maintenance and Comprehensive Maintenance

II. Language Ability Drill(语言能力练习)

(I) Vocabulary Exercise

Study the following words. Then use them correctly in the sentences below.

Verbs	Nouns	Adjectives(形容词)	Adverbs(副词)
experience	experience	experienced	
	inexperience	inexperienced	
doubt	doubt	doubtful	doubtfully
			undoubtedly
	fortune	fortunate	fortunately
	misfortune	unfortunate	unfortunately

1. experience (v.), experience (n.), inexperience, experienced, inexperienced

1) One's _____ can help him to be successful.

2) Young men tend to make a few mistakes because of _____.

3) After _____ so many defeats, finally we gain the success.

4) She is young and _____, but she is good learner.

5) This work needs someone more _____.

6) That night he _____ hunger and coldness.

2. doubt (v.), doubt (n.), doubtful, doubtfully, undoubtedly

1) A _____ look is on his face.

2) I have serious _____ about the wisdom (智慧) of his decision.

3) His friends and doctors very much _____ whether he could do it.

4) Deng Yaping is _____ one of the greatest athletes.

5) We all looked at him _____.

6) If not I had worked very hard, I would have _____ failed the examination.

3. fortune, misfortune, fortunate, unfortunate, fortunately, unfortunately

1) She was a/an _____ girl, because her parents died when she was very young.

2) _____ all the passengers were saved in the car accident.

3) He is loved by anyone who has the _____ to know him.

4) _____ is sometimes a sort of treasure in one's life.

5) We had planned to have a picnic, but _____ it rained that day.

6) You are so _____ to be admitted by that famous university.

(Ⅱ) Cloze

　　Todd was working at his gas station(加油站) at night when he heard over the radio that a 1 in Long Island had been 2 by an armed man who had killed the night guard and got away with $150,000. "One hundred and fifty thousand." Todd whistled. Here's a fellow who just 3 into a bank and helps himself 4 so much money. Todd thought of the 5 with which he man-aged to get the amount of money he 6 to start his gas station. So many papers to 7 , so much money to pay hack. The news 8 twenty minutes later. The gunman had 9 a car for a ride, and then 10 out the driver. He was possibly 11 the Southern State Parkway in a white Ford. License plate(车牌) number LJR1939. The 12 of the announcer continued: " 13 out for white cars. Don't pick up 14 and all you folks in gas stations better not do 15 to a white Ford car." Todd stood up and 16 to see out into the cold night. It was dark but Todd 17 the Southern State Parkway was out there. Just 18 , Todd saw the headlights coming at him and a car pulled in for 19 There it was, a white Ford. He saw the 20 , LJR1939. "What should I do?" Todd had to make a quick 21 "Yes, sir." Todd 22 while making up his mind for sure. " 23 her up." the man said sounding like any other 24 When the tank(油箱) was full, Todd quickly turned and pointed a gun at the man.

"Hands up 25 get out!"

1. A. store　　　　B. bank　　　　C. station　　　　D. house
2. A. searched for　B. held up　　　C. taken over　　 D. broken into

31

3. A. walks	B. looks	C. marches	D. drives
4. A. for	B. by	C. to	D. of
5. A. satisfaction	B. difficulty	C. disappointment	D. spirit
6. A. saved	B. made	C. offered	D. needed
7. A. collect	B. prove	C. sign	D. write
8. A. continued	B. lasted	C. spread	D. arrived
9. A. bought	B. borrowed	C. stolen	D. stopped
10. A. sent	B. found	C. left	D. pushed
11. A. calling from	B. fleeing	C. heading for	D. looking for
12. A. news	B. warning	C. advice	D. voice
13. A. Look	B. Run	C. Call	D. Set
14. A. guests	B. strangers	C. prisoners	D. passengers
15. A. harm	B. favor	C. service	D. business
16. A. tried	B. decided	C. hoped	D. happened
17. A. considered	B. knew	C. recognized	D. learnt
18. A. then	B. there	C. right	D. now
19. A. directions	B. repairs	C. gas	D. parking
20. A. mark	B. number	C. sign	D. name
21. A. decision	B. call	C. movement	D. remark
22. A. wondered	B. stopped	C. waited	D. asked
23. A. Cover	B. Fill	C. Check	D. Tie
24. A. visitor	B. robber	C. driver	D. rider
25. A. or	B. and	C. but	D. to

(Ⅲ) Complete the following sentences, using the words given in brackets

1. I ____ that it was a mistake to let him go. (can't help)
2. After drinking heavily at the New Year's Eve (除夕) party, ____ the next morning with a painful headache. (waken)
3. His classmates tried to ____ swimming across the lake, but he did not listen. (dissuade)
4. After studying Unit One, we all ____ our study habits. (set out)
5. I recognized him as a friend of my father's whom I ____ once or twice. (previously)
6. Of all American cities, San Francisco is considered by many to ____ beautiful. (by far)

Part 2. Dialogue

Move Into the New House
(喜迁新居)

Ⅰ. Typical Sentences (经典短句)

(Ⅰ) Daily Conversations (日常用语)

致歉语: Sorry!

32

对不起！
I'm sorry to keep you waiting.
我很抱歉让您久等.
Sorry. We can't help you.
很抱歉我们不能为您效劳。

致谢语：Thank you. That's very kind of you.
谢谢，您真是太好了。（应答为：That's all right。或 My pleasure。）
It's very kind of you to say so.
谢谢您的夸奖。

祈请语：Just a moment please.
请稍等一下。
May I have your name, please?
请问贵姓？
Would you please fill out this form?
请您填一下这张表,好吗？请您填一下这张表,好吗？
This way, please.
请这边走。

(Ⅱ) Professional Conversation（专业会话）

1. It is forbidden to change the original windows and doors in the apartment.
   单元内原有封阳台和窗户不能更换。
2. Please observe the principle for decoration time, don't disturb other residents here.
   注意装修时间,不能打扰其他业主的正常休息。
3. You must consult the Heat Supply Office before rearranging your heat system.
   改动暖气前您必须向供热站咨询。
4. Please use the cargo elevator to carry the decoration materials.
   运装修材料用货梯。
5. You mustn't floor indoors by using floor stone.
   户内地面不准铺石材。

Ⅱ. Conversation Passages

(Ⅰ) Passage 1.

A：Good morning, sir. Can I help you?
　 早上好,先生。有什么我可以为您效劳的吗？
B：Yes, I want to handle all the procedures of removing.
　 今天我想办一下所有的入住手续。
A：So you have learnt the necessary payment, havent you?
　 您知道要付哪些费用了吗？
B：Oh, yes, I know. But I have no idea of how much money should I pay for this.
　 是的,我知道了。可我还不清楚一共要付多少钱。

A: It's O.K. A moment please. Let me see. Altogether you should pay 500 yuan for these.
没关系,请稍等一下,让我算算,您一共要付 500 元。

B: Here's the money.
给您钱。

A: Thank you. Would you please fill out this form?
谢谢,请您填一下这张表,好吗?

B: Ok. Here you are. Is there anything more should I do?
好的,给您。我还需要作些什么吗?

A: No, that's all. Later people from engineering division will help you with building test.
没有了,等会儿由工程部人员跟您去验房。

(Ⅱ) Passage 2.

A: Hello, I'm sorry to keep you waiting. I'm the person from engineering division, and I will help you with building test today.
您好,抱歉让您久等了。我来自工程部。今天由我带您去验房。

B: That's all right. Glad to meet you. My name is WangGang. May I have your name, please?
没关系,幸会,幸会。我叫王刚,请问您贵姓?

A: My name is Liu Ming. This way, please.
在下刘明。请这边走。

B: Thank you. I would like to know what I should pay attention to when I make decoration of my house.
谢谢,我想了解一下在装修时应注意的事项。

A: Oh, yes. There is something you should pay special attention to when you make decoration, for example: firstly, please observe the principle for decoration time, don't disturb other residents here; secondly, it is forbidden to change the original windows and doors in the apartment; you mustn't floor indoors by using floor stones, neither; lastly, you must consult the Heat Supply Office before rearranging your heat system.
噢,是的。在您装修时还真要注意以下事宜。比如:首先,您要注意装修时间,不能打扰其他业主的正常休息;其次,单元内原有封阳台和窗户不能更换;户内地面也不准铺石材;最后,要改动暖气前您必须向供热站咨询。

B: Oh, I see. Thank you. You're so professional. However, you know, I have bought a lot of decoration material. How can I carry them to my house?
是的,我清楚了。谢谢您。您真专业。可是,您知道我买了许多装修材料,要怎么搬上楼呢?

A: You can use the elevator. And please use the cargo elevator to carry the decoration materials. If you can't move all the material into the elevator by yourself, we can help you. However, to carry those precious things we are sorry we couldn't help you.
您可以使用电梯啊!而且请您用货梯运装修材料。如果您自己不能把材料搬上电梯。我们可以帮您。但是很抱歉我们不能帮您搬那些贵重物品。

B: Thank you. That's very kind of you.
   谢谢,您真是太好了。

III. Exercises for Dialogue

(I) Fill in the following blanks while observing the conversational manner（按照日常会话习惯完成以下填空）

A: I'm sorry to keep you waiting.
B: _____, my name is SunQiang. _____?
A: _____ is WuMei.
B: I was told your English is very good.
A: _____.
B: I wonder are you willing to help me study English?
A: _____.
B: Thank you. _____.
A: You're welcome.

(II) After filling in the blanks, translate the former dialogue into Chinese.

(III) Make a conversation with your partner about asking for what things you should pay attention to when you make a house decoration. (there should be at least 3 turn-taking in the dialogue)

IV. Spoken Language Drill (fill in the blanks according to the Chinese translation)

Dialogue 1.

A: I _____ must be going now.
   现在我真的该告辞了。

B: But you just got here. Can't you stay a little _____?
   不过你刚来呀。不能再呆一会了吗?

A: That's very nice of you, but I really can't.
   谢谢你的好意,但是我实在不能再呆了。

B: Well, it's too bad that you have to go.
   哦,真遗憾,你一定要走。

A: Thanks very much. It was a great party!
   非常感谢。这次聚会好极了。

B: It was our _____.
   这是我们的荣幸。

Dialogue 2.

A: I'd better be going.
   我得告辞了。

B: So _____? Why don't you stay a little longer?
   这么早就走了? 为什么不多呆一会呢?

35

A: I wish I could, but it's already late.
　　我是想多呆一会儿，但是时间已经很晚了。

B: Oh, it's a shame that you have to leave.
　　哦，真遗憾，你非走不可呀。

A: Thank you for a _____ meal.
　　谢谢你的美餐。

Dialogue 3.

A: I really should be on my way.
　　我真的该告辞了。

B: Oh, not yet! At least have one for the _____.
　　哦，还不到时候，至少再喝一杯，以表送行。

A: No. Thanks all the _____.
　　不喝了。不过还是得谢谢你。

B: Well, I'm sorry you have to leave so early.
　　哦，很遗憾，你非得这么早走不可。

A: Thank you very much. We really had a good time.
　　非常感谢你。我确实玩得很痛快。

B: Well, thank you for _____.
　　唔，谢谢你的光临。

Dialogue 4.

A: I think it's about time we got going.
　　我想差不多是该告辞的时候了。

B: What? Already? Won't you have _____ coffee?
　　怎么，已经要走了？要不要再喝点咖啡？

A: I'd love to, but I have to get up[(使)起床]early tomorrow.
　　我是很想再喝一点，但我明天得起早。

B: Oh! I'm sorry. I wish you could stay.
　　哦，真遗憾，要是你能多呆一会儿该多好。

A: Thank you for a very _____ evening.
　　谢谢你，今晚过得真愉快。

B: Don't mention[提起；提到]it. I hope you can come again soon.
　　不用谢，希望你不久能再来。

Part 3. Supplementary Reading:

How To Be True To You
Give wisely and carry a big stick

　　I knew a man, a very tall and spare and gentle man, for several years before I found out that he visited prisoners in our county jail, week in and week out for decades. He would write letters for them, carry messages, fetch clothing or books. But mainly he just

36

offered himself. He didn't preach to them, didn't pick and choose between the likable and the nasty, didn't look for any return on his kindness. All that mattered was that they were in trouble.

Why did he spend time with out-casts when he could have been golfing or watching TV? "I go in case everyone else has given up on them," he told me once. "I never give up." Never giving up is a trait we honor in athletes, in soldiers, in survivors of disaster, in patients recovering from severe injuries. If you struggle bravely against overwhelming odds, you're liable to end up on the evening news. But in less flashy, less news-worthy forms, fidelity to a mission or a person or an occupation shows up in countless lives all around us.

It shows up in parents who will not quit loving their daughter even after she dyes her hair purple and tattoos her belly and runs off with a rock band. It shows up in couples who choose to mend their marriages instead of filing for divorce. It shows up in volunteers at the hospital or library or women's shelter or soup kitchen. It shows up in unsung people everywhere who do their jobs well, not because the supervisor is watching or because they are paid gobs of money but because they know their work matters.

When my son Jesse was in sixth grade, his teacher was diagnosed with breast cancer. She told the children about the disease, about the surgery and therapy, and about her hopes for recovery. Jesse came home deeply impressed that she had trusted them with her news. She could have stayed home for the rest of the year. On mastectomy healed, she began going in to school one afternoon a week, then two, then a full day, then two days and three.

When a parent worried aloud that she might be risking her health for the sake of the children, the teacher scoffed, "Oh, heavens, no! They're my best medicine." Besides, these children would only be in sixth grade once, she said, and she meant to help them all she could while she had the chance.

The therapy must have worked, because ten years later she's going strong. When I see her around town, she always asks about Jesse. Is he still so funny, so bright, so excited about learning? Yes, he is, I tell her, and she beams.

A cause needn't be grand, it needn't impress a crowd to be worthy of our commitment. I have a friend who built houses Monday through Friday for people who could pay him and then built other houses for free on Saturday with Habitat for Humanity. A neighbor makes herself available to international students and their families, unriddling for them the puzzles of living in this new place. Other neighbors coach soccer teams, visit the sick, give rides to the housebound, tutor dropouts, teach adults to read.

I could multiply these examples a hundredfold without ever leaving my county. Most likely you could do the same. Any community worth living in must have a web of people faithful to good work and to one another, or that community would fall apart.

To say that fidelity is common is not to say it's easy, painless or free. It costs energy and time, maybe a lifetime.

And every firm yes we say requires many a firm no. One Sunday I was talking the man who visited prisoners in jail, when a young woman approached to ask if he would join the board of a new peace group she was organizing. In a rush of words she told him why the cause was crucial, why the cause was crucial, why the time was ripe, why she absolutely needed his leadership. Knowing this man's sympathies, I figured the would agree to serve. But after listening to her plea, he gazed at her soberly for a moment, then said, "That certainly is a vital concern, worthy of all your passion. But it is not my concern."

The challenge for all of us is to find those few causes that are peculiarly our own—those to which we are clearly called and then to embrace them with all our heart. By remaining faithful to a calling, we can create the conditions for finding a purpose and a pattern in our days.

If you imagine trying to solve all the world's problems at once, though, you're likely to quit before you finish rolling up your sleeves. But if you stake out your own workable territory, if you settle on a manageable number of causes, then you might accomplish a great deal, all the while trusting that others elsewhere are working faithfully in their own places.

参考译文:

如何真待自我
——明智施助于人与妥善保护自己

 我认识一位先生多年,他修长清瘦,温文尔雅。后来我发现他日复一日,月复一月地访问我们县城监狱的囚犯,已经坚持了几十年。他帮助犯人们写信,递条子,捎带衣物和书籍。然而他仅是帮忙而已。他不会跟他们讲大道理,不会凭个人好恶,挑三捡四地选择帮助的对象,也不会谋求别人对他的好心以任何回报。他所关心是:他们正身陷囹圄。

 他本可以把时间花在玩高尔夫球或看电视上的,为什么要与这些社会的弃儿呆在一起?他立即对我说:"我这样做,是因为其他人都对他们不抱希望,而我永远不会放弃对他们的期望。"

 "永不放弃"是一种高贵品质,我们可以从运动员、士兵、灾祸的幸存者以及康复中的重伤者身上看到它的闪光。假如你能勇敢地和比你强大得多的对手抗争,你的事迹有可能在晚间的新闻中占一席之地。但在那些不是那么惊天动地,不太值得见诸报端的事例中,对人,对使命,对职业的真诚在我们身边无数人身上都得以体现。

 它体现在这样的父母身上,他们的女儿把自己的头发染紫了,在自己的肚子纹身,甚至与摇滚乐队厮混,他们依然深爱着她;它在这样的夫妇身上,他们选择改善婚姻关系而不是离婚;它体现在那些默默无闻的大众身上,他们在自己的工作中尽职尽责,不是因为有人监督或是他们能从中得到大把钞票,而是因为他们知道自己的工作很重要。

 我的儿子杰西上六年级的时候,他的老师被诊断患上了乳腺癌。她把这种疾病的概况、手术、治疗方法和她对未来康复的希望都告诉了孩子们。杰西回家后,对于老师能把自己的病情告诉他们,感触颇深。她本可以请病假,在余下的日子里呆在家中养病,但是她的乳腺切除手术做好以后,她就开始每星期到学校上一下午的班,后来就是两个下午、一整天,直至两天、三天……

一位家长很担心,认为她会为了这些孩子而伤身,这位老师却戏谑地说道:"哦,不!他们是我的最好良药。此外,这些孩子只能上一次六年级。"她想在自己有机会教他们时全力以赴。

她接受的治疗一定很成功,我在十年后见到她时,她挺强健。当我领着她在城中兜圈时,她总是询问杰西的情况:他是否还是那么机灵调皮,对学习充满兴趣?我告诉她,"是的"。她嘴角露出一丝微笑。

一项事业不需要有多壮丽,它不需要给人留下这样的印象:它值得我们去从事。我有一个朋友,他从星期一到星期五为那些愿意出钱的人建房,而星期六则为"人道家居"组织免费建房。我的一个邻居为那些新来到这个陌生地方的外国学生和他们的家人答疑解惑。别的邻居们有的执教足球队,探视病人,有的驱车访问那些羁居于家的人,教育那些悲观厌世的人,教成年人读书。

光从这县城中,我就能举出成百上千个这样的例子,你多半也能同样举出这么多。任何一个值得一住的社区中都一定有很多对工作,对他人真诚相待的人,否则,这个社区就会崩溃。

"真诚待人"是一种普遍现象,但并不是说你能够轻而易举、无痛无扰地做到真诚待人。它需要时间、精力,也许要一辈子的努力。

此外,当我们每坚定地说一次"是"时,要说许多次"不"。一个星期天,我正与那位探视囚犯的先生交谈,一位女士走过来,问他能否加入她正在筹备的一个新的和平组织的理事会。她滔滔不绝地说了许多。说明这一事业为何具有关键意义,为何时机已经成熟,为何她绝对需要接受他的领导。我知道他富有同情心,料想他会同意加入。谁知他在听完她的恳求以后,用一种矜持的眼神盯着她看了一会,然后说:"那自然是极其重要的,值得'你'为其倾尽全力,但它却不是'我'所关心的。"

我们所有人面临的挑战,就是要找到那些能与自己相匹配的事业——我们能清楚地听到它们的召唤,找到以后,我们就要全心全意地去从事它们。如果能忠诚于一个召唤,我们就能为找到自己生活的目标和模式创造条件。

假定你想在片刻之间解决世上的所有问题,那么你有可能在卷起袖子准备大干一场前就知难而退。但如果你只想在自己能力所及的范围内一搏,如果你只致力于些许你所能从事的事业,如果你相信在其他地方,别的人也在自己的领域中辛勤工作,你也许会取得极大的成功。

Exercises for the reading:

1. The good man mentioned in the beginning of this article spent his time _____.
   A. On golf B. In watching TV
   C. On entertainment D. In helping prisoners
2. Never giving up is a trait we honor in _____.
   A. athletes B. soldiers
   C. survivors of disaster D. all of them
3. _____ such examples can be found in the author's county.
   A. A hundredfold B. A thousand of
   C. Tens of thousands of D. We don't know
4. The challenge for all of us is to find those few causes that _____.

  A. make money   B. make fame
  C. are peculiarly our own   D. make a comfortable life
5. How was that teacher of the author's son ten years later?
  A. She died, because she still worked when she had cancer.
  B. She was going strong.
  C. She was still sick in hospital.
  D. She was worse than before.

Part 4. Practical Writing

Invitation

Following the rule given in the passage, you are to write an invitation:

Dear sir/madam:

On [date], we will host an evening of celebration in honor of the retirement of [name], President of [company]. You are cordially invited to attend the celebration at [hotel], [location], on [date] from to p.m. [name] has been the President of [company] since [year]. During this period, [company] expanded its business from to . Now it's our opportunity to thank him for his years of exemplary leadership and wish him well for a happy retirement. Please join us to say Good-bye to [name].

      See you on [date].

                      Sincerely yours,

                          [name]
                          [time]

  With the experience you have gotten to make your own one to invite a person to your party.

Dear sir/madam:

                     Sincerely yours,
                          [name]
                          [time]

Unit 3. Performance of Building Services

Part 1. Text

Performance of Building Services

The performance of the building services is a key factor[1] in the building occupants' assessment of their environment. Quality services which perform well throughout the life of the building will generally minimize the turnover of tenants and assist the building owner to maximize his or her return on their investment.

The building services components generally include:

Air-conditioning and other Mechanical Services
Lifts and Escalators
Electrical Reticulation and Lighting Systems
Fire Protection Services
Communication Systems
Security Systems
Hydraulic Services

All of these services are dynamic and must be continually maintained at an appropriate level if satisfactory performance is to be achieved throughout the life of the building.[2]

These service systems are generally not automatically adaptable to changing tenants' requirements. However, a well designed system will include the flexibility to allow them to be modified to meet a wide range of changing tenant requirements during the life of the building. To optimize the performance of the building services systems, both the day-to-day maintenance of the systems and their adaptation to meet changing tenant requirements must be closely monitored by the Building Manager.

The Traditional Approach

Historically, the maintenance of building services systems has been the responsibility of contracting organizations that provide maintenance services as an adjunct to their primary activity, which is the initial installation of these systems.

The maintenance arrangements that have evolved vary for each of the service disciplines and the most common traditional approach for each discipline may be summarized as follows:

Air Conditioning Systems

The building owner enters a contract with an air-conditioning maintenance contractor.[3] Generally this contractor is part of the initial contract for the supply and installation of the equipment. The maintenance contract may provide comprehensive cover or may simply cover routine maintenance with breakdowns treated as an extra to the base contract.

The building owner is not obliged to continue with the original installation contractor once the 12 months defects liability period on a new installation has expired.

Lifts

At the time of tender for a new lift installation the contractors can offer a comprehensive maintenance agreement for the maintenance of the lift installation for a 10 or 20 year period.[4] The maintenance contract offered includes a formula for escalating the cost of the maintenance throughout the contract period.

The building owner is generally obliged to engage the installation contractor for the ongoing maintenance of the lifts as it is a statutory requirement of the Department of Industrial Relations (or their equivalents in each State) that a maintenance contract on the lift installation be effected.

Fire Protection Systems

The fire protection systems must be maintained in accordance with AS 1851 and the monitoring of compliance with the Standard is the responsibility of the local Council and associated Fire Brigade. At the conclusion of the defects liability period on a new installation the Building Manager is free to enter a contract with any Fire Protection Maintenance Contractor for this work. In New South Wales, under the provisions of the Local Government Act, Part 59 "Essential Services"(which includes Fire Protection Systems) need to be reported on annually.

Electrical Services

Routine maintenance on the electrical services is handled in the following manner:
Replacement of light bulbs in the tenanted space is the responsibility of the tenant.
General routine maintenance of electrical equipment such as checking the work.
undertaken by contractors and the general cable integrity is usually undertaken by the Building Manager. He or she may request an electrical contractor to undertake specific tasks on their behalf.

Special equipment such as generators, UPS systems and emergency lighting are generally covered by maintenance contracts entered into with the suppliers or installers of the particular equipment.

Hydraulics Services

In most instances, routine maintenance is not undertaken on hydraulic services and the major maintenance undertaken is in the form of resolving or correcting specific problems.

Communications, Electronic Security, Building Automation Systems

Maintenance of these systems is generally covered by the Building Manager entering into agreements with the installing contractors. In some instances the maintenance agreement is a comprehensive contract where the contractor takes responsibility not only for routine maintenance, but for correction of all problems and for the replacement of defective parts throughout the course of the maintenance contract.

In Summary

In each instance outlined above, the Building Manager is dependent on a combination of his or her own knowledge, in-house expertise, and/or external consultants. The ability to assess maintenance quality and the diligence of the particular maintenance contractors to ensure that the systems are maintained in a manner that will provide for the optimum operation of these systems is of paramount importance.

The above points briefly cover the routine and breakdown maintenance of various services components. A further important area that requires scrutiny and close management is the tenancy fitout modifications to buildings. In the past there has been a tendency for tenants to alter their fitout layouts without reference to the Building Manager and often without any services design input. This approach inevitably leads to problems with services operation and an increased level of complaints. Fortunately, the increasing sophistication of the tenancy fitout market has reduced the incidence of this type of approach and major modifications are, in most instances, professionally managed.

The successful Building Manager must have the capacity, capability and the systems in place to monitor minor changes in tenancy fitout and to ensure that professional advice is obtained where appropriate so that the integrity and efficiency of the building services systems are maintained.[5]

参考译文：

房屋服务的履行

房屋服务的履行是业主评价居住环境的重要因素。优质的服务能使业主最大限度地延长租期，从而使投资方获得最大的回报。

房屋服务包括：

空调和其他机械设施服务

电梯和扶梯

电路和照明系统

消防系统

通讯系统

安全系统

水力系统

以上这些服务都处于动态运转状况，如果想要令业主满意，就必须及时给予恰当的维护。

通常，这些服务系统并不能根据业主的要求随意改动。但是一个设计完备的系统应当具备一定的灵活适应性来满足业主不同的要求。

为了使房屋服务系统发挥其最大的功用，房屋服务经理必须严格监督对系统的每日维护以及应业主要求所做的改变。

传统方法

一直以来，房屋服务系统的维护是由承包方负责的。除了安装这些系统，他们还要提供对这些设施的维护。

其所涉及的各项维护安排，根据各款服务细则而有所不同，如下是一些最普遍的方法。

空调系统

投资方与空调维护承包方签订合同。通常，该承包方也参与初始合同中有关设备的提供与安装工作。维护合同有两种：提供全面维护或在提供简单常规维护的基础上对突发故障提供额外服务。

在 12 个月的保修期期满之后，投资方不必与原先的安装承包方继续合同。

电梯

在投标一个新的电梯安装工程时，承包方可以提出一个全面维护协议以提供 10 或 20 年的电梯维护。该维护合同包括一个公式用来计算合同期间增长的维护费用。

按照工业关系部（或各州的相应部门）的法规要求：合同双方应确保电梯维护合同的有效性。因此，投资方必须敦促承包方进行日常的维护工作。

消防系统

消防系统必须按照 AS1851 的标准进行维护，并由当地政府联合消防局监督其维护状况。在新安装设施的有效期期满之时，房屋服务经理可以和任何一个消防维护承包者签订合同。在新南威尔士，根据当地政府法案第 59 款，"重要服务"（其中包括消防系统）需要每年上报。

电力服务

常规的电力系统维护是如下进行的：

租用空间中的灯泡更换由业主负责。

电力设施的总体常规维护，如：检查承包方的工作和电路干线是否完好，都是由房屋服务经理来完成。他（或她）可以要求一个电力系统维护承包者代表他完成某些具体工作。一些特殊设施，如：发电机，UPS 系统和应急照明都包括在与供应商或每个设施的安装者所签订的合同之中。

水力服务

大多数情况下，水力服务不进行常规维护。主要的维护工作只是处理某些具体的突发状况。

通讯，电力安全，房屋自动系统。

这些系统的维护都包括在房屋服务经理与安装承包者签订的协议中。有时，维护协议是一个全面的合同，在其履行期中，承包者不仅负责常规维护还要处理所有的问题，以及更换损坏的零件。

小结

在上述各项中，房屋服务经理要依靠自己的综合知识，内部技术人员和外部顾问才能完成本职工作。他们对于维护工作质量的评估和对维护工作者是否勤奋的判断力是至关重要的。因为维护工作的质量和工作者的勤奋程度是保证以上各个系统以最佳状态运行的关键。

以上各点简要概括了各种服务系统的常规以及故障维护。一个更重要的并且需要严格执行管理的环节是业主对房屋的改造。在过去,业主常常不通知房屋服务经理就进行房屋改建,因此房屋中也就没有相应的服务设施。这不可避免地给实施服务带来麻烦,引起越来越多的不满。幸好,越来越完善的装修服务市场减少了此类事件的发生,大多数情况中,房屋的重大改造都是经过专业设计后进行的。

一个成功的房屋服务经理必须具备一定的素质,能力和工作方法来监督业主对房屋任何细小的改动,和提供恰当的专业建议,以确保房屋服务体统的完整性和有效性。

Vocabulary
单词表:

61.	factor	['fæktə]	n.	因素,要素,因数,代理人
62.	occupant	['ɔkju:pənt]	n.	占有者,居住者
63.	assessment	[ə'sesmənt]	n.	(为征税对财产所作的)估价,被估定的金额
64.	assist	[ə'sist]	v.	援助,帮助
65.	component	[kəm'pəunənt]	n.	成分
			adj.	组成的,构成的
66.	reticulation	[ritikju'leiʃ(ə)n]	n.	网状物
67.	hydraulic	[hai'drɔ:lik]	adj.	水力的,水压的
68.	dynamic	[dai'næmik]	adj.	动力的,动力学的,动态的
69.	flexibility	[ˌfleksə'biliti]	n.	弹性,适应性,机动性,挠性
70.	modified	['mɔdifaid]	adj.	改良的,改进的,修正的
			n.	纪律,学科
71.	discipline	['disiplin]	v.	训练
72.	initial	[i'niʃəl]	adj.	最初的,词首的,初始的
			n.	词首大写字母
73.	installation	[ˌinstə'leiʃən]	n.	安装,装置,就职
74.	expire	[iks'paiə]	v.	期满,终止,呼气,断气,届满
75.	escalate	['eskəleit]	vi.	逐步升高,逐步增强
			vt.	使逐步上升
76.	statutory	['stætjut(ə)ri]	adj.	法令的,法定的
77.	compliance	[kəm'plaiəns]	n.	依从,顺从
78.	provision	[prə'viʒən]	n.	供应,(一批)供应品,预备,防备,规定
79.	routine	[ru:'ti:n]	n.	例行公事,常规,日常事务,程序
80.	hydraulics	['hai'drɔ:liks]	n.	水力学
81.	contractor	[kən'træktə]	n.	订约人,承包人
82.	replacement	[ri'pleismənt]	n.	归还,复位,交换,代替者,补充兵员,置换,移位

83. diligence	['dilidʒəns]	n.	勤奋
84. paramount	['pærəmaunt]	adj.	极为重要的规划，设计，（书刊等）编排，版面，配线，
85. layout	['lei‚aut]	n.	企划，设计图案，（工厂等的）布局图版面设计
86. complaint	[kəm'pleint]	n.	诉苦，抱怨，牢骚，委屈，疾病
87. sophistication	[səfistikeiʃən]	n.	强词夺理，诡辩，混合
88. modification	[‚mɔdifi'keiʃən]	n.	更改，修改，修正
89. appropriate	[ə'prəupriit]	adj.	适当的
90. integrity	[in'tegriti]	n.	正直，诚实，完整，完全，完整性

Useful Expressions

be adaptable to 可适应（用）于……
treat as 待……如，当作
be obliged to 不得不做，必须做
in accordance with (to) 根据，按照，与……一致，相适应
in the form of 以……形状（形式、形态），呈……状态
not only ... but (also)... 不但……而且
lead to 导致，通向，通往

Notes

备注：

1. "key factor"：此词中"key"原意是"钥匙或键"而在这里是"关键的、重要的"的意思，所以此词应译为"关键因素或要素"。同样的用法见例句：

"He is the key man in the department. ""他在这个部门里是个关键人物。"

"To learn English well, practice is a key factor. ""要想学好英语，练习是关键。"

2. "All of these services are dynamic and must be continually maintained at an appropriate level if satisfactory performance is to be achieved throughout the life of the building. "："以上这些服务随时可能出现状况，如果想要令业主满意，就必须及时给予恰当的维护。"

此句话中出现了被动语态：

被动语态是相对主动语态而言，表示被动的句式，其基本结构为：be + 动词过去分词。

被动语态的用法：

被动语态表示一种主语和谓语之间的关系，当主语是动作的承受者时，就需要用到被动语态，汉语中所说的，"汽车被撞坏了""钢笔被修好了"等句子就是一种被动语态的句子，在汉语中常用"被""由"等词来表示这种被动语态。在英语中则用动词的被动语态形式来表示。被动语态中还可用 by 短语加在句后表示被动语态中动作的发出者。也就是谓语动词动作的逻辑上的主语，被动语态常用在下列情况。

1) 不知道谁是谓语动词动作的执行者时，或者没有必要说出谁是执行者时。

The glass was broken last night.

玻璃昨天被打破了。

His bike has been stolen.

他的自行车被偷了。

2) 为了强调或突出动作的承受者时。

The plan has been sent to the headmaster.

计划已经送给校长了。

Kilinton was elected the President of U. S. A.

克林顿被选为美国总统。

3) 被动语态也可以说出动作的执行者，构成如下：

动作承受者 + be + 过去分词 + by + 动作执行者。

The picture was praised by everybody.

照片得到了大家的好评。

The classroom was cleaned by us.

教室被我们打扫过。

3. "The building owner enters a contract with an air-conditioning maintenance contractor."："投资方与空调维护承包方签订合同。"在此句中"enters a contract with sb."是一个短语，译为："于某人达成协议/签署合同"。类似的词组还有"make a deal with sb."，"come into a/an contract/agreement with sb."

例句："Tianjin Mobile factory made a deal with Toyota."："天津汽车制造厂与丰田公司达成了一项协议。"

"After several turns of meeting, 2 companies eventually come into an agreement with each other."："经过几轮的磋商，这两个公司终于签署了合同。"

4. "At the time of tender for a new lift installation the contractors can offer a comprehensive maintenance agreement for the maintenance of the lift installation for a 10 or 20 year period."："在投标一个新的电梯安装工程时，承包方可以提出一个全面维护协议以提供10或20年的电梯维护。"中"at the time of ..."译为："在……时"，其意义相当于单词"when"。相同结构的表示时间的短语还有："in the period of ..."："在……的过程中"，"during the time of ..."："在……的期间"。

例句："In the period of war, people ran away from their hometown."："在战争时期，人们都离开了自己的家园。"

"During the time of 20th, many invention were created."："在20世纪，出现了许多发明。"

5. "The successful Building Manager must have the capacity, capability and the systems in place to monitor minor changes in tenancy fitout and to ensure that professional advice is obtained where appropriate so that the integrity and efficiency of the building services systems are maintained."："一个成功的房屋服务经理必须具备一定的素质，能力和工作方法来监督业主对房屋任何细小的改动，和提供恰当的专业建议，以确保房屋服务体统的完整性和有效性。"一句中"... so that ..."是一个词组译为："(做)……以便……"

例句："I got up early this morning so that I can catch the bus."："今天早上我起得很

早,以便赶上公车。"

Ⅰ. **Exercises for the text**(课文练习)

(Ⅰ) Decide whether the following sentences are True or False according to the content of the text.

1. The performance of the building services is a very important factor in the building occupants' assessment of their environment.
2. The building services components generally include: Air-conditioning and other Mechanical Services, Lifts and Escalators, Electrical Reticulation and Lighting Systems, Fire Protection Services, Communication Systems, Security Systems and Hydraulic Services.
3. Only in nowadays, the maintenance of building services systems becomes the responsibility of contracting organizations.
4. The contractor is not part of the initial contract for the supply and installation of the equipment.
5. The building owner is still obliged to continue with the original installation contractor once the 12 months defects liability period on a new installation has expired.
6. The fire protection systems must be maintained in accordance with certain principle.
7. In most instances, routine maintenance is undertaken on hydraulic services and the major maintenance undertaken is in the form of resolving or correcting specific problems.
8. Maintenance of all systems is generally covered by the Building Manager without entering into agreements with the installing contractors.
9. The tenancy fitout modifications to buildings is a more important area.
10. The increasing sophistication of the tenancy fitout market still can't change the problem.

(Ⅱ) Match the words in column A with their corresponding explanation in column B with a bar.

Column A	Column B
1. factor	a. resident
2. occupant	b. element
3. assist	c. improved
4. dynamic	d. active
5. modified	e. help
6. installation	f. proper
7. appropriate	g. setting up
8. layout	h. supply
9. paramount	i. the most important

10. provision   j. plan

(Ⅲ) Choose the best answer（选择最佳答案）
1. He will let you know at once if he _____ any news about the little boy.
   a. get   b. gets   c. will get   d. would get
2. Not only you but also I _____ right.
   a. am   b. have   c. were   d. had
3. She has already gone to school. But before she left, she _____ her breakfast.
   a. had had   b. has had   c. had   d. would have
4. "Sorry, I am a little bit late." "Oh, I _____ here just a few minutes."
   a. am   b. have been   c. had been   d. will be
5. Yesterday an old man found the prisoner, who had run away from the prison four weeks _____.
   a. ago   b. later   c. after   d. before
6. If she _____ ill today, she would join us in the party in the afternoon.
   a. is not   b. were not   c. was not   d. be not
7. A lot of students find the text very hard _____.
   a. understood   b. understanding
   c. to understand   d. being understood
8. In order to get to the garden early, I had my friend _____ a map for me.
   a. drawn   b. to draw
   c. draw   d. drawing
9. We are all looking forward to seeing you again, and we will be very disappointed if you _____.
   a. won't come   b. didn't come
   c. don't come   d. hadn't come
10. Wang Ling is not naturally a morning person, _____ she has four clocks set for about 7:30 a.m.
    a. through   b. because   c. so   d. for

(Ⅳ) Translation
Translate the following Chinese into English：
1. 房屋服务的履行是业主评价居住环境的重要因素。
2. 通常,这些服务系统并不能根据业主的要求随意改动。
3. 一直以来,房屋服务系统的维护是由承包方负责的。
4. 投资方与空调维护承包方签订合同。
5. 一个更重要的并且需要严格执行管理的环节是业主对房屋的改造。
6. 如果想要令业主满意,就必须及时给予恰当的维护。
7. 投资方必须敦促承包方进行日常的维护工作。
8. 有时,维护协议是一个全面的合同。
9. 在过去,业主常常不通知房屋服务经理就进行房屋改建。

10. 房屋服务经理要依靠自己的综合知识、内部技术人员和外部顾问才能完成本职工作。

(Ⅴ) Extra Reading Activity

Extra reading: read the following passage and choose the best answer to complete each of the statements that follow.

PERFORMANCE OF BUILDING SERVICES

THE FUTURE

What does the future hold?

Computerisation is playing an increasing role in all aspects of building design and operations and the maintenance area is no exception. Sophisticated computerised maintenance systems have been developed by major building owners and proprietary software is available for the smaller individual building owner. This software will continue to be further developed and enhanced with the computerised management of building maintenance becoming more commonplace through the 1990's.

The increasing use of CAD in the design of building services provides an ideal avenue for setting up a management system that will allow the changes in services design, necessitated by tenancy fitout, to be monitored and documented throughout the life of the building. By the mid 1990's an on-site CAD system will probably be part of the maintenance management and building management equipment on all major buildings and perhaps many minor buildings. This system, properly managed, will enable all changes in tenancy fitout to be stored on the computer system, thus providing Building Managers, Consultants and Contractors with up to date records on system layouts, revisions etc.

This computerisation, in conjunction with the appropriate levels of professional and technical input, will assist in ensuring that building services systems operate at optimum efficiency (as in fact they were designed to do) throughout the life of the building with the resultant spinoff of tenant satisfaction and high return on investment for building owners.

COMPUTERISED MAINTENANCE MANAGEMENT

Greater efficiencies have resulted through the use of computerised maintenance management systems, particularly in the areas of resource allocation, work scheduling, cost identification and information collation from a comprehensive data base of building engineering activities. (Refer to Annexure A, article from Australian Business, August 24, 1988 "Engineering's Last Frontier", attached).

Essentially maintenance engineering software packages provide a facility for integration of planned maintenance, asset management, engineering works orders and cost control data. The database thus developed can be used as an input to a Property Management System.

Why Use a Computer?

Because this equipment has the capacity to

Efficiently processes and stores large volumes of information

Provide immediate access to vital information

Act as a well structured tool for planning and control

Produce meaningful and accurate reports for management

Not forget-resign, retire or die

The computer based system must be able to perform the following functions.
1. Maintenance of the asset register
2. Incorporation of the maintenance plan
3. Listing of the maintenance status of each item
4. Listing of "maintenance due" items
5. An inspection/service summary report
6. Report on manpower budget
7. System log keeping
8. Periodic servicing schedules
9. Issuing of maintenance worksheets
10. Issuing of defects reports
11. Recording of unscheduled maintenance
12. Planning of major maintenance activities

The compuer based maintenance system is particularly effective when it is under the direct control of the maintenance engineering staff.

Due mainly to the volume of records and the need for cross referencing, collection of statistics, and assigning costs for work to nominated cost centres, the Building and Engineering Service function lends itself to computer based systems.

1. Computerisation is playing an increasing role in all aspects of _____ is no exception.
   a. the building design area
   b. the operations area
   c. the maintenance area
   d. building design and operations and the maintenance area

2. This software will continue to be further developed and enhanced with the com puter-ised _____ becoming more commonplace through the 1990's.
   a. management of comprehensive Maintenance
   b. management of preventative Maintenance
   c. management of building maintenance
   d. management of equipment maintenance

3. _____ an on-site CAD system will probably be part of the maintenance management and building management equipment on all major buildings and perhaps many minor buildings.
   a. Through the 1990's
   b. At the end of 1990's
   c. August 24, 1988
   d. By the mid 1990's

4. This on-site CAD system, properly managed, will enable all changes in tenancy fitout to be stored on the computer system, thus providing _____ with up to date records on system layouts, revisions etc.

    a. Building Managers   b. Consultants

    c. Contractors   d. All of above

5. Greater efficiencies have resulted through the use of computerised maintenance management systems, particularly in the areas of _____.

    a. resource allocation, cost identification and information collation from a comprehensive data base of building engineering activities.

    b. resource allocation, work scheduling, cost identification and information collation from a comprehensive data base of building engineering activities.

    c. resource allocation, work scheduling, and information collation from a comprehensive data base of building engineering activities.

    d. work scheduling, cost identification and information collation from a comprehensive data base of building engineering activities.

II. Language Ability Drill(语言能力练习)

(I) Vocabulary Exercise

1. **The suffix -en can be added to adjectives to form verbs, meaning "make" or "become", e. g.**

    bright + -en → brighten: make or become bright or brighter

    Now complete the following sentences with verbs formed in this way from the adjectives given in brackets:

    1) The internet _____ the distance between the world and us. (short)

    2) Travel can _____ one's horizon. (wide)

    3) Pupils have to _____ their pencils every day. (sharp)

    4) The river _____ at its mouth where it meets the sea. (broad)

    5) As they approached (接近) the finish line, the runners _____ their steps. (quick)

    6) After the sunset, the sky _____. (dark)

2. **Study the following words. Then use them correctly in the sentences below.**

Verbs	Nouns	Adjectives & Participles	Adverbs
excite	excitement	excited exciting	excitedly
disappoint	disappointment	disappointed disappointing	
	patience reluctance efficiency	patient reluctant efficient	patiently reluctantly efficiently

    1) excite, excitement, excited, exciting, excitedly

    ① That Beijing got the chance to hold the Olympic Games was great _____ in China.

② That best seller made every reader very _____.
③ What are you so _____ about?
④ When the pop singer appeared on the stage, all of his fans _____ applauded.
⑤ The news of victory _____ everybody.
⑥ The film winning the Oscar was _____ indeed.

2) disappoint, disappointment, disappointed, disappointing
① To our _____, this summer we had so much rain.
② It was really _____ that her daughter didn't send her a real present for her eightieth birthday.
③ I was very _____ to this book, which was not half so good as I had expected.
④ Her son _____ her, because he had failed again in his final exams.
⑤ Catherine had a very _____ look when she knew her boyfriend couldn't come.

3) patience, patient, patiently
① We should explain everything as _____ as possible, when we help the old people use computers.
② She treated her pupils with great _____.
③ The cat was so _____ that it kept watching the mouse hole for a long time.
④ _____ is a sort of good character.

4) reluctance, reluctant, reluctantly
① He was _____ to do his homework, because he knew little about it.
② The little boy turned off the TV with much _____.
③ The boss _____ agreed to raise the salary of the workers.
④ I was _____ to go to school when I was young.

5) efficiency, efficient, efficiently
① He did the work with great _____ so that he could have a leisure weekend.
② The boss hoped his staff to work in a more _____ way.
③ After two-month training, she now can work as _____ as an experienced nurse.
④ We need more _____ techniques to speed up our production.

(Ⅱ) Cloze
Ella Fant was a middle-aged lady who lived with her only son John in a small house. She 1 John very much. In her 2 he couldn't do anything 3 . Every morning she would give him breakfast 4 bed and bring him the papers to 5 . It isn't really true that he was too 6 to work—in fact he had tried a few 7 . First of all he was a window-cleaner and in his first week he managed to 8 at least six windows. Then he 9 a bus conductor and on his second 10 a passenger stole his bag with all the fares(车费)collected. He 11 lost his job as a postman 12 he sent off all the letters when he should have taken them to people's houses. It seemed that there was 13 suitable work for him. So he 14 to join the army. Mrs. Fant was so 15 about this that she told the

53

16   to all her neighbors. "My John is going to be a soldier," she said. "He is going to be the best soldier there   17   was, I can tell you! "Then the great day came   18   he was to march past the palace in the parade(接受检阅的队伍). His   19   mother traveled to the city early in the morning to be sure of getting a good   20   in the crowd. The parade was full of sound and color. But when John and his   21   came in sight some of the people watching   22   laughing at the one who couldn't keep pace with the others as they marched along. But Ella Fant, who was filled with   23 , shouted at the top of her voice: "Look at   24   ! They're all out of   25   except my John! Isn't he the best !"

1. A. depended on   B. waited on   C. trusted   D. loved
2. A. hope   B. eyes   C. head   D. beliefs
3. A. wrong   B. great   C. good   D. strange
4. A. to   B. at   C. in   D. by
5. A. check   B. read   C. keep   D. sign
6. A. lazy   B. young   C. weak   D. shy
7. A. ones   B. years   C. tasks   D. jobs
8. A. rub   B. drop   C. break   D. clean
9. A. followed   B. met   C. became   D. found
10. A. day   B. try   C. route   D. chance
11. A. thus   B. even   C. once   D. only
12. A. even if   B. so that   C. because   D. though
13. A. some   B. such   C. less   D. no
14. A. began   B. promised   C. managed   D. decided
15. A. excited   B. worded   C. anxious   D. curious
16. A. incident   B. change   C. news   D. matter
17. A. yet   B. ever   C. never   D. just
18. A. where   B. since   C. when   D. till
19. A. proud   B. kind   C. strict   D. lucky
20. A. time   B. position   C. experience   D. impression
21. A. neighbors   B. army officer   C. mother   D. fellow soldiers
22. A. couldn't help B. shouldn't burst out C. stopped   D. kept
23. A. sadness   B. happiness   C. surprise   D. regret
24. A. them   B. those   C. that   D. him
25. A. sight   B. order   C. mind   D. step

(Ⅲ) **Complete the following sentences, using the words given in brackets:**
1. Very few plants and animals _____ heat or cold for a long time. (endure)
2. This was given us as a present _____ our silver wedding (银婚). (occasion)
3. The old lady dropped her spoon and bent _____, causing her to feel a sharp pain in the back. (pick up)

4. If you _____ the word, look it up in the dictionary. (sure of)
5. Mr. Park, a candidate for Mayor of Chicago, _____ at losing the election. (disappointment)
6. _____ with life in his hometown, the young man moved away to the city at the earliest opportunity. (content)

Part 2. Dialogue

Room Decoration
(房屋装修)

Ⅰ. Typical Sentences（经典短句）

（Ⅰ）**Daily Conversations**（日常用语）

应答语：Sure. No worries.
好的，没问题。
Can you do me a favor?
请你帮个忙，行吗？
My pleasure.
非常乐意。
Thank you for your help.
谢谢你的帮助。
With pleasure.
这是我应该做的。

祝贺语：All the best!
祝一切顺利，心想事成！
Good luck to you!
祝你好运！
Take care!
多保重！
Congratulations on your marriage!
祝贺你们喜结良缘！

辞别语：再见！——See you! Goodbye!
下周见！——See you next week!
晚安！——Good night!
保持联系！——Keep in touch!

（Ⅱ）**Professional Conversation**（专业会话）

1. 日常维护只负责公用部位，户内维修由业主自己负责。
General Maintenance work mainly includes the public area. Indoors reparation should be made by the owners.
2. 你报的维修超过保修期，再修就要交纳费用。

You must pay for this reparation due to the expiration of guarantee time.

3. 保修期内由开发商负责。

Within the guarantee time, the developer should be responsible for the work.

4. 具体保修细则请看入住手册。

To learn the detailed reparation guarantee, you should consult the residential instruction.

5. 水表及煤气表移位必须得到自来水维修和煤气站的同意。

You must get the permission from the Water Supply Office and Gas Supply Office, before change the position of water meter and gas meter.

Ⅱ. Conversation Passages

(Ⅰ) Passage 1

A: Good morning, sir. Did you start to decorate your room?
　早上好,先生。你已经开始装修房子了吗?

B: Yes, I did. And there's something I need your help. Can you do me a favor?
　是的,我已经开始了。有些事我还需要您的帮助。请帮个忙,行吗?

A: Sure. My pleasure. What's your problem?
　当然,非常乐意! 您有什么问题?

B: I need some reparation in my house.
　我的房子有些地方需要修理。

A: More specific?
　可以更具体些吗?

B: En, let me have a think. Right, why not let's go to my place and I will show you. Anyway, if you're available.
　嗯,让我想想……对了,如果你有时间,还不如一起去我家,我告诉你。

A: Good idea. I'm OK. Let's go.
　好主意,我有时间. 我们走吧。

B: Thank you for your help.
　谢谢你的帮助。

A: With pleasure.
　这是我应该做的。

(Ⅱ) Passage 2

(After arriving at the owner's house)

A: Oh, your decoration plan is excellent!
　你的装修计划真的很不错!

B: Thank you. I bought this house for my marriage, and I will hold my wedding here.
　谢谢您的夸奖。我买这房子是为结婚用的,婚礼也会在这举行。

A: Really! Congratulations on your marriage!

是吗！祝贺你们喜结良缘！

B: Thank you. The thing needs repairing is right here in the room. Can you help me?

谢谢。需要修理的地方就在屋里,您能帮我修吗？

A: Let me have a look. Sorry, I can't help you this time. General Maintenance work mainly includes the public area. Indoors reparation should be made by the owners. However, if it is still within the guarantee time, the developer should be responsible for the work. To learn the detailed reparation guarantee, you should consult the residential instruction.

让我看看。对不起,这次我帮不了您,日常维护只负责公用部位,户内维修由业主自己负责。但是如果这房子仍在保修期内,开发商应该负责的。具体保修细则请看入住手册。

B: Oh, I see. Thank you. Another thing is that can I change the position of water meter and gas meter by myself?

谢谢,我知道了。另外,我可以自己改变水表和煤气表的位置吗？

A: Sorry, I'm afraid you can't. You must get the permission from the Water Supply Office and Gas Supply Office, before change the position of water meter and gas meter.

对不起,这恐怕也不行。在动工前,您要对水表及煤气表移位必须得到自来水公司和煤气站的同意。

B: Thank you. That's very kind of you.

谢谢,您真是太好了。

A: You're welcome! I have to leave now. All the best!

不客气,我必须走了。祝一切顺利,心想事成！

B: Thank you. Take care!

谢谢,多保重！

Ⅲ. Exercises for Dialogue

(Ⅰ) Fill in the following blanks while observing the conversational manner（按照日常会话习惯完成以下填空）

A: Did you come to my place?

B: Yes. I have something to _____ you.

A: What's up?

B: I'm _____ to marry Vina.

A: Really! _____

B: Thank you, will I see you then?

A: _____. When and where?

B: The wedding will be held in YuHuaTai restaurant this Sunday 3 o'clock p.m.

A: Ok. I see. I will be right there!

(Ⅱ) After filling in the blanks, translate the former dialogue into Chinese.

(Ⅲ) Make a conversation with your partner about asking for a reparation of house. (there should be at east 3 turn-taking in the dialogue)

Ⅳ. **Spoken Language Drill** (fill in the blanks according to the Chinese translation)

Dialogue 1

A: would you _____ if I borrowed your car?
我想借用一下你的汽车可以吗?

B: Well, when _____?
哦,具体什么时候?

A: Until Monday or Tuesday of next week.
借到下周一或周二。

B: I'm sorry, but it's just not _____.
抱歉,实在是爱莫能助。

Dialogue 2

A: Is there any _____ of my borrowing your typewriter?
能不能借用一下你的打字机?

B: For how long?
要借多久?

A: _____ the end of the week.
借到周末。

B: Yes, I guess that would be all right.
行,我想没问题。

Dialogue 3

A: I was _____ if you'd let me stay with you for a few days.
不知道你能否让我在你这里住几天。

B: It really depends on[视……而定]when.
那得看什么时候。

A: Until next weekend, if that's OK.
如果行的话,住到下个周末。

B: Let me _____ it _____, and I'll let you know later.
让我考虑一下,回头再告诉你吧。

Dialogue 4

A: Do you think you could _____ me some of your records/CDs?
请问你能借我几张唱片吗?

B: Until when?
借到什么时候?

A: Oh, just over the _____.
哦,就过完假期。

B: I'm not sure. I'll have to think about it.

我现在不敢说定,我得考虑一下。

Part 3. Supplementary Reading:

British Pub Customs

Visitors to Britain may find the best place to sample local culture is in a traditional pub. But these friendly hostelries can be minefields of potential gaffes for the uninitiated.

An anthropologist and a team of researchers have unveiled some of the arcane rituals of British pubs—starting with the difficulty of getting a drink. Most pubs have no waiters—you have to go to the bar to buy drinks. A group of Italian youths waited 45 minutes before they realized they would have to fetch their own. This may sound inconvenient, but there is a hidden purpose. Pub etiquette is designed to promote sociability in a society known for its reserve. Standing at the bar for service allows you to chat with others waiting to be served. The bar counter is possibly the only site in the British Isles in which friendly conversation with strangers is considered entirely appropriate and really quite normal behavior. "If you haven't been to a pub, you haven't been to Britain."This tip can be found in a booklet, Passport to the Pub: The Tourists' Guide to Pub Etiquette, a customers' code of conduct for those wanting to sample "a central part of British life and culture". The trouble is that if you do not follow the local rules, the experience may fall flat. For example, if you are in a big group, it is best if only one or two people go to buy the drinks. Nothing irritates the regular customers and bar staff more than a gang of strangers blocking all access to the bar while they chat and dither about what to order. Amazingly for the British, who love queues, there is no formal line-up—the bar staff are skilled at knowing whose turn it is. You are permitted to try to attract attention, but there are rules about how to do this. Do not call out, tap coins on the counter, snap your fingers or wave like a drowning swimmer. Do not scowl or sigh or roll your eyes. And whatever you do, do not ring the bell hanging behind to counter—this is used by the landlord to signal closing time. The key thing is to catch the bar worker's eyes. You could also hold an empty glass or some money, but do not wave them about. Do adopt an expectant, hopeful, even slightly anxious facial expression. If you look too contented and complacent, the bar staff may assume you are already being served.

Always say "please" and try to remember some of the British bar staffs pet hates. They do not like people to keep others waiting while they make up their minds. They don't like people standing idly against the bar when there are a lot of customers wanting for service. And they do not like people who wait until the end of the order before asking for such drink as Guinness stout which take considerably longer to pour than other drinks. One Dutch tourist who spent six months visiting 800 of Britain's 61,000 pubs and interviewing 50 publicans and bar workers and more than 1,000 customers said: "I cannot understand how the British ever manage to buy themselves a drink. "But they do, and if you follow these tips you should be able to do so, too. Speaking of tips, you should never offer the bar staff a cash gratuity. The correct behavior is to offer them a drink. Pubs pride themselves on their egalitarian atmosphere. A tip in cash would be a reminder of their service role, whereas the offer of a drink is a friendly gesture. So now you have a drink, but what about meeting the locals? Pub-goers will indicate in unspoken ways if they are interested in chatting. Concentrate on those who have bought drinks and are still loitering at the bar. Those who have moved to sit at tables are probably not seeking company. Look for people with "open" body language, facing outwards into the room. Don't ever introduce yourself with an outstretched hand and a big smile. Natives will cringe and squirm with embarrassment at such brashness. The British, quite frankly, do not want to know your name and shake your hand—or at least not until a proper degree of mutual interest has been well established (like maybe when you marry their daughter) Talk generally about the weather, the beer or the pub and at an appropriate moment, offer to your new found companion a drink. This exchange is key to feeling part of the pub crowd and thereby getting to know more about Britain than its tourists spots. The ritual of sharing—buying round of drinks in turn—is of great significance. This is because the British male is frightened of intimacy, finds it difficult to express friendly interest in other males and can be somewhat aggressive in his manner. If you are having British friends or business contacts, one of your hosts will probably buy the first round, but you should be quick to offer the next. The right time to offer to buy a drink is when their glasses are still a quarter full. The line of "It's my round—What are you having?" may not be in your phrase book, but it is one of the most useful sentences in the English language.

参考译文：

英国酒吧习俗

访问英国的人会发现传统英国酒吧是最能领略当地文化的地方。但对于初来乍到的异国人来说,这些友善的酒吧却犹如潜藏着有惹事危险的"地雷区"。

一位人类学家和一组研究人员揭示了某些鲜为人知的英国酒吧习俗。人们首先遇到的困难是从买酒开始的。大多数英国酒吧都没有酒保,你得到吧台去买酒。一伙意大利年轻人等了三刻钟才明白他们得自己去买。这听上去似乎让人觉得不方便,可却有它深刻的内涵。在因其冷漠而出名的英国社会里,酒吧习俗的形成是为了促进社会交往。排队的时候可以和其他等待买酒的人交谈。在英伦诸岛上,和陌生人亲切地交谈而被认为是完全适宜的正常行为的惟一场所可能就是吧台了。"你如果没去过酒吧,那就等于没有到过英国。"这个忠告可在名为《酒吧护照:旅游者酒吧习俗指南》的小册中找到,它对那些想要领略"英国生活和文化核心部分"的人是一种行为准则。问题是如果你不入乡随俗的话,你将一无所获。譬如说,你们若是团体前往,那最好是一个或两个人前去买酒。酒吧常客和酒保最讨厌的就是一大伙人一边聊着一边又优柔寡断不知喝什么酒好,把通往吧台的路给堵住。就爱排队的英国人而言,酒吧里看不到正式的排队这令人感到惊讶。酒保有本领知道该轮到谁了。你可以做些动作引起酒保的注意,但有规可循。不要大声嚷嚷,不要在吧台面上敲击钱币,不要叭叭地弹手指,不要像快淹死人的那样挥动手臂,不要绷着脸,不要唉声叹气,不要翻动眼珠。在不该干的事当中还绝对不要摇晃挂在吧台后面的铃,那是酒吧老板用的,表示关门时间到了。关键是你要让酒保看见你。你可以举起空杯子或钱,可不要摇晃。你脸上可以流露等待、期望,甚至略带焦急的表情。你如果显得太心满意足的样子,酒保会认为他们已经为你提供服务了。要把"请"字挂在嘴边,要尽量记住一些英国酒保最厌恶的事。他们不喜欢酒客拿不定主意而让别人等着;不喜欢好多客人等着买酒而有人却靠着吧台闲站着;也不喜欢有人等到最后才说要喝像爱尔兰烈性黑啤酒那样的酒,因为比起别的酒来,准备这种酒的时间要长得多。一个曾花了半年的时间,去了英国61000家酒吧中的800个,访谈了50位酒吧老板和酒保以及1000多个酒客的荷兰旅游者说:"我不明白英国人是怎么给自己买到酒的。"可事实上他们就能。如果你按着本文所说的忠告去做,你也能如愿以偿地买到酒。说到"小费",你可千万别给酒保现金以表示谢意。正确的做法是请酒保喝一盅。酒吧为自己的平等气氛感到自豪。现金小费会使人想到酒保是伺候人的,而请喝一杯则是友好的表示。好,你现在喝上酒了,那又怎么和当地人接触呢?上酒吧的人如果有兴趣交谈的话,会用非言语方式表现出来。注意那些已经买了酒可还在吧台前晃荡的人。那些已经离开吧台,找到椅子坐下的人可能只是想独斟。找那些脸朝外,朝屋里人看,用形体语言表示"可接触"的人。千万不要伸出手来笑容满面的自我介绍。对于这种轻率鲁莽,当地人会因尴尬而战战兢兢,坐立不安。坦率地说,英国人不想知道你的姓名,也不想跟你握手——至少在相互间尚未形成某种共同利益(譬如当你娶他们的女儿为妻)之前不会。可以跟人泛泛地谈天气,谈啤酒,或者谈所在的酒吧。在适当的时刻主动提出给你新找到的同伴买酒。这种相互请酒是感受自己是酒吧群体中的一员的关键作法,从而可以更多了解旅游点以外的英国。轮流买酒分担费用的习俗有它重要意义。这是因为英国男人害怕亲密,他们对其他男性表示友好有困难,举止行为上多少有可能不甚和善。你如果和英国朋友在一起或者在洽谈商业合同,接待你的主人中有一位可能买第一轮酒,而你应该很快表示买下一轮的。在对方杯子里的酒还剩下四分之一时,就是你该提出买酒的时候了。"这轮由我买——你喝的是什么?"这句话在你的英语小册里可能没有,但它却是英国语言中非常有用的一句话。

1. The best place for visitors to sample British local culture is _____.
   A. a museum   B. a theater   C. a traditional pub   D. a university
2. Most pubs have _____ waiters.
   A. a lot of   B. a few   C. no   D. some
3. Where is possibly the only site in the British Isles in which friendly conversation with strangers is considered entirely appropriate?
   A. around table   B. at bar counter
   C. outside the pub   D. We don't know.
4. What do British bar staffs hate?
   A. They do not like people to keep others waiting while they make up their minds.

B. They don't like people standing idly against the bar when there are a lot of customers wanting for service.

C. They do not like people who wait until the end of the order before asking for such drink as Guinness stout which take considerably longer to pour than other drinks.

D. All of the above

5. People in the pub talk generally about the following except _____.

    A. the weather   B. the beer   C. the pub   D. their families

Part 4. Practical Writing

个人简历写作参考

一、英文简历撰写注意事项

1. 多用无主句。
2. 年代顺序由近及远。
3. 单项标题大写。
4. 纸张一般为16开或A4。

二、英文简历的基本内容

1. 个人情况：Name, Sex, Date of Birth, Place of Birth, Permanent Domicile, Nationality, Martial Status, Children, Religion, Party Affiliation, Health, Height, Weight, Present Address, Permanent Address.

2. 职业意向：Objective/Position Wanted: A position as English Instructor, preferably handling students from the intermediate to the advanced levels.

3. 资历：Qualifications: Bachelor of Arts in Business Administration, major in marketing.

4. 经历(Job Experience)：一般逆序写。

Job Experience

5/86-12/86   University of California Press, Berkeley, California

Editorial and Marketing Trainee

5/86-8/86   Wyatt and Duncan Interiors, Berkeley, California

Sales Clerk

5. 文化程度(Education)：一般逆序写，可以包括主要课程。例如：

Master of Science with concentration in Electronics,

Massachusetts Institute of Technology, from Sept, 1985 to June, 1987

Bachelor of Science

Beijing University, Department of Electrical Engineering, from Sept, 1981 to July, 1985

6. 技术资历与特长(Technical Qualifications/ Special Skills)。

7. 著作及专利(Publications and Patents)。

8. 社会活动(Social Activity)。
9. 荣誉与奖励(Honors and Awards)。
10. 爱好及兴趣(Hobbies and Interests)。
11. 证明人(References)。

Unit 4. Security

Part 1. Text

Security

WHY DO WE NEED SECURITY?

To provide protection for:

      Tenants
      The General Public
      The Property Asset itself

FACTORS TO BE CONSIDERED

Tenant's Business-Today, for a whole variety of reasons, tenants can and are being targeted for bomb threats, bribery, larceny, computer associated crimes and unfortunately, the list goes on and on. [1]

Tenants using the building in question, during both normal office hours, and after hours, require the knowledge that both they, their property and their own business cannot be interfered or tampered with by outside parties.

Public Access-Members of the public using the building at any time need to be both controlled and provided with the peace of mind, which stems from the observable aspects of building security. By control, it is intended to prevent members of the public gaining access to unauthorized areas and thereby possibly causing the associated problems which may follow. [2]

Asset Design-The building asset itself presents its physical design, aspects of which need to be considered for security purposes. An example of which might be the stairwells, which would require securing in some manner so as to prevent people from accessing tenancies from "the back door" in an unauthorized sense. Also corridors, service bays, lanes, plant rooms, fire corridors etc. all need special consideration.

SECURITY METHODS

A building owner or management team may chose to apply either of, or both, the following security methods.

    In-house security guards or security devices
   Private security company services and security devices and control

Either of the two methods outlined above may employ anyone or a number of the following security elements:

Alarms-Alarms are available in a variety of detection methods, including movement, infrared, vibration, door and window alarms.[3] The purpose of alarms is to detect unauthorized access or movement in, or through a particular area.

Patrols-Patrols can be both internal (within the property) and or external. The tendency today is away from internal night watchman services towards the services of an external security patrol company.

Dogs-Security dogs are highly effective in certain circumstances and can be left on the property overnight or alternatively incorporated with a personal patrol service by a guard as required during the night.[4]

Cameras-Security cameras are simply monitoring devices. It should be remembered they are only as good as the guard or control room personnel that may be watching them.

Police Liaison-A working knowledge of the chain of command and local police network as it would apply to any security problem at your property is very helpful. This knowledge is highly desirable when dealing with an after hours security problem.

Key Systems-Buildings can have both restricted or unrestricted key systems. As the name would indicate, a restricted key system makes it more difficult for people to copy keys for use within a building. Key cutting can only be undertaken with the authorization of the Building Ownership or the Building Manager, and generally only at specialist or nominated facilities.

Building Access Devices-Buildings are now incorporating security card access devices for entry control during particular hours.

These devices offer selective building access. By that, it is meant that the users of those keys may only be given access to the building during designated hours. For example, one of these devices may be given to the Company Principal who should be authorized to enter the building on a 24 hour basis 365 days of the year. Alternatively, another key may be given to the office secretary who is authorized to enter the office between the hours of 6arn and 9pm Monday to Friday, and he or she may also be restricted to certain areas.

This selective keying system allows you to authorize only certain people in the building between certain hours, and into certain areas.

Building Perimeter Security-All exterior parts of the building need to be examined for possible entry or interference. This would include doors, locks, windows and basement areas. Naturally appropriate security devices should be fitted to those doors and windows etc which could both detect and inhibit entry from the outside of the building.

Computer Data Cabling-In buildings today the increasing sophistication of tenancy operation dictates that computer operations and their data cables should be suitably installed within the building structure to prevent tapping and interference from unauthorized parties.[5] This is usually a design component, which needs to be reviewed by the Property Manager at the time of construction of the building with the building's architect.

In existing properties any upgrade of tenancy facilities incorporating computer devices should receive the appropriate scrutiny regarding cabling and restricted access to data cables.

SUMMARY

Security is a unique subject, which applies both to the asset and the building users. The security methods or approach outlined above are general only and would need to be modified or tailored for properties of a specialist nature.

参考译文：

安 全 系 统

为什么我们需要安全系统？
因为我们要保护：
业　　主
一般公众
物业财产

我们考虑的因素：

业主的自身因素——今天，由于诸多原因，业主可能或者正受到炸弹、行贿、受贿、盗窃和计算机犯罪的威胁。不幸的是，新的威胁还在出现。

业主在上班和下班的时间段中都想确保自己的人身安全和财产安全不受侵犯。

公共通道——时时刻刻使用这座大厦的人群在享受由保安系统提供的平静之时，也应接受管理。通过控制，保安系统趋向于避免公众进入非获许区域，因此很有可能随之引发一系列的矛盾。

财产设计——房屋财产本身体现于它的物理设计，其中必须考虑安全因素。楼梯间就是其中一例：它要求某种方式的安全措施，来防止某些人从相连的房间或后门进入。同样，走廊、服务区、过道、机械室和消防通道等都需要特别的考虑。

保安方式

房屋所有者或者管理层可以选择如下两种或一种保安方式：

屋内保安员或安全设备

私人保安公司服务，安全设备及安全控制

以上两种方法可以应用以下一种或几种安全设备：

警报器——警报器的种类很多，有移动警报器、红外线警报器、震动警报器、门窗警报器。使用警报器的目的是为了发现非法进入或通过某一特定地区的人。

巡逻——巡逻可以是内部巡逻（在建筑物中），也可以是外部巡逻。现在，室内的守夜保安员已逐渐被淘汰，取而代之的是安全公司提供的室外巡逻服务。

保安犬——保安犬在一些情况下很实用，他们可以整夜看守财产，或者和保安员一同在夜间巡逻。

监视器—安全监视器就是一种简单的监视设备，应当记住的是它们的功能仅相当于警卫或者监控室里的监控人员。

警力联网——了解指挥工作条例和当地的警方网络非常有帮助,他们会帮你解决所在地区的任何安全问题。当遇到一个已发生了数小时的安全问题时,人们就非常需要这些知识的帮助。

钥匙——大楼对钥匙的管理可以是严格或非严格的。从名字上就可以看出,严格的钥匙系统很难让人配得可以在一座楼里使用的钥匙。钥匙配制只有在得到了大楼所有者或房屋服务经理的许可后方可让专家或授权的机构制作。

大楼进出设备——现在,在特定的时间里,可以使用门卡进出大楼。

这些设备实现了对进出大楼的人员进行选择。这样的系统就意味着那些钥匙的使用者只能在规定的时间里进入大楼。例如,大楼的负责人使用的那种设备可以使他们一年365天每天24小时进入大楼。相比之下,办公司秘书所使用的那种钥匙只能让他们在周一至周五早上6点至晚上9点这段时间里进入办公室,同时他们被限制在特定的区域里活动。

这种有选择的钥匙系统能让你决定哪些人在某个时间段里进入某些区域。

大楼外围安全——大楼外部所有地区都需要被检查是否有进入或打扰的可能,这包括门、锁、窗和地下室区域。当然,适当的安全设施,应当被安装在这些门窗上,他们既能监视又能禁止从大楼外部的进入。

电脑数据线缆——现在,越来越复杂的房屋租赁操作说明了电脑操作及其数据线缆应当被恰当地安装在大楼的架构中,这样就能避免来自外界的骚扰。这通常是在大楼建造之时,由物业经理和建筑师共同商讨的工程设计的一部分。

在现存的建筑中,任何租用设施的升级,特别是电脑设施,都应该得到恰当的实施,这是考虑到线缆和连接电缆特定途径。

小结

安全系统是一个特殊的课题,它既关系到物业财产,也关系到房屋使用者。上述对安全措施的说明,只是一个简要的概括,具体实施应根据不同房屋的特点进行修改完善。

Vocabulary
单词表:

91.	security	[siˈkjuəriti]	n.	安全
92.	bribery	[ˈbraibəri]	n.	行贿,受贿,贿赂
93.	larceny	[ˈlɑːsni]	n.	盗窃罪
94.	interfere	[ˌintəˈfiə]	vi.	干涉,干预,妨碍,打扰
			vi.	干预,玩弄,贿赂,损害,削弱,篡改
95.	tamper	[ˈtæmpə]	vt.	篡改
			n.	捣棒,夯,填塞者
96.	unauthorized	[ʌnˈɔːθəraizd]	adj.	未被授权的,未经认可的
			n.	通路,访问,入门
97.	access	[ˈækses]	n.	存取,接近
98.	asset	[ˈæset]	n.	资产,有用的东西
99.	corridor	[ˈkɔridɔː]	n.	走廊
100.	lane	[lein]	n.	小路,巷,里弄,狭窄的通道,航线

101. perimeter	[pəˈrimitə]	n.	[数]周长，周界
102. sophistication	[səˌfistiˈkeiʃən]	n.	强词夺理，诡辩，混合
103. interference	[ˌintəˈfiərəns]	n.	冲突，干涉
		adj.	合并的，结社的，一体化的
104. incorporate	[inˈkɔːpəreit]	vt.	合并，使组成公司，具体表现
		vi.	合并，混合，组成公司
		vt.	结社，使成为法人组织
105. nominate	[ˈnɔmineit]	vt.	提名，推荐，任命，命名
106. alternatively	[ɔːlˈtəːnətivli]	adv.	做为选择，二者择一地
		n.	细节，详细
107. particular	[pəˈtikjulə]	adj.	特殊的，特别的，独特的，详细的，精确的，挑剔的
108. selective	[siˈlektiv]	adj.	选择的，选择性的
109. indicate	[ˈindikeit]	vt.	指出，显示，象征，预示，需要，简要地说明
110. personnel	[pəːsəˈnel]	n.	人员，职员

Useful Expressions

provide ... with　向……提供；给……装备；把……装到……里
prevent ... from　阻止，制止；妨碍；预防
a variety of　各式各样，各种；各款
be away from...　离开，远离，不在……，向离开……的方向
apply to　适用于，适合，应用到
deal with　做买卖，处理，安排，涉及

Notes

备注：

1. "Today, for a whole variety of reasons, tenants can and are being targeted for bomb threats, bribery, larceny, computer associated crimes and unfortunately, the list goes on and on."："今天，由于诸多原因，业主可能或者正受到炸弹，行贿、受贿，盗窃和计算机犯罪的威胁。不幸的是，新的威胁还在出现。"中的"on and on"是一种习惯用法，表示"越来……越"或"不断……"的意思。

例如：

"He runs on and on."

"他不断得跑啊跑。"

2. "By control, it is intended to prevent members of the public gaining access to unauthorized areas and thereby possibly causing the associated problems which may follow."："通过控制，保安系统趋向于避免公众进入非或许区域，因此很有可能随之引发一系列的矛盾。"一句中，"be intended to do sth."是一个词组，译为："有趋势做某事"。

3. "Alarms-Alarms are available in a variety of detection methods, including move-

ment, infrared, vibration, door and window alarms. ":"警报器的种类很多,有移动警报器、红外线警报器、震动警报器、门窗警报器。"一句中,"be available"的意思是:"有……"。但其还有"可得到"的意思。

4. "Security dogs are highly effective in certain circumstances and can be left on the property overnight or alternatively incorporated with a personal patrol service by a guard as required during the night.":"保安犬在一些情况下很实用,它们可以整夜看守财产,或者和保安员一同在夜间巡逻。"一句中,"be incorporated with sb./sth."是:"与某人或某物(结合在)一起;一同"的意思。

5. "In buildings today the increasing sophistication of tenancy operation dictates that computer operations and their data cables should be suitably installed within the building structure to prevent tapping and interference from unauthorized parties.":"现在,越来越复杂的房屋租赁操作说明了电脑操作及其数据线缆应当被合适地安装在大楼的架构中,这样就能避免来自外界的骚扰。"一句话中,"interference"一词与"from"连用指:"来自……的干扰"。

6. "Either of the two methods outlined above may employ anyone or a number of the following security elements.":"以上两种方法可以应用以下一种或几种安全设备。"一句话中,"a number of"是一个词组,译为"若干,许多"。

例如:
A number of new products have been successfully launched.
许多新产品已成功投放市场。

7. "It should be remembered they are only as good as the guard or control room personnel that may be watching them.":"应当记住的是它们的功能仅相当于保安员或是在监控室里进行监控的监控人员"一句中,"as good as"是一个词组,译为"和几乎一样;实际上等于"。

例如:
The house was as good as sold.
这间房屋等于已经卖掉了。

Ⅰ. Exercises for the text(课文练习):

(Ⅰ) Decide whether the following sentences are True or False according to the content of the text.

1. Patrols only refer to the internal one.
2. Security dogs are highly effective because they can guard the property overnight.
3. All the buildings' key systems should be restricted.
4. People can make the key cutting anywhere after taking the authorization of the Building Ownership or the Building Manager.
5. The selective keying system can only decide the people's entrance time.
6. The computer system along with other devices in the building should be updated properly.
7. Security not only applies to the asset but also to the building users.
8. The security methods approach wouldn't need to be modified or tailored at all no matter

what a specialist nature of the properties is.

(Ⅱ) Connect the word in column A to the explanation which is similar to it in column B with a bar.

Column A   Column B
1. larceny   a. office clerk
2. interfere   b. show
3. access   c. name
4. asset   d. especial
5. nominate   e. gateway
6. alternative   f. substitutive
7. particular   g. property
8. selective   h. of selection
9. indicate   i. disturb
10. personnel   j. stealing

(Ⅲ) Choose the best answer（选择最佳答案）
1. The old man _____ good care of.
   a. is taking   b. is being taken   c. takes   d. has taken
2. Wang Lin drives very fast and is a very careless man, _____ worries his mother very much.
   a. what   b. that   c. who   d. which
3. I was sure that my husband _____ me $100 when he got his salary.
   a. gives   b. would give   c. give   d. will give
4. I borrowed some magazines _____ read on the journey.
   a. so as to   b. that   c. which   d. what
5. The foreigners _____ around the school by our president at the moment.
   a. show   b. are showing
   c. are being shown   d. have shown
6. What my friend would like me to do is _____ silent about it.
   a. keep   b. to keep
   c. keeping   d. kept
7. Next year our teacher will visit the school _____ she taught 30 years ago.
   a. what   b. who   c. when   d. where
8. Mother told me that I was given a week to decide whether I _____ the present.
   a. will accept   b. would accept
   c. have accepted   d. had accepted
9. When _____ in the open air, we often sing English songs.
   a. work   b. working
   c. worked   d. works
10. It was a cold winter morning, and there was not anyone _____ the little girl could

turn to for help.

a. that   b. which   c. whom   d. what

(Ⅳ) Translation

Translate the following Chinese into English:

1. 这样的系统就意味着那些钥匙的使用者只能在规定的时间里进入大楼。
2. 安全系统是一个特殊的课题，它既关系到物业财产，也关系到房屋使用者。
3. 这种有选择的钥匙系统能让你决定哪些人在某个时间段里进入某些区域。
4. 钥匙配制只有在得到了大楼所有者或房屋服务经理的许可后方可让专家或授权的机构制作。
5. 业主在上班和下班的时间段中都想确保自己的人身安全和财产安全不受侵犯。
6. 今天，由于诸多原因，业主可能或者正受到炸弹，行贿、受贿，盗窃和计算机犯罪的威胁。
7. 使用警报器的目的是为了发现非法进入或通过某一特定地区。
8. 这通常是在大楼建造之时，由物业经理和建筑师共同商讨的工程设计的一部分。
9. 同样，走廊，服务区，过道，机械室和消防通道等都需要特别的考虑。
10. 现在，室内的守夜保安员已逐渐被淘汰，取而代之的是安全公司提供的室外巡逻服务。

(Ⅴ) Extra Reading Activity

Extra reading: read the following passage and choose the best answer to complete each of the statements that follow.

OCCUPATIONAL HEALTH, SAFETY AND ENVIRONMENTAL ISSUES INTRODUCTION

The cost of underwriting insurance for occupational and environmental risks are escalating rapidly after recognising the quantum of current settlements.

The costs to the Insurance Industry of Occupational Health, Safety and Environmental Insurance can best be assessed and managed by the effective use of an Independent Audit and Investigation process.

A significant cost and risk reduction tool is an effective independent Audit of the building requiring underwriting so as to highlight it's potential shortcomings and exposures. This independent audit is then used to assist the prospective client to develop a Strategic Plan for the management of Occupational health, Safety and Environmental issues. By developing this plan, it is possible to ensure that the prospective building to be insured manages these critical areas, thereby improving its performance and hence reducing the insurance risk on an ongoing basis.

Accidents and incidents do occur in industry and these can be cosily in terms of litigation and settlements. The quantum of the settlements will be significantly affected by the evidence presented. Objective, independent and specialist investigation provides the best evidence to ensure that the settlements are based on fact.

Audit and investigation in Occupational Health, Safety and Environmental issues is a highly specialised field requiring a specialist's technical knowledge and, importantly, the ability to discuss the key facts and present them in a form that will influence either the potential insurer or those involved in the litigation process.

A specialised, independent consultancy could provide major returns to both the Underwriting Organisation and the property owner.

OCCUPATIONAL HEALTH, SAFETY AND ENVIRONMENTAL MANAGEMENT: A TENANCY PERSPECTIVE

INTRODUCTION

With the introduction of the Occupational Health and Safety legislation, organisations have been required to introduce programs for the effective management of Occupational Health and Safety in the workplace. Generally, these programs all require an investment of funds in order to achieve their aims and objectives. The success of these programs should be judged by their cost effectiveness, as measured by the positive benefits compared to their direct cost.

Nationally, these programs cost billions of dollars, yet the performance return, as measured by workplace accidents, deaths, occupational ill health, workers compensation costs and their consequences, would suggest that this investment has not necessarily been successful nor cost effective. Indeed if organisations were to judge the Return on Funds Invested in these programs, in a similar manner to their Capital Investment Programs, then serious questions would be raised about the Strategic Planning Process invoked to determine this expenditure.

With the exception of certain industries, the Stategic Planning Process has not been applied to the management of Occupational Health, Safety and the Environment due, mainly, to the perception of this aspect of the management role as being a highly technical area, and therefore, not a general management function. If perceived as a key aspect of the business, requiring strategic planning by senior management, then this investment of significant funds would more than likely be very cost effective and indeed provide a significant return on the funds invested.

WHAT THEN ARE THE RETURNS?

Productivity gains
Reduced exposure to litigation
Reduced accident rates
Reduced absenteeism
Reduced workers compensation claims
Increased efficiency of capital equipment
Compliance with legislation
Reduced workers compensation premiums
Improved Industrial Relations
Reduced adverse media exposure
Improved working environment

Reduced environmental impact of processes

THE BENEFITS?

The major benefit anticipated will be a reduced unit cost and hence the potential for greater profitability.

Another significant benefit is the reduced risk of adverse media exposure and hence the protection and/or potential improvement of the corporate image.

Another major benefit is an improvement in the working environment, resulting in a healthier, more stable workforce with reduced Industrial Relations problems.

These benefits are all significant in contributing to profitability and hence return on funds invested for the building user. It is simply good housekeeping.

HOW TO ACHIEVE THESE RETURNS?

The building user could appoint a professional consultancy team to assist the senior management of the organisation to develop and implement a cost effective strategic plan for the management of Occupational Health, Safety and Environmental issues. The consultancy team would work to develop this plan using the following process:

Understand the business and its Strategic Plan.

Understand the organisation, its people and the working environment.

Baseline assessment of the organisation that will include:

workplace visitations and discussions,

objective OHS&E monitoring programs,

review of necessary statistical and financial information,

review of all current programs and their costs,

review of insurance reports,

review of documentation from enforcement authorities,

review of materials used including their storage, use and disposal,

review of the legislative requirements pertaining to the organisation

review of all discharges and their environmental consequences,

review of emergency procedures,

review of the Industrial Relations management including Safety Committees and Safety Representatives.

The production of an objective overview of the current management of Occupational Health, Safety and the Environment, including potential consequences and risks.

Work with the Senior Management Group to develop a Strategic Plan using the above overview as a baseline.

Develop a costed Action Plan for the implementation of the Strategic Plan.

Discussion of the Strategic Plan and Action Program with the organisation and its people.

Implementation of the Action Program.

Production of an Annual Audit of the Program with a Report to identify the Return on

Funds invested.

This process should provide any building user organisation with a cost effective five year Strategic Plan for the management of Occupation Health, Safety and the Environment and an audit process to confirm its success.

1. It can best for _____ to assess and manage the costs to the Insurance Industry of Occupational Health, Safety and Environmental Insurance.
    a. the effective use of an Independent Audit and Investigation process
    b. the effective use of Investigation process
    c. the Property Manager
    d. the asset manager
2. _____ provides the best evidence to ensure that the settlements are based on fact.
    a. Objective and specialist investigation
    b. Independent and specialist investigation
    c. Objective, independent and specialist investigation
    d. Objective, independent investigation
3. The success of these programs for the effective management of Occupational Health and Safety in the workplace should be judged by their cost effectiveness, as measured by the _____ compared to their _____.
    a. benefits ... direct cost
    b. positive benefits ... direct cost
    c. positive benefits ... cost
    d. direct cost ... positive benefits
4. what are the benefits?
    a. The major benefit anticipated will be a reduced unit cost and hence the potential for greater profitability.
    b. Another significant benefit is the reduced risk of adverse media exposure and hence the protection and/or potential improvement of the corporate image.
    c. Another major benefit is an improvement in the working environment, resulting in a healthier, more stable workforce with reduced Industrial Relations problems.
    d. all of above
5. The building user could appoint _____ to assist the senior management of the organisation to develop and implement a cost effective strategic plan for the management of Occupational Health, Safety and Environmental issues.
    a. the asset manager   b. a professional consultancy team
    c. the contracter   d. the Property Manager

II. Language Ability Drill(语言能力练习)

(I) Vocabulary Exercise

Study the following words. Then use them correctly in the sentences below,

Verbs	Nouns	Adjectives & Participles	Adverbs
	honesty	honest	honestly
		dishonest	
	child	childish	childishly
	childhood		
act	act	active	actively
	action		
	activity		
	emotion	emotional	emotionally
		unemotional	
accept	acceptance	acceptable	acceptably
distract	distraction	distracted	
		distracting	

1. honesty, honest, dishonest, honestly
   1) _____ I don't think this dress is suitable to you.
   2) I hate _____ people.
   3) His _____ made him lose all the friends.
   4) Being _____ is one of the most important characters.
   5) My parents always gave me _____ opinions, though some of them were disappointing.

2. child, childhood, childish, childishly
   1) It is _____ for girls to dream of marrying a millionaire.
   2) Mary always behaved so _____ that her boyfriend couldn't bear her anymore.
   3) Every one wants to be a _____ again.
   4) I had a happy _____.
   5) When she was in her _____, she started to play the piano.

3. act (v.), act (n.), action, activity, active, actively
   1) The student union held various _____ last year.
   2) The young man captured (抓到) the murderer single-handed. And for that brave _____ he was given a medal by the local government.
   3) He was so _____ that he was outstanding in almost every field.
   4) Zhang Tielin always _____ as the emperor in TV series.
   5) During his fourth year in the university, Jim _____ took part in social practices.
   6) _____ speak louder than words.
   7) We should exercise ourselves in healthy _____ as much as possible.

4. emotion, emotional, unemotional, emotionally
   1) Someone said that human beings were a kind of _____ animal.
   2) Living with an _____ spouse is a misery.
   3) Not only love but also work needs _____.
   4) _____ speaking, I feel great sympathy (同情) for you although I think you are wrong.

5) His constant fears show that he is suffering from a serious _____ disorder（失调）.

5. accept, acceptance, acceptable, acceptably

1) John was happy the clothes he wore to the party were _____; he was _____ dressed.

2) I think they would _____ our proposal.

3) My proposal gains _____.

4) I don't think Professor Wang will _____ our invitation（邀请）.

6. distract, distraction, distracted, distracting

1) There should be no _____ around the classroom in which an examination is being held.

2) People should learn to work even under being _____.

3) The radio _____ me from paying attention to my work.

4) I find it _____ to study in the street.

5) I can accomplish a great deal more in the library than at home, where there are too many _____.

(Ⅱ) Cloze

People of Burlington are being disturbed by the sound of bells. Four students from Burlington College of Higher Education are in the bell tower of the 1 and have made up their minds to 2 the bells nonstop for two weeks as a protest（抗议）against heavy trucks which run 3 through the narrow High Street. "They not only make it 4 to sleep at night, but they are 5 damage to our houses and shops of historical 6 ," said John Norris, one of the protesters. " 7 we must have these noisy trucks on the roads," said Jean Lacey, a biology student, "why don't they build a new road that goes 8 the town? Burlington isn't much more than a 9 village. Its streets were never 10 for heavy traffic." Harry Fields also studying 11 said they wanted to make as much 12 as possible to force the 13 to realize what everybody was having to 14 "Most of them don't 15 here anyway," he said, "they come in for meetings and that, and Town Hall is sound proof（隔音）， 16 they probably don't 17 the noise all that much. It's high time they realized the 18 ." The fourth student, Liza Vernum, said she thought the public were 19 on their side, and even if they weren't, they soon would be. 20 asked if they were 21 that the police might come to 22 them. "Not really," she said, "actually we are 23 bell-ringers. I mean we are assistant bell-ringers for the church. There is no 24 against practicing." I 25 the church with the sound of the bells ringing in my ears.

1. A. college   B. village   C. town   D. church
2. A. change   B. repair   C. ring   D. shake
3. A. now and then B. day and night C. up and down   D. over and over
4. A. terrible   B. difficult   C. uncomfortable   D. unpleasant
5. A. doing   B. raising   C. putting   D. producing

6. A. scene	B. period	C. interest	D. sense
7. A. If	B. Although	C. When	D. Unless
8. A. to	B. through	C. over	D. round
9. A. pretty	B. quiet	C. large	D. modem
10. A. tested	B. meant	C. kept	D. used
11. A. well	B. hard	C. biology	D. education
12. A. effort	B. time	C. trouble	D. noise
13. A. townspeople	B. other students	C. government officials	D. truck drivers
14. A. stand	B. accept	C. know	D. share
15. A. shop	B. live	C. come	D. study
16. A. but	B. so	C. or	D. for
17. A. notice	B. mention	C. fear	D. control
18. A. event	B. loss	C. action	D. problem
19. A. hardly	B. unwillingly	C. mostly	D. usually
20. A. I	B. We	C. She	D. They
21. A. surprised	B. afraid	C. pleased	D. determined
22. A. seize	B. fight	C. search	D. stop
23. A. proper	B. experienced	C. hopeful	D. serious
24. A. point	B. cause	C. need	D. law
25. A. left	B. found	C. reached	D. passed

(Ⅲ) Complete the following sentences, using the words given in brackets

1. Ted is expected to _____ after he has considered the problem. (come up with)
2. I hear young people under 18 _____ buying cigarettes in that country. (prohibit)
3. Though people of different cultures may experience difficulties in learning _____, cultural awareness and an open mind can reduce these difficulties. (communicate)
4. Efforts _____ of different races (种族) and cultures have not met with (获得) complete success. (bring together)
5. The United States experienced a sharp rise _____ after the Second World War, known as the "baby boom"(生育高峰). (rate)
6. _____ increased awareness, the incidence (发病率) of AIDS has dropped in many U.S. cities. (partly)

Part 2. Dialogue

Parking Car in the Community I
（小区内停车1）

Ⅰ. **Typical Sentences**（经典短句）

（Ⅰ）**Daily Conversations**（日常用语）

办公室接待来电用语：

77

打电话时说：

This is Wang Ming speaking. May I speak to Mr. Li, please?

我是王明，请找李先生.

May I leave a message?

您能帮我捎个信吗？

接电话时说：

Hello, this is _____ from department speaking. What can I do for you?

您好！我是（ ）物业（ ）室（部、处）的（ ）.请问您有什么事？

May I ask who's calling?

请问您哪里？

Hold on a minute. Let me find him.

请等一会，我去叫他.

He is not here right now. May I take your message?

他现在不在，有什么事我可以转告他吗？

(Ⅱ) **Professional Conversation**（专业会话）

1. Please show me your parking card.
   请出示您的车证.

2. Please get the parking card from Property Management department.
   请到物业管理处办理车证.

3. The path in living community is one-way. Please make a round to leave from the back door.
   小区是单行道，绕到后门出车.

4. The cars belonging to the ground parking area are forbidden to park in the underground garage.
   地上车位的车辆不准驶入地下车库.

5. Cars are not in this living community are required to pay management fee, if they stay in the community longer than 15 minutes.
   外来车辆在小区内超过15分钟，需要交纳管理费.

Ⅱ. **Conversation Passages**

(Ⅰ) **Passage 1**

A：Good morning, sir. Please show me your car parking card.
   早上好，先生。请出示您的车证.

B：What kind of card? I'm afraid I don't have it.
   什么样的车证？我恐怕没有.

A：So please take one from Property Management department. Mr. Liu is in charge of it.
   那么请到物业管理处办理车证吧。刘先生负责此事.

B：Would you please just let me drive in, and I will stay for a very short time.
   您能让我先开进去吗？我就停一会儿.

A: Well, cars are not in this living community are required to pay management fee, if they stay in the community longer than 15 minutes.

外来车辆在小区内超过15分钟,交纳管理费。

B: En, OK. I see. I will leave in a minute.

好吧,知道了,我一会就走。

A: Right. Park your car in the place for guests, please.

请将您的车停入来宾车位。

B: Thank you.

谢谢。

A: With pleasure.

这是我应该做的。

(Ⅱ) Passage 2

(After parking the car)

A: Hello., this is Chen Ming from Property Management department speaking. What can I do for you?

您好!我是物业部的陈明,请问您有什么事?

B: May I speak to Mr. Liu, please?

请找刘先生。

A: He is not here right now. May I ask who's calling?

他现在不在,请问您是哪位?

B: I'm an owner in the community. I want to have a car parking card of the community.

我是这的住户,我想办一张小区车证。

A: Oh, I see. But this work must be done by him. He's not here just now. I can take your message for him.

噢,我知道了,办车证只由刘先生负责,我可以帮您留个信。

B: Ok, you're so nice to do so.

您真是太好了。

A: You're welcome. Now please tell me your information.

不用客气,请告诉我您的情况吧。

B: My name is Yang Yong. I live in the Building 3, gate 1, 4th floor, room 1. I want to have a one-year car parking card.

我叫杨勇,我住在3号楼,4楼,1门。我想办一张一年期的车证。

A: Ok, I get it. Now I will repeat it for you. Your name is Yang Yong. You live in 3-1-401, and you want to get a one-year car parking card. Is that right?

好,我听懂了,我现在为您重复一遍,您的姓名是杨勇,您住在3号楼1门401室,您想办一张一年期的车证。对吗?

B: Absolutely right! Thank you again!

完全正确!再一次感谢您!

A: You're welcome. I will tell Mr. Liu when he comes back all about it. And he will call you back. Right, would you please also leave your phone number?

不用客气,刘先生回来后,我会转告他的。那时他再打给您,对了,您可以把电话号码也留一下吗?

B: Sure, my telephone number is 24321567. And my mobile phone number is 13001010101.

当然可以,我的家庭电话是 24321567。我的手机号码是 13001010101。

A: Ok, I have noted it down. Anything else I can do for you?

好,我已经记下来了。还有什么事我可以帮您做的吗?

B: No, I think that's all. Thank you for your help. See you later.

噢,我想没有了。谢谢您的帮助,再见。

A: You're welcome. See you later!

不用谢,再会。

Ⅲ. Exercises for Dialogue

(Ⅰ) Fill in the following blanks while observing the conversational manner(按照日常会话习惯完成以下填空)

A: Hello, _____ Xiao Ming from Property Management department _____. Can _____?

B: Yes. _____ Mr. Liu?

A: _____ a minute. Let me find him.

B: OK.

A: I'm sorry. He's not here now. Anything I can do for you?

B: Yes, _____?

A: Sure, I will note it down.

B: Please tell him Mr. Wang in 1-3-401 has called him. And I'm waiting for his calling back.

A: Ok. I see. Anything else _____?

B: No. _____. Thank you

A: _____. Then, bye.

B: Bye-bye.

(Ⅱ) After filling in the blanks, translate the former dialogue into Chinese.

(Ⅲ) Make a telephone conversation with your partner about anything you like(there should be at least 3 turn-taking in the dialogue).

Ⅳ. Spoken Language Drill (fill in the blanks according to the Chinese translation)

Dialogue 1.

A: I'd like to make an _____ with Professor Smith. Would 9:00 tomorrow be all right?

我想和史密斯教授约个会面时间。明天9点行吗?

B: I'm _____ not. She doesn't have any openings in the morning.
恐怕不行。上午她没有空。

A: Could I _____ make it early in the afternoon?
我可以约在下午一上班的时间吗?

B: No. That's not good either. But give me your number and I'll call you if somebody cancels.
不。也不行。不过请你把电话号码给我,如果有人取消约会,我就打电话通知你。

Dialogue 2.

A: Would Dr. Block be able to see me at 9:30 tomorrow?
明天9点半布洛克医生能给我看病吗?

B: I'm sorry, but she won't have any _____ until 11:00, unless there's a cancellation.
对不起,除非有预约取消,11点以前她没有空。

A: Would 1:00 be _____?
1点钟行吗?

B: Yes, she's free then.
可以,她那时有空。

Dialogue 3.

A: Hello. Can I _____ to Yolanda, please?
喂,我找约兰达讲话,可以吗?

B: _____, please.
请你等一下。

A: Thank you.
谢谢。

B: Sorry, but she is _____.
很抱歉,她出去了。

A: Would you tell her Tom Gray Called?
请你告诉她汤姆格雷来过电话,好吗?

B: I'd be glad to.
好的。

Dialogue 4.

A: Hello. Is Marie Ward there, please?
喂,请问玛丽沃德在吗?

B: I'll see if she's in.
我去看看她在不在。

A: OK.
好的。

B: I'm afraid she's not here.
很抱歉,她不在。

A: Could you give her a _____, please?
请问你能不能带个口信给她？

B: Yes, _____.
当然可以。

Part 3. Supplementary Reading:

Tips on Tipping

Gratuity can be a tricky business: What's just right in one country can be miserly or extravagant in another.

It's every traveler's nightmare. The porter brings your bags to your room and helpfully explains how to access CNN. He shows you how to turn on the lights and adjust the air conditioner. Then he points to the phone and says: "If there's anything else you need, just call." All this time, you have been thinking one thing: "How much should I tip this guy?" Out of desperation you shove a few banknote into his hand, hoping that you're neither given too much or too little.

It's difficult to divine what constitutes an appropriate tip in any country. In Japan, if you leave a couple of coins on the table, the waiter may chase after you to return your forgotten change. In New York, on the other hand, if you leave less than 15%, your reservation might not hold up next time. Asia, with its multiplicity of cultures and customs, is a particularly difficult terrain. To make your next trip a little easier, here's guide to tipping across the region:

Bangkok In general, the more Westernized the place is, the more likely you will be expected to leave a gratuity. Some top end restaurants will add a 10% service charge to the bill. If not, waiters will appreciate you tacking on the 10% yourself. However, if you're eating at a downscale restaurant a tip is not necessary. If you're staying at one of Bangkok's many five star establishments, expect to tip the porter 20 to 50 baht(株), depending on how many bags you have. Taxi are now metered in Bangkok. Local custom is to round the fare up to the nearest five baht(株).

Hong Kong Gratuity is customary in this money mad metropolis. Most restaurants automatically add a 10% service charge to the bill, but the surcharge often ends up in the pocket of the owner. If the service is good, add another 10% to the bill, up to HK $100 in an especially nice restaurant. For HK $20 bill may be more acceptable. When in a taxi, round up to the nearest dollar.

Kuala Lumpur Like Indonesia, tipping in Malaysia is confined to the pricier Westernized joints, which often add a 10% service charge to your meal or hotel room. If you are at a hotel restaurant, expect a 10% service charge. But at local restaurants, there's no need to add a gratuity. At five star hotels, one or two ringgit(林吉特) will suffice a porter. At lower end establishments, don't feel compelled to tip. Like Bangkok, many taxis are now metered, so you can just round up to the nearest ringgit(林吉特).

Seoul Tipping is not part of Korean culture, although it has become a matter of course in international hotels where a 10% service charge is often added. If you're at a Korean barbecue joint, there's no need to add anything extra. But a sleek Italian restaurant may require a 10% contribution. If you are at a top end hotel, international standards apply, so expect to pay 500 to 1,000 won per bag. Taxi drivers don't expect a tip. Keep the change for yourself.

Singapore According to government mandate in the Lion City, tipping is not permitted. It's basically outlawed at Changi Airport and officials encourage tourists not to add to the 10% service charge that many high end hotels tack on to the bill. At restaurants, Singaporeans tend not to leave tips. Nicer restaurants do sometimes levy a 10% service charge. Hotel staff is the one exception to the no tipping rule. As a general guide, S $1 should be adequate for baggage lugging service. Taxi drivers don't expect gratuity, but they won't refuse it.

Taipei Like Japan and China, Taiwan is not a tipping society, even though much of the currency seems to come in coin form. Tipping is not expected in restaurants. However, that rule is changing as American type eateries introduce Western ways. Hotel staff won't be overly offended if you don't tip. Gratuity is not expected in taxicabs.

参考译文:

给小费的窍门

给小费是一件棘手的事情,在一个国家适当数目的小费在另一个国家可能会被认为太吝啬或是太阔绰。

对于每一位旅行者来说,这都像一场噩梦。行李员把你的行李搬到房间,然后开始告诉你解释如何收看CNN,告诉你怎么开灯,怎么把空调调好。最后他指着电话说:"如果你还需要什么,请打电话。"而你却一直在反复思考着一件事:"我到底该给这家伙多少小费?"最终,你近乎绝望地把几张钞票塞进他手里,心中暗暗祷告你的小费不多也不少。

知道在每一个国家该给多少小费并不容易。在日本,如果你在桌上留下几个硬币,服务生会追着还给你留下的零钱。在纽约则恰恰相反。如果你给的小费少于消费额的15%,那么下次你预定的桌子可能就会被人占去。由于亚洲各国文化和风俗习惯差异较大,因此在这里给小费格外困难。为了让你下次旅行较为顺利,我们向你提供一些在这一地区给小费的窍门。

曼谷 总的说来,一个地方西化的程度越高,希望你给小费的可能性就越大。有些高级的饭店会在账单里加收10%的服务费。如果没有的话,侍者会希望你主动加上那10%。不过,如果你在一家低档次的餐馆就餐,就没有必要给小费。如果你住在曼谷的某家五星级饭店,就请准备付给搬运工20到50株,具体的数目得依你的行李多少而定。如今曼谷的出租车都打表计程,当地的惯例是把车费整到最接近的五铢的倍数。

香港　在这个金钱至上的大都市里,给小费是司空见惯的。大多餐馆自动在账单里加了10%的服务费,但这笔额外的收入最后却常常落到雇主手里。如果服务质量确实好的话,在账单以外还要再加上10%。而在一个极好的饭馆里,小费可以多达100港币。对于旅馆的搬运工来说,10元港币的小费已足够。不过在最好的一些饭店,20港币可能更受欢迎。坐出租车的话,车费要凑够最近的整数。

　　吉隆坡　像在印度尼西亚一样,在马来西亚给小费也仅限于那些价格较高的西式场所。在那里,一般在就餐或旅馆房间的费用之外附加10%的服务费。如果你在饭店的餐厅就餐,也得准备给10%的服务费。但在当地的饭馆里,却没有必要附加小费。在五星级饭店,给搬运工一两个林吉特就足够了。在低档次的饭店,不一定非给小费不可。像曼谷一样,多数出租车都按里程计费,所以只要凑足最近的整数就行。

　　汉城　尽管在国际饭店里收取10%的服务费似乎是一件理所当然的事,给小费不是韩国文化的一部分。如果你去一个吃韩国烧烤的地方,那么没有必要付额外的费用。但是在一个雅致的意大利餐馆就餐,可能就要多付10%的小费。如果你下榻的是最高级饭店,就要按国际规范行事。这种地方搬一件行李的小费大概是500到1,000韩元。不用给出租车司机小费,找的零钱你自己留着好了。

　　新加坡　根据狮城政府的规定,给小费是不允许的。在樟宜国际机场,这种行为基本上是违法的。官方鼓励游客拒绝支付一些高级饭店附加在账单上的10%的服务费。在饭馆就餐时,新加坡人一般都不留小费。但一些好的饭馆有时也会收取10%的服务费。饭店员工是不收小费原则的惟一例外。一般的准则是,如有人帮你搬运行李,给一新元就够了。出租车司机是不指望拿小费的,但你给他们,他们也不会拒绝。

　　台北　就像日本和中国大陆一样,尽管有大量硬币用于流通,台湾也是一个无需小费的社会。饭馆里不用给小费。不过,随着一些美式餐馆引进西方做法,这一原则也在改变。饭店的员工如果没有得到你的小费的话,也不会觉得任何损失。坐出租车也不需要给小费。

Exercises for the reading:
1. In which country, if you leave a couple of coins on the table, will the waiter chase after you to return your forgotten change?
   A. New York　　　B. Bangkok　　　C. Japan　　　D. Hong Kong
2. In which country, the more Westernized the place is, the more likely will you be expected to leave a gratuity?
   A. Bangkok　　　B. Seoul　　　C. Taipei　　　D. Singapore
3. In Singapore, where do customers need to leave tips?
   A. At Changi Airport　　　　　B. In average restaurants
   C. To hotel staff　　　　　　　D. To taxi drivers
4. In which country will you pay tips for taxi?
   A. Singapore　　　B. Seoul　　　C. Hong Kong　　D. Taipei
5. What is the rate of service charge customers should pay introduced in this article?
   A. 5%　　　　　　　　　　　　B. 10%
   C. 15%　　　　　　　　　　　　D. It varies from different countries.

Part 4. Practical Writing

求职信（Position Application）

常用句式：

1. Your advertisement in China Daily of July 4th for a secretary prompts me to offer you my qualifications for this position.

7月4日《中国日报》上有一则贵公司招聘秘书的广告，我想应征此工作。

2. It has come to my attention that your current director of public relations is on the verge of retirement, and that position maybe open shortly. If this is true, would you please consider me for the job.

我注意到您的公关部主任即将退休，很快就会有个空位，希望您能考虑我来做此项工作。

3. I refer to your company's advertisement for a computer engineering manager in the April 29 edition of the China Times and attach a résumé to support my application for the position.

贵公司4月29日在《中国时报》上刊登了一则招聘一名电脑工程经理的广告，我写信应聘此职，并附上了我的履历表。

4. The attached résumé details my qualifications and experience in the business.

附上的履历表就本人的能力及经验都已详加说明。

5. Four years' experience on China Daily gives me the confidence to apply for this desirable job.

我在《中国日报》四年的工作经历使我有信心申请这个有吸引力的工作。

My experience as an assistant manager in the office services area and my business administration degree uniquely qualify me for the position you have available.

我过去是经理助理，负责办公行政事务。我的商务行政学位也适合你们的要求。

6. I am a graduate of New York University, majoring in marketing and I have 10 years of successful experience behind me.

我毕业于纽约大学，主修营销学。十年来，我的工作一直非常成功。

7. As you will see from the enclosed C. V., I have had eight years' experience of editing.

正如您从本人履历表上所得知的，我从事编辑工作已八年了。

8. It seems to me that this experience, together with my education, has given me ideal preparation to assume the role of the director of public relations in a firm such as yours.

我的这一经历以及我所受的教育为我在像你们这样的公司担任公关部主任的职位奠定了良好的基础。

9. I hope you will give me opportunity to talk with you in person, I can come to Chicago at any time.

我希望能与您亲自面谈，我随时可以来芝加哥。

10. I hope we may meet soon to discuss the employment opportunity in your company.
我希望很快能与您见面,讨论我为贵公司服务的可能性。

11. May I have the privilege of an interview? If you will let me know when it is convenient for you to see me, I will arrange my calendar accordingly.
您可以给我一次面谈机会吗?如果您愿意告诉我何时方便,我将做好相应安排。

12. You may telephone me on my private line (6-3454) if you prefer calling.
如果您愿意打电话,我的私人电话号码是 6-3454。

13. Please contact me at my address or telephone above.
请按信头地址及电话号码与我联系。

14. I am available for an interview at your convenience.
希望你有空时安排面谈。

Unit 5. Comprehensive Contract Maintennace

Part 1. Text

Comprehensive Contract Maintennace

As with every proper business relationship, there are reciprocal benefits and responsibilities expressed or implied between the owner and specialist contractors with regard to the maintenance of lifts, escalators or moving pathway installation. Comprehensive contract maintenance provides ongoing maintenance, usually on the following basis:

1. Preventative Maintenance Service to be Provided by the Contractor
Should systematically

(a) Inspect the equipment for worm, burnt, broken or other wise unserviceable components and compensate for any evident irregular running or deviation from normal design characteristics.

(b) Repair or replace all parts of the equipment which warrant such action as a result of normal wear and tear.

(c) In respect of lifts, renew all wire ropes when necessary and equalize the tension on all hoisting ropes.

(d) Periodically examine all safety devices and governors and carry out tests as required by relevant statutes, regulation sand requirements.

(e) Keep machine rooms, secondary floors, internal ledges, separating beams, lift, escalator and moving pathway pits in clean condition, excluding rubbish, dust and leakages originating outside these confines.

(f) Perform this preventative maintenance during normal working hours and days, the intervention of holidays, industrial disputes or other events beyond the contractor's control permitting.

(g) Report to the owner whenever it may be necessary to shutdown the equipment to allow the performance of extensive work needed.

(h) Stock such spare parts and materials as are reasonably necessary for performing preventative maintenance.

(i) Use trained and supervised personnel to service and maintain the equipment.

2. Emergency Calls
Specialist contractors should attend to emergency breakdown calls at any hour of the

day or night, without additional charge to the owner, where such a breakdown arises in the course of the equipment being operated normally.

Upon notification of any such emergency breakdown by the owner, the equipment will be serviced as soon as practicable. If attendance is required outside normal working hours, just such adjustment and repairs will be effected as can then be reasonably performed by the attending contractor's representative. They may reserve the right to charge the owner for nuisance calls and calls which are the result of negligence or misuse of the equipment or are required by-reason of any cause beyond control.

3. Work Outside Scope of Service

At the request of the owner and at reasonable notice, the specialist contractor will perform the following additional services, provided said contractor received the additional costs incurred in performing such work:

(a) Make repairs or replacements to the equipment necessitated through negligence, misuse or acts of vandalism, or any cause beyond the contractor's control, except normal wear and tear.

(b) Carry out alterations or additions to the equipment, which may be required by any statutory authority or by variations to existing legal requirements or introduction of new regulations, codes, acts, by-laws or ordinances dealing with the equipment.

(c) Perform any of the works listed (emergency calls excepted) outside normal working hours.

参考译文：

综合性的维修合同

在每个正当的商业关系中,所有人和专业承包商之间关于电梯、自动扶梯或可移动装置的维修都明确表达或暗示了相互的利益和责任。综合性的维修合同提供了现行的维修内容,通常是建立在下面这些内容的基础之上的。

1. 承包商提供的预防性维修服务

应该做如下分类：

(a) 检查设备的磨损件,易损件,或在其他方面不适用的零件,对任何明显的不正常运行或对正常设计性能形成的偏差进行补偿。

(b) 修理或取代设备的各个部位,保证这些机械装置是正常磨损的结果。

(c) 关于电梯,必要时更新所有的钢丝绳,调整提升钢丝绳的张力。

(d) 定期检查所有设备和调速器的安全性能,按照有关的章程、规则和需要进行测试。

(e) 保持车间,多层平台,内部横梁,隔离梁,电梯,自动扶梯和移动走道的凹槽等各部位的清洁,清除垃圾,灰尘和这些边缘外侧开始出现的渗漏物。

(f) 进行预防性维护,可以在正常的工作时间内,也可以在节假日里或发生工业争端的时候,以及其他超出承包商负责范围之外的可能发生的情况。

(g) 不管何时关闭设备以进行必需的维护性工作,都要向业主报告。

(h) 储备一些零件和材料,以备进行预防性维护时的不时之需。

(i) 使用经过培训和管理的人才做售后服务和维修设备。

2. 紧急呼叫

专业承包商应该设立紧急维修服务电话,为业主提供24小时服务,而不收取额外费用,这样在正常操作设备的过程中就出现了这种紧急维修。

业主一拨打紧急维修服务电话,承包商将会尽可能快地到位进行设备维修。如果在正常工作时间以外需要提供维修服务,那么就相应做些调整,由负责维修的承包商的代理人来进行维修。对于比较棘手的维修要求,由于粗心大意或者对设备进行了有误操作而导致的维修,或由于任何无法控制的原因导致的维修要求,代理人可以保留向业主收费的权力。

3. 服务范围之外的工作

应业主的要求,并给予合理的通告,专业承包商将会提供以下附加的服务,但提供服务的承包商也会在承担下述服务的同时收取附加成本费:

(a) 对于疏忽、误操作、破坏性行为、或承包商无法控制的原因(正常磨损除外)导致的设备损坏,进行必要的维修和更换。

(b) 对设备进行更换或扩建,以满足司法当局的需要;满足现行法律变化的需要;满足介绍与设备相关的新规则、新标准、新条例、新法规、新规章的需要。

完成正常工作时间之外列出的工作项目(紧急维修服务除外)。

Vocabulary
单词表:

111. comprehensive	[kɔmpri'hensiv]	a.	内容广泛的,综合的,承包的
112. contract	['kɔntrækt]	n.	契约,合同
113. maintenance	['meintinəns]	n.	维修,保养
114. proper	['prɔpə]	a.	正当的,规矩的;出色的,极好的
115. relationship	[ri'leiʃənʃip]	n.	关系,联系;家属关系,亲属关系
116. reciprocal	[ri'siprəkə]	a.	相互的
117. responsibility	[ris'pɔnsəbiliti]	n.	责任,责任心;职责,任务
118. imply	[im'plai]	vt.	含有…的意思;暗指,暗示,意指
119. owner	[əunə]	n.	所有人,物主
120. specialist	['speʃəlist]	n.	专家
121. escalator	['eskəleitə]	n.	(建)自动扶梯
122. ongoing	['ɔngəuiŋ]	a.	正在进行的,前进的,
		n.	进行,行动,事物
123. preventative	[pri'ventətiv]	a.	预防性的
124. systematically	[,sisti'mætikəli]	ad.	有系统地,成体系地,有秩序地,有规则地,有组织地;分类(上)地,分类学地
125. worn	[wɔ:n]	a.	耗尽的,变得衰弱的

126.	otherwise	[ˈʌðəwaiz]	ad.	另外,别样;在其他方面;要不然,否则
127.	unserviceable	[ʌnˈsəːvisəbl]	a.	不能使用的,不适用的,无用的;不耐用的
128.	compensate	[ˈkɔmpenseit]	vt.	补偿,赔偿,酬报;(机)补整,补偿
129.	evident	[ˈevidənt]	a.	明显的
130.	deviation	[diviˈeiʃən]	n.	偏差
131.	characteristic	[kæriktəˈristik]	n.	性能
132.	warrant	[ˈwɔrənt]	v.	保证
133.	wear	[wɛə]	v.	磨损
134.	tear	[tɛə]	v.	撕裂
135.	respect	[risˈpekt]	n.	关于
136.	equalize	[ˈiːkwəlaiz]	v.	调整
137.	hoist	[hɔist]	v.	提高,提升
138.	tension	[ˈtenʃən]	n.	(物)张力,拉力,牵力;(蒸汽等的)膨胀力,压力
139.	governor	[ˈgʌvənə]	n.	调速器
140.	statute	[ˈstætjuːt]	n.	法令,章程
141.	periodically	[piəriˈɔdikəli]	ad.	定期地,周期地
142.	relevant	[ˈrelivənt]	a.	有关的、贴切的,中肯的,恰当的;成比例的,相应的
143.	ledge	[ledʒ]	n.	(自墙壁突出的)壁架;架状突出物
144.	exclude	[iksˈkluːd]	v.	拒绝,隔绝,排除
145.	leakage	[ˈliːkidʒ]	n.	渗漏物
146.	originate	[əˈridʒineit]	n.	起源,开始出现
147.	confine	[kənˈfain]	n.	(常用复)境界,边缘,区域,范围
148.	intervention	[intəˈvenʃən]	n.	介入,干涉
149.	dispute	[disˈpjuːt]	n.	争论,辩论;争执,争端
150.	stock	[stɔk]	vt.	储备,备有;给(商店)办货
151.	supervise	[ˈsjuːpəvaiz]	vt. & vi.	监督,管理
152.	specialist	[ˈspeʃəlist]	n.	专家;专业人员
153.	charge	[tʃɑːdʒ]	n.	费用;靠人赡养的人;主管;充电
154.	notification	[nəutifiˈkeiʃən]	n.	通知,通报;布告;通知单
155.	attendance	[əˈtendəns]	n.	参加,出席;出席率;护理,照料
156.	representative	[repriˈzentətiv]	n.	典型;代表,代理人;继承人;众议院议员
157.	reserve	[riˈzəːv]	vt.	储备;保留;推迟;预定
158.	nuisance	[ˈnjuːsns]	n.	麻烦的事;讨厌的事;多余的事
159.	negligence	[ˈneglidʒəns]	n.	忽视,疏忽;粗心大意
160.	scope	[skəup]	n.	范围,余地,机会;眼界;导弹的射程;

目的，意图
Useful Expressions
with regard to　关于
on the basis　在……基础上
as a result of　作为……的结果
in respect of　关于
attend to　专心，照顾，照料
in the course of　在……的过程中，在……期间
at the request of　应……要求，请求

Notes
备注：

1. Preventative Maintenance Service to be Provided by the Contractor 承包商提供的预防性维修服务

此句中，Preventative Maintenance Service 指预防性维修服务

to be Provided 是动词不定式的被动形式。当动词不定式逻辑上的主语是动词不定式所表示的动作的承受者时，一般要用被动形式。

例如，

That young man seems to be trusted by everyone.

那年轻人看起来博得了大家的信任。

2. In respect of lifts, renew all wire ropes when necessary and equalize the tension on all hoisting ropes. 关于电梯，必要时更新所有的钢丝绳，调整提升钢丝绳的张力。

此句中，renew all wire ropes when necessary 和 equalize the tension on all hoisting ropes 是由 and 连接的两个并列句。

3. Report to the owner whenever it may be necessary to shutdown the equipment to allow the performance of extensive work needed. 不管何时有必要关闭设备以进行必需的延续性工作，都要向业主报告。

此句中，whenever it may be necessary to shutdown the equipment to allow the performance of extensive work needed 是由 whenever 引导的时间状语从句；在从句中，it 是形式主语，to shutdown the equipment to allow the performance of extensive work needed 是真正的主语；needed 是过去分词做定语，修饰前面的名词 extensive work。

4. Specialist contractors should attend to emergency breakdown calls at any hour of the day or night, without additional charge to the owner, where such a breakdown arises in the course of the equipment being operated normally. 专业承包商应该设立紧急维修服务电话，为业主提供 24 小时服务，而不收取额外费用，这样在正常操作设备的过程中就出现了这种紧急维修。

本句中，关系副词 where 引导的是非限定性定语从句。对先行词不起限定修饰作用，只是进行补充说明，去掉后也无损先行词意思完整的定语从句称为非限定性定语从句。非限定性定语从句中关系代（副）词的用法与限定性定语从句的基本相同（如：who，whom，whose，which，和 where，when，皆不可省略），只是不可用 that 和 why。

例如：
Shakespeare, whose works are world-famous, is well known in my country.

莎士比亚的作品世界闻名，他在我国家喻户晓。

He has left for Water Park, where he has to give a speech.

他去水上公园了，他要在那里发表演讲。

5. They may reserve the right to charge the owner for nuisance calls and calls which are the result of negligence or misuse of the equipment or are required by-reason of any cause beyond control. 对于比较棘手的维修要求，由于粗心大意或者对设备进行了误操作而导致的维修，或由于任何无法控制的原因导致的维修要求，代理人可以保留向业主收费的权力。

在此句中，nuisance calls 和 calls which are the result of negligence or misuse of the equipment or are required by-reason of any cause beyond control 是并列句，做介词 for 的宾语；其中，关系代词 which 引导的是定语从句，修饰前面的名词 calls。在此定语从句中，又含有两个由 or 连接的并列句 are the result of negligence or misuse of the equipment 和 are required by-reason of any cause beyond control。

6. Carry out alterations or additions to the equipment, which may be required by any statutory authority or by variations to existing legal requirements or introduction of new regulations, codes, acts, by-laws or ordinances dealing with the equipment. 对设备进行更换或扩建，以满足司法当局的需要；满足现行法律变化的需要；满足介绍与设备相关的新规则、新标准、新条例、新法规、新规章的需要。

本句中，关系代词 which 引导的是非限定性定语从句。有一种非限定性定语从句，由 which 引导，其先行词不是主句中的某一个名词，而是整个句子（或其中的一部分）。

例如：
He won the first prize, which we had never expected.

他赢得了头等奖，这我们根本没有想到。

Ⅰ. Exercises for the text(课文练习)：

(Ⅰ) Decide whether the following sentences are True or False according to the content of the text.

1. As with every proper business relationship, there are reciprocal benefits and responsibilities expressed or implied between the owner and specialist contractors with regard to the maintenance of lifts, escalators or moving pathway installation.
2. Inspect the equipment for worm, burnt, broken or other wise unserviceable components and compensate for any evident regular running or deviation from normal design characteristics.
3. This preventative maintenance can not be performed during normal working hours and days.
4. Don't report to the owner whenever it may be necessary to shutdown the equipment to allow the performance of extensive work needed.
5. Use trained and supervised personnel to service and maintain the equipment.

6. The property manager should attend to emergency breakdown calls at any hour of the day or night, with additional charge to the owner, where such a breakdown arises in the course of the equipment being operated normally.
7. Upon notification of any such emergency breakdown by the owner, the equipment will be serviced as soon as practicable.
8. They may not reserve the right to charge the owner for nuisance calls and calls which are the result of negligence or misuse of the equipment or are required by-reason of any cause beyond control.
9. The contractor didn't receive the additional costs incurred in performing such additional work.
10. Make repairs or replacements to the equipment necessitated through negligence, misuse or acts of vandalism, or any cause beyond the contractor's control, except normal wear and tear

(Ⅱ) **Match the English words with their Chinese translations, choose the appropriate words to complete the sentences below and translate them into Chinese.**(将下列英语单词与其中文意思相匹配,选择合适的词将下列句子补充完整并译成中文。)

    1. responsibility   a. 保证,(正当)理由,根据
    2. imply   b. 适合的,正当的,规矩的;出色的,极好的
    3. unserviceable   c. 责任,责任心;职责,任务
    4. proper   d. 另外,别样;在其他方面;要不然,否则
    5. warrant   e. 关系,联系;家属关系,亲属关系
    6. relationship   f. 不能使用的,不适用的,无用的;不耐用
    7. otherwise   g. 磨损
    8. worn   h. 明显的
    9. wear   i. 含有…的意思;暗指,暗示,意指
    10. evident   j. 耗尽的,变得衰弱的,用坏的

1. Do as you think _____.
2. The _____ between the army and the people is as close as fish to water.
3. This is the grave _____ of the Party and government workers.
4. Do you realize what his words _____?
5. That is a _____-out coat.
6. He reminded me of what I should _____ have forgotten.
7. They are replacing _____ equipment.
8. That is an _____ mistake.
9. He said so without _____.
10. The dripping water _____ a hole in the stone.
11. I will be very busy in the _____ of the next two or three weeks.

(Ⅲ) **Choose the best answer**(选择最佳答案)
1. He spoke too quickly _____.
    a. understand   b. to be understood

c. not to understand   d. not to be understood

2. Try your best _____ you'll certainly succeed this time.
   a. so   b. and   c. or   d. for

3. I'm sure that he'll appreciate the chance _____ to him. He really wants to visit your country.
   a. to be given   b. is given   c. giving   d. to give

4. I feel it an honour _____ to speak here.
   a. to ask   b. to be asked   c. asking   d. having asked

5. Wet umbrellas are not allowed _____ into the hall.
   a. to be taken   b. to take
   c. taken   d. taking

6. _____ he saw her, he was always all smiles.
   a. whatever   b. whenever
   c. however   d. whichever

7. _____ is still unknown when the president is going to make a public speech.
   a. Which   b. That   c. It   d. What

8. _____ doesn't matter what you do at this point.
   a. That   b. This   c. It   d. What

9. Many things _____ impossible in the past are quite common today.
   a. having been considered   b. to be considered
   c. considering   d. considered

10. My wife is planning to have the furniture _____ light green.
    a. paint   b. painting
    c. to paint   d. painted

11. Mr. Wang took us to a small town, _____ he set up his first factory.
    a. where   b. here   c. which   d. that

12. Our concert turned out to be a great success, _____ they had never expected.
    a. what   b. that   c. when   d. which

(Ⅳ) Translation

Translate the following Chinese into English:

1. 综合性的维修合同提供了现行的维修内容。
2. 检查设备的磨损件、易损件,对任何明显的不正常运行或对正常设计性能形成的偏差进行补偿。
3. 关于电梯,必要时更新所有的钢丝绳,调整提升钢丝绳的张力。
4. 定期检查所有设备和调速器的安全性能,按照有关的章程、规则和需要进行测试。
5. 储备一些零件和材料,以备进行预防性维护时的不时之需。
6. 业主一拨打紧急维修服务电话,承包商将会尽可能快的到位进行设备维修。
7. 代理人可以保留向业主收费的权力。
8. 应业主的要求,并给予合理的通知,专业承包商将会提供附加的服务。

9. 完成正常工作时间之外列出的工作项目。

10. 承包商也会在承担下述服务的同时收取附加成本费。

(Ⅴ) Topic Extra Reading

Read the following passage and choose the best answer to complete each of the statements that follow.

Owner's Responsibilities

(*a*) Equipment and its Accommodation

The owner will be responsible for keeping the following in good repair and proper working order:

(ⅰ) Machine rooms, secondary floors or supporting structures, means of access thereto and lift wells in their entirety.

(ⅱ) Electric light and power mains and switches elsewhere on the supply side of the equipment circuit breakers.

(ⅲ) Machine room and lift well ventilation and associated control equipment. The owner will confer with the specialised contractor before effecting any alterations, servicing or repairs to such equipment.

(ⅳ) Sump pumps, syphons and the like installed to remove water from lift pits or other machinery areas. The owner will confer with the specialist contractor before effecting any alterations, servicing or repairs to such equipment.

(ⅴ) Buried hydraulic caissons.

(ⅵ) Landing door (excluding mechanical and electrical attachment), landing door surfaces, frames, transom panels and sills.

(ⅶ) Car superstructures including fixed or removable panels, doors, car gates, ceilings, light fittings (including fluorescent or incandescent lamps), handrails, ventilation fans, floor surfaces and other architectural features and accessories.

(ⅷ) General purpose power outfits, light globes/tubes fitted to escalator and moving pathway balustrades, lift wells, pits and machinery rooms.

(ⅸ) Car and landing push button, indicator and control panel faceplates.

(ⅹ) Telephone, television, communication, audio and security equipment and any wiring thereto not supplied and installed by the specialist contractor.

(ⅺ) Internal and external balustrades, deck panels, skirtings and floor plates of escalators and moving pathways.

(ⅻ) Any equipment added from the date of original installation other than equipment added by the specialist contractor.

(*b*) Access to Premises and Equipment

The owner should afford the specialist contractor's personnel and agents reasonable access to the equipment during the contractor's normal working hours. Access to equipment outside normal working hours should be as mutually agreed between the owner and the specialist contractor. The owner should provide proper, safe and convenient means of access to enable the specialist contractor's personnel and agents to maintain the equipment.

(c) Owner not to make Repairs

For safety reasons, the owner should not, without the specialist contractor's prior written consent, permit any other party to maintain, repair or make alterations to the equipment.

1. _____ will be responsible for keeping in good repair and proper working order.
    a. The specialist contractor
    b. The owner
    c. The Property Manager
    d. The attending contractor's representative
2. The owner will confer with _____ before effecting any alterations, servicing or repairs to such equipment.
    a. the attending contractor's representative
    b. the Property Manager
    c. the contractor
    d. the specialised contractor
3. Any equipment added _____.
    a. from the date of original installation
    b. by the specialist contractor
    c. by the attending contractor's representative
    d. by the contractor
4. Which of the following statements is true?
    a. The owner should afford the specialist contractor's personnel and agents reasonable access to the equipment outside the contractor's normal working hours.
    b. The owner should afford the contractor's personnel and agents reasonable access to the equipment during the contractor's normal working hours.
    c. The owner should afford the specialist contractor's personnel and agents reasonable access to the equipment during the contractor's normal working hours.
    d. The Property Manager should afford the specialist contractor's personnel and agents reasonable access to the equipment during the contractor's normal working hours.
5. The owner should provide _____ means of access to enable the specialist contractor's personnel and agents to maintain the equipment.
    a. proper
    b. safe
    c. convenient
    d. proper, safe and convenient

Ⅱ. Language Ability Drill(语言能力练习)

(Ⅰ) Vocabulary Exercise

Some compound adjectives (复合形容词) are formed by a noun + an adjective, e.g.

brand＋new—brand-new
air＋sick—airsick(晕机的)

Now form compound adjectives with the nouns and adjectives given below and then complete each of the following sentences with a proper compound adjective.

nouns	adjectives
age	blind
care(忧虑)	cold
color	deep
duty(关税)	free
grass	green
ice	long
knee	old
life	sick
nation	thin
paper	white
sea	wide
skin	
snow	
world	

1. His hair has become _____ as a result of hard working.
2. The two old men have been _____ friends.
3. It's very difficult for a _____ to tell redness from green.
4. What they are doing has attracted(吸引) _____ attention.
5. They spent a _____ summer in Qingdao during the summer vocation.
6. This river is only _____ in winter.
7. The foreigners bought a lot of souvenirs in the _____ shop at the airport.
8. Since you are _____, we'd better go to Shanghai by train.

Make the italicized words emphatic(强调的) after the model:
Model: I wanted boots. —I did want boots.
1. They gave up halfway. What a shame!
2. Be more careful next time.
3. Come and join us in the discussion.
4. The pen writes smoothly.
5. I hope you will stay for lunch.

(Ⅱ) **Cloze**

At the beginning of this century, medical scientists made an interesting discovery: we are built not just of flesh(肌肉) and blood but also of time. They were __1__ to show that we all have a "body clock" __2__ us, which controls the __3__ and fall of our body energies, __4__ us different from one day to the next. The __5__ of a 'body clock' should not

97

be too   6   since the lives of most living things are controlled   7   the 24-hour night-and-day cycle(循环). We feel   8   and fall asleep at night and become   9   and energetic during the day. If the 24-hour cycle is   10   most people experience unpleasant   11   . For example, people who are not   12   to working at night can find that   13   of sleep causes them   14   badly at work.   15   the daily cycle of sleeping and   16   , we also have other cycles which   17   longer than one day. Most of us would   18   that we feel good on some days and not so good on   19   ; sometimes our ideas seem to flow and at other times, they   20   do not exist.

1. A. anxious   B. able   C. careful   D. proud
2. A. inside   B. around   C. between   D. on
3. A. movement   B. supply   C. use   D. rise
4. A. showing   B. treating   C. making   D. changing
5. A. invention   B. opinion   C. story   D. idea
6. A. difficult   B. exciting   C. surprising   D. interesting
7. A. from   B. by   C. over   D. during
8. A. dull   B. tired   C. dreamy   D. peaceful
9. A. regular   B. excited   C. lively   D. clear
10. A. disturbed   B. shortened   C. reset   D. troubled
11. A. moments   B. feelings   C. senses   D. effects
12. A. prevented   B. allowed   C. expected   D. used
13. A. miss   B. none   C. lack   D. need
14. A. perform   B. show   C. manage   D. control
15. A. With   B. As well as   C. Except   D. Rather than
16. A. working   B. moving   C. living   D. waking
17. A. repeat   B. remain   C. last   D. happen
18. A. agree   B. believe   C. realize   D. allow
19. A. other   B. the other   C. all other   D. others
20. A. just   B. only   C. still   D. yet

(Ⅲ) Complete the following sentences, using "could(not) have ＋ p.p.":

1. Mary _____（本来可以买件大衣）, but she choose to lend the money to a needy neighbor.
2. If it hadn't been for your help, we _____（不可能在这么短的时间里就在实验上取得成功）.
3. You _____（本来可以制订）a more detailed（详细的）plan.
4. I _____（本来可以借你）the money. Why didn't you ask me?
5. Her husband _____（本来可以帮助她的）, but he did not choose.

Part 2. Dialogue

Parking in the Community Ⅱ
（小区内停车 2）

Ⅰ. Typical Sentences（经典短句）

（Ⅰ）Daily Conversations（日常用语）

车辆管理服务用语：

(1) 车辆进入管理区时：

Please exchange your driving license to car parking card.

请用您的驾驶证换取车位牌。

Sorry for making you wait for me so long!

对不起，久等了！

(2) 发现车辆违章停放时：

Sir, excuse me, please park your car in the proper position.

先生，对不起，请您按位泊车。

Please don't park the sidewalk.

请不要停在人行道。

Please don't park in the grass.

请不要停在绿化地。

(3) 发现车辆未关好门时：

Sir, please shut the door and window of your car.

先生请关好车门、窗。

Please lock your car.

请锁好车。

（Ⅱ）Professional Conversation（专业会话）

1. Parking area in the living community is full. No more cars are allowed to park in the community.

   小区车位已满，不再停放外来车辆。

2. You have park your car in a wrong place. Please drive into your own parking place.

   您的车放错车位了，请调回自己的车位。

3. You should put your bike into the garage for bicycle but not here.

   自行车不能放在这，要放到自行车库。

4. The parking fee in community is taken by observing the Tianjin Parking Management Charge Principle.

   小区车场收费标准按照《天津市停车场管理收费标准》执行。

5. You should put your car parking card on the upper right corner of the car front window.

   您应当把车证置于前挡风玻璃右上角。

II. Conversation Passages

(I) Passage 1

  A: Good afternoon, may I speak to Mr. Yang, please?
   下午好,我想找一下杨先生。
  B: Yes, here's Mr. Yang speaking. Who's that?
   我就是。您是?
  A: This is Mr. Liu who is in charge of the car parking management.
   我是负责车辆停放管理的刘先生。
  B: Oh, it's you.
   噢,是您哪。
  A: Yeah, sorry for making you wait for me so long!
   是的,对不起,让您久等了!
  B: It doesn't matter. Does the lady in your department tell you all about my matter?
   您部门中的那位小姐把我的事都告诉您了吗?
  A: Yes, Miss. He has told me you want to have a one-year car parking card. And I have manage that for you. When can you come to get it?
   是的,何小姐告诉我您想办一张一年期的车证,我已经帮您办好了,您什么时候可以来取一下?
  B: Really! Thank you very much. I will go to your place and get it now.
   是吗? 谢谢您,我现在就去您那里拿。
  A: Alright. I will be here waiting for you.
   那好吧. 我在这等您。
  B: Thank you for your kindness.
   谢谢您。
  A: You're welcome.
   不用谢。

(II) Passage 2

(After getting the certificate)

  A: Good afternoon, sir. Do you have a car parking card? If you do not have one, Please exchange your driving license to car parking card.
   下午好,先生,您有停车卡吗? 如果没有请用驾驶证换取车位牌。
  B: Yes, I have it. Where should I park?
   是的,我有。我应该把车停在哪呢?
  A: Please don't park in the grass or the sidewalk. There's an area for parking in community. May I see your parking card?
   请不要停在绿化地或人行道上。小区有专门的停车位,我可以看一下您的停车证吗?
  B: Sure, here it is.

当然了,给您。

A: Let me see. Your parking area is No. 9. You can park there. Do you need my help to find it?
让我看看。您的停车位在9号,您可以把车停在那,您需要我帮您找吗?

B: No, I think I can do that. Anyway, thank you very much.
不用了,我自己找就行了,谢谢你。

A: You're welcome.
不用客气。

(after a while)(过了一会)

B: Execuse me, sir. I found my parking place, but it has been taken by another car.
先生,我找到了我的车位,但已经有车停那了。

A: Really? It's impossible! I will find it out for you.
真的吗? 这不可能! 我会帮您查清楚的。

B: Ok. Sorry for bothering you.
好的。真不好意思给您添麻烦了。

A: No, not at all. It's my job.
不,一点也没有。这是我的工作。

B: It's right there.
就在那。

A: Oh, sorry, sir. I'm afraid you have made a mistake. This is not No. 9 but No. 6. So your parking place is over there.
噢,先生,恐怕是您搞错了。这不是9号停车位,而是6号,所以您的车位在那边。

B: Oh, sorry for my carelessness.
对不起,我太粗心了。

A: That's all right. By the way, please lock your car, shut the door and window of your car.
没关系,顺便说一句,请留意锁好车关好车门和车窗。

B: Thank you.
谢谢你。

Ⅲ. Exercises for Dialogue

(Ⅰ) Fill in the following blanks by considering Chinese.(按照中文完成以下填空)

A: Good afternoon, sir. _____? If you do not have one. Please _____ to car parking card.
下午好,先生。您有停车卡吗?如果没有请用驾驶证换取车位牌。

B: Yes, I have it. Where should I park?
是的,我有。我应该把车停在哪呢?

A: Please don't park _____. There's an area for parking in community. May I see your parking card?

101

请不要停在绿化地或人行道上。小区有专门的停车位。我可以看一下您的停车证吗？

B: Sure, here it is.
当然了，给您。

A: Let me see. ＿＿＿＿＿＿＿. You can park there. Do you need my help to find it?
让我看看，您的停车位在 9 号，您可以把车停在那，您需要我帮您找吗？

B: No, I think I can do that. Anyway, thank you very much.
不用了，我自己找就行了，谢谢你。

(Ⅱ) After filling in the blanks, translate the former dialogue into Chinese.

(Ⅲ) Make a conversation with your partner about finding a parking place. (there should be at least 3 turn-taking in the dialogue)

Ⅳ. **Spoken Language Drill** (fill in the blanks according to the Chinese translation)

Dialogue 1

A: It seems to be ＿＿＿＿＿＿＿ up.
看来天要放晴了。

B: It's such a nice change.
真是令人高兴的转变。

A: I really don't think this weather will ＿＿＿＿＿＿＿.
我确实认为这样的好天长不了。

B: Let's just ＿＿＿＿＿＿＿ it doesn't get cold again.
但愿不会再冷。

Dialogue 2

A: ＿＿＿＿＿＿＿ day, isn't it?
今天天气真好，是不是？

B: Yes, it's not like what the radio said at all.
是的，一点也不像收音机里说的那样。

A: I wish it would ＿＿＿＿＿＿＿ this way for the weekend.
但愿整个周末都能保持这样的好天气。

B: As long as it doesn't snow!
只要不下雪就行啊！

Dialogue 3

A: It looks like it's going to be ＿＿＿＿＿＿＿.
今天看来像是个晴天。

B: Yes, it's much ＿＿＿＿＿＿＿ than yesterday.
是的，比昨天好多了。

A: They say we're going to get some rain ＿＿＿＿＿＿＿.
据说待会儿要下雨。

B: Oh, let's just hope it stays(维持某种状态)warm.

哦,我只希望一直暖和下去。

Dialogue 4

　　A: I think it's going to be a nice day.

　　　我想今天会是一个好天。

　　B: It's certainly a big _____ over yesterday.

　　　肯定比昨天大有好转。

　　A: But it's supposed to get cloudy and windy again this afternoon.

　　　但是,据说今天下午又要转阴刮风了。

　　B: Well, the worst of the winter should be _____.

　　　不过,冬天最糟糕的一段日子总该过去了。

Part 3. Supplementary Reading:

If Only

　　Having worked at a 7-Eleven store for two years, I thought I had become successful at what our manager calls "customer relations". I firmly believed that a friendly smile and an automatic "sir", "madam", and "thank you" would see me through any situation that might arise, from soothing impatient or unpleasant people to apologizing for giving out the wrong change. But the other night an old woman shattered my belief that a glib response could smooth over the rough spots of dealing with other human beings.

　　The moment she entered, the woman presented a sharp contrast to our shiny store with its bright lighting and neatly arranged shelves. Walking as if each step were painful, she slowly pushed open the glass door and hobbled down the nearest aisle. She coughed dryly, wheezing with each breath. On a forty degree night, she was wearing only a faded print dress, a thin, light beiges sweater too small to button, and black vinyl slippers with the backs cut out to expose calloused heels. There are no stocking or sock on her splotchy, blue veined legs.

　　After strolling around the store for several minutes, the old woman stopped in front of the rows of canned vegetables. She picked up some corn nib lets (玉米粒罐头) and stared with a strange intensity at the label. At that point, I decided to be a good, courteous employee and asked her if she needed help. As I stood close to her, my smile became harder to maintain; her red rimmed eyes were partially closed by yellowish crusts; her hands were covered with layer upon layer of grime, and the stale smell of sweat rose in a thick vaporous cloud from her clothes.

　　"I need some food," she muttered in reply to my bright "Can I help you?"

　　"Are you looking for corn, madam?"

　　"I need some food," she repeated. "Any kind."

　　"Well, the corn is ninety five cents," I said in my most helpful voice. "Or, if you like, we have a special on bologna today."

　　"I can't pay," she said.

　　For a second, I was tempted to say, "Take the corn." But the employee rules flooded into my mind: Remain polite, but do not let customers get the best of you. Let them know that you are in control. For a moment, I even entertained the idea that this was some sort of test, and that this woman was someone from the head office, testing my loyalty. I responded dutifully, "I'm sorry, ma'am, but I can't give away anything for free."

The old woman's face collapsed a bit more, if that were possible, and her hands trembled as she put the can back on the shelf. She shuffled past me toward the door, her torn and dirty clothing barely covering her bent back.

Moments after she left, I rushed out the door with the can of corn, but she was nowhere in sight. For the rest of my shift, the image of the woman haunted me. I had been young, healthy, and smug. She had been old, sick, and desperate. Wishing with all my heart that I had acted like a human being rather than a robot, I was saddened to realize how fragile a hold we have on our better instincts.

参考译文：

情 理 之 间

在一家7—11连锁店工作了两年后，我觉得我在经理所说的"客户关系"方面已经做得老道圆熟了。我深信，友好的微笑、张口就来的"先生"、"夫人"、"谢谢"已足已帮我应付任何情况——从应付急性子、讨厌鬼到为找错零钱而道歉。但是，那天晚上，一位老妇人的出现彻底瓦解了我的信念：嘴巴乖巧并不意味着就能顺利与人打交道。

老妇人一进门，便与店中灯火通明、货架整齐、明晃晃的环境形成强烈反差。她缓慢地推开玻璃门，步履蹒跚地走到离她最近的货架之间，迈出每一步似乎都在忍受着疼痛。老妇人干咳着，费劲地喘着每一口气。那天夜里的气温只有华氏40度，可她只穿着一件褪色的印花连衣裙，一件薄薄的浅米色毛衣，小得连扣子都扣不上；脚上穿着剪掉后鞋帮的黑色塑料便鞋，露出了长满硬茧的脚后跟；她连双袜子都没穿，污迹斑斑、青筋凸暴的双腿裸露在外。

在店里徘徊片刻之后，老妇人停在蔬菜罐头架前，她拿了一个玉米粒罐头，双眼使劲盯着标签，神情怪异。这时，我决意做一个有礼貌的好店员，去问问老妇人是否需要帮忙。

当我站到她身边时，我觉得要保持微笑更难了。她眼圈通红，黄乎乎的眼屎几乎遮住了眼睛，双手积满了一层层厚重的污垢，衣服上散发的一阵阵强烈的汗酸臭味扑鼻而来。

我轻快地问："能为您效劳吗？"老妇人嗫嚅道："我需要一点吃的。"

"你是不是在找玉米，夫人？"

"我需要一点吃的，"她又说了一遍，"什么都行。"

"哦，这罐玉米9毛5。"我说话的声音听起来十分乐意助人。"如果您需要的话，今天有特价的大红肠。"

"我没有钱。"老妇人说。

有那么一瞬间，我真想说"把玉米拿走吧"。但是，脑海里开始回响起员工守则：保持礼貌,但是不要让顾客利用你,让他们明白是你在控制局面。一时间,我甚至还冒出了这样的想法:这是一种测试,老妇人是公司总部派来的,考验我是否忠于职守。于是,我尽职尽责地回答道:"对不起,夫人,我不能给您免费。"

老妇人的脸一下子变得更加干瘪了,如果有这种可能的话。她双手颤抖着,把罐头放回货架上。然后曳步从我身边挪过,朝门口走去。她那又脏又破的衣服几乎都无法遮住她佝偻的背。

过了一会儿,我拿着一罐玉米冲出门外,但老妇人已无影无踪。在余下当班的时间里,老妇人的影子一直在我脑海里挥之不去。我年轻、健康、自我感觉良好;她却风烛残年、疾病缠身、孤立无援。我真希望我在老妇人面前的所作所为能更像一个人,而不是机器。意识到人类如此易于失去自己的善良本性,我感到深深的悲哀。

Exercises for the reading:

1. Which one is not true about the old woman's appearance?

    A. She wore a faded print dress.

    B. She wore black vinyl slippers with the backs cut out to expose calloused heels.

    C. She wore a pair of dirty socks.

    D. She walked slowly as if each step were painful.

2. What did the author do when the old woman asked for food without money?

    A. He refused her immediately.

    B. He bought her the food later.

    C. Both A and B

    D. Neither A nor B

3. Why didn't the author help the old woman at first?

    A. Because it was a test taken by head office to test his loyalty.

    B. Because he didn't have money himself.

    C. Because he was a mean person.

    D. Because the employee rules reminded him that do not let customers get the best of him.

4. Why did the author buy food for the old woman at last?

    A. His boss told him to do so.

    B. Other customers paid for it.

    C. His heart told him to do it.

    D. We don't know.

5. What did the author think of as highly important?

    A. Good instincts of human beings.

    B. Following the employee rules.

    C. Working as a robot.

    D. Both A and B

Part 4. Pratical Writing

求职信范例

范例一：

Changjian Road 23, Hefei
Anhui Province
China
Dear Mr. Li:
We acknowledge receipt of your letter of 29th May. We have pleasure in enclosing our latest prospectus. If you require further information, please do not hesitate to contact us.

Sincerely,
Professor Cook
July 20, 2000

范例二：

Dear Sir,

    I have obtained your address from the British Council. I intend to study English next year, and I am interested in your summer school English class. I would be most grateful if you could send me your latest prospectus.

    I look forward to hearing from you.

Yours truly,
Jame Li
July 20, 2000

范例三：

Dear Sir,

    I am writing in reference to the recent order I placed with your company. I was most disappointed to note that on examining the set of wine I ordered, four of them were badly damaged.

    I request that replacement be sent as soon as possible. It is essential that I receive these goods as soon as possible as they are intended as a wedding gift for a relative.

    I have previously received a high standard of service from your company and I trust that this matter may be brought to a swift and satisfactory conclusion.

Yours truly,
Cester Chen
July 20, 2000

范例四:

Dear Miss Wilson,

　　We have received your letter of 10th May in which you say that you are in receipt of fault goods. We have investigated the matter and found that the damage was cause by an oversight on our part. A new set of six wine glasses has now been dispatched to you and you should receive them by the end of this week.

　　We apologize for any inconvenience caused by this problem and will endeavor to prevent it happening again.

Yours truly,
CHESTER CHEN
July 20, 2000

范例五:

Dear Mrs. Smith,

　　My name is Chencheng. I am a final student of Anhui Agricultural University. I am currently seeking employment in which I could make full use of my English language skills. For this reason, I would be interested in any job vacancies available in your company. I am confident and enthusiastic, so although I have little work experience, I believe that my personal qualities will allow me to make a valuable contribution to your company.

　　I wish to work for Haier in particular because as a newly opened joint venture company in Hefei, I feel you could offer me the chance to work among Chinese and overseas employees in a modern and friendly environment.

　　I enclose my curriculum vitae; I am available for interview at any time. If there are no positions available at this time, I would be most grateful. If my application could be considered for future vacancies.

Yours sincerely,
Chencheng
July 20, 2000

期 中 测 试

Part 1. 专业练习（总共四题，满分150分）

一、Translate the following sentences into English.（共10小题，每小题3分，满分30分）

1. 租金和运行开支很大程度上由市场力量决定。
2. 物业管理是监督物业运行和维护以实现业主目标的过程。
3. 更加重视对房屋的维护与保养是为了能够降低修换房体所带来的高额开销。
4. 自动控制系统是任何大楼空调系统中最重要的一个环节。
5. 在过去，业主常常不通知房屋服务经理就进行房屋改建。
6. 如果想要令业主满意，就必须及时给予恰当的维护。
7. 使用警报器的目的是为了发现非法进入或通过某一特定地区。
8. 同样，走廊、服务区、过道、机械室和消防通道等都需要特别的考虑。
9. 业主一拨打紧急维修服务电话，承包商将会尽可能快的到位进行设备维修。
10. 检查设备的磨损件、易损件，对任何明显的不正常运行或对正常设计性能形成的偏差进行补偿。

二、Fill in the following blanks while observing the conversational manner（按照日常会话习惯完成以下填空）

（一）Patterns（共15小题，每小题2分，满分30分）

1. Welcome _____ our school.
   Welcome _____ become one of members in this school.

2. How are you!
   _____, thank you! _____?
   _____, too.

3. _____ some tea, please.

4. I'm _____ to keep you waiting.

5. A: That's very _____ of you.
   B: That's all right.

6. May I _____ your name, please?

7. _____ you please fill out this form?

8. A: Can you do me a favor?
   B: _____.（非常乐意）

9. A: Thank you for your help.
   B: _____.（这是我应该做的.）

10. Congratulations _____ your marriage!

11. Keep _____ touch!
12. A: _____ Wang Ming speaking. May I speak to Mr. Li, please?
    B: He is not here right now.
    A: May I leave a message?
    B: _____.
13. _____ can I do for you?
14. A: Please exchange your driving license _____ car parking card.
    B: Sorry _____ making you wait for me so long!
15. Sir, _____, please park your car in the proper position. Please don't park the sidewalk.

(二) **Dialogues**(共 3 小题,每小题 15 分,满分 45 分)

Dialogue 1

A: Good morning, _____?
B: Yes, here's Mr. Wang speaking. _____?
A: This is Mr. Zhang who is in charge of the car parking management.
B: Oh, _____.
A: Yeah, sorry for making you wait for me so long!
B: _____. Does the lady in your department tell you all about my matter?
A: Yes, Miss. Shen _____ you want to have a one-year car parking card. When can you come to get it?
B: Really! _____. I will go to your place and get it now.
A: All right. _____.
B: Thank you for your kindness.
A: _____.

Dialogue 2

A: Good afternoon, sir. Please show me your car parking card.
B: _____? I'm afraid I don't have it.
A: So please take one from Property Management department. Mr. Liu is in charge of it.
B: _____, and I will stay for a very short time.
A: Well, cars are not in this living community are required to pay management fee, if they stay in the community longer than 15 minutes.
B: _____. I will leave in a minute.
A: Right. Park your car in the place for guests, please.
B: Thank you.
A: _____.

Dialogue 3

A: Good morning, sir. Did you start to decorate your room?
B: Yes, I did. And there's something I need your help. _____?
A: Sure. My pleasure. _____?

109

B: I need some reparation in my house.

A: _____? (可以更具体些吗？)

B: En, let me have a think. Right, why not let's go to my place and I will show you. Anyway, if you're available.

A: _____. (好主意.) I'm OK. Let's go.

B: Thank you for your help.

A: _____.

三、Choose the best answer（选择最佳答案）(共 10 小题；每小题 2.5 分，满分 25 分)

1. I have about five or six weeks in English, which seems a long holiday _____ you realize how quickly the days pass.
   a. in which   b. until   c. on which   d. that

2. Mr. Brown _____ me a present next week for my fifteenth birthday.
   a. gives   b. gave   c. is giving   d. will give

3. He _____ to the movies, had he known that Jane would be there.
   a. would have gone   b. had gone
   c. should have gone   d. would go

4. He _____ a Teachers' Day card yesterday afternoon.
   a. makes   b. will make
   c. is going to make   d. made

5. The exhibition has a modern layout and many of the lifelike figures are modeled in a _____ pose.
   a. relaxing   b. relax
   c. relaxation   d. relaxed

6. Hi, Mary! Where _____ you _____?
   a. did...go   b. do...go   c. were going   d. are...going

7. _____ in Washington, Helen turned on the radio in her hotel room to listen to the weather report.
   a. Arrived   b. Having arrived
   c. After arrived   d. On having arrived

8. I will tell you about his news as soon as I _____ it in the newspaper.
   a. read   b. see   c. will see   d. will read

9. Lucy usually _____ to school at 7:00 o'clock in the morning.
   a. go   b. will go   c. went   d. goes

10. I completely forgot _____ the front door last night and feel fortunate that nothing is stolen.
    a. locking   b. to have locked
    c. being locked   d. to lock

四、Read the following passage and choose the best answer to complete each of the statements that follow.(共 10 小题；每小题 2 分，满分 20 分)

(一) CAR PARKING: AN ESSENTIAL SERVICE
INTRODUCTION

Every city is virtually dependent for its existence upon adequate car parking. This has become a vital component of CBD and urban property development.

In small and medium sized cities, car parking is essential for the conduct of all civic, cultural, social, business and shopping activities, while in large cities with developed public transportation it must still be provided for people who travel by private vehicle.

Savage restrictions on car usage could have disastrous economic consequences for a city. It has been suggested that the banning of private cars would at the very least cause severe social and economic disruption. Many consumers could respond by going elsewhere.

NOT THE END OF THE JOURNEY

While car parks are the normal and natural termination for access roads and city streets, they are by no means the end of the journey. They are an interchange where the motorist becomes a pedestrian. Therefore, they must be functional and meet the needs of their customers, all of whom wish to park in well designed facilities, as close to their destinations as practical.

The location of a car park influences the design, parking charges and type of services provided.

Preferably it should be within comfortable walking distance of the principal destination of its patrons. Some buildings today incorporate public car parking facilities within the building itself or associated areas.

The cost of providing parking in any locality should be balanced against the estimated extent of use and revenue. This in turn will depend upon the location of the car parking in relation to the centers of attraction and road networks and on the ease of parking in the facility itself. The provision of low cost peripheral parking areas, for example, may be of little value if drivers do not patronise them, preferring alternatives closer to the CBD.

The rate of egress from a car park will almost entirely depend upon the absorption capacity of the traffic flow in the street or streets in which the car park exit is located. The number of entrances and exits should be kept to a minimum, as a large number will not necessarily contribute to alleviating traffic problems and could on the contrary, create chaos resulting in tremendous operational difficulties and needlessly increase security problems.

Car park entry points should extend as far as possible into the building in order to allow queuing of cars within a holding area between the building alignment and the check-in point or boom gate. This would prevent the cars from queuing back into the street.

LONG SPAN VERSUS SHORT SPAN

The tendancy today is to construct long span multi-storey parking structures. The long span structure permits column free floors, which is an important consideration from the stand point of safety. Visibility is improved, interior lighting is more efficient, cleaning and day to day maintenance are easier, and a substantially increased economical utilisation of parking areas is achieved.

Long span structures facilitates the alteration of parking space sizes if necessary without significant loss of efficient floor space, thus providing greater flexibility in design as well as operation. However, long span structures are more expensive than short span structures. Short span construction is found more frequently in parking areas where air rights above are devoted to some other use such as offices. The principal reason for using short span in self standing car parks is that a cost saving in the order of about 10% may be achieved.

Short span construction generally requires parking between columns or another car and a column, with all the associated inconvenience and hazards. There may well be less utilisation of the parking facility because people park improperly, using part of a second space in their efforts to avoid a column and effectively denying its use to another customer.

Car parking is not just a question of creating a space for a vehicle while complying with parking regulations regarding such matters as the width in entrances and exits, car parking spaces and the depth of reservoir areas. It is a service and it would be wise to bear in mind that it is the people who use it that will determine its success or failure.

1. _____, car parking is essential for the conduct of all civic, cultural, social, business and shopping activities.
    a. In small sized cities
    b. In medium sized cities
    c. In small and medium sized cities
    d. In large cities
2. The location of a car park influences _____.
    a. the design and parking charges
    b. parking charges and type of services provided
    c. the design and type of services provided
    d. the design, parking charges and type of services provided
3. The cost of providing parking in any locality will depend upon _____.
    a. the location of the car parking in relation to the centers of attraction and road networks and on the ease of parking in the facility itself
    b. the design, parking charges and type of services provided
    c. within comfortable walking distance of the principal destination of its patrons
    d. facilities within the building itself or associated areas
4. The number of entrances and exits should be _____.
    a. kept to a minimum
    b. a large number
    c. small sized
    d. medium sized
5. Which of the following statements is not true?

a. Car parking is not just a question of creating a space for a vehicle while complying with parking regulations.
b. Car parking should be regarded such matters as the width in entrances and exits, car parking spaces and the depth of reservoir areas.
c. Car parking is a service and it would be wise to bear in mind that it is the people who use it that will determine its success or failure.
d. Car parking is just a question of creating a space for a vehicle while complying with parking regulations.

(二) TENANCY IDENTIFICATION
INTRODUCTION

Imagine a large office complex or an industrial estate without signs. Total confusion. Quite clearly from a purely functional view point, signs are an essential element of any large property development. They are needed to identify a facility and its various parts and to give directions.

A good signage program will move people efficiently through the facility, prevent them from becoming lost, assist in reducing accidents and encourage further visits.

Signs are more than just a practical necessity, they should in fact be an integral part of a corporate identification program, reinforcing the graphic style of an organisation, stationary, advertisements, and printed literature. It is important therefore that the Property Manager consider how a signage program can be best utilised in a building so as to project the image of the businesses and the building itself.

Under normal circumstances the Building Manager/Building Ownership, would need to provide signs such as building directory, floor directories, various exit signs, fire hydrant, toilet and other service signs stipulated by rule and health regulations.

Unless a tenant has naming rights, the Building Ownership will also supply name, and number signage to the building to identify the premises.

LEGIBILITY AND STYLE

Whether the premises in question is a central business district office tower or an office park development in a suburban location, a retail store in a shopping complex, or a building in an industrial estate, a number of factors need to be taken into account in developing effective signage.

Most importantly, any sign must be legible and to be legible it must first of all be visible. This means that it must be correctly located so that obstacles do not obscure the sign.

Legibility depends upon several factors including the size of the sign and the letters. Another consideration comes into play if a sign involves several words or long words, it may need to be visually compact. Other factors influencing legibility include colour and brightness. Correct selection of type face is especially important because as well as its influence on legibility the type face also helps to project a business or building "personality".

CHANGING FASHION IN SIGNS

For many years the fashion in signs was the simple lettering styles with clean cut block letters. Relatively recently however, more elaborate lettering styles have been implemented which has meant a change from a fairly standard approach to one providing a much greater individuality in sign design. As a result, signs are now being regarded more as an integral part in overall design rather than serving a merely functional purpose.

Neon signs have been making a comeback recently with new technologies in their design and usage. Another trend evident over recent years has been the computerised directory. This is typically used in department stores, shopping complexes and office foyers. It enables a visitor to press a lettered button on a computer system to call up the location details of the destination required.

Not every tenant wants an illuminated sky sign or computerised directory but they all need signs. An effective signage program will not just happen, it demands planning and it may require the services of a sign specialist.

1. "It is important therefore that the Property Manager consider how a signage program can be best utilised in a building so as to project the image of the businesses and the building itself." In this sentence, "it" means _____.
    a. Signs are more than just a practical necessity, they should in fact be an integral part of a corporate identification program, reinforcing the graphic style of an organisation, stationary, advertisements, and printed literature
    b. A good signage program will move people efficiently through the facility, prevent them from becoming lost, assist in reducing accidents and encourage further visits
    c. The Property Manager consider how a signage program can be best utilised in a building so as to project the image of the businesses and the building itself
    d. They are needed to identify a facility and its various parts and to give directions
2. Under normal circumstances the Building Manager/Building Ownership, would need to provide signs such as _____.
    a. building directory, floor directories
    b. various exit signs, fire hydrant
    c. toilet and other service signs stipulated by rule and health regulations
    d. all of above
3. _____ is most important.
    a. It must be correctly located so that obstacles do not obscure the sign
    b. Any sign must be legible and to be legible it must first of all be visible
    c. A number of factors need to be taken into account in developing effective signage
    d. Unless a tenant has naming rights, the Building Ownership will also supply name, and number signage to the building to identify the premises
4. Legibility depends upon several factors including _____.

a. if a sign involves several words or long words, it may need to be visually compact
   b. the size of the sign and the letters
   c. color and brightness
   d. all of above
5. Signs are now being regarded more as _____.
   a. an integral part in overall design
   b. serving a merely functional purpose
   c. a comeback recently with new technologies in their design and usage
   d. planning and it may require the services of a sign specialist

Part 2. 能力练习(总共四题,满分 120 分)

一、单项填空(共 15 小题;每小题 1 分,满分 15 分)

从 A、B、C、D 四个选项中,选出可以填入空白处的最佳选项,并在答题卡上将该项涂黑。

1. ——The exam wasn't difficult, was it?
   ——No, but I don't think _____ could pass it.
   A. somebody   B. anybody   C. everybody   D. nobody

2. ——_____ Mr. Hopkins _____ this week? ——No. He is on holiday.
   A. Does, work   B. Is, working
   C. Has, worked   D. Will, work

3. _____ in the chimney for five hours, the thief looked very pale and tired.
   A. Trapping   B. Being trapped
   C. Having trapped   D. Having been trapped

4. I had been puzzled over the problem for over an hour without any result, _____ all at once the solution flashed across my mind.
   A. while   B. when   C. then   D. as

5. _____ every word of his were true, what action would the teacher wish to take?
   A. As if   B. Since   C. Suppose   D. when

6. _____, he could not cover the whole distance in 15 minutes.
   A. As he ran fast   B. If he ran fast
   C. Since he ran fast   D. Fast as he ran

7. She needed to borrow some money. She tried _____ Gerry but he was short of money, too.
   A. asking   B. to ask   C. to have asked   D. to be asking

8. In some countries, _____ are called "public schools" are not owned by the public.
   A. which   B. as   C. what   D. that

9. The roof fell _____ he had time to dash into the house to save his baby.
   A. as   B. after   C. until   D. before

10. Over time, she _____ all the hardships and gradually learns the meaning of life.
    A. gets through   B. goes by

115

C. finds out   D. breaks into

11. The speaker referred to his notebook _____ when he gave the talk.
    A. now and then   B. for a while
    C. here and there   D. all over

12. ——Is there a flight to London this evening?
    ——There _____ be. I'll phone the airport and find it out.
    A. must   B. will   C. might   D. can

13. I was so familiar with him that I recognized his voice _____ I picked up the phone.
    A. while   B. after   C. in case   D. the moment

14. Bamboo grows best _____ it is warm and it rains often.
    A. in the place which   B. in places where
    C. in which   D. there where

15. ——We'll have four guests altogether.
    ——So 15 bottles of beer _____ be enough.
    A. may   B. might   C. should   D. would

二、完形填空(共 20 小题;每小题 1.5 分,满分 30 分)

阅读下面短文,掌握其大意,然后从 16—35 各题所给的 A、B、C、D 四个选项中,选出最佳选项。

Having passed what I considered the worst obstacle(障碍), our spirits (16). We made our way towards the left cliff(悬崖), where the going was better, though (17) steeper(steep 陡峭). Here we found (18) snow, as most of it seemed (19) blown off the mountain. We could see (20) mountains in the distance because (21) were forming all round us.

About one o'clock a storm (22) suddenly. We should have noticed its coming but we were concentrating on cutting steps and before we had time to do anything, we were (23) by snow. We could not move up or down and had to wait motionless, getting colder and colder. (24) my hood(兜帽), my nose and cheeks were nearly frozen but I dare not (25) a hand out of my glove to (26) them.

After two hours of this, I realized we would have to do something to (27) being frozen to death. We stood from time to time through the snow. I had (28) the outline of a butterss(扶垛) just above us. Our only (29) was to climb up to the buttress, and dig out a platform at the foot of it on which we could put up our (30). We climbed to this place and started to cut away the ice. At first my companion seemed to regard this situation as (31) but gradually the wind died away and he (32) up. At last we made a platform big enough to pitch the tent, and we did this as best as we could. We (33) into our sleeping bags fell asleep, (34) that we were lucky to be still (35).

16. A. rose   B. raised   C. calmed   D. lowered
17. A. quite   B. very   C. rather   D. hardly

116

18. A. few	B. much	C. tiny	D. little
19. A. it had	B. to have been	C. it was	D. to be
20. A. no	B. continuous	C. grey	D. beautiful
21. A. winds	B. rains	C. clouds	D. fogs
22. A. turned up	B. sped up	C. grew up	D. came up
23. A. frightened	B. tired	C. blinded	D. excited
24. A. Although	B. With	C. Even if	D. In spite of
25. A. take	B. pick	C. give	D. send
26. A. feel	B. help	C. warm	D. cover
27. A. forbid	B. defend	C. protect	D. avoid
28. A. made out	B. found out	C. worked out	D. figured out
29. A. way	B. helper	C. hope	D. mind
30. A. tent	B. bed	C. sleeping bags	D. luggage
31. A. funny	B. hopeless	C. dangerous	D. courageous
32. A. turned	B. cheered	C. looked	D. stood
33. A. rushed	B. jumped	C. crawled	D. crowded
34. A. knowing	B. feeling	C. realizing	D. understanding
35. A. alive	B. warm	C. happy	D. comfortable

三、阅读理解(共 20 小题;每小题 2 分,满分 40 分)

(一)

When my first wartime Christmas came, I was in basic training in New Jersey and not sure if I would make it home for the holidays. Only on the afternoon of December 23 was the list of men who would have three-day passes posted. I was one of the lucky soldiers.

It was Christmas Eve when I arrived home, and a little snow had fallen. Mother opened the front door. I could see beyond her, into the corner of the living room where the tree had always stood. There were lights, all colors, and ornaments shining against the green of a pine.

"Where did it come from?" I asked.

"I asked Gates boy to cut it," my mother said. "I wouldn't have had one just for myself, but when called-on, such a rush! He just brought it in this afternoon...."

The pine reached to the proper height, almost to the ceiling, and the Tree Top Crystal Star was its place. A few green branches reached about a little awkwardly (难看) at the side, I thought, and there was a bit of bare trunk showing in the middle. But the tree filled the room with warm light and the whole house with the pleasant smell of Christmas.

"It's not like the one you used to find," my mother went on. "Yours were always in good shape. I suppose the Gates boy didn't know where to look. But I couldn't be fussy (挑剔)."

"Don't worry," I told her. "It's perfect."

It wasn't, of course, but at the moment I realized something for the first time: all

117

Christmas trees are perfect.

36. From the passage we can infer that _____.
    A. the writer spent his first Christmas during the war
    B. soldiers did not all go home for Christmas during the war
    C. all the soldiers had three-day passes
    D. the writer could not go home for Christmas

37. From the passage, we can conclude that _____.
    A. the writer used to cut very beautiful Christmas trees
    B. his mother didn't like Christmas trees
    C. his mother didn't want to have a Christmas tree because it was wartime
    D. the writer didn't like the tree cut by someone else

38. The best title for this passage would be _____.
    A. How to Choose a Christmas Tree
    B. How Soldiers Spent Their Christmas
    C. The Perfect Christmas Tree
    D. The Christmas with an Ugly Christmas Tree

(二)

Scientists found that our Earth is not cold, hard rock all the way through. Not at all. Only the crust, the outside of the earth is cold, solid rock.

Below this cold solid crust of the Earth, there is hot rock that melts in places. Every now and then some of the hot, melted rock is pushed out.

This hot, melted rock expands, and can push its way out through a weak spot in the Earth's crust. When this happens, a volcano is made.

The melted rock below the Earth's crust can flow, like toothpaste (牙膏), if it is squeezed. If you squeeze a partly filled tube of toothpaste in one place, what happens?

The toothpaste flows to another part of the tube. If you press down on one part of the tube with a finger, what happens? This tube rises in another place, as the toothpaste flows there, making a hill.

Strangely enough, when a volcano forms, the Earth may be behaving like a tube of toothpaste. If the Earth is pressed down in one place, it may rise in another place. Hot, melted rock within the Earth may flow to another place as the Earth is pressed down. When this hot, melted rock breaks through the Earth's crust, a volcano forms.

A volcano is only one kind of mountain. Other kinds of mountains form when the Earth's crust is raised. But each time the Earth is raised in one place, something is pressing against the Earth in another place.

39. Scientific findings have proved that _____.
    A. the earth is cold with hard rock being everywhere
    B. the earth is hot
    C. the earth is neither hot nor cold

D. the outside of the earth is cold while there is hot rock below this cold hard rock

40. What is a volcano?
    A. It is a tube of toothpaste.
    B. It is a kind of mountain.
    C. When the cold hard rock becomes hot and melts, it is a volcano.
    D. When the cold hard rock becomes hard and melts, it is pushed out. Thus a volcano is formed.

41. Which of the following is true?
    A. If there is hot and melted rock, there will be a volcano.
    B. A mountain is formed when the hot and melted rock pushes out.
    C. A volcano is like a tube of toothpaste.
    D. A mountain is formed when the melted rock below the Earth's crust flows.

(三)

Last week, I bought an alarm system for about $450. It consisted of a control unit with three small units. I put the control unit in the sitting-room and fastened the other units by the front door, back door and living-room windows. The instructions told us to choose three numbers, so we chose 491, the last three numbers of our telephone number.

Now I must explain how the alarm works:

1. There is a power siren in the control unit. It makes a very loud noise.

2. Each of the small units sends out beams or rays in different directions. If anything moves, it breaks a beam. This sends a signal to the control unit. The siren makes a noise which you can hear 50 meters away.

3. When we go to bed, I press the three buttons numbered 4, 9 and 1. Then we have 30 seconds to get out of the room before the alarm starts to work.

That might I slept soundly because I was sure that no burglar could get into our house. However, at about 2:10a.m., I woke up and heard the siren.

"There must be a burglar in the house," Mary said. "What shall we do?"

"I'll go and see who's there," I said. "Stay here. Don't make a noise."

I went downstairs quietly. When I reached the living-room, I switched on my torch and looked round the room. Then I turned the light on. I switched the siren off and searched the rooms downstairs. There was nothing wrong except that the back door was unlocked. I locked it, re-set the alarm and went back to bed.

About an hour later, the alarm started again. I jumped out of bed, fell over a chair in the dark and bumped into the bedroom door. Mary woke up and started hitting me with a torch. "Hey! Wait a minute!" I whispered. "It's only me. I'm going downstairs to see what's wrong."

I went down into the living-room and listened for a moment. The only sound I could hear was the siren. I turned on the light and then switched the siren off. As I did so, I glanced across at the curtains in front of the windows. I saw a house lizard (a kind of small animal) disappear behind the curtains.

"Oh!" I said to myself. "That's our burglar."

When the lizard moved, it started the siren. I guessed that the alarm had been made in Europe, where there are no house lizards.

Well, I won't finish this story but if you want an alarm system free of charge, let me know. I'll send you ours. We bought a dog this morning. It knows the difference between a lizard and a burglar.

42. The writer bought an alarm system to _____.
  A. make sure that he got up early every day
  B. warn him when there were lizards in his house
  C. frighten burglars and tell him that somebody had got into the house
  D. make Mary feel safe to live in the large room

43. The writer used numbers 4,9,1 to _____.
  A. set the alarm system
  B. make a telephone call
  C. give numbers to each of the three units in the downstairs rooms
  D. name his alarm system

44. The purpose of the three units was to _____.
  A. send a message to the control unit and start the siren
  B. sound their own sirens when the control unit told them to
  C. check that the control unit worked properly all the time
  D. give them enough light

45. If the writer set the alarm and remained in the room for more than half a minute, _____.
  A. nothing would happen   B. the control unit would not work
  C. the siren would make a noise   D. the dog would bark

46. The purpose of the writer in writing the passage is to _____.
  A. tell us that the alarm system doesn't work
  B. tell us an interesting experience
  C. show us how the alarm system works
  D. make it clear that he wants to give away his alarm system

(四)

Professor Martin's report says that children who attend a number of different schools, because their parents have to move around the country, probably make slow progress in their studies. There are also signs, says Professor Martin, that an unusually large number of such children are mentally affected.

The professor says "It's true, my personal feeling is that children should stay in one school. Our findings are based on research and not on any personal feelings that I or many assistants may have on the subject."

Captain Thomas James, an Army lecturer for the past 20 years and himself a father of two, said, "I've never heard of such rubbish. Taking me for example, no harm is done to the education of my children, who change schools regularly——if they keep to the same system, as in our Army schools. In my experience——and I've known quite a few of them——Army children are as well adjusted as any others, if not more so. What the professor doesn't appear to appreciate is the fact that in such situation children will adapt (适应) much better than grown-ups."

When this was put to Professor Martin, he said that at no time had his team suggested that all children were backward or mentally affected in some way, but simply that in their experience there was a clear tendency (倾向性).

"Our findings show that while the very bright children can deal with regular changes without harming his or her general progress in studies, the majority of children suffer from constantly having to enter a new learning situation".

47. Professor's Martin's report suggests that _____.
    A. it may not be good for children to change schools too often
    B. parents should not move around the country
    C. the reason of children making slow progress is that they have changed schools
    D. more and more children are mentally affected

48. According to the passage, Professor Martin's personal feeling _____.
    A. is the opposite of what his report has shown
    B. is in a way supported by his research
    C. has played a big part in his research
    D. is based on the experience of his own children

49. From the passage, we can conclude that Captain James' children _____.
    A. have been affected by changing schools
    B. go to ordinary state schools
    C. can get used to the Army school education
    D. discuss their education regularly with their father

50. About children and grown-ups, Captain James says that children _____.
    A. are generally well-adjusted   B. are usually less experienced
    C. can adapt much more easily   D. can deal with changes quickly

51. According to Professor Martin, _____ suffer from changing schools regularly.
    A. army children   B. quite a few children
    C. bright children   D. slow children

(五)

Maureen stood by the lake. Suddenly the other children came running through the trees with sharp cries of excitement. They rushed up to the lake, leaning over the crystal-clear water, watching the crowds of tiny fish. Some children demanded loudly to go to the boats, but all at once those who had been left behind at the ice-cream stall (小摊) came

121

running up to make some announcement or other, and they all left the water and dashed back the way they had come. With growing excitement, Maureen ran after them.

When she saw what they had been running for, she stopped running. They were buying things again. The toy stall was open and they were crowded around it. Behind the stall a calm middle-aged woman was selling a great variety of small rubbish. She took money from the forest of small hands in exchanging for little boats, plastic dolls, yellow pencils and rubbers, anything. Maureen leaned against a tree, looking on. The idea of spending washed against her face like a strong current, trying to draw her in.

Nona Parker pushed out to the edge of the group and laid what she had bought on the ground so that she could see what money she had left in her white purse. Under Maureen's eyes lay a boat, a mouth oran, and little plates of doll's food in colored plaster——a brown load of bread, a joint of beef, a pink pudding——all tiny and terribly desirable. Maureen was so full of the wish for the things like that she couldn't bear to look at it. She turned her head sharply. Her face against the tree, she shut her eyes and prayed eagerly for some money, for the price of a set of toy plates.

In a moment, she opened her eyes, but she didn't turn back to the stall. It was too painful to see the others buying whatever they wanted. She rubbed almost round the tree, her eyes on the ground. And there at her very feet was a ten pence piece.

52. Maureen stopped running after the other children because she _____.
    A. was too shy to push her way in
    B. thought the other children were rich
    C. knew the stall was selling rubbish
    D. couldn't afford to buy anything

53. Maureen's strong desire for the plates of doll's food grew when _____.
    A. she happened to see what Nona had bought
    B. Nona showed off her things to other children
    C. she saw other children buying things freely
    D. she was pushed to the edge of the group

54. When the children reached the toy stall _____.
    A. they were disappointed at the badly-made toys
    B. they were excited by the unusual toys
    C. they carefully chose what they were going to buy
    D. they were eager to get whatever they were offered

55. Seeing the others buying so many wonderful things, Maureen felt _____.
    A. ashamed   B. helpless
    C. hurt   D. discouraged

四、写作(共两题,满分35分)

(一) 短文改错(共10小题,每小题1分,满分10分)

此题要求改正所给短文中的错误。对标有题号的每一行作出判断:如无错误,在该行右

122

边横线上画一个勾(√);如有错误(每行只有一个错误),则按下列情况改正:

该行多一个词:把多余的词用斜线划掉(\),在该行右边横线上写出该词,并也用斜线划掉。

该行缺一个词:在缺词处加一个漏字符号(∧),在该行右边横线上写出该加的词。

该行错一个词:在错的词下划一横线,在该行右边横线上写出改正后的词。

注意:原行没有错的不要改。

British public libraries linked by computers. If your nearest   1. _____
library in London doesn't have the book you want to borrow,   2. _____
a librarian will go on-line to see whether some of the other   3. _____
nearby libraries have. If no library has the book in store, the   4. _____
librarian will search for further, connecting libraries in other   5. _____
city like Manchester. If a copy of the book is located, an   6. _____
arrangement will be made for it to be sent your library, and   7. _____
in a day and two, you will be able to check it out. It is also   8. _____
possibly for keen readers to borrow books from university   9. _____
and college libraries, even if we are not students.   10. _____

(二)书面表达(计分25分)

提示:你校学生会将为来访的美国朋友举办一个晚会,要在学校广播中宣布此事,并欢迎大家参加。为使美国朋友听懂,请你用英语写一篇广播通知。要点如下:

宗旨: 欢迎来访的美国朋友
组织者: 学生会
时间: 8月15日(星期六)晚7:30
地点: 主楼屋顶花园
活动内容:音乐、跳舞、唱歌、游戏、交换小礼品(请包装好、签名并在包装外面写上几个祝愿词)

注意:
□ 广播稿约100词。
□ 应包括以上要点,但不要逐字翻译,要组织成一篇通顺连贯的短文。
□ 开头语已为你写好。May I have your attention please? I have an announcement to make.

生词:交换礼品——to exchange gifts
　　　学生会——the Student Union

123

Unit 6. Reducing Cost

Part 1. Text

Reducing Cost

Property owners are increasingly seeking ways to minimize the total owning cost of air-conditioning systems. Key factors influencing cost include:

a. The energy efficiency of the facade in terms of solar gain. conductive gain and loss, and natural lighting ability.

b. The efficiency of artificial lighting systems.

c. The efficiency of the cooling and beating plant.

d. The effective cost of operating equipment using varying energy sources purchased under particular tariff structures.

Air-conditioning designers are becoming more heavily involved in the assessment of the energy implications of alternative building facades.

The capital and operating costs of air-conditioning systems have intensified the effort to improve the passive design of buildings. Capital is more commonly invested in double glazing, external shading and reflective glazing.

While the former two techniques involve little risk, there is a significant degress of apprehension in the use of reflective glazing. Although reflective glazing docs present a useful thermal facade solution, the problems of reflection of heat to neighbours, possible disruption due to glare and night time internal light reflection, must be considered.

To complement the design efficiencies of improved building thermal performance and air distribution systems, the efficiency and cost effectiveness of producing heating and cooling have also been improved in recent years. Engineers are now considering a building system as a totally interactive energy equation.

Cooling equipment is being analyzed more thoroughly for its pan load energy performance. As this is generally very low compared to its full load efficiency, thermal storage in the form of ice making equipment is being installed to allow cooling machines to operate at efficiency high load levels by severing the relationship between instantaneous or pan building load and cooling production.

Outside air cooling cycles are being viewed more critically to ensure that air transport energy costs do not outweigh the benefits of the reduced cost of cooling and the wasting of potential useful internal heat. The inclusion of thermal storage, particularly cold storage, can substantially reduce the cost of producing cooling for buildings by reducing electrical demand.

The installation of ice storage in recent projects has produced a more even electrical demand on peak summer cooling days. Tariff savings result because the cooling is produced in a controlled fashion over 24 hours rather than by an instantaneous demand.

Most recent designs have enabled the incorporation of ice storage, without a capital cost penalty, by reducing the capital cost of refrigeration equipment, cooling towers, pipe work and refrigeration compressor electrical supplies. Costs for electrical demand can be reduced by up to 50% using this design technique.

Increasing energy costs will continue the trend towards designs that produce more efficient systems in buildings into the future.

参考译文：

降低成本

财产所有者正在日益寻找降低空调系统总成本的方法。影响成本的主要因素包括：

a. 从太阳光的利用角度看表层的能效。

传导的获得和损失，以及自然的采光能力。

b. 人造照明系统的效率。

c. 制冷和采暖设备的效率。

d. 操作设备的有效成本：在特定的税率结构之下购买设备所需的不同能源。

在建筑物表层材料的选择上，空调设计者越来越多地参与其在能源应用方面的评估。

空调系统的投资的和操作的成本已经加强了要在改进建筑物被动设计方面做出努力。资金更多的投在双层玻璃，外部遮阳玻璃和反射玻璃上。

尽管前面的二项技术很少有什么风险，人们还是对使用反射玻璃普遍存在担心，虽然反射玻璃的确提供了一个建筑表面向外反射热能的办法，但是必须考虑到由于眩目的光和夜里室内光的反射造成的可能的破坏。

近几年来，为了进一步改善建筑物热性能和空气分配系统的设计效率，加热和冷却装置的效率和成本的有效利用也得到了改进。现在工程师们正在考虑把建筑物系统作为完全地相互作用的能量平衡系统。

对冷却设备的部件承载能量的性能正在进行更彻底地分析。由于这与全部承载效率相比一般很低，因此用制冷设施贮藏热量制成的设备，通过切断瞬间或部分建筑物载荷与冷却产品之间的联系以安装到允许冷却机器以高效和高承载水平进行操作。

更密切地注视外面空气冷却周期以确保空气传送能量的成本不超过减少冷却成本的收益和潜在的有用的内部热量的浪费。包括热的贮藏，特别是冷藏，实质上能通过减少电能来降低给建筑物制冷的成本。

在最近的项目中，安装贮藏冰块的设备使得夏季制冷高峰期对电的需求量比较平稳。这样就节省了电费,因为制冷需要 24 小时进行而不是瞬间的需求,而用电高峰期的电税是很高的。

最近大部分设计都考虑到了冰块的贮藏问题,没有投资成本损失,而是通过降低冰箱设备,冷却塔,管道工作和冷却压缩机的供电设备的资金成本等这样的手段。用这项设计技术。可使所需电量的成本最多降低 50%。

递增的能量成本将使未来社会的建筑物继续沿着创建更有效的系统的趋势发展。

Vocabulary
单词表:

161.	facade	[fə'sɑːd]	n.	(房屋的)正面,立面;表面,外观,(掩饰真相的)门面
162.	solar	['səulə]	a.	太阳的,日光的,利用太阳光的
163.	conductive	[kən'dʌktiv]	a.	传导性的,传导上的
164.	particular	[pə'tikjulə]	a.	特殊的,特别的,特指的;独特的,异常的;详细的;挑剔的
165.	tariff	['tærif]	n.	关税(率);收费表,价目表
166.	assessment	[ə'sesmənt]	n.	估价,评价;估计数
167.	implication	[ˌimpli'keiʃən]	n.	含有……的意思;牵连;影响
168.	alternative	[ɔː'ltəːnətiv]	a.	两者(或两者以上)挑一的;选择的;
			n.	抉择;可供选择的办法(或方案)
169.	capital	['kæpitl]	n.	资本,资方;a. 资本的;基本的,首要的,重要的;致死的;第一流的
170.	intensify	[in'tensifai]	vt.	加强,加剧;vi. 强化
171.	passive	['pæsiv]	a.	被动的,受动的,消极的;无利息的
172.	glazing	['gleiziŋ]	n.	窗用玻璃;(总称)玻璃窗;玻璃装配工作;磨光
173.	reflective	[ri'flektiv]	a.	反射的,反映的思考的,沉思的
174.	significant	[sig'nifikənt]	a.	有意义的,意义(或意味)深长的;表明……的;重要的,值得注意的;有效的;非偶然的
175.	apprehension	[ˌæpri'henʃən]	n.	理解,领悟;担心,忧虑
176.	present	['preznt]	vt.	介绍,引见;提出,呈递;出示,上演
177.	disruption	[dis'rʌpʃən]	n.	分裂,瓦解;破坏
178.	complement	['kɔmplimənt]	n.	补足物;vt. 补充,补足
179.	thermal	['θəːməl]	a.	热的,由热造成的;温泉的;
			n.	上升暖气流
180.	performance	[pə'fɔːməns]	n.	履行,执行,完成;成绩;演出
181.	distribution	[ˌdistri'bjuːʃən]	n.	分配,销售;分布;分配装置,分配系统;区分,分类
182.	effectiveness	[i'fektivnis]	n.	有效,生效;有力;实在,实际
183.	interactive	[ˌintər'æktiv]	a.	相互作用的,相互影响的
184.	equation	[i'kweiʃən]	n.	均衡,平均;(个别或综合的)因素
185.	install	[in'stɔːl]	vt.	任命,安装,安置

186. production	[prəˈdʌkʃən]	n.	生产；制作；演出；提供
187. view	[vju:]	vt.	看，检查，估计
188. critically	[ˈkritikəli]	ad.	评论性地；对……感到不满地；关键性地；应急所必须地
189. outweigh	[autˈwei]	vt.	在重量上超过；在价值上超过
190. storage	[ˈstɔ:ridʒ]	n.	保管；库存量；仓库
191. saving	[ˈseiviŋ]	n.	节约；挽救；(复)储蓄(金)；存款
192. fashion	[ˈfæʃən]	n.	方式；风尚
193. incorporation	[inˌkɔ:pəˈreiʃən]	n.	结合，合并，社团，公司；混合
194. penalty	[ˈpenlti]	n.	惩罚，罚款；困难，不利后果

Useful Expressions

in terms of 用……的话说；从……的角度(或观点)
be involved in... 包括在……中，被卷入
due to 由于，起因于，归于

Notes
备注：

1. Property owners are increasingly seeking ways to minimize the total owning cost of air-conditioning systems. 财产所有者正在日益寻找降低空调系统总成本的方法。

在句中，to minimize the total owning cost of air-conditioning systems 是动词不定式短语做定语，修饰前面的名词 ways。

例如：

That is our house to stay in during the holiday.
那就是我们假期呆的房子。

2. Key factors influencing cost include：影响成本的主要因素包括：

在句中，influencing cost 是现在分词短语做定语，修饰前面的名词 factors。

例如：

He lived in a room overlooking the sea.
他住在一个朝海的房间里。

3. The capital and operating costs of air-conditioning systems have intensified the effort to improve the passive design of buildings. 空调系统的投资和操作的成本已经强化了要在改进建筑物被动设计方面所做的努力。

在句中，have intensified 构成的是现在完成时态，表示到现在为止已经完成的行为。

例如：

Have you been to that country before?
你以前去过那个国家吗？

I have read the book.
我读过这本书。

to improve the passive design of buildings 是动词不定式短语做定语，修饰前面的名词 effort。

4. Although reflective glazing docs present a useful thermal facade solution, the problems of reflection of heat to neighbours, possible disruption due to glare and night time internal light reflection, must be considered. 虽然反射玻璃的确提供了一个对周围物体的热反射问题有用的热学表层的解决办法,但是必须考虑到由于眩目的光和夜里室内光的反射造成的可能的破坏。

在句中,助动词 does 起强调作用。Although 引导的是让步状语从句,表示在某种相反的条件下主句谓语行为仍然发生。

注意:在让步状语从句中,有 although 就不能用 but,有 but 就不能用 although。

例如:

Although/Though he is still young, (不用 but) he is going very grey.

他虽然还年轻,但已快满头斑白了。

must be considered 是含有情态动词的被动语态。

例如:

These exercises should be finished by the students in class.

学生们应该在课上完成这些练习。

Meat should always be kept cool.

肉应该总是保存在低温下。

5. To complement the design efficiencies of improved building thermal performance and air distribution systems, the efficiency and cost effectiveness of producing heating and cooling have also been improved in recent years. 近几年来,为了补充改进的建筑物热性能和空气分配系统的设计效率,加热和冷却装置的效率和成本的有效利用也得到了改进。

在句中,to complement the design efficiencies of improved building thermal performance and air distribution systems,是动词不定式短语做目的状语,例如:

(In order) to save the child, he dived into the river.

为了救那个孩子,他跳进了河里。

have also been improved 构成的是现在完成时态的被动语态,经常和 in recent years 这样的时间状语连用。

例如:

The boy has been made to work long.

那个男孩已经被迫工作很长时间了。

6. Cooling equipment is being analysed more thoroughly for its part load energy performance. 对冷却设备的部件承载能量的性能正在进行更彻底地分析。

在句中,is being analysed 构成的是现在进行时态的被动语态。

例如:

The child is being taken good care of. (Good care is being taken of the child.)

那个孩子正在受到精心照料。

Ⅰ. Exercises for the text(课文练习):

(Ⅰ) Decide whether the following sentences are True or False according to the content of the text.

1. Air-conditioning designers are becoming more heavily involved in the assessment of the

energy implications of alternative building facades.
2. Capital is less commonly invested in double glazing, external shading and reflective glazing.
3. Although reflective glazing does present a useful thermal façade solution, the problems of reflection of heat to neighbours, possible disruption due to glare and night time internal light reflection, must be considered.
4. Engineers are now considering a building system as a totally interactive energy equation.
5. Costs for electrical demand can be reduced by up to 50% without this design technique.
6. Property Managers are increasingly seeking ways to minimize the total owning cost of air-conditioning systems.
7. The capital of air-conditioning systems has intensified the effort to improve the passive design of buildings.
8. Cooling equipment is being analysed more thoroughly for its part load energy performance.
9. Outside air cooling cycles are being viewed more critically to ensure that air transport energy costs outweigh the benefits of the reduced cost of cooling and the wasting of potential useful internal heat.
10. Increasing energy costs will continue the trend towards designs that produce more efficient systems in buildings into the future.

(Ⅱ) **Match the English words with their Chinese translations, choose the appropriate words to complete the sentences below and translate them into Chinese**(将下列英语单词与其中文意思相匹配,选择合适的词将下列句子补充完整并译成中文):

1. particular	a. 任命,安装,安置
2. capital	b. 估价,评价;估计数
3. install	c. 在重量上超过;在价值上超过
4. facade	d. 介绍,引见;提出,呈递;出示,上演
5. reflective	e. 特殊的,特别的,特指的;独特的,异常的;详细的;挑剔的
6. passive	f. 两者(或两者以上)挑一的;选择的;n. 抉择;可供选择的办法
7. present	g. (房屋的)正面,立面;表面,外观,(掩饰真相的)门面
8. outweigh	h. 资本,资方;a. 资本的;基本的,首要的,重要的;致死的;第一流的
9. assessment	i. 反射的,反映的;思考的,沉思的
10. significant	j. 被动的,受动的,消极的;无利息的
11. alternative	k. 履行,执行,完成;成绩;演出
12. performance	l. 有意义的,意义(或意味)深长的;表明……的;重要的,值得注意的;有效的;非偶然的

1. He only assumes a _____ of neutrality.
2. The cocoanut is _____ to the tropics.
3. We should have a correct _____ of historical figures.

4. We have no _____ in the matter.

5. _____ comes dripping from head to foot, from every pore, with blood and dirt.

6. They put the enemy in a _____ position.

7. That is _____ glare of the beach.

8. Statistically _____ correlation exists between vitamin deficiency and disease.

9. Allow me to _____ Mr. Brown to you.

10. This novel is really a remarkable _____.

11. He _____ himself in a front-row seat.

12. The advantages _____ the disadvantages.

(Ⅲ) **Choose the best answer**(选择最佳答案)

1. I want the article _____ two days before the meeting opens.
   a. to type   b. to be typed   c. be typed   d. type

2. All those _____ to go to the football match, please raise your hands.
   a. will wish   b. wish   c. wishing   d. wished

3. He's already gone home. But before he left, he _____ all the mistakes in his translation.
   a. had corrected   b. has corrected   c. corrected   d. would correct

4. Why is the rubbish still here? It ought to _____ yesterday.
   a. be thrown away   b. have thrown away
   c. have been thrown away   d. throw away

5. The city _____ its birth-rate by almost 60% in the past 20 years.
   a. has cut   b. cuts   c. have cut   d. has been cut

6. Your question _____ soon(by me).
   a. can answer   b. can be answered
   c. can have answered   d. answer

7. He does more reading than you do, doesn't he? ——Yes, he _____ do much more than me.
   a. do   b. does   c. did   d. done

8. _____ he is already over sixty, he's active in physical labour.
   a. Although   b. /   c. But   d. As

9. The city government must take action _____ the increasing population.
   a. to control   b. controlling   c. controls   d. controlled

10. A lot of buildings _____ and the place _____ very noisy ever since we moved here.
    a. have been built; has become   b. have been built; became
    c. were built; has become   d. were built; became

(Ⅳ) **Translation**:

Translate the following Chinese into English:

1. 财产所有者正在日益寻找降低空调系统总成本的方法。

2. 空调设计者越来越密切的关注对建筑物表层所选材料是否节能的评价。

3. 资金更多的投资在双层玻璃,外部遮阳玻璃和反射玻璃。

4. 虽然反射玻璃的确提供了一个对周围物体的热反射问题的有用的热学表层的解决办法,但是必须考虑到由于眩目的光和夜里室内光的反射造成的可能的破坏。

5. 现在工程师们正在考虑把建筑物系统作为完全地相互作用的能量平衡系统。

6. 实质上能通过减少电能来降低给建筑物制冷的成本。

7. 制冷需要 24 小时而不是瞬间的控制方式。

8. 用这项设计技术可使所需电量的成本最多降低 50%。

9. 递增的能量成本将使未来社会的建筑物继续创建更有效的系统这种趋势。

10. 最近大部分设计都考虑到了冰块的贮藏问题。

(V) Extra Topic Reading:

Extra reading: read the following passage and choose the best answer to complete each of the statements that follow.

ADVANCES IN AIR-CONDITIONING

Air-conditioning systems are no longer simply mechanical means of providing some measure of dry bulb temperature control within enclosed spaces. The modem air-conditioning is an integral part of a building design, aimed at producing an environment in which human tasks can be undertaken with maximum efficiency.

The concept of a total internal environment has enabled designers to better satisfy the wide range of human psychological and physiological demand.

The integral approach to environment design has produced a significant trend in recent years towards the specialist designing of systems for individual buildings so that they will perform satisfactorily for a wide range of internal activities and allow for a greater divergence of occupants.

Competition For Tenants

A driving force behind the progression in environment design has been the competition between properties to secure increasingly sophisticated tenants. The challenge for air-conditioning systems' designers has been to provide internal environments for discerning tenants with a cost structure that will enable Building Owners to be financially competitive.

The need for a safe, fresh and healthy environment devoid of stress inducing temperatures, noise and vibration has long been established. For discerning tenants the major features required from a modem air-conditioning system include:

a. Occupant Safety - the ability to control the spread and effect the removal of smoke under all emergency conditions is of fundamental life saving importance.

Recently built major office towers which are air-conditioned in vertical stages to maximize the space efficiency of the building service core, discharge smoke horizontally at intermediate locations at the tower. For increased safety, smoke discharge must be possible in two alternative directions.

b. Environmental Freshness - the sensation of environmental freshness is determined by the inter-relation of air cleanliness, air oxygen content and air movement. This is an area which has

131

historically offered the major scope for design improvement. Each of the components contributing to freshness, if improved, adds significant capital and operating costs.

Design techniques have had to be developed to satisfy tenant demand for improvement whilst minimizing cost penalties to Building Owners. Operating costs were reduced by developing variable air volume (VAV) systems which reduced air circulation energy but this was at the expense of environmental freshness.

More recent design techniques have combined the operating costs advantages of VAV systems with developments in electronic control capability and electrostatic filters to produce a vastly improved environmental freshness.

c. Accurate Temperature Control - the most significant recent influences on ability of air-conditioning systems to maintain accurate temperature control have been the rapidly increasing automation of work stations and the emergence of micro processor based direct digital control systems.

Zoning of air-conditioning systems must take account of the varying internal influences but must also recognize that highly concentrated heat sources will occur at work stations and that the ability to deal with the changing location of heat sources must be flexible through the life of the building.

Rapid reductions in cost have enabled advanced electronic controls to be applied to small sub systems controlling small sub zones throughout a total complex.

d. After Hours Service -tenant demand for a fully controlled environment, outside normal business hours, for relatively small floor areas has increased with the growing use of automated commercial equipment and the need for 24 hour international communications.

The use of electronic speed controls to maintain ventilating fans serving VAV systems, has enabled after hours ventilation to be provided at reasonable operating cost. The provision of temperature control for low after hours loads is accommodated by the installation of thermal equipment of a range of sizes such that large machinery does not then have to operate at very inefficient low load conditions.

1. The modern air-conditioning is the following except _____.
   a. an integral part of a building design
   b. aimed at producing an environment in which human task can be undertaken with maximum efficiency
   c. simple mechanical means of providing some measure of dry bulb temperature control within enclosed spaces
   d. no longer simple mechanical means of providing some measure of dry bulb temperature control within enclosed spaces

2. "The integral approach to environment design has produced a significant trend in recent years ." In the sentence "a significant trend" means _____.
   a. the specialist design of systems for individual buildings so that they will perform satisfactorily for a wide rang of internal activities and allow for a greater

      divergence of occupants

    b. an integral part of a building design

    c. no longer simple mechanical means of providing some measure of dry bulb temperature control within enclosed spaces

    d. producing an environment in which human task can be undertaken with maximum efficiency

3. A driving force behind the progression in environment design has been _____.

    a. to provide internal environments for discerning tenants with a cost structure that will enable Building Owners to be financially competitive

    b. the competition between properties to secure increasingly sophisticated tenants

    c. the specialist design of systems for individual buildings

    d. perform satisfactorily for a wide rang of internal activities and allow for a greater divergence of occupants

4. For discerning tenants the major features required from a modern air-conditioning system include _____.

    a. Occupant safety and Environmental Freshness

    b. Accurate Temperature Control

    c. After Hours Service

    d. All of above

5. _____ has enabled after hours ventilation to be provided at reasonable operating cost.

    a. The use of electronic speed controls to maintain ventilating fans serving VAV systems

    b. A driving force behind the progression in environment design

    c. The challenge for air-conditioning systems' designers

    d. Provide internal environments for discerning tenants with a cost structure

II. Language Ability Drill(语言能力练习)

(I) Vocabulary Exercise

Study the following words. Then try to use them correctly in the sentences below.

Verbs	Nouns	Participles
manage	management manager	managing
inspect	inspection inspector	inspected
consult	consultation consultant	consulting
bore	bore boredom	boring bored
assemble	assembly	assembled

133

1. As neither _____ nor labor would give in, the union organized a strike. (manage)

2. The factory will be much more productive if it is properly _____. (manage)

3. They _____ her car at the garage (汽车修理厂). (inspect)

4. I gave the bicycle set a thorough _____ before I bought it. (inspect)

5. Before making any decision, Jane _____ with her father. (consult)

6. Hans went to his dentist (牙医) for _____ because of a bad toothache. (consult)

7. John is such a _____ that no one likes to talk to him. (bore)

8. _____ with detective (侦探的) stories, Jimmy has now taken an interest in modern poetry. (bore)

9. Understandably Ann was so nervous. After all it was the first time that she ever spoke before an _____ crowd. (assemble)

10. They were busy _____ a tractor (拖拉机) when the accident happened. (assemble)

(Ⅱ) Cloze

My Experience in a Free School

At first I couldn't believe it! There were no 1 in rows; no bells rang; no one had to go to 2 . Although we all lived "in", 3 made us go to bed at a certain time; there was no "lights out". The 4 thing was that practically all the students went to class, 5 very few people stayed up late at night. Only the new people stayed up or 6 class. The new ones always went wild 7 , but this never lasted long. The 8 took some getting used to. Our teachers treated us like 9 ; never did we have to 10 "stand up", "sit down", "speak out". I don't 11 one student who didn't try his best. The subjects were the same as those in 12 school, but what a difference in the approach (方式)! For example, in bo-tany (植物学) we had 13 classes in the spring or fall, but instead we 14 two gardens, a vegetable garden and a flower garden. 15 In winter we each studied a few 16 things about what we had grown. In math the students built three different kinds of storerooms-small ones 17 , but usable. They did this instead of having lessons in the classroom. They really had a 18 time too, designing everything, drawing the blueprints, 19 the angles (角度) and so on. I didn't take 20 . I can't stand it! Besides, I could do the basic things with numbers. That's 21 ! 22 I think I am a 23 person for having gone to the school. I can read and write as well as anyone else my age, and I can think better. That's probably a real big 24 between the free school and regular school the amount of 25 .

1. A. desks   B. lights   C. students   D. buildings
2. A. home   B. bed   C. class   D. work
3. A. anybody   B. nobody   C. teachers   D. parents
4. A. sad   B. last   C. good   D. strange
5. A. and   B. but   C. so   D. yet
6. A. attended   B. took   C. missed   D. studied
7. A. from then on B. at first   C. once more   D. just then

134

8. A. freedom	B. habit	C. time	D. people
9. A. workers	B. pupils	C. gardeners	D. grown-ups
10. A. understand	B. study	C. play	D. say
11. A. hear from	B. feel like	C. think about	D. know of
12. A. night	B. regular	C. small	D. real
13. A. all	B. short	C. no	D. indoor
14. A. planted	B. studied	C. drew	D. toured
15. A. Still	B. Then	C. Yet	D. Next
16. A. wild	B. successful	C. usual	D. particular
17. A. as well	B. after a while	C. of course	D. as a result
18. A. funny	B. great	C. convenient	D. thoughtful
19. A. looking out	B. taking out	C. finding out	D. figuring out
20. A. math	B. care	C. botany	D. notice
21. A. dull	B. interesting	C. enough	D. dangerous
22. A. On the whole	B. Once again	C. Sooner or later	D. After a while
23. A. careful	B. better	C. busier	D. lovely
24. A. problem	B. chance	C. difference	D. change
25. A. reading	B. gardening	C. teaching	D. thinking

(Ⅲ) **Complete the following sentences, using the words given in brackets:**

Example: The sight of the Golden Gate Bridge in San Francisco is often a great surprise to visitors.

Visitors to San Francisco .... (amaze)

Visitors to San Francisco are often amazed at the sight of the Golden Gate Bridge.

1. Any good relationship between nations is based on mutual（相互的）trust and respect.

    Mutual trust and respect... (basis)

2. Few mothers would be surprised to find boys' bedrooms untidy（不整洁的）.

    For many boys, it seems almost impossible to .... (neat)

3. A thick fog（雾）over the airport kept our plane from taking off on schedule.

    The take-off of our plane... (hold up)

4. In its history the city has been hit by two earthquakes（地震）that caused great damage, one in 1906 and the other in 1989.

    The city has experienced.. (major)

5. The professor was an outstanding scientist, yet in his personal life he was often forgetful.

    Though an outstanding scientist, ... (absent-minded)

6. An employee（雇员）can hardly expect to keep his job if he fails to report to work on time.

    Failure to report to work on time will often result in .... (fire).

Part 2. Dialogue

Welcoming the Visitors
（接待访客）

Ⅰ. Typical Sentences(经典短句)

（Ⅰ）Daily Conversations(日常用语)

要求重复：

1. Pardon (me)? (or Beg your pardon?)
   请再说一遍好吗？
2. I'm sorry. I didn't understand you.
   抱歉，我不了解您的意思。
3. Would you mind repeating your question?
   麻烦您再说一遍（您的问题），好吗？
4. Would you please speak more slowly?
   可否请您讲慢一点？
5. I'm afraid I can't explain it in English.
   恐怕我没办法用英语解释。
6. Excuse me. What did you say?
   抱歉，您说什么？
7. Excuse me. What do you mean by '…'?
   对不起，您说'…'是什么意思？
8. Is that so? I see.
   是这样吗？我明白了。
9. Would you please say it again?
   请您再说一次好吗？
10. Do you follow me?
    你懂我的意思吗？

（Ⅱ）Professional Conversations（专业会话）

1. Would you please tell me which resident you are going to visit?
   请告诉我您要找哪户？
2. Please fill in this form of record for visitors.
   请您填写来访记录。
3. Please park your car in the area for guests.
   请将您的车停于客人车位。
4. The No. 3 building is right behind the fountain.
   3号楼在喷泉后。
5. Taxi is forbidden to enter the community.
   出租车严禁驶入小区。

Ⅱ. **Conversation Passages**

Passage 1.

A: Good evening, sir. Would you please tell me which resident you are going to visit?
晚上好,先生。请告诉我您要找哪户?

B: Yes, I think it is 10-1-501.
是10号楼1门501室。

A: Pardon?
请再说一遍好吗?

B: It's Room 1-501, Building 10.
是10号楼1门501室。

A: Oh, I see.
是这样,我明白了。

B: Can I park my car inside the community.
我可以把车停在小区里面吗?

A: Yes, of course, you can. But please park it in the guest area.
是的,当然可以,但请将您的车停于客人车位。

B: Thank you.
谢谢。

A: With pleasure.
这是我应该做的。

Passage 2.

(After parking the car)

A: Hello, is this YueYang Community?
您好,请问这是岳阳小区吗?

B: Yes, are you visiting someone?
是的,您来串门的吗?

A: Yes. He lives in Building 3.
是的,就住在3号楼。

B: Welcome! But the taxi is forbidden to enter the community.
欢迎!但出租车严禁驶入小区。

A: Oh, I see.
噢,我知道了。

B: So, would you please tell me which resident you are going to visit?
请告诉我您要找哪户?

A: I only know he lives in Building 3, and his name is YangYong.
我只知道他住在3号楼,叫杨勇。

B: Oh, you're looking for Mr. Yang. Didn't he tell which floor and room he lives in?
您是来找杨先生的,他没告诉您他住在哪层哪室吗?

137

A: Yes, he did. But I forget it. What a memory!
不,他跟我说了。可是我忘了,瞧我这坏记性。

B: Ok, would you please fill in this form of record for visitors?
请您填写一下来访记录吧。

A: All right.
好吧。

B: Mr. Yang lives in 3-1-401.
杨先生住在 3 号楼 1 门 401 室。

A: Would you please speak more slowly?
可否请您讲慢一点?

B: Of course, he lives in the No. 1 room on Floor 4.
当然,他住在 4 楼 1 室。

A: Thank you very much.
非常感谢!

B: You are welcome. And Building No. 3 is right behind the fountain.
不用谢,3 号楼就在喷泉后。

Ⅲ. Exercises for Dialogue

(Ⅰ) Fill in the following blanks by considering Chinese.
(按照中文完成以下填空)

A: Welcome! _____.
但出租车严禁驶入小区。

B: Oh, I see.

A: So, _____?
请告诉我您要找哪户?

B: I only know he lives in Building 3-1, and his name is YangYong.
我只知道他住在 3 号楼 1 门,叫杨勇。

A: Oh, you're the visitor to Mr. Yang. Didn't he tell which _____?
他没告诉您他住在哪层哪室吗?

B: Yes, he did. But I forget it. What a bad memory!
不,他跟我说了,可是我忘了。瞧我这坏记性。

A: _____?
请您填写一下来访记录吧。

B: All right.
好吧。

A: Mr. Yang lives in 3-1-401.

(Ⅲ) Make a telephone conversation with your partner about anything you like. (there should be at least 3 turn-taking in the dialogue)

Ⅳ. Spoken Language Drill (fill in the blanks according to the Chinese translation)

Dialogue 1.

A: I like your new coat.
我喜欢你的新外套。

B: Do you think it _____ OK?
你看合身吗?

A: Yes. It looks _____!
很合身,看上去好极了!

B: I bought it at half price.
我花了半价买来的。

A: You were _____ to find it.
你的运气真好。

Dialogue 2.

A: What a beautiful sweater!
多漂亮的毛衣!

B: Do you think it looks good on me?
你看我穿着好看吗?

A: Yes, and it _____ beautifully _____ your pants.
好看,配上你的这条裤子美极了。

B: You won't believe it, but it was really cheap.
你不会相信的,但这条裤子确实很便宜。

A: I wish I could find one just like it.
要是我也能碰到这样一件就好了。

Dialogue 3.

A: I love that shirt.
我喜欢这件衬衫。

B: Do you really like it?
你真的喜欢吗?

A: Yes, it fits _____.
是的,合身极了。

B: It wasn't very expensive either.
而且也不太贵。

A: That's _____! It sure looks expensive.
真想不到! 看上去肯定以为很贵。

Dialogue 4.

A: That's a very nice jacket.

这件茄克衫真漂亮呀!
B: Does it really _____ OK?
看上去真的不错吗?
A: Yes, and I like the color too. It _____ your hat.
是的,我也喜欢这颜色。和你的帽子很相配。
B: And I got it on _____.
我在大减价时买的。
A: That's incredible!
简直难以相信!

Part 3. Supplementary Reading:

Passage A
China to Improve Community Health Service System

China is expected to set up a nationwide framework for its **community** health service system by 2005, said officials from China's health and civil affairs departments Friday. China has decided to take measures to improve its community health service system, according to **officials** attending an inauguration ceremony for building pilot communities with a better health service system. Vice minister of China's Health Ministry Zhu Qingsheng said that the community health service networks made great **contributions** to the prevention and control of severe acute respiratory syndrome (SARS) this spring. Zhu said the service networks did a lot in surveilling and reporting SARS cases, in screening and transferring SARS patients and in disease contact tracing, which helped a lot in **combating** SARS. About 100 pilot communities are to be set up in the next two years, including 20 that will employ traditional Chinese medicine, under the guidance of the Ministry of Health, the Ministry of Civil Affairs and the State Administration of Traditional Chinese Medicine, Zhu added. He said community health service is very important for better social and **economic** development, and the service system is expected to cover the whole country in the future. According to statistics from the Ministry of Health, 358 **cities had** started a community health service by the end of 2002, accounting for 54 percent of China's total.

参考译文:

我国将要改善社区健康服务体系

国家健康及国内事务部门官员于周五透露,我国准备在2005年以前,建立起一个全国性的社区健康服务体系。出席试点社区建筑奠基仪式上的国家健康及国内事务部门官员表示,我国已经决心要采取措施改善全民社区健康服务体系。国家卫生部副部长朱庆生说中国的社区健康服务网络对预防和控制今年春季爆发的非典型性肺炎疫情,做出很大贡献。

朱庆生说,该服务网络在挽救和报导 SARS 事件中做了很大努力,他们放映和广播患病的 SARS 病人的情况,跟踪他们的病情,这些在与 SARS 的斗争中起了很大的作用。朱补充说,大约有一百个试点社区将会在未来的两年内建立,二十个将会在卫生部和国家中医药管理局的指导下雇佣中国的传统中医师。他说社区卫生服务对于社会安定和经济发展都非常的重要,该体系在未来将会覆盖全国。根据卫生部的数字统计:到 2002 年底,共有 358 个城市开展了社区健康服务,占据了全国城市总数的 54%。

Passage B

President George W. Bush

President George W. Bush is not what you'd call a poster child for life in the fast lane. As governor of Texas, he had little tolerance for briefings that ran too long, and made sure there was plenty of space in his schedule to work out and play video games. Since moving to the White House, he's still in bed by 10 p.m. By contrast, his predecessor, Bill Clinton, was notorious for burning the midnight oil, holding marathon meetings and packing activity into every minute of his day.

But though the new President may prefer to take life at a leisurely pace, that doesn't mean he's ineffective.

The truth is, we all move at our own personal speed, and for the most part, that suits us just fine. The ones who juggle 10 balls in the air at once and don't know the meaning of downtime don't necessarily get more done, nor are they more tense, unhappier or even unhealthier than those who prefer marching to a slower drummer. Where we go wrong, say experts, is when we expect everyone around us to conform to our own preferred tempo.

Doing what comes naturally The speed at which we move through life seems to be hardwired into us right from the start.

In scientific terms, people who enjoy keeping a busy schedule are known as polychromic (多元惯性者), while their more single minded counterparts are monochromic (单一贯性者). What's interesting is that polychromic people, more than monochromic ones, tend to feel they accomplish in a day just about everything they set out to do. They also perceive themselves as handing pressure better than monochromic people, who are more methodical and don't like change.

While you might expect that a leisurely paced person would be better organized than a multitasker, in fact monochromic folks actually have trouble getting their act together, and tend to put off things because of their focus on accomplishing tasks in a certain order.

Several decades ago, some highly publicized studies indicated that fast track, "Type A" personalities were the ones most at risk for heart disease and other stress related illnesses. However, researchers today seem to be moving away from the notion that pace by itself affects health. Instead, they're looking to other factors, such as hostility level and negative emotions like guilt.

Indeed, many multitaskers enjoy their active lives. And the monochromic folks of the world don't necessarily wish they could pick up their pace. It is fire to take what come naturally K. B.

When speed becomes a problem where fast and slow people alike run into trouble is when they live or work with people who operate at a speed different from theirs. A multi-tasker may despair of a slow lane husband who doesn't get many chores done on the weekend, or a child who takes her time getting ready for school.

For the unhurried, the office can be a particular source of frustration. With workplaces becoming increasingly high tech and high speed, it's easy to feel left behind if you don't work well in that atmosphere.

But still, the less speedy among us are often valuable staff members. A multitasker may overlook details in her rush to accomplish 10 things by quitting time, but a less hurried worker will make sure all the facts are in place before turning in a project. And while being a speed demon may be an advantage in some professions, there are other jobs where a methodical approach is preferred. Slow people tend to be the inner focused philosophers and artists.

Getting in sync What can you do about the people in your life who don't share your preferred pace? First, acknowledge the fact that their style is their own, and that it's not wrong to be a fast or slow person.

A better solution is to figure out others' natural rhythm and make it work to everyone's advantage. If you're a meticulous type with a go-getter manager, ask her which projects she consider top priority so you can give yourself plenty of time to finish them, and ask for a precise deadline for each one. If you're the speediest member of a low key team, delegate appropriate tasks, such as research, to the slower staffer. Still, if the pace of your job consistently makes you miserable, you might look into a line of work better suited to your own style.

Mixed pace couples can avoid driving each other crazy by finding ways to accommodate each other's tempos. When possible, chores should be classified by their urgency, with the faster person responsible for the more pressing tasks. For a joint project such as planning a vacation, the slower spouse could spend an afternoon comparing airline prices online while the quicker one could make the hotel reservations, jot down a packing list and arrange to have the mail delivery suspended.

While the important thing is to feel good about the pace you were born with, it's still not a bad idea to try a temporary change once in a while. If you're the full Filofax（备忘录）type, taking a slow down day can give you a new perspective.

参考译文：

乔治·W·布什

乔治·W·布什总统不是人们所说的那种"快车道上的慢孩子"。身为得克萨斯州州长的他,很少有耐心去听长篇大论的简况介绍,他要确保时间表中有充足的时间来编、玩视频游戏。入主白宫后,他仍然每天早上10点钟以后才起床。与此相反,他的前任比尔·克林顿以熬夜、召开马拉松会议并把一天中的每一分钟安排得满满当当而著称。

尽管新总统可能喜欢缓慢的生活节奏,但这并不意味着他碌碌无为。

事实上,我们每人都有自己的生活节奏,而且大多数情况下,这一节奏对我们来讲,恰好合适。同时在空中要10个球,而不知道休息的意义的人比起那些更喜欢按慢节奏行进的人来,并不一定会干得更多,同样也不一定更紧张,更不快乐甚至是身体更差。专家认为问题就出在我们期望周围的每一个人都能遵从我们自己喜欢的节奏上。

顺其自然 我们的生活节奏似乎从一开始就像硬件一样安到了我们身上。

科学术语中,喜欢把时间安排得很满的人被称为多元惯性者,而与他们对应的头脑较为简单的人被称为单一惯性者。有趣的是,多元惯性者比单一惯性者更倾向于认为在一天中几乎完成了他们所要做的一切,他们还觉得自己比单一惯性者更能承受压力,而单一惯性者做事更有条理而且不喜欢变化。

你可能会以为一个生活节奏缓慢的人将会比身兼数职者更易于组织,事实上,由于单一惯性者注重按某一程序完成任务,因而他们难于共同行动并有拖延倾向。

几十年前,一些广为宣传的研究表明快节奏即"A型"人最易患心脏病及其他与压力有关的疾病。然而,今天的研究人员似乎不再认为节奏本身影响健康,而是着眼于其他因素,比如敌对程度及像负疚感的消极情绪。

的确,许多身兼数职者喜欢积极的生活。而世界上单一惯性者并不一定希望加快生活节奏。顺其自然就好。

当节奏成为问题时 无论是快节奏还是慢节奏者,在和与其生活节奏不同的人们一起生活或工作时,都会遇到麻烦。一个身兼数职者可能对慢吞吞在周末干不了多少活的丈夫感到绝望,或是对慢条斯理准备上学的孩子感到绝望。

对于那些慢条斯理的人来说,办公室可能是产生挫败感的一个特殊的源泉。随着办公场所越来越高科技化、高速度化,如果在这种氛围中工作干得不是很好的话,很容易感觉被落在了后面。

但是,我们中速度较慢的人通常是很有价值的工作人员。一个身兼数职者可能由于急于在下班之前做好10件事而忽略了细节,但是一个较为从容的工作人员将会在交工前确保所有的事实都很适当。尽管有些职业中大刀阔斧可能是一种优势,其他的工作却更要求有条不紊的做事方法。慢性子的人倾向于成为注重内心世界的哲学家和艺术家。

学会协调,对于你的生活中有着不同于你所喜欢的节奏的人们,你能做些什么呢?首先,承认这是他们自己的方式这一事实,而且承认做一个快节奏或慢节奏的人都没有错这一事实。

一个更好的解决办法是找出他人的自然节奏,而且使其有利于每个人。如果你属于过分仔细的那一类,而且你的经理是一个能干而有进取心的人,你就要问一下她认为哪些项目最重要,以便拿出足够的时间来完成这些项目,并问清每个项目的确切截止时间。如果你是一个慢节奏团队中最快的一个,你就要把如研究工作等的相应工作委派给较为缓慢的人员。还有,如果你的工作节奏一直让你觉得很难受,你可以探求一种更适合你自身方式的工作。

节奏不同的夫妻可以找到容纳双方节奏的方式避免使对方发疯。如果可能的话,家务活应该按缓急程度来分类，快性子的人负责更为紧迫的任务。对于一个如度假计划等的联合项目，慢性子的一方可以花上一个下午的时间联系比较航空公司的价格，而急性子的另一方可以预定旅馆，草草列出打包清单，并安排邮件暂停投递。

尽管最重要的是要对你与生俱来的节奏感觉良好，偶尔尝试一下暂时的变化仍是一个不错的主意。如果你要靠备忘记事本来理顺你繁忙的生活节奏，那放慢节奏会让你有一个新的视点。

Exercises for the reading:

1. Bill Clinton was notorious for the followings, except _____?
   A. burning the midnight oil
   B. holding marathon meetings
   C. packing activity into every minute of his day
   D. play video games

2. Which of the followings is not true?
   A. slow people tend to be the inner focused philosophers and artists.
   B. a leisurely paced person would be better organized than a multitasker.
   C. researchers today seem to be moving away from the notion that pace by itself affects health.
   D. people who enjoy keeping a busy schedule are known as polychromic.

3. If you're a meticulous type with a go-getter manager, what should you do?
   A. ask her which projects she consider top priority so you can give yourself plenty of time to finish them.
   B. ask for a precise deadline for each one.
   C. both A and B
   D. neither A nor B

4. When a mixed pace couple planning a vacation, the slower spouse could _____.
   A. jot down a packing list
   B. make the hotel reservations
   C. spend an afternoon comparing airline prices online
   D. arrange to have the mail delivery suspended

5. What can you do about the people in your life who don't share your preferred pace?
   A. acknowledge the fact that their style is their own, and that it's not wrong to be a fast or slow person.
   B. figure out others' natural rhythm and make it work to everyone's advantage.
   C. find ways to accommodate each other's tempos.
   D. all of the above

Part 4. Practical Writing

常用句首短语及句式（**Phrases and Sentences Used to Start an Essay**）

1. **With the (rapidly) growing popularity of** Internet surfing (computers/cars/mobile

phones/pagers/PDP television/...) **in China, the quality of our lives is improving for the better.**

2. **With the (rapid) growth of our economy** (heavy industries/transportation system/market economy/population/private enterprises/housing industry/...), **an increasing number of problems, such as** (water shortages/traffic jams/industrial pollution/waste of energy/desert spreading/...), **are beginning to surface.**

3. **With the (rapid) development of science and technology** (market economy/electronic industry/information industry/higher education/...) **an increasing number of people come to realize that** (knowledge is power/a weak nation has no international prestige/education is of vital importance...).

4. **There is a wide concern that** many large state-owned companies are in deficit (quite a few Chinese cities face the problem of water shortages, industrial pollution and waste of energy/various kind of superstition flare up/...).

5. **Currently, there is a widespread concern over** drug abuse (high unemployment rate / wildlife extinction /environmental pollution/desertification/organized crime/widespread corruption /energy crisis/water shortages/traffic jams/increasing traffic accidents/...).

6. **In the past two decades** (In the past five years), **millions of** private enterprises (private schools / supermarkets / fast food restaurants/...) **have mushroomed all over China**

7. **There are three major values of** owning a car (a computer/an apartment/a mobile phone/a beeper/...). **To begin with ... Next ... Last ... There are, on the other hand, more reasons against it. First(ly) ... Second(ly) ... Finally...**

8. **Different people have different attitudes towards** the biding of the 29th Olympic Games (access to WTO/private cars/high unemployment rate/Internet surfing/private schools/state monopoly of telecommunication/urbanization/stock/...) **Some are in favor of... while others are against...**

9. **When it comes to the access to WTO** (Internet surfing/private schools/brain-drain/e-business/high rate of unemployment/China's football / recycling / widespread corruption ...) **most people believe that... But other people argue that...**

10. **Recently, extensive studies** (statistics/surveys/investigations/...) **show** (reveal/indicate/demonstate/prove/...) **that** 107 Chinese cities and 1231 small towns suffer water shortages.

Unit 7. Maintenance

Part 1. Text

Maintenance

Regular preventive maintenance of mechanical services plant is essential to minimize operating costs, minimize breakdowns with as a consequence inconvenience to building occupants and to satisfy authorities that the systems are not hazardous to health and will operate correctly for smoke control in a fire situation.

The initial specification for mechanical services installation generally also incorporates the requirement for the mechanical services contractor to provide routine maintenance on a monthly basis during the twelve month warranty period. During this period the consulting engineer generally sees copies of maintenance reports and ensures that maintenance is performed properly.

However, on many projects the consulting engineers responsibility ends at the expiry of the warranty period and at this stage in many buildings mechanical services maintenance starts to deteriorate.

This is where the consulting engineers energy and plant management department can assist by becoming involved in:

- inspecting buildings which have been allowed to deteriorate and recommending remedial measures.
- preparing detailed maintenance specifications, putting them to tender and recommending the appropriate service contractor.
- assessing energy consumption records to determine whether the plant is operating as it should.
- assisting managing agents with trouble shooting in the mechanical services area.

Mechanical services maintenance is usually performed by a mechanical services contractor. However, there are some areas where it is essential that the mechanical services contractor engages specialist assistance. The main areas where this is necessary are:

- water treatment and cooling tower cleaning
- chiller sets
- controls

Annual preventive maintenance costs for office buildings administered by experienced consulting engineering firms are usually in the range of $1.20 to $3.50/m air-conditioned space. Breakdown maintenance is additional to this and varies considerably with the age and condition of the plant.

ASSESSING AN AIR-CONDITIONING MAINTENANCE AGREEMENT

As a Property Manager, air-conditioning will no doubt play a significant role in your day to day activities. Tenants will require assistance in securing reputable service contractors to provide regular maintenance and breakdown service.

In the event of a system malfunction or discomfort experienced by building occupants, the Property Manager often receives the complaint and is then required to place service calls and the like so as to rectify the problems.

It all sounds pretty easy so far, however, the Property Manager is also required to track and control the costs associated with air-conditioning maintenance and breakdown service. Regular break-downs are costly, periodic planned maintenance can also be costly. Obviously, the higher the quality of preventative maintenance, the less likelihood of regular equipment breakdowns.

Therefore, the selection of an organization to provide air-conditioning service should not be taken lightly.

There are many things which must be considered in the selection process. They are:

a) Cost of the maintenance program

b) Hours to be spent on-site

c) Inclusions/exclusions

d) Use of sub-contractors

e) Hourly rates and other costs

f) Response time to calls

g) After hours service

h) Insurance

Often there is pressure to accept a tender based solely on price. In some cases, the lowest price may offer the best value for money. In other cases, it may lead to excessive breakdowns and/or tenant aggravation through poor response times to calls, constant discomfort, high breakdown costs, lost productivity and so on.

There are two key points to a successful selection process:-

1. Understanding the basic building requirements.

2. Providing a tender document that allows you to compare, on an equal footing, submissions for service for the same site.

Without a tender document, it becomes too easy for the service contractor to manipulate a service program so as to lower the tendered price.

Once the agreement is awarded to the lowest tenderer, it is assumed that the breakdown service, at non-discounted prices, will make the agreement economically viable. Again, sometimes the lowest price does, in fact, represent the best value for money, but experience suggests that caution should be used.

参考译文：

设备维护

机械维修厂的定期预防性维护是非常重要的,它可以减少运行成本,降低因故障而给建筑物所有者带来的不便,此外,通过保证系统对健康无害并在发生火情时正确地控制烟雾,以使相关主管满意。

机械维修装置的原始说明(附有约定条件)通常也体现对机械维修承包商的需求,在十二个月担保期内每月提供定期的维护。在此阶段咨询工程师通常查看维护报告的副本来确保维护工作的正常运行。

然而在许多工程中,咨询工程师的职责要履行到担保期满才结束,在此阶段许多建筑物的机械维护开始恶化。

这就是咨询工程师能源和设备管理部能提供帮助之处。

- 检查已被认为恶化的建筑物并提出补救的措施。
- 准备详细的维护说明,组织投标并推荐适合的维修承包商。
- 对能源消耗记录进行评估以确定该设备是否按要求操作。
- 协助管理人员解决机械维护区域出现的问题。

机械设备维护通常由机械维护承包商来完成。然而有一些区域,机械维修承包商保证提供专业帮助是很必要的。有这种需要的主要的区域是:

- 水处理和冷却塔清洁装置
- 冷却装置
- 控制装置

富有经验的咨询工程公司管理的办公大楼每年的预防性维护费用通常是在装有空调的空间 \$1.20 到 \$3.50/m。故障维修对预防性维护是个补充,随设备的使用时间和情况而改变。

对空调维修协议进行估价

作为一个物业经理,空调设备在日常工作中必定将发挥重要的作用.住户需要可靠的规范的承包商提供定期的养护和维修服务.

如果系统发生故障或者大楼的业主感觉不舒适,物业经理经常会收到投诉,于是接下来还需要设置服务电话,以便整顿存在的问题。

尽管听起来很容易,物业经理还需要跟踪和控制与空调养护和维修服务密切相关的成本。经常性的维修费用是昂贵的,而定期的计划内养护费用可能也是昂贵的。但显而易见的是,预防性维护的质量越高,设备出事故的可能性就越低。

因此,不应该轻视选择空调服务机构的问题。

在选择空调服务机构过程中,要考虑许多因素。这些因素包括:
养护成本

现场操作时间
包含的/不包含的服务项目
分包商的使用
每小时的费用和其他成本
对报修电话的反应时间
维修后服务
安全性能

要接受只建立在价格基础上的投标经常是有压力的。在某种情况下,最低的价格可能提供最高的价值。而在其他情况下,也可能导致过多的维修和/或住户的不满,主要是因为报修时间很长也得不到服务、经常出现不舒适的感觉、维修成本很高、生产率很低等等。

要想在选择过程中获得成功,有两个关键因素:
1. 了解基本的建筑要求。
2. 同时提供投标文件,允许你平等地进行比较。

没有投标文件,服务承包人很容易窜改服务程序以降低投标价格。

一旦与价格最低的投标者签定了协议,维修服务就由它来不折不扣地承担,这会使协议在经济学角度更可行。况且,实际上,有时最低的价格的确能体现最高的价值,但以往的经验告诉我们仍然要谨慎从事。

Vocabulary
单词表:

195.	preventive	[pri'ventiv]	a.	预防的,防止的
196.	maintenance	['meintinəns]	n.	维修,保养
197.	essential	[i'senʃəl]	a.	必要的,必不可少的
198.	minimize	['minimaiz]	vt.	使减到最少,使缩到最小
199.	breakdown	['breikdaun]	n.	(机械等的)损坏;故障;倒塌
200.	consequence	['kɔnsikwəns]	n.	结果,后果
201.	occupant	['ɔkjupənt]	n.	占有人,占有者;居住者
202.	authority	[ɔː'θɔriti]	n.	[复]当局,官方
203.	hazardous	['hæzədəs]	a.	危险的,冒险的
204.	initial	[i'niʃəl]	a.	最初的,开始的
205.	specification	[ˌspesifi'keiʃən]	n.	(载有约定条件等的)说明书;列入说明书的一个项目
206.	contractor	[kən'træktə]	n.	承包人,承包商,包工头
207.	warranty	['wɔrənti]	n.	保证(书),担保(书);保单
208.	responsibility	[risˌpɔnsə'biliti]	n.	责任;责任心;职责,任务
209.	expiry	[iks'paiəri]	n.	(期限、协定等)满期,终止
210.	deteriorate	[di'tiəriəreit]	vt.	使恶化;
			vi.	恶化
211.	inspect	[in'spekt]	vt.	检查,审查
212.	recommend	[ˌrekə'mend]	vt.	推荐,介绍;劝告,建议

213.	tender	[tendə]	vi.	投标
214.	assess	[ə'ses]	vt.	对（人物、工作等）进行估价，评价
215.	consumption	[kən'sʌmpʃən]	n.	消费(量)；消耗
216.	assist	[ə'sist]	vt.	援助，帮助
			vi.	援助，帮助
			n.	援助，帮助
217.	chiller	[tʃilə]	n.	冷却装置
218.	agreement	[ə'gri:mənt]	n.	协定，协议；同意，一致
219.	tenant	['tenənt]	n.	租户，房客；不动产占有人；居住者
220.	assistance	[ə'sistəns]	n.	帮助；援助
221.	secure	[si'kjuə]	vt.	使安全，保卫；保证；关紧；招致
222.	reputable	['repjutəbl]	a.	规范的，声誉好的，可尊敬的
223.	contractor	[kən'træktə]	n.	订约人；承包人；收缩物
224.	breakdown	['breikdaun]	n.	（机械等的）损坏，故障；衰竭
225.	malfunction	[mæl'fʌŋkʃən]	vi.	失灵，发生故障，机能失常；
			n.	失灵，故障
226.	rectify	['rektifai]	vt.	纠正，整顿；调整，校正
227.	costly	['kɔstli]	a.	昂贵的，代价高的；价值高的，豪华的
228.	periodic	[ˌpiəri'ɔdik]	a.	周期的，定期的，循环的；一定时间的
229.	likelihood	['laiklihud]	n.	可能(性)；可能发生的事物；可能成功的迹象
230.	exclusion	[iks'klu:ʒən]	n.	被排除在外的事物；排斥
231.	inclusion	[in'klu:ʒən]	n.	包含，包括；内含物
232.	subcontractor	['sʌbkən'træktə]	n.	转包人，分包者；转包工作的承包者
233.	hourly	['auəli]	a.	每小时的，每小时一次的；时时刻刻的
234.	rate	[reit]	n.	价格；比率；速率；等级；房地产税率
235.	insurance	[in'ʃuərəns]	n.	安全保障；保险单；保险费；保险业
236.	solely	[soul]	ad.	单独地，惟一地
237.	excessive	[ik'sesiv]	a.	过多的；过分的；极度的
238.	aggravation	[ˌægrə'veiʃən]	n.	恼火，恶化
239.	productivity	[ˌprɔdʌk'tiviti]	n.	生产率；生产能力；丰饶，多产
240.	footing	['futiŋ]	n.	立足点；地位，基础；关系；总额
241.	compare	[kəm'pɛə]	vt.	比较，对照；比喻；n. 比较
242.	submission	[səb'miʃən]	n.	提出，提交；谦逊；服从
243.	manipulate	[mə'nipjuleit]	vt.	窜改，伪造账目等；熟练地使用；摆布；操作器
244.	assume	[ə'sju:m]	vt.	承担；设想；采取
245.	discount	['diskaunt]	vt.	打折；贴现；对……持怀疑态度；看轻
246.	economically	[ˌi:kə'nɔmikəli]	ad.	节约地；节俭地；在经济学上
247.	viable	['vaiəbl]	a.	可行的；生存的；n. 生存性；生活力

248. caution　　　　[ˈkɔːʃən]　　　　n.　小心,谨慎;警告;与众不同的人或物

Useful Expressions

warranty period　　担保期,保修期
consulting engineer　　顾问工程师
be involved in　　包括在……中,被卷入
in the range of　　在射程内,在……范围内
breakdown maintenance　　故障性维护
in additional to　　除……之外(还)
at the expiry of　　在……期满,终止时
no doubt　　无疑地,必定
play a ... role　　起……作用
in the event of　　如果,万一
on an equal footing　　以一个平等的关系

Notes
备注:

1. Regular preventive maintenance of mechanical services plant is essential to minimize operating costs, minimize breakdowns with as a consequence inconvenience to building occupants and to satisfy authorities that the systems are not hazardous to health and will operate correctly for smoke control in a fire situation. 机械维修厂的定期预防性维护是非常重要的,它可以减少运行成本,降低因故障而给建筑物所有者带来的不便,此外,通过保证系统对健康无害并在发生火情时,正确地控制烟雾,以使相关主管满意。

此句中,minimize breakdowns with as a consequence inconvenience to building occupants 前面省略了动词不定式的符号 to,与 minimize operating costs 共用一个 to;to satisfy authorities that the systems are not hazardous to health 与 to minimize operating costs, minimize breakdowns with as a consequence inconvenience to building occupants 并列,由 and 连接。

preventive maintenance 预防性维护

2. During this period the consulting engineer generally sees copies of maintenance reports and ensures that maintenance is performed properly. 在此阶段咨询工程师通常看维护报告的副本来确保维护工作的正常运行。

此句中,that maintenance is performed properly 是由从属连词 that 引导的宾语从句,做 ensures 的宾语。在复合句中做宾语的从句,称为宾语从句。可以引导宾语从句的有:从属连词 that(无词义,口语中常省略),if, whether(是否);连接代词 who, whom, whose, which, what(有词义,在从句中担任一定的成分);连接副词 when, where, how, why(有词义,在从句中作状语)。

例如:
All of us consider (that) the problem is very serious.
我们都认为这个问题很严重。
I do not care whether you like the plan or not.
我不管你是否喜欢这个计划。

I do not know if it is raining.
我不知道天是否在下雨。
We can learn what we did not know.
我们能够学会我们原来所不懂的东西。
Please tell him why the meeting was put off.
请告诉他会议为什么延期。

"is performed"是一般现在时态的被动语态。

例如：

A new type of truck is produced by the plant.
一种新型卡车是由该厂制造的。
The period of the Tenth Five-Year Plan can be divided into two stages. 第十个五年计划可以分为两个阶段。

句中，consulting engineer 咨询工程师

3. This is where the consulting engineers energy and plant management department can assist by becoming involved in;以下就是顾问工程师能源和设备管理部能提供帮助之处。

此句中，where the consulting engineers energy and plant management department can assist by becoming involved in 是由连接副词 where 引导的表语从句，在 is 后构成系表结构。在句中担任表语成分的从句称为表语从句，可以引导表语从句的有：从属连词 that，whether；连接代词和连接副词；关系代词 what。

例如：

The fact is that he is much cleverer than his brother.
事实是他比他的兄弟聪明得多。
The reason for his failure is that he did not work hard.
他失败的原因是他工作不努力。
The truth is that they refused all the suggestions.
真实情况是他们拒绝了所有的建议。
The question is whether there is anyone to help us.
问题是是否有人来帮助我们。
The problem is where we can get fresh vegetables.
问题是我们在什么地方能弄到新鲜蔬菜。
This is not what I expected.
这不是我所期望的。

4. Inspecting buildings which have been allowed to deteriorate and recommending remedial measures. 检查已被认为恶化的建筑物并推荐补救的措施。

此句中，which have been allowed to deteriorate 是由关系代词 which 引导的定语从句，修饰前面的名词 buildings。定语从句是修饰名词的从句，起形容词的作用。可以引导定语从句的有：关系代词 who，whom，whose，that，which；关系副词 where，when，why。

例如：

The teacher gave those copies to the students who were interested.

老师把那些副本给了感兴趣的学生。
The worker (whom/who) you mentioned has not come.
你提到的那个工人没有来。
I just bought the magazine whose format is similar to that of yours.
我刚买了版式和你的相似的杂志。
This is the book about which I told you last week.
这就是我上星期对你们说的那本书。
This is the best novel that I have ever read.
这是我读过的最好的小说。
The office where he works is on the second floor.
他工作的办公室在二楼。
I will never forget the day when I joined the Party.
我永远忘不了我入党的那一天。
This is the reason why I am leaving tomorrow.
这就是我明天离开的原因。

原句中,recommending remedial measures 与 inspecting buildings which……为并列结构;have been allowed 是现在完成时态的被动语态。

例如:

A large number of personnel has been trained by our school.
大量人才从我们学校培养出来。
The policy of "one country, two systems" has been discussed.
"一国两制"的政策已经讨论了。

5. assessing energy consumption records to determine whether the plant is operating as it should.
对能源消耗记录进行评估以确定该设备是否按要求操作。

此句中,to determine whether the plant is operating as it should 作目的状语;whether the plant is operating as it should 是由 whether 引导的宾语从句,作 determine 的宾语。

6. However, there are some areas where it is essential that the mechanical services contractor engages specialist assistance. 然而有一些区域,机械维修承包商保证提供专家帮助是很必要的。

此句中,where it is essential that the mechanical services contractor engages specialist assistance 是由 where 引导的定语从句,修饰前面的名词 areas;在此定语从句中,it 作形式主语,真正的主语是 that 引导的后置了的主语从句:that the mechanical services contractor engages specialist assistance. 在句中担任主语成分的从句称为主语从句。可以引导主语从句的有:从属连词 that, whether;连接代词 who, whom, whose, which, what;连接副词 when, where, how, why;关系代词 what, whatever。(主语从句经常放在句子后部,用代词 it 作形式主语)。

例如:

It is widely believed that milk and eggs are nutritious.

人们普遍认为牛奶和鸡蛋是有营养的。
It is doubtful whether they will be able to come.
他们是否能来还有疑问。
Who will be elected is still a question.
谁将当选还是个问题。
What he said is interesting. 他所说的很有趣。

7. The main areas where this is necessary are:有这种需要的主要的区域是:

此句中,where this is necessary 是由 where 引导的定语从句,修饰前面的名词 areas.

8. Annual preventive maintenance costs for office buildings administered by experienced consulting engineering firms are usually in the range of $1.20 to $3.50/m air-conditioned space. 富有经验的顾问工程公司管理的办公大楼每年的预防性维护费用在装有空调的空间 通常是 $1.20 到 $3.50/m。

此句中,administered by experienced consulting engineering firms 是过去分词短语作定语,修饰前面的名词 office buildings.

Ⅰ. Exercises for the text(课文练习)

(Ⅰ) Decide whether the following sentences are True or False according to the content of the text.

1. Regular preventive maintenance of mechanical services plant is not essential to minimize operating costs.
2. The initial specification for mechanical services installation generally also incorporates the requirement for the mechanical services contractor to provide routine maintenance on a monthly basis during the twelve month warranty period.
3. On many projects the consulting engineers responsibility doesn't end at the expiry of the warranty period and at this stage in many buildings mechanical services maintenance starts to deteriorate.
4. Mechanical services maintenance is usually performed by a mechanical services contractor.
5. Breakdown maintenance is additional to this and varies considerably with the age and condition of the plant.
6. The Property Manager will require assistance in securing reputable service contractors to provide regular maintenance and breakdown service.
7. In the event of a system malfunction or discomfort experienced by building occupants, the Property Manager often receives the complaint and is then required to place service calls and the like so as to rectify the problems.
8. Obviously, the higher the quality of preventative maintenance, the more likelihood of regular equipment breakdowns.
9. In other cases, it may lead to excessive breakdowns and/or tenant aggravation through poor response times to calls, constant discomfort, high breakdown costs, lost productivity and so on.

10. With a tender document, it becomes too easy for the service contractor to manipulate a service program so as to lower the tendered price.

(Ⅱ) **Match the English words with their Chinese translations, choose the appropriate words to complete the sentences below and translate them into Chinese**(将下列英语单词与其中文意思相匹配,选择合适的词将下列句子补充完整并译成中文):

 1. preventive   a. 维修,保养
 2. maintenance   b. [复]当局,官方,许可
 3. essential   c. 保证(书),担保(书);保单,理由
 4. consequence   d. 援助,帮助 vi. 援助,帮助 n. 援助,帮助
 5. authority   e. 预防的,防止的
 6. initial   f. 结果,后果
 7. warranty   g. 检查,审查
 8. assist   h. 推荐,介绍;劝告,建议
 9. inspect   i. 必要的,必不可少的
10. recommend   j. 最初的,开始的
11. caution   k. 每小时的,每小时一次的;时时刻刻的;
12. exclusion   l. 纠正,整顿;调整,校正;
13. assume   m. 立足点;地位,基础;关系;总额
14. discount   n. 小心,谨慎;警告;与众不同的人或物
15. secure   o. 价格;比率;速率;等级;房地产税率
16. hourly   p. 比较,对照;比喻;n. 比较
17. submission   q. 承担;设想;采取
18. compare   r. 被排除在外的事物;排斥
19. rectify   s. 打折;贴现;对……持怀疑态度;看轻
20. footing   t. 使安全,保卫;保证;关紧;招致
21. rate   u. 提出,提交;谦逊;服从

 1. The leadership of the Party is _____ to socialist revolution and socialist construction.
 2. It's of no _____.
 3. Do you know the _____ issue of the magazine?
 4. The militiamen did much to _____ the frontier guards' search for the enemy.
 5. On whose _____?
 6. Take a _____ measure against rats.
 7. _____ of way is important.
 8. I wonder what _____ they have for refusing us admittance.
 9. You must _____ outgoing baggage.
10. He _____ me for Party membership.
11. A million signatures have been _____.
12. It is necessary to _____ the style of work.

155

13. Never concentrate all your attention on one or two problems, to the _____ of others.
14. There is an _____ train service in the suburbs.
15. The train was going at the (a) _____ of 80 kilometres an hour.
16. There's no _____ about it.
17. Keep your _____!
18. The results have been carefully checked and _____.
19. We have received more _____ than we can possibly publish.
20. The motion of matter always _____ certain forms.
21. His rich experience is not to be _____.
22. When operating a machine, we must use _____.

(Ⅲ) **Choose the best answer**(选择最佳答案)

1. _____ is true that the price of land in Tokyo is high.
   a. It   b. That   c. What   d. This
2. This is _____ our plan has failed.
   a. what   b. that   c. why   d. which
3. Can you tell me _____ the train will arrive?
   a. where   b. when   c. what   d. who
4. The engineer about _____ you asked will come here tomorrow.
   a. whom   b. that   c. what   d. which
5. People _____ are in the sunlight get warm.
   a. which   b. that   c. what   d. who
6. Do you know _____ her name is?
   a. who   b. that   c. what   d. which
7. _____ is suitable for you may not be suitable for me.
   a. It   b. That   c. What   d. This
8. _____ did that should be praised.
   a. Whichever b. Whoever   c. Whatever   d. Wherever
9. The professor told me _____ I could find those magazines.
   a. where   b. that   c. what   d. who
10. One reason _____ women live longer than men after retirement is that women can continue to do something they are used to doing.
    a. where   b. that   c. what   d. why

(Ⅳ) **Translation**:

Translate the following Chinese into English:

1. 在此阶段顾问工程师通常看维护报告的副本来确保维护工作的正常运行。
2. 准备详细的维护说明，组织投标并推荐适合的维修承包商。
3. 机械设备维护通常由机械维护承包商来完成。
4. 富有经验的顾问工程公司管理的办公大楼每年的预防性维护费用在装有空调的空间通常是 $1.20 到 $3.50/m 。

5. 故障维修对预防性维护是个补充,随设备的使用时间和情况而改变。

6. 尽管听起来很容易,然而物业经理还需要跟踪和控制与空调养护和维修服务密切相关的成本。

7. 预防性维护的质量越高,定期设备维修的可能性就越低。

8. 在某种情况下,最低的价格可能提供最高的价值。

9. 没有投标文件,服务承包人很容易窜改服务程序以降低投标价格。

10. 但以往的经验告诉我们仍然要谨慎从事。

(Ⅴ) Extra Reading Activity:

Extra reading: read the following passage and choose the best answer to complete each of the statements that follow.

Case History

A seven storey office building has a central plan chilled water and heating water system, which is reticulated to multi-zone air handling units on each floor. The control system is a complex electronic type, designed to provide five different comfort zones on each floor. The building also has a car-park and toilet exhaust system.

Two contractors tender for the maintenance agreement. One has held the expired agreement for the past several years, the second is called in by the new Property Manager to provide a comparison price (the property is new to the management company).

The existing contractor provides a price reflecting the Previous year's agreed price, plus a small increase of three percent to cover the Consumer Price Index. The second contractor inspects the site for the first time and provides a price based on their Perceived needs of the building. The two Prices are as follows:

Contractor "A" (existing contractor) $5,800.00 per annum
Contractor "B" (new contractor) $8,712.00 per annum

The Property Manager is provided with the following information from contractor "B".

1. Monthly service proposed @ 6 hours/visit, a total of 72 hours per annum.

2. Controls to be maintained separately twice per annum @ 32 hours per visit, a total of 64 hours per annum.

3. An annual overhaul of the chiller and boiler plant will be carried out, where oil will be changed in the compressors, tubes will be cleaned and filters will be changed. A total of 50 hours will be spent performing this service.

4. Parts required to carry out all routine maintenance has been included and the cost is $900.00 per annum.

As contractor "A" has been maintaining the plan for several years, they have simply provided their price on a renewal notice, which omits the details other than the previous cost, the increase amount and the new cost.

The Property Manager contacts contractor "A" and asks for a breakdown of their proposed agreement. The response is as follows:

1. Monthly service proposed @ 8 hours/visit, a total of 96 hours per annum.

2. Controls to be maintained separately on an annual basis @ 64 hours per annum.

3. An annual overhaul of the chiller and boiler plant will be carded out as per contractor "B".

4. Parts have been included, but the value not disclosed.

The Property Manager also receives the following information from contractors:

Contractor "A"		Contractor "B"	
Hourly Rate(normal)	$45.00/hour	Hourly Rate	$42.00/hour
Hourly Rate(O/T)	$60.00/hour	Hourly Rate(O/T)	$58.00/hour
Travel Time	$45.00/hour	Travel Time	$42.00/hour
After Hours Callout (first four hours)	$240.00	After Hours Callout (first four hours)	$220.00
Service Charge	$45.00/call	Service Charge	Nil
Kilometre Charge	$0.40/km	Kilometre Charge	Nil

The true comparison is now made. The Property Manager totals the hours to be spent on-site by each contractor and divides it into the tendered sum, with the following results:

Contractor "A"		Contractor "B"	
Total Hours	200 per annum	Total Hours	186 per annum
Tendered price	$5,800.00	Tendered Price	$8,712.00
Calculated Rate	$29.00/hour	Calculated Rate	$42.00/hour
Tendered Hourly Rate	$45.00/hour	Tendered Hourly Rate	$42.00/hour

Contractor "A" is contacted and given an opportunity to explain their submission. The hourly rate of less than $29.00/hour, when parts are taken into consideration, is well below the tendered hourly rate and considered to be below the tenderer's actual operating costs. The response by the contractor "A" being that they "always provide maintenance at a much reduced rate" to their competitors.

The Property Manager awards the agreement to contractor "B", as the hours to be spent on-site are consistent with what is needed in the building and the tendered price is a true reflection of the requirements. The ongoing breakdown costs tendered are significantly lower than that of contractor "A", showing uniformity in their tender submission. Finally, a check of the building history shows a high incidence of breakdowns not covered by the maintenance agreement.

1. The control system is a complex electronic type, designed _____.
    a. to have a central plan chilled water and heating water system
    b. to be reticulated to multi-zone air handling units on each floor
    c. to provide five different comfort zones on each floor
    d. to have a car-park and toilet exhaust system
2. Which statement the following is not true?
    a. Contractor "A" is existing contractor, Contractor "B" is new contractor.
    b. Contractor "A" provides a price reflecting the Previous year's agreed price, plus

a small increase of three percent to cover the Consumer Price Index.

   c. Contractor "B" inspects the site for the first time and provides a price based on their perceived needs of the building.

   d. Contractor "A" is called in by the new Property Manager to provide a comparison price (the property is new to the management company).

3. What information is the Property Manager provided with from contractor "B"?

   a. Monthly service proposed @ 6 hours/visit, a total of 72 hours per annum; controls to be maintained separately twice per annum @ 32 hours per visit, a total of 64 hours per annum.

   b. An annual overhaul of the chiller and boiler plant will be carried out, where oil will be changed in the compressors, tubes will be cleaned and filters will be changed. A total of 50 hours will be spent performing this service.

   c. Parts required to carry out all routine maintenance has been included and the cost is $900.00 per annum.

   d. All of above.

4. The Property Manager contacts contractor "A" and asks for a breakdown of their proposed agreement. The response that is different from Contractor "B" is _____.

   a. Monthly service proposed @ 8 hours/visit, a total of 96 hours per annum; Parts have been included, but the value not disclosed

   b. Controls to be maintained separately on an annual basis @ 64 hours per annum

   c. An annual overhaul of the chiller and boiler plan will be carried out as per contractor "B"

   d. Monthly service proposed @ 6 hours/visit, a total of 72 hours per annum; controls to be maintained separately twice per annum @ 32 hours per visit, a total of 64 hours per annum

5. Which of the following statements is not true?

   a. Contractor "A" is contacted and given an opportunity to explain their submission.

   b. (Contractor "A") The hourly rate of less than $29'00/hour, when parts are taken into consideration, is well below the tendered hourly rate and considered to be below the tenderer's actual operating costs.

   c. The Property Manager awards the agreement to contractor "A", as the hours to be spent on-site are consistent with what is needed in the building and the tendered price is a true reflection of the requirements.

   d. Finally, a check of the building history shows a high incidence of breakdowns not covered by the maintenance agreement.

II. Language Ability Drill（语言能力练习）

(I) Vocabulary Exercise

1.1 The suffixes -er, -or, and -ar can be added to verbs to form agent nouns←names of persons or things performing an act, e. g. visitor←visit, singer←sing, operator←operate. Can you explain how the following words are formed?

    actor←   sailors←
    beggar←   sampler←
    beginner←   shopper←
    liar←   translator←

Now complete the following sentences with the above agent nouns.

1. Nowadays, there're many _____ along the street in the commercial area.

2. I have studied English only for 3 weeks. I am a _____.

3. A _____ is someone who always tells lies.

4. Most people walking in the stores are more visitors than _____.

5. Those people do not beg publicly cannot be regarded as _____.

6. I like watching plays and I am an amateur(业余的) _____.

7. Francis Chichester sailed around the world single-handed in a small boat. He is recognized as one of the greatest _____ of the century.

8. Fu Lei translated many French novels into Chinese. He was one of the greatest _____ of modern China.

1.2 Study the following words. Then use them correctly in the sentences below:

Nouns	Adjectives	Adverbs
evidence	evident	evidently
kindness	kind	kindly
eagerness	eager	eagerly
sincerity	sincere	sincerely
occasion	occasional	occasionally

1. evidence, evident, evidently

1) Do you have any _____ that it is Marry who stole the jewels(宝石)?

2) _____, they have just left, for the seat is still warm.

3) It is _____ that the elderly gentleman has been greatly hurt and will never come back to the store to sample puddings any more.

4) The old man looked at his grand daughter with _____ pride.

2. kindness, kind, kindly

1) It's very _____ of you to invite me to tea.

2) Would you _____ turn down the radio?

3) _____ is one of the qualities we would look for in a friend.

4) The policeman treated the lost child very _____.

3. eagerness, eager, eagerly

1) The old man began _____ to sample one after another of the puddings as soon as he accepted the spoon.

2) He is always _____ to see new places and keen(渴望的) to meet new people.

3) They looked forward to the occasion with great _____.

4) All the children listened to the story with _____ attention.

4. sincerity, sincere, sincerely

1) Was he _____ in his offer to purchase a pudding for the old man?

2) The narrator _____ wished that he could take back his tactless words.

3) I may say in all _____ that I did not mean to hurt you.

4) Please give my _____ regards(问候的) to all the members of your family.

5. occasion, occasional, occasionally

1) We had fine weather all through July except for an _____ thunder-storm.

2) Prof. Wilson's daughter teaches at a high school in California, and she _____ flies to New York to see him.

3) I can't recall(想起) the _____, but I did meet her before.

4) In the past two years, Myra has come to see her mother only _____.

(Ⅱ) Cloze

I climbed the stairs slowly, carrying a big suitcase, my father following with two more. By the time I got to the third floor, I was 1 and at the same time felling lonely. Worse still, Dad 2 a step and fell, sending my new suitcases 3 down the stairs. "Damn!" he screamed, his face turning red. I knew 4 was ahead. Whenever Dad's face turns red, 5 . How could I ever 6 him to finish unloading the car 7 screaming at me and making a scene in front of the other girls, girls I would have to spend the 8 of the year with? Doors were opening and faces peering out(探出), as Dad walked 9 close behind. I felt it in my bones that my college life was getting off to a(n) 10 start. " 11 the room, quickly," I thought. "Get him into a chair and calmed down." But 12 , would there be a chair in Room 316? Or would it be a(n) 13 room? 14 I turned the key in the lock and 15 the door open, with Dad 16 . complaining(抱怨) about a hurting knee or something. I put my head in, expecting the 17 . But to my 18 , the room wasn't empty at all! It had furniture, curtains, a TV, and seven paintings on the walls. And there on a well-made bed sat any new 19 , dressed neatly, greeting me with a nod, she said in a soft voice, "Hi, you must be Cori." Then, she 20 the music and looked over at 21 , "And of course, you're Mr. Faber," she said 22 . "Would you like a glass of iced tea?" Dad's face turned decidedly 23 before he could bring out a "yes." I knew 24 that Amy and I would be 25 and my first year of college would be a success.

1. A. helpless   B. lazy   C. anxious   D. tried
2. A. took   B. minded   C. missed   D. picked
3. A. rolling   B. passing   C. dropping   D. turning
4. A. suffering   B. difficulty   C. trouble   D. danger
5. A. go ahead   B. look out   C. hold on   D. give up
6. A. lead   B. help   C. encourage   D. get

7. A. after	B. without	C. while	D. besides
8. A. best	B. beginning	C. end	D. rest
9. A. with difficulty	B. in a hurry	C. with firm steps	D. in wonder
10. A. fresh	B. late	C. bad	D. unfair
11. A. Search	B. Find	C. Enter	D. Book
12. A. in fact	B. by chance	C. once more	D. then again
13. A. small	B. empty	C. new	D. neat
14. A. Finally	B. Meanwhile	C. Sooner or later	D. At the moment
15. A. knocked	B. forced	C. pushed	D. tried
16. A. yet	B. only	C. even	D. still
17. A. worst	B. chair	C. best	D. tea
18. A. regret	B. disappointment	C. surprise	D. knowledge
19. A. roommate	B. classmate	C. neighbour	D. companion
20. A. turned on	B. turned down	C. played	D. enjoyed
21. A. Dad	B. me	C. the door	D. the floor
22. A. questioning	B. wondering	C. smiling	D. guessing
23. A. red	B. less pale	C. less red	D. pale
24. A. soon	B. there	C. later	D. then
25. A. sisters	B. friends	C. students	D. fellows

(Ⅲ) Answer the following questions after the model：

Model：Do you think this pudding has plum(葡萄干) in it?　　　　　　(taste)
Well, it tastes as if it has plum in it.

1. Do you think James is putting on weight?　　　　　　　　　　　(look)
2. Do you think this shirt is made of cotton?　　　　　　　　　　　(feel)
3. Do you think those women come from New York?　　　　　　　(sound)
4. Do you think they know each other?　　　　　　　　　　　　　(look)
5. Do you think this milk is fresh?　　　　　　　　　　　　　　　(smell)
6. Do you think these puddings are homemade?　　　　　　　　　(taste)
7. Do you think Lennie is hungry?　　　　　　　　　　　　　　　(look)
8. Do you think the music is African?　　　　　　　　　　　　　(sound)

Part 2. Dialogue

Pets Management
(宠物管理)

Ⅰ. **Typical Sentences**(经典短句)

(Ⅰ) Daily Conversations（日常用语）

制止语：

1. Don't ...

请不要……

2. Would you please stop...
请停止……

3. It is forbidden to...
禁止……

4. You mustn't...
您绝对不可以……

5. No...
不可以……

建议语：

1. Would you please...
您可以……吗？

2. How about...?
……怎么样？

3. Why don't you...?
为什么您不……？

4. It is more proper for you to...
您还不如……

5. You are required to....
您必须……

(Ⅱ) Professional Conversation（专业会话）

1. Pets in community should be registered.
小区内的宠物需要登记。

2. Walking dogs is forbidden in or around the Kids' Garden.
禁止在儿童游乐园里或附近遛狗。

3. No pissing or shiting for pets on the path.
宠物禁止在道路上大小便。

4. Pets should receive injection regularly.
宠物应规律的接受疫苗注射。

5. Pets should be fasten with belt when walk outside room.
宠物在屋外应拴带子。

Ⅱ. Conversation Passages

(Ⅰ) Passage 1.

A: Good afternoon, Mr. Yang. Oh, what a cute puppy!
下午好，杨先生。多可爱的一只小狗啊！

B: Yes, it is bought for my wife. I really hope she will like it, too.
是啊，这是给我太太买的，真希望她也能喜欢。

A: Certainly! She will.

她准能喜欢!

B: Right, shall I do something before raising this dog in our community?
我如果想在咱小区养狗是不是要先办一些手续?

A: That's right, you should. Firstly you should register for it. Any pets in community should be registered.
是的,首先您要先为它登记,小区内的宠物都要记录在案的。

B: En, OK. I see. I will do that.
好,我知道了。一定会照办的。

A: Then you should have it received injection regularly.
然后,您要让它定期接受疫苗注射。

B: Thank you for your help.
谢谢你的帮助。

A: With pleasure.
这是我应该做的。

(Ⅱ) Passage 2.

(After parking the car)

A: Good morning, Mr. Yang. Does your wife like your gift?
早上好,杨先生。您太太喜欢您的礼物吗?

B: Yeah, she treats him as our son. And we even gave him a boy's name yesterday.
是的,她把它当成我们的孩子。我们昨天还给它起了个男孩的名字。

A: Really? What's it?
是吗?叫什么呀?

B: Dingding. It sounds as cute as he is, doesn't it?
叫丁丁。这名字就像他一样可爱吧?

A: It is really a good name. By the way, have you registered for him?
真是个好名字。对了,您给他把手续都办了吗?

B: Yes, I have. And I will have him injected regularly.
是的,我都办好了,而且我会按时带他去打针的。

A: Thank you for your cooperation.
谢谢您的合作。

B: I have just done what I should do.
我只是做了我应该做的。

A: Anyway, there're also some other things you should pay attention to.
可是还有一些事请您需要注意的。

B: Ok, for example?
是吗?例如?

A: For example pets should be fasten with a belt when walk outside room.
例如宠物在屋外应拴带子。

B: Anything else?

还有吗?

A: Also walking dogs is forbidden in or around the Kids' Garden, and no pissing or shiting for pets on the path.
还有宠物禁止在道路上大小便,而且在儿童游乐园里或附近遛狗也是不允许的。

B: Thanks, I see. And I will obey these principles.
谢谢你,我知道了,我会按要求办的。

A: Thank you for your cooperation with our work.
谢谢您配合我们工作。

Ⅲ. Exercises for Dialogue

(Ⅰ) Fill in the following blanks by considering Chinese
(按照中文完成以下填空)

A: For example _____.
例如:宠物在屋外应拴带子。

B: Anything else?
还有吗?

A: Also _____, and _____.
还有宠物禁止在道路上大小便,而且在儿童游乐园里或附近遛狗也是不允许的。

B: Thanks, I see. And I will obey these principles.
谢谢你,我知道了,我会按要求办的。

A: _____.
谢谢您配合我们工作。

(Ⅱ) Make a telephone conversation with your partner about anything you like.. (there should be at least 3 turn-taking in the dialogue)

Ⅳ. Spoken Language Drill (Fill in the blanks according to Chinese Translation)

Dialogue 1.

A: Would you _____ some tea?
你想喝点茶吗?

B: Yes, please.
好的。

A: Would you like _____ to eat?
你想吃点什么吗?

B: No, thanks. Just tea.
不用了,谢谢。喝茶就好了。

A: OK. Would you like to watch some television?
好吧。你想看电视吗?

B: No. Not _____.
不太想看。

165

Dialogue 2.

A: Why don't we go to a movie tonight?
今晚我们去看电影怎么样?

B: I'd love to but I _____. I have to study.
我想去但不能去。我必须学习。

A: But it's just two hours.
可电影就只有两个小时呀。

B: No. I have a test tomorrow morning. I have no _____.
不行,我明早要考试。我别无选择。

Dialogue 3.

A: I can't _____ whether to go to university or get a job.
我没法决定是去上大学还是工作。

B: If I were you, I would continue _____.
如果我是你,我就继续学习。

A: I don't know what I want to study.
我不知道我想学什么。

B: You're good at English. Maybe you should study English.
你英语不错。也许你该学英语。

A: That's what my parents want me to do.
那正是我父母想让我做的。

Dialogue 4.

A: Why do you look so _____?
你怎么看起来这么难过?

B: I failed my English examination.
我英语考试不及格。

A: oh, that's too _____.
哦,太糟了。

B: If only I had _____.
要是我及格了该有多好。

A: Take it easy. I'll help you.
放轻松点儿。我会帮你的。

Part 3. Supplementary Reading:

Passage A
Country & Town

For centuries town and country have been regarded as being in opposition to each other. It has been suggested that the superficial differences between the two—wide-open spaces contrasting with brick and concrete are less important than the contrasting attitudes of town and country.

I am one of the many city people who are always saying that given the choice would prefer to live in the country away from the dirt and noise of a large city. I have managed to convince myself that if it weren't for my job I would immediately head out for the open spaces and go back to nature in some sleepy village buried in the country. But how realistic is this dream?

Cities can be frightening places. The majority of the population live in massive tower blocks, noisy, squalid and impersonal. The sense of belonging to a community tends to disappear when you live fifteen floors up. All you can see from your window is sky, or other blocks of flats. Children become aggressive and nervous cooped up at home all day, with nowhere to play; their mothers feel isolated from the rest of the world. Strangely enough, whereas in the past the inhabitants of one street all knew each other, nowadays people on the same floor in tower blocks don't even say hello to each other.

Country life, on the other hand, differs from this kind of isolated existence in that a sense of community generally binds the inhabitants of small villages together. People have the advantage of knowing that there is always someone to turn to when they need help. But country life has disadvantages, too. While it is true that you may be among friends in a village, it is also true that you are cut off from the exciting and important events that take place in cities. There's little possibility of going to a new show or the latest movie. Shopping becomes a major problem, and for anything slightly out of the ordinary you have to go on an expedition to the nearest large town. The city-dweller who leaves for the country is often oppressed by a sense of unbearable stillness and quiet.

What, then, is the answer? The country has the advantage of peace and quiet but suffers from the disadvantage of being cut off: the city breeds neurosis and a feeling of isolation-constant noise batters the senses. But one of its main advantages is that you are at the centre of things, and that life doesn't come to an end at half past nine at night. Some people have found a compromise between the two; they have expressed their preference for the quiet life by leaving the suburbs and moving to villages within commuting distance of the large conurbations. They generally have about as much sensitivity as the plastic flowers they leave behind they are polluted with strange ideas about change and improvement which they force on to the unwilling original inhabitants of the villages.

What then of my dreams of leaning on the cottage gate, chewing a piece of grass and murmuring "morning" to the locals as they pass. I'm keen on the idea, but you see there's my cat, Toby. I'm not at all sure that he would take to all that fresh air and exercise in the long grass. I mean, can you see him mixing with all those hearty males down on the farm? No, he would rather have the electric imitation—coal fire any evening.

参考译文：

城镇与农村

若干世纪以来,城市和农村一直被认为是相互对立的。曾经有这样的说法:两者之间的表面差异,即开阔的场地和砖石混凝土的对照并没有对两者所持的不同态度那样重要。

许多城里人总是说如果给予选择,我们宁愿住在农村,远离大城市的灰尘和噪音。我也是这些人中的一员。我努力说服了自己,要不是因为工作的缘故,我将立刻搬迁到开阔的农村,回到大自然的怀抱,回到隐藏在乡间那寂静的村庄。但这一梦想又有多现实呢?

城市有可能是使人害怕的地方。大多数人住在又闹又脏又没有人情味的高楼大厦里。如果你住在十五层以上高的楼上,就丧失了属于某一社会群体的感觉。从窗户里能够看到的就是天空或其他一排排的房屋。孩子们变得好斗、紧张,因为成天关在家里没处玩;他们的母亲们也感到与周围世界隔离开了。更奇怪的是过去一条街的居民彼此都认识,而今住在高楼大厦同一层楼的人甚至从不相互问好。

农村生活却不同于这种孤立生活,地方感情把小村庄的居民广泛地联系了起来。他们有这样的好处,即需要帮助时,知道总会有人出来关照的。但乡村生活也有不足之处。在一个村子里,周围都是你的朋友,虽然这是事实,但你却与发生在城里的振奋人心的重要事情隔离开了,这也是事实。几乎没有可能看一场新的演出或一部最新影片。去商店买东西成了主要问题,只要是稍微有点特殊的商品,你就得远征到相距最近的大城市。搬迁到农村来的城市居民常因一种不能忍受的宁静与沉寂而感到压抑。

那么,结论如何呢?农村具有宁静之优点,但却要受与城市隔断这一缺点之苦,城市会引起神经官能症和孤独感。因为持续不断的噪音有损人的理性。但其主要优点之一是你处在事物的中心;晚上九点半之前整个城市总是充满了生机。有的人在二者之间找到了折衷的办法,他们离开城郊搬到了能乘车往返于大城市和农村之间的村庄,以表达他们对"平静生活"的向往。这些人大概就像他们所遗弃的塑料花一样,缺乏感受,他们的脑子里沾染了些关于改变和改进农村的奇怪思想,并将这些强加给不愿接受的当地村民。

那么我的梦想是:靠在一幢农舍门前,嘴嚼着一根小草,向路过的当地人喃喃说一声"早上好"——又怎么样呢?我迷恋这一想法,但你看我还有一只小猫——托比。他会不会喜欢那里所有的新鲜空气,喜欢在那长得很深的杂草中活动,我毫无把握。我的意思是,你能想象他会下去与农庄里那些活蹦乱跳的雄猫混在一起吗?不,他宁愿天天晚上见到有如炭火似的电灯光。

Passage B
Thanks and Apologies

As the American people's concept of being polite is different from that held here, I'd like to discuss with you the use of "please", "excuse me" and "thank you". I have noticed that the Chinese people use "please" as often as we do on most occasions. But on some occasions they don't use this word. For instance, Chinese teachers rarely say "please sit down" when their students have answered their questions and the traffic police here are also not accustomed to using "please" when they are on duty. We say "please pass me the salt" instead of stretching out our arms to reach for it. So don't forget to say "please" whenever the situation requires it if you are in the United States. I believe we say "excuse me" more often and on more occasions than the Chinese people. We say "Excuse me" when we need to pass in front of someone, to leave a party or the dinner table or when we want to excuse ourselves from company or find ourselves late for an appointment and so on. "Thank you" means that you appreciate what someone has done for you, very often very small and most ordinary things. So we in the West thank people all day long.

参考译文:

致谢与道歉

美国人对礼貌的概念与中国有所不同。在这里,我想和你们一起讨论一下"请(please)"、"对不起(excuse me)"和"谢谢(thank you)"的用法。我注意到,在大多数场合,中国人和我们一样常常用"请"这个词,但在某些场合你们又不用。比如,中国教师在他们的学生回答问题后很少说"请坐",中国的交通警在他们值勤时也不太习惯用"请"这个词。在餐桌上,我们说"请把盐递给我",而不是自己伸手去拿。假如你们去美国,那么,当情况需要时可别忘了说"请"。我相信,我们美国人说"对不起"的时候要比中国人多得多或更为普遍。当我们要经过某人的面前、要离开宴会或餐桌,或者是当我们要离开同伴(或约会迟到等等)时,我们都要说声"对不起"。"谢谢你"意味着你在某人为你做了什么事后表示谢意,那通常是一件无足轻重和极其普通的事情。所以,我们西方人真是从早到晚谢不离口。

Exercises for Text B

1. What the difference between American people and Chinese in using "please"?

    A. Chinese people doesn't use "please" at all.

    B. American People doesn't use "please" at all.

    C. Chinese people always use "please" on all the occasions, while American people on some occasions don't.

    D. American people always use "please" on all the occations, while Chinese people on some occasions don't.

2. When an American people say "thank you" to you, you should take it as:

    A. a very serious one, and become very happy.

    B. a meaningless thing, and ignore it.

    C. a usual thing, and accept it while offering "You're welcome".

    D. a thing should be rejected. (拒绝)

Part 4. Practical Writing

常用句尾短语及句式(Phrases and Sentences Used to End and Essay)

1. **Without** computer (cell telephone/PDP television/cars/microelectronics/telecommunication/Internet/genetics advances/...), **it would be difficult to imagine modern life.**

2. **We should redouble our efforts to build China into** a powerful (prosperous/better...) **nation with international prestige.**

3. **It is imperative for us to take effective measures to correct the situation** (fight corruption/hold back a tidal wave of crime/terminate excessive exploitation of natural resources/ease water shortages/...)

4. **In order to make our world a better place in which to live, we must** learn to live in harmony with all wildlife species (stop polluting our environment right away/conscientiously follow family planning).

5. **In short,** (population explosion, environmental pollution and exhaustion of natural resources) **are the major problems to be solved to** make our world a better place in which to live.

6. **I want to be a teacher** (a doctor/or to do something) **not only because..., but also because.**

7. **It goes without saying that** science and technology constitute primary productive force (knowledge is something/creativity is everything/cheating never pays/...).

8. **Living in harmony with nature (wildlife) has become a part of modern civilization.**

9. The state-enterprises (The township enterprises) **have only two choices: solve these longstanding problems through reforms or go bankrupt.**

10. We should not let the golden opportunity slip by. On the contrary, we should seize any opportunity and face the challenge with confidence, courage and wisdom.

Unit 8. Monitoring The Cleaning Contract

Part 1. Text

Monitoring The Cleaning Contract

It is essential to develop a professional relationship between the Property Manager and the cleaning contractor. This will involve regular inspections to ensure that the contractor is maintaining the required or specified cleaning standards. It is suggested that the cleaning contractor prepare a regular report on a weekly or perhaps monthly basis, outlining what has been done, what periodical cleaning tasks need to be done, and any problems encountered by the contractor.

Inspections should be carried out as early as possible in the morning, ideally before the tenants have commenced work. Periodicals should be scheduled and the schedule made available so that these items may be inspected after completion.

Good and honest communication between the Property Manager and the cleaning contractor is essential in obtaining a quality service which is ongoing.

PERFORMANCE AND QUALITY OF WORK

The cleaning contract should specify the minimum standard of performance. The contractor will execute/perform the specified cleaning tasks to the reasonable satisfaction of the Property Manager/Building Owner. Payment for the work will be made on the basis of twelve monthly payments. The cleaning contract may be cancelled at any time upon 30 days by written notice.

Should the quality and standard of cleaning deteriorate as a result of the contractor not acting in a diligent and competent manner, the Property Manager/Building Owner may serve the contractor with a written notice of default specifying the problem and what actions need to be taken. If the contractor does not remedy the default within 7 days from the date of notice, the contract may be cancelled.

CLEANERS' AWARD

The Cleaners' Award is the legislative basis which affects cleaning contract prices and regulates the industry. The award is extensive in the range of issues that it addresses. These issues include annual leave, meal allowance, first aid, uniform, toilet cleaning allowance, current rates of pay, classification structure and wage rates, penalty rates, overtime, superannuation, hours of work, terms of engagement, redundancy and structural efficiency. At the time of preparing these notes, the amended award states that the basic rate of pay per week for adult full time cleaners range between $356.10 and $400.60, plus appropriate penalties.

COMMON CLEANING CONTRACT CLAUSES

Default

If the work is not carried out to the satisfaction of the Property Manager, the following remedies may be available:

Have the work performed or redone by others in respect of the default.

Reassess the fair and reasonable cost involved in the default, and deduct such costs.

Direct the contractor to rectify or satisfactorily carry out work within specified time and withhold any payment until work is satisfactorily carried out.

Variation of Space to be Cleaned

The Property Manager may at any time by notice in writing, vary the portions of the building to be cleaned under the contract. In the event of such variation, the amount payable to the contractor shall be varied in the same manner as the initial contract amount agreed upon between the parties. If they are unable to agree within 28 days, the Property Manager may terminate the contract by giving the contractor 7 days notice in writing.

Extension of Contract

If, upon expiration of the contract period, the Property Manager and the contractor agree to extend the contract period, the extended contract shall be under terms and conditions as set out in the previous contract document, or as subsequently agreed.

Insurance

The contractor should provide public liability insurance of at least $5,000,000 for accidents/ incidents arising out of, or caused by a non performance of the contract, to any person or damage to the property. The contractor may be called upon to provide evidence of continuity of his insurance policy either at a renewal of the contract or as requested. The contractor must effect and keep the appropriate Occupational Health and Safety insurance such as either workcare or comcare.

参考译文：

保洁合同的管理

物业经理和保洁工作承包商之间建立业务关系是很必要的。这将需要定期的检查以确保承包商按照约定的具体标准做好保洁工作。建议合同承包商定期准备一份报告，(可以是每周或每月一份报告)，简要说明已完成的保洁工作，日后需要完成的定期的保洁任务，以及承包商在工作中遇到的问题。

应该在上午尽可能早地进行检查,最理想的时间是在住户上班之前。定期要做的工作应该列表,而且表格应置于显著位置,这样便于完成后大家进行检查。

物业经理和保洁工作承包商之间进行良好、诚实的合作,对于获得高质量的服务是非常重要的。

保洁工作的操作和质量

保洁合同应该规定最低操作标准。承包商完成规定的保洁任务才会达到物业经理/业主的满意。保洁费用是按 12 个月的付款方式进行缴纳。书面通知 30 天以上可以取消保洁合同。

如果承包商工作不勤奋,不能胜任工作,而导致保洁工作质量和标准的降低,物业经理/业主可以给承包商提出书面通知,指出他没有履行职责的错误,以及需要采取的措施。如果承包商在声明之日起 7 天内不纠正这个错误,可以取消合同。

保洁工的报酬

保洁工的报酬是立法的基础,它会影响保洁合同的价格和工作任务的确定。在核拨范围内报酬是多方面的,包括一年一度的假期,伙食补助,急救,统一服装,卫生间保洁补助,当月的薪水,级别结构和薪水标准,罚款标准,加班费,退休金,工作时间,合同期限,年终奖和结构效益工资。在准备这些说明时,应该声明给予成年保洁工每周的基本工资标准在 356.10 美元和 400.60 美元之间,再加上适当的奖金。

普通的保洁合同条款

违约

如果保洁工作没有达到物业经理的满意,可采取以下做法:
- 由别人来承担这项工作以示惩罚。
- 重新评估违约造成的损失,并且扣除这些费用。
- 直到承包商在规定的时间内进行整顿并令人满意地完成了工作,再继续支付报酬。

保洁区域的变更

物业经理可以在任何时间以书面通知的方式,在合同允许的范围内调整大楼的保洁区域。万一这个调整使得付给承包商的酬金金额与最初协商好的合同金额有变化,如果在 28 天之内双方没有达成一致,物业经理可以给承包商用书面通知一周的方式终止合同。

合同期的延长

如果在合同期满时,物业经理和承包商协商延长合同期,延长期的合同将遵照以前的合同文件执行,或按其后的协议执行。

保险

承包商应该提供至少 5000000 美元公开的责任保险,以赔偿意外的,或没按合同操作而引起的事故给人身和财产带来的损失。可以要求承包商提供保险政策规定的连带责任的证据,既可以在延长合同时这样做,也可以现在要求它来做。承包商必须投保适当的职业健康安全险。

Vocabulary
单词表：

249.	monitor	['mɔnitə]	v.	控制,管理;探索;报警;调节
250.	professional	[prəˈfeʃnl]	a.	业务的,专业的,职业的
			n.	专业人员,内行
251.	involve	[inˈvɔlv]	vt.	免不了,需要;包含;遍及;占用
252.	inspection	[inˈspekʃən]	n.	检查,调查,验收,监督
253.	specify	[ˈspesifai]	vt.	确定,规定;详细说明
254.	outline	[ˈautlain]	vt.	概述,画轮廓
255.	encounter	[inˈkauntə]	v.	遭遇,碰见,打击,冲突
256.	commence	[kəˈmens]	v.	开始;得……学位
257.	performance	[pəˈfɔːməns]	n.	性能,效能,效率;生产力(率)
258.	deteriorate	[diˈtiəriəreit]	v.	降低,变坏,衰退;损坏
259.	diligent	[ˈdilidʒənt]	a.	勤劳的,勤奋的,努力的,刻苦的
260.	competent	[ˈkɔmpitənt]	a.	胜任的,有能力的;应该做的;适当的;权限内的
261.	default	[diˈfɔːlt]	n. v.	不履行,拖欠;缺乏;错误
262.	remedy	[ˈremidi]	n. vt.	补救;改善,纠正;治疗;赔偿
263.	award	[əˈwɔːd]	n.	决断;判决;奖品
264.	legislative	[ˈledʒislətiv]	a. n.	立法的;立法机关
265.	extensive	[iksˈtensiv]	a.	彻底的,粗放的,延伸的,扩大的,大范围的
266.	issue	[ˈiʃ(j)uː]	n.	拨发,流出,争论,发行,结果,收获
267.	allowance	[əˈlauəns]	n.	补助,津贴,供给量;允许;考虑
268.	superannuation	[sjuːpəˌrænjueiʃən]	n.	退休,废弃,淘汰
269.	engagement	[inˈgeidʒmənt]	n.	约定,契约;衔接;交战,接近
270.	redundancy	[riˈdʌndnsi]	n.	多余,剩余度;过多,重复
271.	amend	[əˈmend]	v.	改善,修正,修订,更改
272.	clause	[klɔːz]	n.	条款,项目,从句
273.	reassess	[ˈriːəses]	vt.	对……再估价,再鉴定,再征收
274.	deduct	[diˈdʌkt]	vt.	扣除,减去,折扣;推论
275.	rectify	[ˈrektifai]	vt.	改正,纠正,整顿,清除
276.	withhold	[wiðˈhould]	vt.	抑制,扣留,拒绝给予
277.	variation	[ˌvɛəriˈeiʃən]	n.	变化,调整
278.	terminate	[ˈtəːmineit]	v.	终止,满期;接在端头上
279.	extension	[iksˈtenʃən]	n.	延伸,广度;扩展;附加;大学公开演讲
280.	subsequently	[ˈsʌbsikwəntli]	ad.	其后,其次,接着
281.	continuity	[ˌkɔntiˈnjuiti]	n.	连锁,连续;节目说明
282.	renewal	[riˈnjuəl]	n.	更新,恢复;修补;重做;续订

283. occupational [ɔkju'peiʃən] a. 职业的,与职业有关的

Useful Expressions

between... and...   ……和……之间
on... basis/on the basis of...   根据,以……为基础,在……基础上,以……为度;以……为条件
carry out   执行,实现,贯彻,落实,了结
as... as possible   尽可能地……
at any time   在任何时候
as a result (of)...   作为(……的)结果
in a manner   在某种意义上,在一定程度上,有点
with a written notice   以书面通知的形式
from the date of notice   从通知之日起
in the range of   在……范围内
at the time of   当……时候
first aid   急救
in respect of   关于,就……而论,相对于
(be, become) involved in   包含在……中,与……有关,被卷入,处于……之中,专心的做
withhold any payment   不予支付
in writing   以书面形式
in the event of   万一,即使
be unable to   不能
set out   出发,开始;装饰;宣布;打算;设计布局;系统的安排
at least   至少
call upon   要求,请求
as requested   按照要求

Notes
备注：

1. It is essential to develop a professional relationship between the Property Manager and the cleaning contractor. 物业经理和保洁工作承包商之间建立业务关系是很必要的。
在句中,it 是形式主语,真正的主语是动词不定式短语 to。
例如：
It is not an easy thing to support a large family.
养活一大家人是不容易的。

2. This will involve regular inspections to ensure that the contractor is maintaining the required or specified cleaning standards. 这将会需要定期的检查以确保承包商进行必要的,保洁工作标准指定的维修。
在句中,指示代词 this 指上文提到的事物；动词不定式短语 to 做目的状语,其中又包含了一个由 that(that 被省略)引导的宾语从句,做及物动词 ensure 的宾语。

例如：

Tom borrowed some books so as to read on the journey.

汤姆借了一些书，以便在旅途中阅读。

The boy promised her that he would never be late for school any more.

那个男孩向她保证，上学不会再迟到了。

3. It is suggested that the cleaning contractor prepare a regular report on a weekly or perhaps monthly basis, outlining what has been done, what periodical cleaning tasks need to be done, and any problems encountered by the contractor. 建议合同承包商定期准备一份报告，(可以是每周或每月一份报告)，简要说明已完成的保洁工作，日后需要完成的定期的保洁任务，以及承包商在工作中遇到的问题。

在句中，it 是形式主语，真正的主语是 that 引导的主语从句，注意：当主句谓语为 suggest, command, demand, insist, order, require, 等动词的被动语态，主句含有要求，建议等语意时，谓语用动词原形或 should＋动词原形，所以句中 prepare 用的是动词原形，而不用其他形式。

例如：

It is suggested that each of them (should) write an article.

建议他们每人写一篇文章。

在句中，是由 what 引导的宾语从句，做现在分词 outlining 的宾语，在此宾语从句中，has been done 是现在完成时态的被动语态；过去分词短语 encountered by the contractor 做定语，修饰前面的名词 problems。

例如：

She explained(to him) what he had to do to start the car.

她(向他)讲解要启动汽车得怎么做。

The man killed by a tiger was a hunter.

那个被老虎咬死的人是个猎人。

4. Periodicals should be scheduled and the schedule made available so that these items may be inspected after completion. 定期要做的工作应该列表，而且表格应容易看到，这样便于完成后大家进行检查。

在句中，so that 引导的是目的状语，经常和情态动词连用，如：can/could, will/would, may/might, should。

例如：

He arranged everything so that we could get there at one o'clock.

他安排好了一切，以便我们能一点到达那里。

5. Good and honest communication between the Property Manager and the cleaning contractor is essential in obtaining a quality service which is ongoing. 物业经理和保洁工作承包商之间进行良好的、诚实的合作，对于获得高质量的服务是非常必要的。

在句中，是主语部分，比较长，需要注意；is 是谓语，essential 是表语。

6. Should the quality and standard of cleaning deteriorate as a result of the contractor not acting in a diligent and competent manner, the Property Manager/Building Owner may

serve the contractor with a written notice of default specifying the problem and what actions need to be taken. 如果承包商工作不勤奋,不能胜任工作,而导致保洁工作质量和标准的降低,物业经理/业主可以给承包商提出书面通知,指出他没有履行职责的错误,以及需要采取的措施。

在句中,should 引导的是句。在 if 引导的真实条件句中,如果 should＋动词原形表示不大可能实现的条件,此时 if 可省去,而将 should 挪至句首,构成倒装语序。

例如:

If we should fail this time, everything will be quite different.

如果我们这次失败了,一切就完全不同了。

可改写为:

Should we fail this time, everything will be quite different.

7. Have the work performed or redone by others in respect of the default 为了处罚而重做,或由别人来承担这项工作。

本句中使用了 have sth. done 的结构,表示某事被做,或让别人做某事,过去分词 done 做宾语补足语,用于表示感觉、致使等动词(如:see, watch, hear, feel, find, discover, have, get, make, want 等)后。

例如:

I had my hair cut yesterday.

我昨天理发了。

Ⅰ. Exercises for the text 课文练习:

(Ⅰ) Decide whether the following sentences are True or False according to the content of the text.

1. It is essential to develop a professional relationship between the Property Owner and the cleaning contractor.
2. It is suggested that the cleaning contractor prepare a regular report on a weekly or perhaps monthly basis, outlining what has been done, what periodical cleaning tasks need to be done, and any problems encountered by the contractor.
3. Inspections should be carried out as early as possible in the morning, ideally after the tenants have commenced work.
4. The cleaning contract should specify the maximum standard of performance.
5. If the contractor docs not remedy the default within 7 days from the date of notice, the contract may be cancelled.
6. The Cleaners' Award is the legislative basis which affects cleaning contract prices and regulates the industry.
7. The award is not extensive in the range of issues that it addresses.
8. At the time of preparing these notes, the amended award states that the basic rate of pay per month for adult full time cleaners range between $356.10 and $400.60, plus appropriate penalties.

9. If they are unable to agree within 28 days, the Property Manager may terminate the contract by giving the contractor 7 days notice in writing.
10. The contractor may not be called upon to provide evidence of continuity of his insurance policy either at a renewal of the contract or as requested.

(Ⅱ) **Match the English words with their Chinese translations, choose the appropriate words to complete the sentences below and translate them into Chinese.**(将下列英语单词与其中文意思相匹配,选择合适的词将下列句子补充完整并译成中文。)

    1. inspection   a. 确定,规定;详细说明;
    2. issue   b. 概述,画轮廓
    3. involve   c. 勤劳的,勤奋的,努力的,刻苦的
    4. outline   d. 检查,调查,验收;监督
    5. specify   e. 拨发,流出,争论,发行,结果,收获
    6. diligent   f. 免不了,需要;包含;遍及;占用

1. There can be no force unless two bodies are _____.
2. That is China Commodity _____ Bureau(CCIB).
3. The contract _____ steel sashes for the windows.
4. This is _____ of process.
5. He is _____ in his work.
6. This is the burning _____ of the day.

(Ⅲ) **Choose the best answer**(选择最佳答案)

1. They found the house _____ down to the ground.
  a. burn   b. burned   c. burns   d. burning
2. _____ he is still alive is quite true.
  a. That   b. What   c. Which   d. Who
3. You should speak slowly _____ your students can follow you.
  a. so...that   b. to   c. so that   d. for fear that
4. The time _____ was quite enough.
  a. allow   b. allowed   c. allows   d. allowing
5. He was afraid of _____ she might say if she found him out some day.
  a. that   b. who   c. where   d. what
6. It is suggested that the visitors _____ to the Great Wall first.
  a. go   b. went   c. going   d. gone
7. A lot of people find modern art very hard _____.
  a. understood   b. understanding   c. to understand   d. being understood
8. The city government must take action _____ the increasing population.
  a. to control   b. controlling   c. controls   d. controlled
9. He didn't believe _____ such things mattered much.
  a. what   b. that   c. which   d. where
10. _____ is a pity that you have missed such a good chance.

a. That　　　　b. What　　　　c. It　　　　d. Who

(Ⅳ) Translation:

Translate the following Chinese into English:

1. 物业经理和保洁工作承包商之间建立业务关系是很必要的。
2. 应该在上午尽可能早地进行检查,最理想的时间是在住户上班之前。
3. 物业经理和保洁工作承包商之间进行良好的、诚实的合作,对于获得高质量的服务是非常必要的。
4. 承包商完成规定的保洁任务才会达到物业经理/业主的满意。
5. 如果承包商在声明之日起7天内不纠正这个错误,可以取消合同。
6. 为了处罚而重做,或由别人来承担这项工作。
7. 物业经理可以在任何时间以书面通知的方式,在合同允许的范围内调整大楼的保洁区域。
8. 承包商必须投保适当的与职业有关的健康安全险。
9. 直到承包商在规定的时间内进行整顿并令人满意地完成了工作,才继续支付报酬。
10. 如果保洁工作没有达到物业经理的满意,就可能得到赔偿。

(Ⅴ) Topic Extra Reading: read the following passage and choose the best answer to complete each of the statements that follow.

COMMON CLEANING CONTRACT CLAUSES

Indemnity

The contractor will usually be required to indemnify the proprietor from all claims, demands, writs, summons, actions, suits, proceedings, judgements, orders, decrees, costs, losses and expenses whatsoever the Property Manager/Building Owner may incur. This includes claims for loss of life, personal injury and/or damage to the property arising out of the performance or non-performance of the contractor under the contract.

Discrepancies in Documents

A draft clause to cover this topic may include the following wording:

"Documents which evidence the contract shall be taken as mutually explanatory and anything contained in one but not in the other shall be equally binding as if contained in all."

Any discrepancies, ambiguities or inconsistencies should be put in writing by the cleaning contractor to the Property Manager/Building Owner to clarify the interpretation.

Security Deposit

If a cleaning contract exceeds $100,000 the contractor may, as evidence of his commitment to fulfill the contract, be required to deposit 5% of the contract price in the form of cash, bank guarantee, government bonds or shares within 14 days of acceptance of the tender and prior to actually being awarded the contract.

Assignment/Subletting of the Cleaning Contract

The cleaning contractor shall not without prior written approval of the Property Manager/Building Owner, and except on the terms and conditions as agreed between the parties, encumber, assign or charge on the contract.

SUMMARY

The Property Manager needs to acquire a level of expertise when arranging and maintaining a cleaning contract for his or her clients. This involves understanding the client's requirements, preparing a specification based on a detailed inspection of all parts of the building including tenancies in occupation, inviting cleaning contractors to submit tenders, awarding the contract, being aware of insurance requirements and changes to the contract, and maintaining the standard of cleaning negotiated.

An important observation is that if the Property Manager spends the time and the effort to research and write the specification, this then forms the basis of a well performing cleaning contract and goes a long way towards avoiding many of the problems that can arise between the parties as a result of a misunderstanding of the duties to be performed as specified.

1. The contractor will usually be required to indemnify the proprietor from all claims, demands, writs, summons, actions, suits, proceedings, judgements, orders, decrees, costs, losses and expenses whatsoever _____ may incur.
    a. the Property Manager/Building Owner
    b. the Property Manager
    c. Building Owner
    d. themselves
2. Which of the following statements is not true?
    a. Any ambiguities should be put in writing by the cleaning contractor to the Property Manager/Building Owner to clarify the interpretation.
    b. Any inconsistencies should be put in writing by the cleaning contractor to the Property Manager/Building Owner to clarify the interpretation.
    c. Any topic should be put in writing by the cleaning contractor to the Property Manager/Building Owner to clarify the interpretation.
    d. Any discrepancies should be put in writing by the cleaning contractor to the Property Manager/Building Owner to clarify the interpretation.
3. If a cleaning contract exceeds _____ the contractor may, as evidence of his commitment to fulfill the contract, be required to deposit 5% of the contract price in the form of cash, bank guarantee, government bonds or shares within 14 days of acceptance of the tender and prior to actually being awarded the contract.
    a. $500,000   b. $100,000   c. $10,000   d. $5,000,000
4. "The cleaning contractor shall not without prior written approval of the Property Manager/Building Owner, and except on the terms and conditions as agreed between the parties, encumber, assign or charge on the contract." This sentence means _____.
    a. The cleaning contractor shall without prior written approval of the Property Manager/Building Owner, and except on the terms and conditions as agreed between the parties, encumber, assign or charge on the contract

b. The cleaning contractor shall not with prior written approval of the Property Manager/Building Owner, and except on the terms and conditions as agreed between the parties, encumber, assign or charge on the contract

c. The cleaning contractor shall not have prior written approval of the Property Manager/Building Owner, and except on the terms and conditions as agreed between the parties, encumber, assign or charge on the contract

d. The cleaning contractor shall have prior written approval of the Property Manager/Building Owner, and except on the terms and conditions as agreed between the parties, encumber, assign or charge on the contract

5. The Property Manager needs to acquire _____ when arranging and maintaining a cleaning contract for his or her clients.
   a. the client's requirements
   b. preparing a specification based on a detailed inspection of all parts of the building including tenancies in occupation
   c. a level of expertise
   d. inviting cleaning contractors to submit tenders, awarding the contract

II. Language Ability Drill(语言能力练习)

(I) Vocabulary Exercise

1.1 You already know that the suffix -ly can be added to adjectives to form adverbs, but it can also be added to nouns to form adjectives, with the meaning "like in manner, nature, or appearance", e.g.

saint+-ly   saintly: like a saint; very holy
friend+-ly   friendly: of a friend; kind

Now form adjectives by adding -ly to the nouns listed below and then use them in the following sentences.

beast   brother   father
man   scholar(学者)   coward(懦夫)

1. Jack was _____ enough and respected by many.
2. To run away at the first sign of danger is a _____ action.
3. The local people gave the visitors some _____ advice.
4. There's always a _____ smile on Dr. Adams' face.
5. Cathy wears a pair of glasses, which gives her a _____ look.
6. The _____ behavior of Japanese army angered the whole world.

1.2 Study the following words. Then use them correctly in the sentences below:

Verbs	Nouns	Adjectives & Participles	Adverbs
imply	implication	implied	
surprise	surprise	surprising	surprisingly
		surprised	

Verbs	Nouns	Adjectives & Participles	Adverbs
respond	response	responsible	
	responsibility	irresponsible	
correct	correctness	correct	correctly
		incorrect	incorrectly
smooth	smoothness	smooth	smoothly
die	death	dead	deadly
		deadly	

1. imply, implication, implied

   1) The _____ is to criticize the darkness of the society.

   2) Are you _____ that she loves me?

   3) Can you figure out the _____ meaning of this sentence?

   4) The teacher smiled, with the _____ that he did agree with me.

2. surprise (v.), surprise (n.), surprising, surprised, surprisingly

   1) I was _____ to find he was in Beijing.

   2) The birthday party should be a _____ one.

   3) _____, Chinese soccer team has won this match.

   4) The news _____ all of us.

   5) It is not _____ that Jack got fired since he was always daydreaming at work.

   6) A look of _____ came into his eyes as he read the telegram.

3. respond, response, responsibility, responsible, irresponsible

   1) The suggestions we put forward at the meeting met with little _____.

   2) Tom _____ to the pain by crying.

   3) It is _____ of her to leave the children alone in the house.

   4) Who should be _____ for the mistake?

   5) Mr. Black was fully aware that his new post as general manager was a position of great _____.

   6) Teachers are _____ for the students' security when they're in school.

4. correct(v.), correctness, correct(a.), incorrect, correctly

   1) A/An _____ translation of a single word could lead to misunderstanding.

   2) The teacher was busy _____ our exercise books when we called at his house.

   3) You are _____ in thinking that he is little bit lazy.

   4) Facts have proved the _____ of this theory.

   5) I kept practising until I was able to pronounce these words _____.

   6) He spent a lot of time _____ my pronunciation.

5. smooth (v.), smoothness, smooth (a.), smoothly

   1) The plane landed _____.

182

2) Mother is _____ the sheets so that the bed may be more comfortable.

3) It's not a very good thing for a young man to have a path in life that is quite _____.

4) Many Western visitors are impressed by the _____ of Chinese silk and satin(缎子).

5) The old lady _____ the wrinkled paper and read on.

6. die, death, dead, deadly (a.), deadly (ad.)

1) One winter morning the old beggar was found lying _____ in the snow.

2) Peace-loving people all over the world want these _____ weapons(武器) done away with(废除).

3) He is _____ curious about others' matters.

4) Liu Hulan _____ for the people. Her _____ is weightier than Mount Tai(泰山).

5) The bear was already _____ as a result of shortage of food.

(Ⅱ) Cloze

A land free from destruction, plus wealth, natural resources, and labor supply-all these were important 1 in helping England to become the center for the Industrial Revolution. 2 they were not enough. Something 3 was needed to start the industrial process. That "something special" was men-4 individuals who could invent machines, find new 5 of power, and establish business organizations to reshape society.

The men who 6 the machines of the Industrial Revolution 7 from many backgrounds and many occupations. Many of them were 8 inventors than scientists. A man who is a 9 scientist is primarily interested in doing his research 10 . He is not necessarily working 11 that his findings can be used.

An inventor or one interested in applied science is 12 trying to make something that has a concrete use. He may try to solve a problem by 13 the theories 14 science or by experimenting through trial and error. Regardless of his method, he is working to obtain a 15 result: the construction of a harvesting machine, the burning of a light bulb, or one of 16 other objectives.

Most of the people who 17 the machines of the Industrial Revolution were inventors, not trained scientists. A few were both scientists and inventors. Even those who had 18 or no training in science might not have made their inventions 19 a groundwork had not been laid by scientists years 20.

1. A. cases   B. reasons   C. factors   D. situations
2. A. But   B. And   C. Besides   D. Even
3. A. else   B. near   C. extra   D. similar
4. A. generating   B. effective   C. motivating   D. creative
5. A. origins   B. sources   C. bases   D. discoveries
6. A. employed   B. created   C. operated   D. controlled
7. A. came   B. arrived   C. stemmed   D. appeared
8. A. less   B. better   C. more   D. worse
9. A. genuine   B. practical   C. pure   D. clever

10. A. happily	B. occasionally	C. reluctantly	D. accurately
11. A. now	B. and	C. all	D. so
12. A. seldom	B. sometimes	C. all	D. never
13. A. planning	B. using	C. idea	D. means
14. A. of	B. with	C. to	D. as
15. A. single	B. sole	C. specialized	D. specific
16. A. few	B. those	C. many	D. all
17. A. proposed	B. developed	C. supplied	D. offered
18. A. little	B. much	C. some	D. any
19. A. as	B. if	C. because	D. while
20. A. ago	B. past	C. ahead	D. before

(Ⅲ) **Complete the following sentences, using the words in brackets:**

1. Now many households in this city use electric stoves (炉子) instead of gas rings(煤气灶).
   Electric stoves ....
   (take the place of)

2. Divorce has become more acceptable now; in earlier times, however, people took it as a shame to a family.
   In earlier times, divorce ....
   (disgrace)

3. Catching sight of a policeman walking toward him, the thief grew very fearful.
   The sight of a policeman ....
   (nervous)

4. The way the law was broken caused angry surprise among all the women in our neighborhood.
   All the women in our neighborhood ....
   (shock)

5. His impatience to get started was written on his face.
   The expression on his face showed that..
   (extremely eager)

6. She hates being disturbed, because she is studying for an exam tomorrow.
   She is studying for an exam tomorrow, so you'd better ....
   (interrupt)

Part 2. Dialogue

Cleaning Service in Community I
(小区清洁服务1)

Ⅰ. **Typical Sentences**（经典短句）

(Ⅰ) **Daily Conversations**（日常用语）

To Echo

（随声附和）
1. Exactly.
   正是那样。
2. I've got it.
   我明白了。
3. Of course.
   当然。
4. Sure. /Certainly.
   当然可以。
5. I think so.
   我想是的。
6. I am sure.
   我敢肯定。
7. That's good.
   那很好啊。
8. You are right. /You are quite right on this point.
   你说得很对。
9. That's it.
   是的，正是如此。
10. So do I.
    我也这么认为。

(Ⅱ) Professional Conversation（专业会话）
清洁员用语：
1. Sir, please don't smoke. Please put out the cigarettes!
   先生，请不要吸烟，请将烟熄灭！
2. Would you mind not smoking here?
   请您别在这里吸烟好吗？
3. Excuse me. Would you mind smoking in the lounge?
   抱歉，请您到吸烟室去抽，好吗？
4. Would you please leave your umbrella outside the door?
   请您把伞放在门外好吗？
5. You can leave the dust bag right here.
   你可以把垃圾袋就放在这。

Ⅱ. Conversation Passages

(Ⅰ) Passage 1
A: Good afternoon, can I help you?
   下午好.您有什么事吗?
B: Yes, is it the pets' hospital?

185

这是宠物医院吗？

A: Yes, it is.
是的，就是这。

B: Can you help me to give my dog an injection?
您能给我的狗种个疫苗吗？

A: Sorry, I'm the cleaner here. The vet is over there.
对不起，我是这的清洁工. 兽医在那边呢。

B: Sorry for the interruption.
对不起，打扰了。

A: It doesn't matter. But sir, would you please leave your umbrella out of the door? And please don't smoke, put out the cigarettes, please!
没关系。可是，先生，请您把伞放在门外好吗？而且请不要吸烟，请将烟熄灭！

B: Oh, sorry.
噢，对不起。

A: Thank you for your cooperation. And you can smoke in the lounge.
感谢您的合作，您可以到吸烟室去抽。

B: Thank you for your kindness.
谢谢您。

A: You're welcome.
不用谢。

(Ⅱ) Passage 2

A: Hello, this is Chen Ming from Property Management department speaking. What can I do for you?
您好！我是物业部的陈明. 请问您有什么事？

B: Hello. I'm an owner who lives in the Building 3, gate 1, 4th floor, room 1. This morning, I found the trash channel was locked. Is it under reconstruction?
您好，我是住在3号楼1门401室的住户。今天早上我发现垃圾管道被锁上了，是不是正在整修呢？

A: Yes, it is. Some bricks inside the trash channel fell off yesterday. We're going to give the notice by this noon. Anyway, sorry for the inconvenience to you.
噢，是的。昨天夜里垃圾管道内部的砖掉下来了。我们本想赶在中午之前就出通知的。真对不起，给您带来了不便。

B: It's ok.
没关系的。

A: Anything else I can do for you?
我还可以帮您什么忙吗？

B: Right. During the time of reconstruction, where should I leave the rubbish?
对了，在修理期间我应当把垃圾丢在哪呀？

A: Would you please put them into a bag? Then you can leave the dust bag right outside your door. We will send someone to collect them.

请您把垃圾装到一个袋子里,好吗?你可以把垃圾袋就放在门外,我们会派人收的。

B: No problem!

没问题!

A: Thank you for supporting our work.

感谢您支持我们的工作。

B: It's my pleasure. By the way, how long will the work take?

荣幸之至. 顺便问一句,修理要花多长时间?

A: It depends on how serious the problem is.

这要取决于问题究竟有多严重了。

B: I see.

我明白了。

A: Anyway, we'll try our best to save the time.

我们会抢分夺秒的。

B: I'm sure you will. Good luck!

我相信你们一定会的,祝您们好运!

A: Thank you for your kindness. Bye!

谢谢您的宽宏大量,再见!

B: Bye-bye.

再见。

Ⅲ. Exercises for Dialogue

(Ⅰ) **Fill in the following blanks by considering Chinese.**(按照中文完成以下填空)

A: Hello,_____. What can I do for you?

您好!我是物业部的陈明。

B: Hello. I'm an owner who lives in the Building 3, gate 1, 4th floor, room 1. This morning, I found the trash channel was locked. Is it under reconstruction?

您好,我是住在3号楼1门401室的住户,今天早上我发现垃圾管道被锁上了,是不是正在整修呢?

A: Yes, it is. Some bricks inside the trash channel fell off yesterday. _____. Anyway, sorry for the inconvenience to you.

我们本想赶在中午之前就出通知的。

B: It's OK.

没关系的。

A: _____?

我还可以帮您什么忙?

B: Right. During the time of reconstruction, where should I leave the rubbish?

对了,在修理期间我应当把垃圾丢在哪呀?

187

A: Would you please put them into a bag? Then you can leave the dust bag right outside your door. _____.
你可以把垃圾袋就放在门外,我们会派人收的。

B: No problem!
没问题!

(Ⅱ) After filling in the blanks, translate the former dialogue into Chinese.

(Ⅲ) Make a conversation with your partner about finding a parking place. (there should be at least 3 turn-taking in the dialogue)

Ⅳ. **Spoken Language Drill** (fill in the blanks according to the Chinese translation)

Dialogue 1

A: I'd like to say _____ to everyone.
我要向诸位告别了。

B: What time are you going?
你什么时候走?

A: My plane leaves at 7:25.
我乘的飞机7点25分起飞。

B: Well, goodbye and have a _____ trip!
那么,再见,祝你一路顺风。

A: Goodbye. _____ to look me up [看望;探访] if you're ever in Washington.
再见。要是你光临华盛顿的话,别忘了来看我。

Dialogue 2

A: I've come to _____ goodbye.
我是来告别的。

B: When are you off [离开;离去]?
你什么时候动身?

A: I'm _____ home on Sunday afternoon.
我星期四下午乘飞机回家。

B: Well, goodbye. See you soon.
那么,再见。后会有期。

A: Please don't forget to say goodbye to the rest of the family for me.
请别忘了代我向你的家人告别。

Dialogue 3

A: I just dropped in to say goodbye.
我只是来告别的。

B: What time are you leaving?
你几点钟走?

A: I'm going to _____ to leave by 10:00.

188

我争取 10 点以前离开。

B: _____ and give my best to your parents.

多保重,代我向你的父母问候。

A: Goodbye. Hope to see you again next year.

再见。希望明年再见到你。

Dialogue 4

A: I'm _____ to say goodbye.

我打电话向你告别来了。

B: When do you leave?

你何时起程?

A: I'm catching [及时赶上] the 11:00 train.

我准备赶 11 点火车。

B: Take care of yourself and don't forget to keep in _____.

多多保重。别忘了保持联系。

A: Goodbye. Thanks again for _____.

再见了,再次感谢你所做的一切。

Part 3. Supplementary Reading:

Passage A

The Standard of Living

The "standard of living" of any country means the average person's share of the goods and services which the country produces. A country's standard of living, therefore, depends first and foremost on its capacity to produce wealth. "Wealth" in this sense is not money, for we do not live on money but on things that money can buy: "goods" such as food and clothing, and "services" such as transport and entertainment.

A country's capacity to produce wealth depends upon many factors, most of which have an effect on one another. Wealth depends to a great extent upon a country's natural resources, such as coal, gold, and other minerals, water supply and so on. Some regions of the world are well supplied with coal and minerals, and have a fertile soil and a favourable climate; other regions possess none of them. The U.S.A. is one of the wealthiest regions of the world because she has vast natural resources within her borders, her soil is fertile, and her climate is varied. The Sahara Desert, on the other hand, is one of the least wealthy.

Next to natural resources comes the ability to turn them to use. Sound and stable political conditions, and freedom from foreign invasion, enable a country to develop its natural resources peacefully and steadily, and to produce more wealth than another country equally well served by nature but less well ordered. Another important factor is the techni-

189

cal efficiency of a country's people. Old countries that have, through many centuries, trained up numerous skilled craftsmen and technicians are better placed to produce wealth than countries whose workers are largely unskilled. Wealth also produces wealth. As a country becomes wealthier, its people have a large margin for saving, and can put their savings into factories and machines which will help workers to turn out more goods in their working day.

A country's standard of living does not only depend upon the wealth that is produced and consumed within its own borders, but also upon what is indirectly produced through international trade. For example, Britain's wealth in foodstuffs and other agricultural products would be much less if she had to depend only on those grown at home. Trade makes it possible for her surplus manufactured goods to be traded abroad for the agricultural products that would otherwise be lacking. A country's wealth is, therefore, much influenced by its manufacturing capacity, provided that other countries can be found ready to accept its manufactures.

To calculate the average standard of living of any country, one divides its "national income" by the number of people in it. Strictly, the term "national income" means the total of goods and services produced for consumption in that country in a year; but such a total cannot be divided unless it is expressed in money.

Exercise

1. A country's wealth depends upon _____.
    a. its standard of living
    b. its money
    c. its ability to provide goods and services
    d. its ability to provide transport and entertainment
2. The main idea of the second paragraph is that _____.
    a. the U. S. A. is one of the wealthiest countries in the world
    b. the Sahara Desert is a very poor region
    c. a country's wealth depends on many factors
    d. natural resources are an important factor in the wealth or poverty of a country
3. The third paragraph is about _____.
    a. how wealth produces wealth
    b. peaceful development of a country's natural resources
    c. the importance of the technical efficiency of a country's people
    d. all of the above
4. The word "margin" in "... a large margin for (line 8, para 3) ..." means _____.
    a. the space at the side of the page
    b. the edge
    c. the amount earned but not needed for living

    d. any money deposited in a savings account
5. Which of the following about Britain's wealth is true according to the passage?
    a. Britain's wealth is entirely produced and consumed within its borders.
    b. Britain is more dependent upon trade than any other country in the world.
    c. Britain manufactures more than it needs for home consumption.
    d. Britain's wealth lies only in what it can manufacture.

Passage B

What does an astronaut look like?

    Should astronauts wear slippers? Should they be able to watch the evening news?
    These issues came up when a NASA researcher interviewed 10 former astronauts, collecting information for planning future space-flight missions such as the space station.
    William K. Douglas, who was the flight surgeon for the seven original Mercury astronauts, interviewed at least one astronaut from each of NASA's manned space-flight programs (excluding shuttle missions), gathering a wide variety of opinions of such topics as health, food, clothing, morale, personal hygiene, psychological support, and chain of command.
    Among the findings:
    Food. One respondent noted that people lose their ability to taste food when in zero gravity, probably because convection currents carry aromas away from the nose. He suggested that this problem could be overcome by providing stronger condiments such as pepper and hot mustard.
    Clothing. Two-piece garments were favored so that the top part could be easily removed in warmer sections of the space station. Morale could be boosted by providing a "dress" uniform for special occasions or allowing a variety of colors and styles. One astronaut suggested slippers for off-duty wear.
    Hygiene. Shaving with electric razors becomes a problem in space because of whisker dust near the user's face. Douglas recommends that studies on animals be performed to determine whether harmful effects on the lungs might result inhalation of such dust over extended periods of time.
    Privacy. Most of the respondents said a private line of communication with their families was important, as was the ability to communicate privately with one another-i. e., without being overheard by other crew members, ground control, or the press. One thought that long periods spent in space might make it necessary for an astronaut to have a private line of communication to his stock broker. Privacy was also thought necessary for sleeping and for quiet times.
    Sleeping. One respondent expressed concern about the long-term effects of intermittent sleep, in which a person wakes up and goes back to sleep several times during a sleep

period-a phenomenon that occurs more frequently in space flight than on Earth. The resulting loss of REM sleep may not cause problems over short periods but might if continued for two months or longer. Difficulty in sleep also resulted from free-floating which allows the head and hands to move about at random.

Death in space. What should be done if a crew member dies during a long-term mission on the space station? The idea of shooting bodies "into the Sun" is not acceptable in today's society, though some form of on-orbit disposal was suggested.

Bringing a body back to Earth in a condition suitable for an open-casket funeral poses such problems as interim preservation and storage. Suggests Douglas: "One of the modern methods of taxidermy is to place the animal in a lifelike pose and freeze it in that position. A vacuum is then drawn on the container, and the animal is completely desiccated. The desiccated specimen is then placed in a sealed case. This technique could be adapted to the space station as a method of preserving the body of a deceased crew member until a relief vessel makes contact."

Physical requirements. In zero gravity there is less of a need for astronauts who are physically strong, so NASA should relax the physical requirements of crew members, suggested one respondent. This may eliminate arbitrary age limits.

参考译文：

宇航员应该什么样

宇航员能穿拖鞋吗？能看到晚间新闻吗？

这些问题是在一位美国国家航空和航天局研究人员采访十名前宇航员时被提出来的。采访的目的是为筹划将来的太空飞行任务（如建立太空站）而收集资料。

威廉·K·道格拉斯是七名飞往水星的宇航员的航天飞机上的外科医生，他几乎访问了国家航天局每项载人太空飞行计划中的一位宇航员（航天飞机飞行任务除外），就健康、衣服、士气、个人卫生、心理支持以及连锁指令等话题广泛收集了意见。

调查结果是：

食物：一位被访者注意到人处于无引力状态时就丧失了辨味能力，这大概是由于空气对流从鼻子那儿把香味刮跑了。他认为这个问题可以通过提供较辣的调味品，如胡椒和芥末来解决。

衣服：两节式衣服很受欢迎，它的上面部分在太空站较暖的地方容易脱下来。在特殊场合下穿"军礼服"或允许穿各种颜色和款式的服装可提高人的士气。一位宇航员建议在非工作时间穿拖鞋。

卫生：在太空中用电动剃须刀修面由于须沫会靠近修面者的脸而成了一个难题。道格拉斯建议在动物身上进行研究以弄清在较长时间内每天吸入这种须沫是否对肺有害。

私事：大多数被访者都说与家人的私人通话线很重要，即能够私下相互交谈而不被机组其他人员、地面控制站或报界偷听到。有一位认为,宇航员长期呆在太空,也许有必要拥有一个同他的证券经纪人保持联系的私人通话线。睡觉和清静之时不受干扰也认为很有必要。

睡眠:一个被访者对断断续续的睡眠引起的长期后果表示关注,人处于这种睡眠时会在睡觉期间醒来若干次。这种现象在太空飞行中比在地球上更常发生。眼球迅速跳动的睡眠所造成的损失在短期内也许不会构成问题,但如持续两个月或更长的时间,就有可能出毛病。自由漂浮令人的头和手胡乱摆动,因此也能导致睡眠困难。

空中死亡:如果一位机组人员在太空站执行长期任务期间丧生该怎么办?尽管有人提出过某种轨道运行中的尸体处置法,但那种把尸体"射入太阳"的主意在当今社会还不可取。

把尸体在合适的情况下装入敞盖棺材送回地面又带来了尸体的暂时防腐和存放这类问题。道格拉斯建议说:"动物标本剥制术的现代方法之一是把动物摆成栩栩如生的姿式并按这种姿式把它冷冻起来,然后在容器上制成一个真空状态并使动物完全脱水,再把制干的标本放进密封盒里。这种方法可能适合于太空站在救援机到达前用来保存死亡机组人员的尸体。"

体力要求:一位被访者说,在无引力状态下,宇航员不必身强体壮,因此,国家航空和航天局应放宽对机组人员的体力要求,这可能取缔专断的年龄限制。

Part 4. Practical Writing

有关抱怨函的回复(Reply)

1. We regret to see from your letter of …that case of our shipment arrived in a badly damaged condition.

    贵公司……月……日来函中提到,有一箱货物在抵达时严重受损,我们深感歉意。

2. We regret to learn from your letter of … that you have experienced such trouble with the computer system that we have sold to your bank.

    从您……月……日的信中,我们深感难过,因为我们出售给贵银行的电脑系统竟带给你们如此困扰。

3. We have read carefully your letter of complaint on the discrepancy of goods with the original sample. Apparently this is caused by the oversight of our production department, please accept our apologies for your inconvenience.

    我们已仔细读过您抱怨本公司货样不符的信件。显然这是本公司生产部门疏忽而导致您的不便,请接受我们的歉意。

4. It is very surprising and regrettable to us that these … problems have occurred and caused you so much trouble.

    因……问题而造成贵公司莫大的麻烦,我们甚为惊讶,也非常遗憾。

5. We have shipped the replacement goods and we trust that this will insure your satisfaction.

    我们已运出更换品,相信能使您满意。

6. We have received your letter complaining our delay of shipment, and we are sorry that we have not been able to deliver your order on time.

收到您方有关延期交货的报怨信,没能如期交货我们实感抱歉。

7. Please accept our apologies for this mistake, and let us know if we can serve you further.

   对所发生的错误我们表示由衷的歉意,并希望今后仍能为您服务。

8. In closing we would like to ask you for patience and understanding as we work to solve your problem.

   最后,希望在我方竭力解决问题期间,恳请贵方忍耐、谅解。

9. We apologize for any trouble/inconvenience you have been put to by our error, and will do our best to prevent any reoccurrence of this sort of error.

   对于此次失误给贵公司带来的麻烦,我们表示由衷歉意。今后我们一定尽力,使这类错误不再发生。

Unit 9. Emergency Evacuation

Part 1. Text

Introduction

In large commercial buildings, shopping centres and industrial properties there are certain circumstances where it is essential that a building be evacuated. It may well be considered the Property Manager's responsibility to put in place procedures to enable the quick and safe evacuation of premises in the event of an emergency arising. What then are some of an emergency arising. What then are some of the circumstances that would or could lead to evacuation?

They might include:

- Fire
- Threat of an explosion - a bomb or gas leak
- Electrical problem(s)
- Petroleum or other flammable liquids leak
- Structural problem caused by earthquake

When placed in the position, it may be difficult to make the decision to evacuate a major property. However, it is worth remembering that the authorities indicate that the action taken in the first five minutes after the incident may have a very serious bearing on the ability to prevent or reduce injury and loss of life.

WHY DO WE NEED EVACUATION PROCEDURES

To protect the occupants-Buildings whether be retail, commercial or industrial all have aspects Of occupancy and public access which need to be considered at all times.

To protect the asset- The primary concern in all building emergency situations must be people, Although once the people factor in the equation has been satisfied, the asset needs to be protected as best as possible.

To satisfy safety codes, both local and national - Throughout Australia authoritative bodies from Local Council right through to State and Federal Governments apply various safety controls which need to be considered and complied with.

These include such issues as;

extinguisher placement, sprinkler installation, stairwell pressurization devices, smoke spill fans and fire rated doors. These are only some of the aspects which are controlled by regulations and which need to be maintained correctly in order to preserve their operational ability in the event of an emergency.

As you can see from the three factors above, it is therefore essential that emergency procedures are in place. The greatest hazard to human life in fires is the smoke and hot gases that rise through a building. Research has found that in almost every situation where a life has been lost in a fire, death was due to the effects of smoke and toxic gases. In most cases research indicates that the victims were overcome within an estimated two to five minutes of the discovery of the fire and were in fact overcome by the volume of smoke and other toxic hot gases rising from the area of the fire.

Correct fire and emergency response procedures supported by trained personnel, fully aware of how to respond in the critical first five minutes before professional help arrives, are invaluable to any strategy for the critical first five minutes before professional help arrives, are invaluable to any strategy for the minimization of injury and death from this situation.

参考译文：

紧急疏散

在大型的商业建筑,购物中心和工业财产聚集地,当有某种情况发生时有必要对建筑物进行疏散。在紧急情况发生时,人们认为采取措施对建筑进行迅速而安全的疏散是物业经理的职责。那么什么是紧急发生的情况呢？什么情况发生时需要疏散呢？

包括下面一些情况：
- 着火
- 爆炸的威胁——炸弹或气体泄漏
- 电路问题
- 石油或其他可燃液体泄漏
- 由地震引起的结构问题

发生紧急情况的地方,做出对主要建筑物进行疏散的决定可能是困难的。然而,必须记住负责人提出的在事故发生后的第一个五分钟之内要采取的措施,否则防止和减少生命财产损失会更加困难。

我们为什么需要疏散程序呢？

保护居住者—不管建筑物是搞零售的,商业的还是工业的,都有随时都需要考虑的居住和公共通道各方面的情况。

保护财产—在所有建筑物发生紧急情况时主要关注的一定是人,一旦人员的疏散问题都妥当解决之后,还是需要尽可能地保护好财产安全。

满足当地的和国家的安全法规的要求—整个澳大利亚的权力机构从地方议会到州政府、联邦政府都对安全工作有许多规定,必须认真参照执行。

这些规定涉及如下问题:

  灭火器的放置,喷水设备的安置,楼梯井的压力输送装置,排烟风扇和控火门. 以上只是需要按规章进行控制和正确维护的其中一些方面,以保证设备在紧急情况下能正常发挥作用。

  正如你能从以上三个因素中看出的那样,紧急疏散程序在特定的场合是非常必要的。在火情发生时对人的生命威胁最大的就是建筑物中不断上升的烟和热气。研究发现,出现人身伤亡的火灾事故中,差不多每个案例都是烟和有毒气体导致的死亡。在绝大多数案例中,遇难者都是在发现火情的2~5分钟之内被着火区域的烟柱和有毒的热气窒息而死的.

  由受训人员支持的正确的火灾紧急反应程序,在紧急情况发生的最关键的头五分钟而专业救助尚未到达时知道如何反应的正确意识,对于专业救助未到的头五分钟极其主要,对于减少伤亡也极其重要。

Vocabulary
单词表:

284.	property	['prɔpəti]	n.	(集合用法)财产;资产;拥有之物;地产,房地产
285.	circumstance	['səːkəmstəns]	n.	(通常用复数)与某事件或某人有关的情况、事实等;环境;情势
286.	evacuate	[i'vækjueit]	vt.	疏散
287.	evacuation	[i'vækju'eiʃən]	n.	撤离,疏散
288.	petroleum	[pi'trəuljəm]	n.	石油
289.	structural	['strʌktʃərəl]	a.	构造的;结构的
290.	premise	['premis]	n.	[复]房屋(及其附属建筑、基地等)
291.	procedure	[prə'siːdʒə]	n.	过程,步骤;程序
292.	occupant	['ɔkjupənt]	n.	居住者;占有人,占有者
293.	retail	['riːteil]	a.	零售的;零售商品的
294.	commercial	[kə'məːʃəl]	a.	商业的,商业上的;商务的;商品化的
295.	aspect	['æspekt]	n.	(建筑物等的)方向,方位
296.	access	['ækses]	n.	接近;进入;通路
297.	asset	['æset]	n.	(单项)财产;宝贵的人(或物)
298.	satisfy	['sætisfai]	vt.	符合,达到(要求,标准,规定等);满足,使满足,使满意
299.	throughout	[θru(ː)'aut]	ad.	到处;始终;彻头彻尾
300.	authoritative	[ɔː'θɔritətiv]	a.	官方的,当局的;有权威的,可相信的
301.	body	['bɔdi]	n.	团体,机关;主体,正文
302.	council	['kaunsil]	n.	政务会;理事会;委员会;地方自治会;地方议会
303.	federal	['fedərəl]	a.	联邦的,联合的;联邦制的
304.	comply	[kəm'plai]	vi.	照做
305.	issue	['isjuː]	n.	结果,结局;问题,争端,争论点;(土地,地产等)收益
306.	extinguisher	[iks'tiŋgwiʃə]	n.	熄灭者,消灭者;熄灯器,灭火器

307.	placement	['pleismənt]	n.	放置,布置;(人员的)安排,安插;(足球等的)定位踢
308.	sprinkler	['spriŋklə]	n.	洒水器,洒水车,喷水设备
309.	a sprinkler system			洒水灭火系统(屋内的管道系统,通常在火灾时因温度激增而自动洒水或喷出其他灭火液)
310.	installation	[ˌinstə'leiʃən]	n.	安装,设置,安置;装置,设备;(军事)设施
311.	stairwell	['stɛwel]	n.	(建)楼梯井
312.	pressurization	[ˌpreʃərai'zeiʃən]	n.	压力输送;挤压;气密;密封;增压,加压
313.	spill	[spil]	vi.	溢出,溅出;充满;泄密;
			n.	溢出,溅出,溢出量,溢出的东西
314.	fan	[fæn]	n.	扇子,风扇,鼓风机
315.	rate	[reit]	vt.	调整快慢差率;对……估价,对……评定,对……评价
316.	regulation	[ˌregju'leiʃən]	n.	规则,规章,法规
317.	maintain	[men'tein]	vt.	维持,保持,继续;维修,保养
318.	toxic	['tɔksik]	a.	有毒的,有毒性的
319.	victim	['viktim]	n.	受害者,牺牲者,受骗者
320.	strategy	['strætidʒi]	n.	战略,战略学;策略,计谋
321.	minimization	['minimai'zeiʃən]	n.	极度轻视,把……估计得最低

Useful Expressions

lead to　(道路等)通往;导致,致使,引起
whether ... or ...　不论……或……;不管……还是……;或者……或者……
at all times　无论何时,一直
comply with　照做,遵守
in place　在适当的位置
in the event of　如果……发生
as ... as possible　尽可能……,尽量……
both ... and ...　既是……又是……,不仅……而且,……和……两者都
such as ...　如同,例如,诸如……之类的
in order to　为了,为的是要
due to　由于,起因于,归于
in fact　实际上,事实上,其实(＝as a matter of fact)

Notes
备注:

1. In large commercial buildings, shopping centres and industrial properties there are certain circum stances where it is essential that a building be evacuated. 在大型的商业建筑,购物中心和工业财产聚集地,当有某种情况发生时有必要对建筑物进行疏散。

此句中,where it is essential that a building be evacuated 是由关系副词 where 引导的

定语从句,修饰前面的名词 circumstances。在定语从句中,that a building be evacuated 又是由 that 引导的后置了的主语从句;it 作形式主语。

2. However, it is worth remembering that the authorities indicate that the action taken in the first five minutes after the incident may have a very serious bearing on the ability to prevent or reduce injury and loss of life. 然而,必须记住负责人提出的在事故发生后的第一个五分钟之内要采取的措施,否则防止和减少生命财产损失会更困难。

此句中,that the authorities indicate that the action taken in the first five minutes after the incident may have a very serious bearing on the ability to prevent or reduce injury and loss of life 是由 that 引导的后置了的主语从句;it 作形式主语;在主语从句中,that the action taken in the first five minutes after the incident may have a very serious bearing on the ability to prevent or reduce injury and loss of life 又是由 that 引导的宾语从句;taken 是过去分词做定语,修饰前面的名词 action。

3. To protect the occupants-Buildings whether be retail, commercial or industrial all have aspects of occupancy and public access which need to be considered at all times. 保护居住者——不管建筑物是零售的、商业的还是工业的都有随时需要考虑的居住和公共通道各方面情况。

此句中,which need to be considered at all times 是由关系代词 which 引导的定语从句,修饰前面的名词 access。

4. To protect the asset- The primary concern in all building emergency situations must be people, although once the people factor in the equation has been satisfied, the asset needs to be protected as best as possible 保护财产——在所有建筑物发生紧急情况时主要关注的一定是人,一旦人员的疏散问题都解决妥当之后,还是需要尽可能地保护好财产安全。

此句中,must 表示推测,意为"一定",一般只用于肯定的陈述句。例如:

You must be tired after your long walk.

走了这么长的路你一定累了吧。

"to be protected"是动词不定式的被动形式,表示动词不定式逻辑上的主语是动词不定式所表示的动作的承受者。

例如:

That young man seems to be trusted by everyone.

那年轻人看起来博得了大家的信任。

He went into the office to be examined orally.

他进办公室去接受口试。

注意:在 although 或 though(虽然,尽管)引导的让步状语从句后,不能用 but(但是)

5. To satisfy safety codes, both local and national - Throughout Australia authoritative bodies from Local Council right through to State and Federal Governments apply various safety controls which need to be considered and complied with. 满足当地的和国家的安全法规的要求——整个澳洲的权力机构,从地方议会到州、联邦政府都实施了必须被考虑和遵守的安全措施。

此句中,which need to be considered and complied with 是由关系代词 which 引导的定语从句,修饰前面的名词 controls;to be considered 是动词不定式的被动形式。

6. These are only some of the aspects which are controlled by regulations and which

need to be maintained correctly in order to preserve their operational ability in the event of an emergency. 以上只是需要按规章进行控制和正确维护的其中一些方面,以保证设备在紧急情况下能正常发挥作用。

此句中,which are controlled by regulations and which need to be maintained correctly 是由关系代词 which 引导的定语从句,修饰前面的名词 aspects;which are controlled by regulations 和 which need to be maintained correctly 是并列的两个定语从句,共同修饰前面的名词 aspects;are controlled 是一般现在时态的被动语态。

7. As you can see from the three factors above, it is therefore essential that emergency procedures are in place. 正如你能从以上三个因素中看出的那样,紧急疏散程序在特定的位置是非常必要的。

此句中,as 引导的是方式状语从句;that emergency procedures are in place 是由 that 引导的后置了的主语从句;it 作形式主语。

8. The greatest hazard to human life in fires is the smoke and hot gases that rise through a building. 在火情发生时对人的生命威胁最大的就是建筑物中不断上升的烟和热气。

此句中,greatest 是形容词的最高级,其前必须加定冠词 the;that rise through a building 是由关系代词 that 引导的定语从句,修饰前面的名词 the smoke and hot gases。

9. Research has found that in almost every situation where a life has been lost in a fire, death was due to the effects of smoke and toxic gases. 经调查发现差不多每个案例中,由于火灾去世的人当中,死因都是烟和有毒气体作用的结果。

此句中,that in almost every situation where a life has been lost in a fire, death was due to the effects of smoke and toxic gases 是由从属连词 that 引导的宾语从句;where a life has been lost in a fire 是由关系副词 where 引导的定语从句,修饰前面的名词 situation。

10. In most cases research indicates that the victims were overcome within an estimated two to five minutes of the discovery of the fire and were in fact overcome by the volume of smoke and other toxic hot gases rising from the area of the fire. 在绝大多数案例中,经研究显示估计受害者都是在发现火情的 2~5 分钟之内遇难的,而事实是被着火区域的烟柱和有毒的热气的侵害。

此句中,that the victims were overcome within an estimated two to five minutes of the discovery of the fire and were in fact overcome by the volume of smoke and other toxic hot gases rising from the area of the fire 是由从属连词 that 引导的宾语从句;were overcome 是一般过去时态的被动语态;rising from the area of the fire 是现在分词短语作定语,要放在所修饰词 the volume of smoke and other toxic hot gases 的后面;and 连接了两个并列谓语 were overcome within an estimated two to five minutes of the discovery of the fire 和 were in fact overcome by the volume of smoke and other toxic hot gases rising from the area of the fire。

Ⅰ. Exercises for the text 课文练习:

(Ⅰ) Decide whether the following sentences are True or False according to the content of the text.

1. It may not be considered the Property Manager's responsibility to put in place proce-

dures to enable the quick and safe evacuation of premises in the event of an emergency arising .

2. What then are some of the circumstances that would or could lead to evacuation? They might include: fire; threat of an explosiona bomb or gas leak ; electrical problem(s); petroleum or other flammable liquids leak ; structural problem caused by earthquake .

3. When placed in the position, it may be easy to make the decision to evacuate a major property.

4. It is worth remembering that the authorities indicate that the action taken in the first ten minutes after the incident may have a very serious bearing on the ability to prevent or reduce injury and loss of life.

5. The greatest hazard to human life in files is the smoke and hot gases that rise through a building.

6. Buildings whether be retail, commercial or industrial all have aspects of occupancy and public access which need to be considered at some times.

7. Although once the people factor in the equation has been satisfied , the asset doesn't need to be protected as best as possible

8. As you can see from the three factors above, it is therefore essential that emergency procedures are in place.

9. In most cases research indicates that the victims were overcome within an estimated in the first ten minutes of the discovery of the fire and were in fact overcome by the volume of smoke and other toxic hot gases rising from the area of the fire.

10. Correct fire and emergency response procedures supported by trained personnel, fully aware of how to respond in the critical first five minutes before professional help arrives.

(Ⅱ) **Match the English words with their Chinese translations, choose the appropriate words to complete the sentences below and translate them into Chinese.**（将下列英语单词与其中文意思相匹配,选择合适的词将下列句子补充完整并译成中文。）

1. circumstance   a. 居住者；占有人，占有者
2. commercial   b. 符合,达到(要求,标准,规定等)；满足,使满足,使满意
3. procedure   c. 照做
4. satisfy   d. 与某事件或某人有关的情况、事实等；环境；情势
5. access   e. (建筑物等的)方向,方位
6. evacuate   f. 过程,步骤；程序
7. occupant   g. 接近；进入；通路
8. comply   h. 商业的,商业上的；商务的；商品化的
9. aspect   i. 疏散
10. issue   j. 结果,结局；问题,争端,争论点；(土地,地产等)收益

1. Act according to _____ .
2. _____ the sick and wounded from a combat area.

3. His first _____ was to make a thorough investigation.
4. The _____ of the seat was Li Hong.
5. He is a student of a _____ college.
6. The house has a southern _____.
7. This is the _____ to a building.
8. The result of the experiment _____ us.
9. You must _____ with the library rules.
10. This is the burning _____ of the day.

(Ⅲ) **Choose the best answer**（选择最佳答案）

1. Next week he will visit the airbase _____ he worked 25 years ago.
   a. when   b. as   c. where   d. which
2. _____ is quite true that he is still alive.
   a. It   b. That   c. This   d. What
3. She required _____ he (should) get there before dark.
   a. what   b. which   c. that   d. how
4. The time _____ was quite enough.
   a. allows   b. allowed   c. allow   d. allowing
5. Have you seen the new machine the parts of _____ are too small to be seen?
   a. that   b. which   c. what   d. who
6. "Why isn't John in class?" "He _____ be sick, or he'd have been here already."
   a. should   b. may   c. must   d. would
7. Nothing at the exhibition is _____ by visitors.
   a. to touch   b. to be touched
   c. to have been touched   d. touch
8. Although it is raining, _____ continue working in the fields.
   a. so they   b. and they   c. but they   d. they
9. My car _____ near our house.
   a. parking   b. is parked   c. parked   d. to park
10. He is _____ man I've ever known.
    a. old   b. older   c. the oldest   d. the older

(Ⅳ) **Translation**：

Translate the following Chinese into English：

1. 发生紧急情况的地方，做出对主要建筑物进行疏散的决定可能是困难的。

2. 一旦人员的疏散问题都解决妥当之后，还是需要尽可能地保护好财产安全。

3. 灭火器的放置，喷水设备的安置，楼梯井的压力输送装置，排烟风扇和控火门需要按规章进行控制和正确维护，以保证设备在紧急情况下能正常发挥作用。

4. 在绝大多数案例中，经研究显示受害者都是在发现火情的2～5分钟之内被着火区域的烟柱和有毒的热气窒息而死的。

5. 紧急疏散程序在特定的场合是非常必要的。

6. 在紧急情况发生时,人们认为采取措施对建筑进行迅速而安全的疏散是物业经理的职责。

7. 然而,必须记住负责人提出的在事故发生后的第一个 5 分钟之内要采取的措施,否则防止和减少生命财产损失会更困难。

8. 不管建筑物是零售的,商业的还是工业的都有居住的方位和随时都需要的公共通道。

9. 在火情发生时对人的生命威胁最大的就是建筑物中不断上升的烟和热气。

10. 任何轻视伤亡的策略是毫无价值的。

(Ⅴ) **Extra Reading Activity**:

Read the following passage and choose the best answer to complete each of the statements that follow.

FACTORS TO CONSIDER

Business activities of the tenants-Tenancies today can be broad in their daily business activities. This means that you can often observe a variety of dangerous substances which are being stored or used in tenancy areas. An example of this would be a dental laboratory where for instance chemicals and heating devices are commonly used. Industrial properties are also prone to extremes of tenancy usage involving dangerous chemicals and devices.

Number of building occupants-Within any emergency evacuation scheme design and implementation you need to be aware of the number occupants that at any given time could be involved in an evacuation from the building.

Further to this you must take account of members of the public who may attend the building and not be familiar with any of the set evacuation procedures.

Building design and built-in safety factors -The building design and its safety features need to be incorporated into the method of evacuation. For example fire rated stairs and number of doors that can be opened at any one time within the fire rated stairs might be an element requiring control in an emergency evacuation.

Sprinklers and other fire prevention devices need be understood and their operations incorporated into warden training.

Safety code requirements - of more recent times new building tend to have stringent current safety code requirements built into them at time of construction. The order buildings are of further concern in that they need to be maintained to acceptable levels of safety especially if and when they are modified.

Building environment(exterior) -The exterior of the building needs to be considered together with the surrounding properties in any design of the evacuation procedures. Failure to do could have evacuated personnel from a building entering an unsafe area at the time of evacuation.

Example of such would be occupants of building alighting onto a busy major traffic thoroughfare with no place to gather in a marshalling area.

1. In this passage "Tenancies today can be broad in their daily business activities." This

means that _____.
   a. this would be a dental laboratory where for instance chemicals and heating devices are commonly used
   b. you can often observe a variety of dangerous substances which are being stored or used in tenancy areas
   c. industrial properties are also prone to extremes of tenancy usage involving dangerous chemicals and devices
   d. the building design and its safety features need to be incorporated into the method of evacuation
2. Within any emergency evacuation scheme design and implementation you need to be aware of _____.
   a. the number occupants that at any given time could be involved in an evacuation from the building
   b. members of the public who may attend the building and not be familiar with any of the set evacuation procedures
   c. the number occupants that not be familiar with any of the set evacuation procedures
   d. both a and b
3. "Fire rated stairs and number of doors that can be opened at any one time within the fire rated stairs might be an element requiring control in an emergency evacuation." Which of the factors to consider does it belong to?
   a. Business activities of the tenants.
   b. Number of building occupants.
   c. Building design and built-in safety factors.
   d. Safety code requirements.
4. The exterior of the building needs to be considered together with _____.
   a. fire rated stairs and number of doors that can be opened at any one time
   b. the surrounding properties in any design of the evacuation procedures
   c. the number occupants that at any given time could be involved in an evacuation from the building
   d. a variety of dangerous substances which are being stored or used in tenancy areas
5. "Failure to do so could have evacuated personnel from a building entering an unsafe area at the time of evacuation." In this sentence, "so" means _____.
   a. example of such would be occupants of building alighting onto a busy major traffic thoroughfare with no place to gather in a marshalling area
   b. the older buildings are of further concern in that they need to be maintained to acceptable levels of safety especially if and when they are modified
   c. the exterior of the building needs to be considered together with the surrounding properties in any design of the evacuation procedures
   d. you must take account of members of the public who may attend the building and not

be familiar with any of the set evacuation procedures

Ⅱ. Language Ability Drill(语言能力练习)

(Ⅰ) Vocabulary Exercise

1.1 Study the following pairs of words and use them correctly in the given sentences:

1. heart / mind
   1) The bad news broke my _____.
   2) Jane works very hard and never loses _____ in face of difficulties.
   3) I promise that I will always keep your warnings in _____.
   4) To my _____, this guy is a good-for-nothing(无用的人).
   5) Were you in your right _____ when you did such a foolish thing?
      I think you must have been out of your _____.
   6) Don't take his rude words too much to _____. He often speaks like that.

2. find / find out
   1) He became so interested in her life story that he decided to _____ more about her.
   2) The librarian promised to _____ me the book I wanted.
   3) I'll try and _____ who broke the transistor(晶体管收音机).
   4) I _____ this to be true in all the cities I visited.
   5) Two of the young men were sent to town to _____ about the situation there.
   6) The wind was blowing all night. But the next morning, I _____ the rice shoots(秧苗) standing up straight, not a bit damaged.

1.2 Study the following words. Then use them to rewrite the given sentences without changing their meaning.

   findings   writings   teachings   savings   earnings

1. What the committee(委员会) finds will be published in the Daily News.
2. At the beginning, he gave all the money he earned to his mother.
3. It took all the money he had saved to buy the house.
4. What Darwin wrote on evolution(进化) produced a tremendous impact(巨大影响) on the development of biology.
5. What Comrade Mao Zedong taught us about the united front is still of great significance(重要性) today.

(Ⅱ) Cloze

A boy walked along Carver Street, singing a sad song. He walked with his head down. Once he looked up and noticed the sign across the empty street, painted on the side of an old house. On the sign a big woman with yellow hair and a five-mile smile held out a big bottle. "Coca-Cola. Drink Coca-Cola," the sign said. "Boy!" the silence was cut by a sudden cry. He turned around quickly to see who had called. An old woman was standing at her door. "You boy! Come here this minute"

Slowly the boy __1__ onto the cold flat stones leading to the old woman's house. When he arrived at her house, she 2 out her hand and wrapped(缠住) her 3 old fingers around his arm. "Help me inside, boy", she said. "Help me 4 to my bed. What's your name?" "Joseph," he said. The old woman on the bed tried to 5 up, raising herself on her elbow(肘). Water 6 from her eyes and mouth. The sight of her made Joseph feel 7 . "I'm dying, Joseph. You can see that, can't you? I want you to write a 8 for me. There's paper and pencil on the table there." Joseph looked down at the 9 , and then looked out the window. He saw the sign again: "Coca-Cola. Drink Coca-Cola." "I want my silver pin to 10 to my daughter." Joseph bent his small body over the table and 11 the pencil slowly across the paper.

"There's my Bible(圣经)," the old woman said. "That's for my daughter, too. I want a 12 Christian burial(基督葬礼) with lots of singing. Write that down, too. That's the last 13 of a poor old woman." The boy laboured over the paper. Again he looked out the window. "Here. Bring it here so I can 14 it." Joseph found the Bible, and, 15 the paper inside, laid it next to the bed. " 16 me now, boy," she sighed. "I'm tired." He ran out of the house. A cold wind blew through the 17 window, but the old woman on the bed 18 nothing. She was dead. The paper in the Bible moved back and forth in the wind. 19 on the paper were some childish letters. They 20 the words: "Coca-Cola. Drink Coca-Cola."

1. A. rushed   B. struggled   C. hurried   D. stepped
2. A. reached   B. let   C. pushed   D. pointed
3. A. firm   B. smooth   C. dry   D. fresh
4. A. back   B. over   C. away   D. ahead
5. A. sit   B. get   C. stand   D. wake
6. A. rolled   B. burnt   C. burst   D. ran
7. A. ill   B. sick   C. unpleasant   D. funny
8. A. letter   B. note   C. will   D. message
9. A. table   B. pen   C. paper   D. woman
10. A. send   B. go   C. belong   D. come
11. A. moved   B. drew   C. used   D. pulled
12. A. great   B. merry   C. splendid   D. real
13. A. hope   B. chance   C. opinion   D. wish
14. A. sign   B. read   C. remember   D. copy
15. A. setting   B. hiding   C. placing   D. laying
16. A. Hold   B. Leave   C. Excuse   D. Pardon
17. A. large   B. open   C. small   D. pretty
18. A. did   B. saw   C. felt   D. knew
19. A. Described   B. Printed   C. Recorded   D. Written
20. A. formed   B. spelled   C. organized   D. repeated

(Ⅲ) Complete the following sentences, using the words in brackets:

1. It seems that he cannot understand the simplest instructions.

    He seems...(unable)

2. Even teachers of the same subject often have very different teaching styles.

    Teaching styles often .... (differ)

3. Chinese cities are bigger in terms of population than most American cities.

    Most American cities .... (compared to)

4. No other animal but man is able to learn and use language.

    Man alone .... (ability)

5. It is far from simple to communicate with people of different cultures, but not impossible.

    Communication with .... (complex)

6. The place where we had agreed to meet escaped from my memory.

    I could .... (recall)

Part 2. Dialogue

Cleaning Service in Community Ⅱ
（小区清洁服务2）

Ⅰ. Typical Sentences（经典短句）

(Ⅰ) Daily Conversations（日常用语）

　　To Echo
　　（随声附和）

1. That's a good idea.
    那真是个好主意。
2. That sounds good.
    听起来倒不错。
3. Indeed.
    一点也不错。
4. OK.
    好。
5. Absolutely.
    绝对是。
6. You said it!
    说的是！
7. Me, too.
    我也是。
8. Yeah? /Really?
    是吗？/真的吗？

9. Really? I can't believe it.
   真的吗？我不敢相信。
10. Oh, yeah?
    哦,是吗？

（Ⅱ）**Professional Conversation**（专业会话）

清洁员用语：

1. Excuse me, please keep the place clean!
   对不起,请爱护公共卫生！
2. Please don't spit everywhere!
   请不要随地吐痰！
3. Please do not throw the garbage everywhere!
   请不要随手扔垃圾！
4. Please throw the garbage into the dustbin!
   请扔到垃圾桶内！
5. Kid, obedient, behave yourself, don't doodle. (No scripts.)
   小朋友,听话,不要乱涂、乱画。

Ⅱ. **Conversation Passages**

（Ⅰ）**Passage 1**

A: Good afternoon, Mr. Yang.
   下午好,杨先生。
B: Good afternoon. How about the reconstruction?
   下午好,修理的活干完了吗？
A: Yes, we have just finished it. Sorry for the inconvenience to you.
   是的,刚刚干完。真对不起,给您带来了不便。
B: That's all right. You must have been working very hard.
   没关系。你们肯定工作得很辛苦吧？
A: Just so so. Anyway, that's our job. By the way, are you going out?
   还可以吧。不管怎么说,那是我们的工作。您这是要出门吗？
B: Yes, I'm going to visit my sister. My nephew is in winter vocation. I will take him here to review lessons.
   是的,我要去我姐姐家。我的小侄子放寒假了,我把他带到这来复习功课。
A: Oh. Take care on the way.
   噢,是这样啊。在路上多小心。
B: Thank you very much. See you!
   谢谢。再见！
A: See you.
   再见。

(Ⅱ) Passage 2

A: Good evening, Mr. Yang. Oh, is this your nephew?
晚上好,杨先生,这就是您的小侄子吗?

B: Yes. Call "uncle"!
是的,叫叔叔。

C: Good evening, uncle.
叔叔,晚上好。

A: What a lovely boy! What's your name?
多可爱的小家伙呀! 你叫什么名字呀?

C: My name is Zhang Liang.
我叫张梁。

A: Did you have a good time when going out with your uncle?
和你舅舅在外面玩的开心吗?

C: Yes, I did. And my uncle bought the color chalks for me.
是的可开心了。舅舅还给我买彩色粉笔了呢。

A: How beautiful they are! What are you going to do with them?
真漂亮! 你要用他们干什么呀?

C: I want to paint the wall with the green one, then draw little flowers on it.
我想用笔把墙画成绿色,然后在上面画花。

A: That must be a lovely picture. But good kids will never do that on the wall or on the floor.
那肯定会很漂亮的。可是好孩子从来都不在墙上或地上画画的。

C: Really?
真的吗?

A: And good kids don't spit everywhere, throw the garbage into the dustbin instead of throwing them everywhere.
而且,好孩子从不随地吐痰,将垃圾丢到垃圾桶里,而不是随手扔。

C: But where do they draw with chalk?
那他们在哪用粉笔画画呢?

A: Oh, they will do it on the blackboard. I have a small one, and I can give it to you.
他们在黑板上画呀。我这就有一块小黑板。给你吧。

C: Thank you, uncle.
谢谢,叔叔。

B: Thank you.
谢谢你。

A: You are welcome. Bye-bye, little Zhang Liang. Remember: keep the place clean.
不用谢。再见,小张梁。记得要爱护公共卫生呀。

B: I will. Thank you. Bye-bye.
我会的。谢谢您,再见。

Ⅲ. Exercises for Dialogue

(Ⅰ) Fill in the following blanks by considering Chinese.（按照中文完成以下填空）

  A：Good kids will never _____.
    好孩子从来都不在墙上或地上画画的。
  B：Really?
    真的吗？
  A：And good kids _____.
    而且，好孩子从不随地吐痰，将垃圾丢到垃圾桶里，而不是随手扔。
  B：But where do they draw with chalk?
    那他们在哪用粉笔画画呢？
  A：Oh, they will do it on the blackboard. _____.
    他们在黑板上画呀。我这就有一块小黑板。给你吧。

(Ⅱ) Make a conversation with your partner about finding a parking place. (there should be at least 3 turn-taking in the dialogue)

Ⅳ. Spoken Language Drill (fill in the blanks according to the Chinese translation)

Dialogue 1.
  A：Do you think you can get me to Union Station by quarter after?
    你看你能否在一刻前把我送到联合车站？
  B：We shouldn't have any _____ if the traffic isn't too heavy.
    如果交通不太拥挤的话，我们不会有什么困难。
  B：You've got _____ of time. That's $7.65.
    你还富有很多时间，请付 7 元 6 角 5 分。
  A：Thank you very much. Here's $10.00. Give me $1.00 _____, please.
    太谢谢你了。这是 10 元钱，找我 1 元就行了。

Dialogue 2.
  A：Kennedy Airport, please. I _____ be there by 7：00.
    请到肯尼迪机场。我得在 7 点前赶到那儿。
  B：I can't _____ anything, but I'll do my best.
    不敢保证，不过我尽力而为。
  B：OK. That'll be $12.00, please.
    到了。请付 12 元。
  A：Thanks a lot. Here.
    多谢。这是车费。

Dialogue 3.
  A：Grand Central Station, please. I want to try to _____ a 6：00 train.
    请到中央火车站。我要赶 6 点的火车。
  B：I think you'll make it if we don't get _____ in a traffic _____.

我想,如果我们不碰上交通阻塞,你是可以赶到的。

B: This is it. That's $9.15, please.
到了。请付9元1角5分。

A: Here.
给你。

Dialogue 4.

A: The Hilton hotel, please. I have a 10:30 _____.
请到希尔顿旅馆,10点半我有一个约会。

B: You'll be there in plenty of time.
你可以很方便地到达那里。

B: Here we are. $8.50, please.
我们到了。请付8元5角。

A: Thank you. Here's $10:00. Keep the _____.
谢谢你。这是10元,不用找了。

Part 3. Reading Activity:

A boy with a Mission

In 1945, a 12-year-old boy saw something in a shop window that set his heart racing. But the price-five dollars-was far beyond Reuben Earle's means. Five dollars would buy almost a week's groceries for his family.

Reuben couldn't ask his father for the money. Everything Mark Earle made through fishing in Bay Roberts, Newfoundland, Canada. Reuben's mother, Dora, stretched like elastic to feed clothe their five children.

Nevertheless, he opened the shop's weathered door and went inside. Standing proud and straight in his flour-sack shirt and washed-out trousers, he told the shop keeper what he wanted, adding, "but I don't have the money right now. Can you please hold it for me for some time?"

"I'll try," the shopkeeper smiled. "Folks around here don't usually have that kind of money to spend on things. It should keep for a while."

Reuben respectfully touched his worn cap and walked out into the sunlight with the bay rippling in a freshening wind. There was purpose in his loping stride. He would raise the five dollars and not tell anybody.

Hearing the sound of hammering from a side street, Reuben had an idea.

He ran towards the sound and stopped at a construction site. People built their own homes in Bay Roberts, using nails purchased in Hessian sacks from a local factory. Sometimes the sacks were discarded in the flurry of building, and Reuben knew he could sell them back to the factory for five cents a piece.

211

That day he found two sacks which he took to the rambling wooden factory and sold to the man in charge of packing nails.

The boy's hand tightly clutched the five-cent pieces as he ran the two kilometres home.

Near his house stood the ancient barn that housed the family's goats and chickens. Reuben found a rusty baking soda tin and dropped his coins inside. Then he climbed into the loft of the barn and hid the tin beneath a pile of sweet smelling hay.

It was dinner time when Reuben got home. His father sat at the big kitchen table, working on a fishing net. Dora was at the kitchen stove, ready to serve dinner as Reuben took his place at the table.

He looked at his mother and smiled. Sunlight from the window gilded her shoulder-length blonde hair. Slim and beautiful, she was the centre of the home, the glue that held it together.

Her chores were never-ending. Sewing clothes for her family on the old Singer treadle machine, cooking meals and baking bread, planting and tending a vegetable garden, milking the goats and scrubbing soiled clothes on a washboard. But she was happy. Her family and their well being were her highest priority.

Every day after chores and school, Reuben scoured the town, collecting the Hessian nail bags. On the day the two-room school closed for the summer, no student was more delighted than Reuben. Now he would have more time for his mission.

All summer long, despite chores at home-weeding and watering the garden, cutting wood and fetching water-Reuben kept to his secret task.

Then all too soon the garden was harvested, the vegetables canned and stored, and the school reopened. Soon the leaves fell and the winds blew cold and gusty from the bay. Reuben wandered the streets, diligently searching for his Hessian treasures.

Often he was cold, tired and hungry, but the thought of the object in the shop window sustained him. Sometimes his mother would ask: "Reuben, where were you? We were waiting for you to have dinner."

"Playing, Mum. Sorry."

Dora would look at his face and shake her head. Boys.

Finally spring burst into glorious green and Reuben's spirits erupted. The time had come! He ran into the barn, climbed to the hayloft and uncovered the tin can. He poured the coins out and began to count.

Then he counted again. He needed 20 cents more. Could there be any sacks left where in town? He had to find four and sell them before the day ended.

Reuben ran down Water Street.

The shadows were lengthening when Reuben arrived at the factory. The sack buyer was bout to lock up.

"Mister! Please don't close up yet." The man turned and saw Reuben, dirty and sweat stained.

"Come back tomorrow, boy."

"Please, Mister. I have to sell the sacks now-please." The man heard a tremor in Reuben's voice and could tell he was close to tears.

"Why do you need this money so badly?"

"It's a secret."

The man took the sacks, reached into his pocket and put four coins in Reuben's hand. Reuben murmured a thank you and ran home.

Then, clutching the tin can, he headed for the shop.

"I have the money," he solemnly told the owner.

The man went to the window and retrieved Reuben's treasure.

He wiped the dust off and gently wrapped it in brown paper. Then he placed the parcel in Reuben's hands.

Racing home, Reuben burst through the front door. His mother was scrubbing the kitchen stove. "Here, Mum! Here!" Reuben exclaimed as he ran to her side. He placed a small box in her work-roughened band.

She unwrapped it carefully, to save the paper. A blue-velvet jewel box appeared. Dora lifted the lid, tears beginning to blur her vision.

In gold lettering on a small, almond-shaped brooch was the word Mother.

It was Mother's Day, 1946.

Dora had never received such a gift; she had no finery except her wedding ring. Speechless, she smiled radiantly and gathered her son into her arms.

参考译文：

一个男孩的心愿

1945年,12岁的男孩鲁本在一家商店橱窗里看到一样令他动心的东西,但那5美元的价钱远远超出了鲁本·厄尔的支付能力。5美元几乎是他家里一星期饭食的开销。

鲁本不能向父亲要钱。全家就靠父亲马克·厄尔在加拿大纽芬兰罗伯茨湾捕鱼维持生计,母亲多拉也终日为他们5个孩子的衣食操劳。

尽管如此,鲁本还是推开了商店那扇久经风雨的门走了进去。他穿着面粉袋改做的衬衫和洗得褪了色的裤子,自豪地站得笔直,告诉店主他想要的东西,并说:"我现在还没有钱买它,能请您为我留一段时间吗?"

"我尽量吧,"店主微笑着说道。"这儿的人一般不花钱买这种东西,一时半会儿卖不出去。"

鲁本有礼貌地碰了碰他的破帽子,走出店外,沐浴在阳光下。清新的微风吹得罗伯茨湾的海水泛起阵阵涟漪。鲁本有所企盼地迈着大步。他要攒足那5美元,而且不告诉任何人。

听到小街传来的铁锤声,鲁本有了主意。他顺着那声音跑过去,来到一处建筑工地。罗伯茨湾的人喜欢自建房屋,用的钉子是从本地一家工厂买的,都装在麻袋里。有时干活一忙乱,麻袋就被随手丢弃了,而鲁本知道工厂按5分钱一个回收这种麻袋。

那天,他找了两条麻袋,拿到杂乱的木建筑构件工厂,卖给了负责钉子装袋的人。

那孩子紧紧地攥着那两个5分的硬币,跑了两公里回家。

他家房子附近有个古老的谷仓,里面圈着山羊和小鸡。鲁本在那里找到一个生锈的小苏打铁罐,并把两枚硬币放了进去。然后,他爬上谷仓的阁楼,把钱罐藏在一堆散发出甜香味的干草下面。

晚饭时分,鲁本跨进家门。父亲正坐在厨房大饭桌旁摆弄渔网,母亲多拉在厨房炉边忙碌着,准备开饭。鲁本就在桌旁坐下了。

他微笑地看着妈妈。窗户透进的些许夕阳将她亚麻色的披肩长发染成了金色。修长、漂亮的母亲是这个家的中心,是凝聚这个家所有成员的粘合剂。母亲的家务活永远也没个完。她要在那台旧的脚踏缝纫机上为家人缝缝补补;要做饭和烤面包;要种草和照看菜园;要挤羊奶;还要用洗衣搓洗衣服。可母亲是快乐的,家人和他们的幸福在她心目中是最重要的。

每天放学,做完家务事后,鲁本就在镇上搜寻和收集装钉子的麻袋。只有两间教室的学校开始放暑假那天,鲁本比谁都高兴。因为现在他有更多时间完成他的任务了。

整整一个夏天,鲁本除了干家务——给菜园锄草、浇水、砍柴和打水外,始终为完成他那秘密使命而不懈努力。

时间飞逝,转眼菜园收获季节来到,蔬菜装罐腌制后储藏起来,学校也重新开学了。不久,树叶纷纷飘零,海湾刮来阵阵寒风。鲁本在街头四处逛荡,努力寻找着被他视为宝物的麻袋。

他经常又冷又累又饿,但是一想到商店橱窗里的那件东西,他就能坚持下去。有时妈妈会问:"鲁本,你上哪儿啦?我们等你吃晚饭呢!"

"玩去啦,妈妈。对不起。"

多拉总会瞧着他的脸,无奈地摇摇头,心想男孩究竟是男孩。

春天终于来了,大地一下子变得一片绿油油,鲁本的精神也随之振奋起来。是时候了!他跑到谷仓,爬上草垛,打开铁罐,倒出所有硬币清点起来。

他又数一遍,还差20美分。镇上还会有丢弃的麻袋吗?他必须在傍晚前找到4条去卖掉。

鲁本沿着沃特街走着。

天色渐暗,影子越拉越长,鲁本来到了工厂。收购麻袋的人正要锁门。

"先生!请先不要关门。"那人转过身来,看到了脏兮兮、汗涔涔的鲁本。

"明天再来吧,孩子。"

"求您了,先生,我必须现在把麻袋卖掉——求您啦。"那人听出了鲁本声音中的微颤,知道他快要哭了。

"你为什么这么急着要这点钱?"

"这是个秘密。"

那人接过麻袋,手伸进口袋,掏出4个硬币放在鲁本手里。鲁本轻声说了声"谢谢"就往回跑。之后,他紧紧抱住钱罐,直奔那商店。

"我有钱啦!"他一本正经地告诉店主。

店主走向橱窗,取出鲁本梦寐以求的东西。

他掸去灰尘,用棕色厚纸把东西小心包好。然后,他把这个小包放在鲁本手中。

鲁本一路跑回家,冲进前门。妈妈正在厨房擦洗炉子。"瞧,妈妈!瞧!"鲁本一边跑向她一边大叫着。他把一个小盒子放在她因劳作而粗糙的手上。为了省下那种包装纸,她小心翼翼地把它拆开。一个蓝色天鹅绒的首饰盒映入眼帘。多拉打开盒盖,泪水顿时模糊了双眼。

在一个小巧的扁桃状胸针上刻着金字:母亲。那是1946年的母亲节。

多拉从未收到过这样的礼物;除了结婚戒指外,她没有别的饰物。她一时说不出话来,脸上洋溢着喜色,笑着把儿子揽入怀中。

Part 4. Practical Writing

海报启事范例

例1: Serial Lectures (1)

Subject: The Comprehension and Translation of Advertisements
Speaker: Professor Zhou Fangzhu from the Dept. of Foreign Language & Literature
Time: At 7:00 p.m., Tuesday, Oct. 17, 1995
Place: Room No. 410, Wenxilou Building
Sponser: The Department of Foreign Language & Literature and the Scientific Research Office

October 12, 1995

例2: English Speech Contest

Hosted by the Student Union of FLD (The Department of Foreign Language & Literature), the 2nd English Speech Contest will be held in the classroom No. 410 of Wenxilou Building at 7:00 p.m., Thursday, October30, 1992.

All are cordially welcome.

The Student Union
The Dept. of FLD
Anhui University
October 28, 1992

例3：Contributions Wanted

In celebration of the fortieth aniversary of the founding of the People's Republic of China, this magazine, China Youth, has decided to publish a special issue for high school students with the title "I love My Motherland". Teachers, students, soldiers, cadres and workers are warmly welcome to send in their contributions in whatover form and style.

Deadline for such contributions will be on July 31, 1989. Contributions should be sent directly to the editiorial board of the magazine.

The Editorial Board
China Youth, Beijing 100842
April 4, 1989

Unit 10. Improvements in Efficiency

Part 1. Text

Improvements in Efficiency

Improvements in efficiency may involve identifying and evaluating ways to reduce energy consumption, while maintaining or even improving services.

Methods of reducing costs might include:

Fuel substitution

    Same fuel, different appliance

    Same fuel, different method

    Shorter running times

    Improved controls

    Rescheduling

    Better procedures

    Revised level of service-matched to that required for the task

    Elimination of the activity (100% saving).

    Tariff changes

Reducing the building's demand for services could be achieved by changing the:

    use of space, or zoning in the building

    time of use

    insulation, shading, windows, etc.

Of course, the energy manager should be mindful of the most important "part" of any building: the PEOPLE who occupy it.

THE SAVING METHODS

Fuel Substitution

Fuels vary in price, according to factors such as supply and demand, cost of conversion or delivery, and government regulations. Pick the most appropriate, cheapest, convenient fuel for the purpose, with an eye to future trends in cost and supply issues.

Same Fuel, Different Appliance

Pursue the correct sizing of equipment for the intended duty. Bear in mind that both under-sizing and over-sizing waste energy.

Efficiencies vary between apparently similar models, and price is certainly not the best guide.

Lighting, for example, offers many options for providing appropriate levels of service, while controlling costs, by considering:
- more efficient lamps
- more efficient light fittings, including reflectors
- task lighting

Same Fuel, Different Method

Heating, for example, can be effected by:
- Heat pumping
- Radiant heating
- Localized heating
- Combined heat and power plants

Shorter Running Time

This may sound obvious, but there are many causes of excessive running times, and even more possible solutions. For example, many buildings use the same equipment for comfort heating and hot water, so a large boiler must operate all year just to provide hot water for hand washing, etc. Providing a small, separate, heater for hot water would overcome this problem.

Often, more efficient controls can be used to reduce the running time of equipment, eg:
- Calendar time-switches
- Optimal start time-switches
- Timers for some functions; for example switched ON manually, OFF automatically
- Lighting   Occupancy sensing controls
              Daylight switching
              Timers (limited safe applications). 51, 739
              Localized switching

Improved Controls

Other examples of improved controls include thermostatic controls that are better at matching plant operation to the demand imposed by the weather and internal equipment.

These controls are intended to minimize the heating-fighting-cooling syndrome, as well as reducing operating times.

Rescheduling

Automatic (or manual) rescheduling of some operations can reduce costs by:
- using cheaper energy, depending on the tariff structure,
- reducing peak electrical or gas demand, depending on tariff,
- using a more efficient or appropriate appliance.

Better Procedures

Changes to routines may reduce operating costs. Consider for instance whether:

the cleaning can be done at a different time, or in less time.

the office "switch-on" routine adds to office efficiency.

Revised Levels of Service

There is no point in providing a level of service efficiently, if that level of service is simply not required. In some cases, providing too "high" a level of service can actually reduce comfort and/or utility, as well as increasing energy and maintenance costs. For example:

Over-cooling in the summer or over-heating in the winter, when most people dress appropriately for the conditions. This is particularly so in public buildings, such as shops, and the public sections of government and other buildings.

Lighting. Different tasks require different levels of illumination. There is no benefit in providing a higher level than is really needed.

Elimination of the Activity

Often, activities in a building change, and a service which was once provided is now no longer required. It is easy to overlook this when there are major changes occurring. For example, an office area may be converted to a storage area which does not required air-conditioning or perhaps the previous high level of lighting.

Occupancy switching of the lights in empty rooms, and daylight switching of external and perimeter lighting are two examples of eliminating unnecessary activities, already mentioned.

Tariff Changes

This method of reducing costs has deliberately been placed at the end of this rather long list. Some people only look at tariffs, and think that there is nothing else of significance which can reduce energy costs. While this approach may be lucrative for "tariff analysts", it can be VERY expensive in the long run depending upon the energy used. So BEWARE!

参考译文：

提高效率的措施

提高效率会涉及到如何鉴定和评估既能降低能耗，又能保持甚至提高服务水平的方法措施。降低成本的方法可能包括：

替换燃料

同样的燃料，使用不同的应用设备

同样的燃料，不同的使用方法

缩短运转时间

改进控制方式

调整时间表

优化操作规程

修订服务标准—与工作任务的需求相匹配

消除不必要的开支

税率的调整

要想减少建筑对于服务的需求,可以考虑调整:

空间的利用,建筑物的分区管理

合理利用时间

隔离物,遮蔽,窗户,等等。

当然,能源管理者应当意识到建筑物中最重要的部分——人,即建筑物的拥有者.

节能措施

替换燃料

各种燃料价格上的不同,取决于如下因素:供求关系,运输费用,政府的相关政策。挑选符合要求的最适合的、最便宜的、使用最方便的燃料,同时要考虑成本和能源问题的未来的发展趋势。

同样的燃料,不同的应用设备

按照预期的要求,选择正确的使用设备,要记住,无论设备过大或过小都是浪费。型号相同但效率可能不同,价格肯定不是最好的指南。

例如照明,可选择许多不同的方案以提供适合的服务,同时要考虑控制成本:

- 使用效率更高的灯具;
- 使用效率更高的电灯附件,包括反射物;
- 按需设定额定和工作参数。

同样的燃料,不同的使用方法

例如,供热可通过下列方法获得:

- 加热泵送热;
- 辐射送热;
- 局部供热;
- 综合供热和发电厂供热。

缩短运转时间

听起来可能很浅显,但有许多运转时间过长的情况,也有许多可以解决问题的方法。例如,许多建筑物取暖和给水加热都用同样的设备,所以大型的锅炉只为提供洗手的热水也必须全年运转,等等。提供一个小型的、分离式的加热器来供应热水将能克服这个问题。

通常使用更有效的控制元件以缩短设备的运转时间,例如:

- 日历定时开关;
- 优化启动定时开关;
- 选用具备一定功能的定时器,例如手动开,自动关的开关装置。

照明装置——感应物体存在的传感器

　　　　——供白天使用的开关

　　　　——定时器(有限的安全装置)

　　　　——局部开关装置

改进控制方式

改进控制方式的其他的例子包括温控装置,它能根据天气和内部设备的要求更好地控制设施的运行。

这些控制装置的使用是为了减少冷热不均及温度不稳定的矛盾,也为了减少操作时间。

重新调整计划表(程序表、时间表)

某些自动的(或人工的)调整可以通过如下三个方面降低成本:
- 使用更经济的能源,这要取决于税制结构;
- 降低高峰期对用电量或用气量的要求,这要取决于税率;

使用更有效或更适合的设备。

优化程序

日常工作方面所做的必要的调整也可以降低操作成本。例如可考虑如下因素:
- 清洁工作是否能在不同的时间或用更少的时间来进行。
- 办公室日常工作的处理是否增进办公效率。

修订服务标准

如果服务标准不是必需的,那么提供一个再有效的服务标准也是毫无意义。在某些情况下,提供过高的服务标准实际上只能降低舒适度和/或实用性,也会浪费能源和增加维修成本。例如:

当大多数人们的穿着适合于环境温度时,(如果服务标准过高,就会出现)在夏天过冷或冬天过热的情况。特别是在公共建筑里尤会如此,例如商店和政府的对外窗口部门以及其他建筑。

照明,不同的工作任务需要不同的照明度标准。如果提供比实际需要更高的照明标准则毫无意义。

消除不必要的开支

通常情况下,一个建筑物里的变化可能很频繁,以前曾经提供的服务现在可能不再需要了。当出现一些重大变化时很容易体会到这一点。例如:一个办公区域可能被变成一个存储区,这样就不再需要空调或以前也许是很高的照明标准。

空屋子照明,白天的室外照明及周边照明是消除不必要开支的两个极端例子,这在前面已经提过。

税率的调整

这种降低成本的方法被有意列在上述相当长的条目最后。因为一些人们只看税款,认为其他降低能源成本的举措没什么意义,这种方法对"税率分析家"来说可能颇有吸引力,但从长远角度来说,它的代价是相当高的,这取决于使用的能源。因此,对这种方法要谨慎为妙。

Vocabulary
单词表:

322.	improvement	[im'pru:vmənt]	n. 改进,改良,增进;改进措施
323.	efficiency	[i'fiʃənsi]	n. 效率,功效,效能,实力
324.	identify	[ai'dentifai]	vt. 认为……一致;识别,鉴定
325.	evaluate	[i'væijueit]	vt. 评价,估……的价
326.	maintain	[men'tein]	vt. 维持,保持;维修,保养
327.	substitution	[ˌsʌbsti'tju:ʃən]	n. 代替,替换
328.	appliance	[ə'plaiəns]	n. 应用,适用;用具,装置;器械

329.	schedule	['skedʒul]	vt. 将……列表,将……列入计划表;安排
330.	procedure	[prə'si:dʒə]	n. 过程,步骤;程序;礼节
331.	revise	[ri'vaiz]	vt. 修订,校订;修改;对……重新分类
332.	elimination	[i,limi'neiʃən]	n. 排除,消除,消灭
333.	activity	[æk'tiviti]	n. 活动性,能动性,敏捷,活跃;活动
334.	saving	['seiviŋ]	n. 节约,节俭;储蓄(金),存款
335.	insulation	[,insju'leiʃən]	n. 隔离,孤立,绝缘,绝热
336.	mindful	['maindful]	a. 留心的,注意的,记住的,不忘的
337.	conversion	[kən'və:ʃən]	n. 变换,转化;更换
338.	delivery	[di'livəri]	n. 交付,交货;投递,传送;发出;释放
339.	issue	['isju:]	n. 流出,放出;出口;结果,结局;发行;问题,争端(土地.地产等的)收益
340.	diesel	['di:zəl]	n. 内燃机,柴油机; a. 柴油发电机的
341.	pursue	[pə'sju:]	vt. 追赶,追击;追随,跟随;追求,寻求;进行,从事;vi. 追赶;继续进行
342.	size	[saiz]	vt. 依一定的尺寸制造. n. 规模,尺寸
343.	sizing	['saiziŋ]	n. 填料,上胶,上浆
344.	intended	[in'tendid]	a. 打算中的,预期的;故意的,有意的
345.	duty	['dju:ti]	n. (机器在给定条件下所做的)功,能率,负载,工作状态;责任,义务
346.	apparently	[ə'pærəntli]	ad. 明显地,显而易见地;表面上地,貌似地,外观上地
347.	lighting	['laitiŋ]	n. 照明,照明设备;点火,发火;(画面的)明暗分布
348.	option	['ɔpʃən]	n. 选择,选择权;选择自由;(供)选择的事物;在规定时间内要求履行合同的特权;被保险人对赔款方式的选择权
349.	pump	[pʌmp]	vt. 用抽机抽液体;用打气筒打气;盘问,追问;倾注;使疲惫;使劲地握手(pumping 抽水,泵送)
350.	radiant	['reidjənt]	a. 放射的,辐射的;发出辐射热的;喜悦的;光辉灿烂的
351.	localize	['ləukəlaiz]	vt. 集中,使限制于局部
352.	power plant		发电站,发电厂;(机动车辆等的)动力设备
353.	excessive	[ik'sesiv]	a. 过多的,过分的,极度的
354.	boiler	['bɔilə]	n. 锅炉,热水贮槽;煮器
355.	calendar	['kælində]	vt. 把……列入表中;(为文件等)作排列,分类和索引
356.	timer	['taimə]	n. 定时器,自动按时操作装置;跑表,计时员

357. occupancy	[ˈɔkjupənsi]	n.	占有,占用,居住;占有期间;建筑物的被占用部分;占有率
358. sensing	[ˈsensiŋ]	n.	测向,偏航显示
359. thermostatic	[ˌθəːməsˈtætik]	a.	恒温的;(灭火设备等)根据温度自动启动的
360. impose	[imˈpouz]	vi.	施影响;利用;欺骗;vt. 征税;把……强加
361. syndrome	[ˈsindroum]	n.	同时存在的事物
362. intend	[inˈtend]	vt.	打算使……成为;意思是;想要
363. peak	[piːk]	a.	最高的,高峰的;v. 达到高峰
364. routine	[ruːˈtiːn]	n.	日常工作,惯例;程序 a. 日常的
365. point	[pɔint]	n.	意义,目的,用途;论点;地点;特征
366. comfort	[ˈkʌmfət]	n.	舒适,安逸;安慰;使生活舒适的事物;盖被
367. utility	[juːˈtiliti]	n.	实用,效用;有用的东西;公用事业
		a.	实用的;有多种用途的
368. illumination	[iˌljuːmiˈneiʃən]	n.	照明,照明度;解释;灯饰
369. previous	[ˈpriːvjəs]	a.	以前的;过早的
370. occupancy	[ˈɔkjupənsi]	n.	占有;被占用的建筑物;占有率
371. external	[eksˈtəːnl]	a.	外部的;客观的;外用的;表面的;外国的
372. perimeter	[pəˈrimitə]	n.	周边,周长;(兵营或工事外的)环形防线
373. deliberately	[diˈlibəritli]	ad.	审慎地,故意地;蓄意地
374. significance	[sigˈnifikəns]	n.	意义,意味;重要性,重大
375. lucrative	[ˈljuːkrətiv]	a.	有利的,生利的,赚钱的;值得作为目标的
376. beware	[biˈwɛə]	vt.	(用于祈使句,或与 must, should 等连用)谨防,当心

Useful Expressions

as well as   也,又,和,同样
power plant   发电站,发电厂;(机动车辆等的)动力设备
of course   当然
at the time of   在……的时候
according to   根据,按照
such as   如同,例如,诸如……之类的
for the purpose of   为了……的目的,为了……起见
with an eye to   留心看着,注意,留神
bear in mind   把……记在心里,牢记
both ... and ...   既是……又是……;不但……而且……;……和……两者都……
for example   例如
add to   增加;增进
no point in doing sth.   做某事毫无意义
in some cases   在某些情况下

depend on（或 upon） 依靠；依赖；取决于
no longer 不再（＝not any longer）
at the end of 在……末端；在……最后；到……尽头

Notes
备注：

1. Reducing the building's demand for services could be achieved by changing the use of space, or zoning in the building... 要想降低建筑物对于服务的需求，可以做如下改变：空间的利用，或在建筑物里分区管理……

在句中，could be achieved 是含有情态动词的被动语态，例如：
These exercises should be done by the students themselves.
这些练习应该由学生们自己来做。
Those magazines may be put on the floor.
那些杂志可以放在地板上。
The man must be sent to hospital at once.
那个人必须立刻送到医院去。

2. Of course, the energy manager should be mindful of the most important "part" of any building: the PEOPLE who occupy it. 当然，能源管理者应当意识到任何建筑物中最重要的部分——人，拥有并居于其中的人。

在句中，the most important 是形容词 important 的最高级，多音节形容词在其前面加 most 构成最高级，形容词最高级前要加定冠词 the，例如：
He was (much) the most handsome of the Smith boys.
他是史密斯家的男孩中最帅的。
who occupy it 是由关系代词 who 引导的定语从句，修饰前面的名词 PEOPLE。
例如：
He is the person who is going to give a concert on the century square.
他是那个要在世纪广场上举行音乐会的人。

3. Pick the most appropriate, cheapest, convenient fuel for the purpose, with an eye to future trends in cost and supply issues. 挑选符合要求的最适合的、最便宜的、使用最方便的燃料，同时要考虑成本和供应问题的未来的发展趋势。

本句是一个祈使句。祈使句是表示命令、要求、请求等的句子，谓语动词用动词原形，可分为第二人称祈使句、第一人称祈使句和第三人称祈使句三种。本句是一个第二人称祈使句。
例如：
Please calm yourself!
请镇静！（第二人称祈使句）
Let each man decide for himself!
让每个人自己做决定。（第三人称祈使句）
Let us help you somehow. 让我们怎么帮帮你。
（第一人称祈使句）

4. Other examples of improved controls include thermostatic controls that are better

at matching plant operation to the demand imposed by the weather and internal equipment. 改进控制方式的其他的例子包括温控装置,它能更好地根据受天气和内部设备影响的操作要求来配合对设施的控制操作。

在句中,that are better at matching plant operation to the demand imposed by the weather and internal equipment 是由关系代词 that 引导的定语从句,修饰前面的名词 controls. 而 that 在从句中用做主语。例如:

He is the famous scientist that will give us a lecture next Thursday.
他是下周四将要给我们做报告的那个著名的科学家。

5. ... using cheaper energy, depending on the tariff structure, reducing peak electrical or gas demand, depending on tariff, using a more efficient or appropriate appliance. 使用更经济的能源,这要取决于税制结构,降低高峰期对用电量或用气量的要求,这要取决于税率,使用更有效或更适合的设备。

在句中,cheaper 和 more efficient 都是形容词的比较级。绝大多数单音节形容词是用加-er 构成比较级;多音节形容词是用在前面加 more 构成比较级。例如:

Days are longer in summer than in winter.
夏天白天比冬天长。
Cities are becoming more and more crowded as the population is increasing.
伴随着人口的增加,城市变得越来越拥挤。

6. Often, activities in a building change, and a service which was once provided is now no longer required. 通常情况下,一个建筑物里的变化可能很频繁,以前曾经提供的服务现在可能不再需要了。

在句中,which was once provided 是由关系代词 which 引导的定语从句,修饰前面的名词 service,而 which 在从句中用做主语。例如:

It is a problem which needs very careful consideration.
这是一个需要非常认真考虑的问题。

For example, an office area may be converted to a storage area which does not required air-conditioning or perhaps the previous high level of lighting.
例如,一个办公区域可能被变成一个存储区,这样就不再需要空调或以前也许是很高的照明标准。

7. Occupancy switching of the lights in empty rooms, and daylight switching of external and perimeter lighting are two examples of eliminating unnecessary activities, already mentioned. 在空屋与照明,白天的室外照明和周边照明是两个减少不必要开支的典型例子,这在前面已经提过。

在句中,Occupancy switching of the lights in empty rooms, and daylight switching of external and perimeter lighting 是整个句子的主语,它是由 and 连接的两个并列句构成的。

8. Some people only look at tariffs, and think that there is nothing else of significance which can reduce energy costs. 因为一些人们只看到了税款,就认为没有什么别的重大举措能降低能源成本。

在句中,and 连接了两个并列谓语 look at tariffs 和 think that there is nothing else of significance which can reduce energy costs; that 引导的是宾语从句,做及物动词 think 的宾语。

例如:

He promised me that he wouldn't do that again.

他向我保证再也不干那事了。

在宾语从句中,which can reduce energy costs 是由关系代词 which 引导的定语从句,修饰前面的名词 significance。

Ⅰ. Exercises for the text 课文练习:

(Ⅰ) Judge the following sentences are True or False according to the content of the text.

1. Improvements in efficiency may involve identifying and evaluating ways to reduce energy consumption, while only maintaining.
2. Of course, the energy manager should be mindful of the most important "part" of any building: the people who occupy it.
3. Pick the most appropriate, expensive, convenient fuel for the purpose, with an eye to future trends in cost and supply issues.
4. Many buildings use the same equipment for comfort heating and hot water, so a large boiler must operate all year just to provide hot water for hand washing, etc. Providing a small, separate, heater for hot water would overcome this problem.
5. Often, more efficient controls can be used to reduce the running time of equipment, eg: calendar time-switches ,optimal start time-switches, timers for some functions; - for example switched ON manually, OFF automatically.
6. Methods of reducing costs might not include: tariff changes.
7. Reducing the building's demand for maintenance could be achieved by changing the use of space, or zoning in the building.
8. Efficiencies vary between apparently similar models, and price is certainly not the best guide.
9. More efficient controls can not be used to reduce the running time of equipment.
10. There is no point in providing a level of service efficiently, if that level of service is simply not required.

(Ⅱ) Match the English words with their Chinese translations,choose the appropriate words to complete the sentences below and translate them into Chinese.(将下列英语单词与其中文意思相匹配,选择合适的词将下列句子补充完整并译成中文。)

    1. delivery   a. 应用,适用;用具,装置;器械
    2. pursue   b. 改进,改良,增进;改进措施
    3. issue   c. 效率,功效,效能,实力
    4. identify   d. 代替,替换
    5. improvement   e. 节约,节俭;储蓄(金),存款
    6. revise   f. 留心的,注意的,记住的,不忘的
    7. schedule   g. 修订,校订;修改;对……重新分类

8. substitution   h. 交付,交货;投递,传送;发出;释放
9. saving   i. 流出,放出;出口;结果,结局;发行;问题,争端(土地.
                               地产等的)收益
10. efficiency   j. 认为……一致;识别,鉴定
11. appliance   k. 将……列表,将……列入计划表;安排
12. mindful   l. 追赶,追击;追随,跟随;追求,寻求;进行,从事;vi. 追
                               赶;继续进行
13. intend   m. 施影响;利用;欺骗;vt. 征税;把……强加
14. point   n. 意义,目的,用途;论点;地点;特征
15. Impose   o. (用于祈使句,或与 must, should 等连用)谨防,当心
16. beware   p. 打算使……成为;意思是;想要
17. peak   q. 同时存在的事物
18. Syndrome   r. 舒适,安逸;安慰;使生活舒适的事物;盖被
19. comfort   s. 以前的;过早的
20. Previous   t. 最高的,高峰的;v. 达到高峰

1. Much _____ has been made in the safety devices of the factory.
2. He lives in an _____ apartment.
3. We have always _____ the revolutionary struggle of the world's people with our own.
4. I want the _____ of tea for coffee.
5. This is an _____ for opening cans.
6. _____ your receipts and expenditures.
7. He has _____ his opinions of me.
8. _____ is getting.
9. Be _____ of your duty.
10. There are three _____ every day.
11. This is the latest (November) _____ of China Reconstructs.
12. Illness _____ him till his death.
13. I am not to be _____ upon.
14. This word possesses a _____ of meanings.
15. Our dictionary is _____ for students.
16. Production _____ from July to September.
17. There is no _____ in doing so.
18. Be of good _____.
19. He was a little too _____ in making the decision.
20. _____ (of) dangers!

(Ⅲ) **Choose the best answer**(选择最佳答案)
1. Be careful next time,_____?
   a. don't you   b. are you   c. will you   d. aren't you

2. Mary is the _____ of the four girls in the family. And she is the _____.
   a. pretty...diligent   b. prettier...more diligent
   c. prettiest...most diligent   d. most pretty...most diligent
3. Let's do the cleaning right after class, _____?
   a. will you   b. shall we   c. do you   d. can we
4. Water _____ into ice.
   a. can be changed   b. can change
   c. change   d. changes
5. The books in the reading-room _____ away.
   a. must not take   b. must not be taken
   c. must take   d. must be taken
6. He is a person _____ is always kind to everybody around him.
   a. who   b. which   c. what   d. whom
7. Cars _____ into the park.
   a. can not be driven   b. can be driven
   c. can drive   d. can not drive
8. _____ to take medicine as the doctor told yesterday.
   a. Not forget   b. Not to forget
   c. Don't forget   d. forget not
9. It is _____ than all the other mountains in Europe. It is the _____ in Europe.
   a. high...high   b. higher...higher
   c. highest...highest   d. higher...highest
10. She _____ in the park.
    a. can not see   b. not see
    c. can not be seen   d. don't see
11. The new rules made the selection even _____, so his mind was much _____.
    a. possible...easy   b. more possible...easier
    c. more possible...more easier   d. possibler...easier
12. Judy is _____ than Mary. She is the _____ of the children.
    a. old...old   b. older...older
    c. older...oldest   d. oldest...oldest
13. The concert has already begun. You should have come a little bit _____.
    a. early   b. much earlier   c. more earlier   d. earlier
14. There is no benefit in providing a _____ level than is really needed.
    a. higher   b. high   c. highest   d. more higher
15. This is the only English-Chinese dictionary _____ could be found in the teachers' reading-room.
    a. what   b. which   c. it   d. that
16. She keeps her keys and money in the handbag _____ she takes with her everywhere.

228

a. which   b. so   c. therefore   d. when

17. The manager invited me here. Could you tell me _____, please?
    a. his office where is
    b. where his office is
    c. where is his office
    d. his office is where

(Ⅳ) Translation:

Translate the following Chinese into English:

1. 在效率方面的改进措施可能包括维修或改进服务时所降低的能量消耗的鉴定和评价方式。

2. 当然,能源管理者应当意识到任何建筑物中最重要的部分——人,拥有并居于其中的人。

3. 各种燃料价格上的变化,要考虑如下因素:供与求,变换燃料或交货的成本,政府的相关政策。

4. 按照预期的负载寻求设备正确的填入量。

5. 许多建筑物取暖和给水加热都用同样的设备,所以大型的锅炉只为提供洗手的热水也必须全年运转。

6. 挑选符合要求的最适合的、最便宜的、使用最方便的燃料,同时要考虑成本和供应收益的未来的发展趋势。

7. 表面上相似的东西之间效率可能不同,价格肯定不是最好的指南。

8. 提供一个小型的、分离式的加热器来供应热水将能克服这个问题。

9. 日常工作方面所做的必要的调整也可以降低操作成本。

10. 在长期经营的依靠能源的领域税款可能是非常昂贵的,而这种"税款分析"的方法可能是非常有利的。

(Ⅴ) Extra Reading Activity:

Read the following passage and choose the best answer to complete each of the statements that follow.

CONTROLLING ENERGY COSTS

INTRODUCTION

Energy Management could be said to represent one of the best investments available to today's property owners and managers. The importance of energy efficiency in the market is increasing NOW, as:

~ energy prices rise
~ tenants become more sophisticated
~ occupancy rates decrease, and
~ environmental concerns and regulations increase
~ market rentals fall or remain at a relatively low level

WHAT IS ENERGY MANAGEMENT?

A few common myths regarding energy management must be dispelled in order to reap the benefits it has to offer.

Energy management is NOT about finding ways to reduce creature comforts; having people sitting in a cold dark room, drinking warm beer.

Energy Management could be said to enable the Property Manager to do more with less, by using the most efficient and appropriate, equipment, methods, and fuels. A Property Manager who applies the principles of energy management can "out-perform" those who do not.

Reducing energy costs can dramatically improve profits, and thereby increase the capital value of the building.

IMPROVING INVESTMENTS WITH ENERGY MANAGEMENT
How it Works - Investment Performance

Investment Performance = (the return)/inputs

$$= \frac{\text{Rent} + \text{capital gains} + \text{prestige}}{\text{Outgoings} + \text{maintenance} + \text{time} + \text{managerial effort}}$$

To maximize the investment performance, we clearly need to maximize the top line, while minimizing the bottom line. Rent will be a function of the building, the market, and the outgoings (tenants will not be keen to pay even market rents if the outgoings are higher than the market average).

OUTGOINGS, are about: 45% fixed, eg. land tax, Water Board, etc

55% manageable, eg. energy, maintenance

ENERGY COSTS account for approximately: 33% of the owners outgoings

or to put it another way

60% of the manageable costs

Size of the Investment Opportunity

You will see therefore that there is scope to reduce energy costs by up to 40%, with a 40% return in this area on investment. This gives an indication of the size of the benefit available, but this is only a part of the reason that energy management offers one of the best investments available.

The Best Investment Available

How could anyone in their right mind claim that energy management offers one of the best investments available to most Property Managers?

Energy management is one of the best investments available because:

* of the confidence of receiving a return. As long as the building continues to operate, the savings will be realised. Compare this to an investment in a refurbishment, promotion, or similarly speculative investment where a return depends upon a successful "product" and market acceptance and possible continued expenditure to provide consistent returns.

* it yields a very high Nett Present Value. The high confidence level in the investment means that a low discount rate can be applied. The very high Nett Present Values result from the:

low discount rate.

high return on investment (typically 50%~100%) and long life (often the life of the building) of energy management opportunities.

* of the opportunity to multiply your money ten-fold in six months. In simple terms, if a building is worth about 15 times its annual earning potential, a reduction in energy costs of $70,000 per year will add $70,000 to the annual profit a building returns to its owner, thus increasing its market value by over $1,000,000. If the simple payback period is 17 months, the investment required is about $100,000 for an increase in nett present value of $1,000,000.

Business Competitiveness

If your competitors reduce their costs by using energy efficiently and you don't look out. In a market over-charged with rentable opportunities and low on quality prospective and sitting tenants, building owners who do not pursue energy management policies will not be able to pass on the cost of energy inefficiency. In simple terms, these costs will come out of their bottom line.

Ease of Acceptance

Unlike many cost-cutting measures, nobody minds energy management. It actually CREATES employment. Even the suppliers of energy want you to use less of it! The Federal Government will also encourage you down the path of energy efficiency. Who knows, you may even receive an award for energy reduction policies and systems.

You will be helping to reduce pollution, and the drain on our limited fossil fuels. Energy efficiency helps the economy by reducing the demand for power station equipment mostly imported, and by lowering the on-costs to Australian businesses, some of whom will be your tenants or suppliers.

Measurable Results

Energy management allows you to see your success as raw numbers. This allows the investment performance to be checked, as well as facilitating investment quality control. This can be very satisfying.

HOW IS THIS IMPROVEMENT POSSIBLE?

You need to firstly research or study the current situation. This initial study or "energy audit" includes:

~ Collection of the energy bills for at least 12 months
~ Collation of consumption data

Analysis of trends, including:
- total consumption Vs targets
- seasonal trends,
- daily patterns (off-peak compared with on-peak),
- long term trends, and
- comparison with other buildings and targets
- standards

On-site Survey of:
- equipment
- capacity

condition, wear, leaks, etc,
time-scheduling and other automatic controls
metering, and
levels of service (temperature, lighting, etc.)

You should then be in a position to undertake calculations involving reconciling actual, anticipated and observed energy use.

1. "Energy Management could be said to represent one of the best investments available to today's property owners and managers." The importance of energy efficiency in the market is increasing now because of _____.
   a. energy prices rise and tenants become more sophisticated
   b. occupancy rates decrease, and. environmental concerns and regulations increase
   c. market rentals fall or remain at a relatively low level
   d. all of above

2. Energy management is _____.
   a. about finding ways to reduce creature comforts; having people sitting in a cold dark room, drinking warm beer
   b. Energy Management could be said to enable the Property Manager to do more with less, by using the most efficient and appropriate, equipment, methods, and fuels
   c. must be dispelled in order to reap the benefits it has to offer
   d. improve profits, and thereby increase the capital value of the building

3. To maximize the investment performance, we clearly need to _____.
   a. maximize the top line, while minimizing the bottom line
   b. minimize the top line, while maximizing the bottom line
   c. maximize the top line, while maximizing the bottom line
   d. minimize the top line, while minimizing the bottom line

4. "This gives an indication of the size of the benefit available, but this is only a part of the reason that energy management offers one of the best investments available." In the sentence, "this" means _____.
   a. There is scope to reduce energy costs by up to 45%, with a 40% return in this area on investment
   b. There is scope to reduce energy costs by up to 33%, with a 40% return in this area on investment
   c. There is scope to reduce energy costs by up to 40%, with a 40% return in this area on investment
   d. There is scope to reduce energy costs by up to 55%, with a 60% return in this area on investment

5. The reason that energy management is one of the best investments available is the following except _____.

a. of the confidence of receiving a return

b. it yields a very high Nett Present Value

c. of the size of the benefit available

d. of the opportunity to multiply your money ten-fold in sir months

6. "If your competitors reduce their costs by using energy efficiently and you don't, look out." Because _____.

   a. you will see therefore that there is scope to reduce energy costs by up to 40%, with a 40% return in this area on investment

   b. this gives an indication of the size of the benefit available, but this is only a part of the reason that energy management offers one of the best investments available

   c. to maximize the investment performance, we clearly need to maximize the top line, while minimizing the bottom line

   d. in a market over-charged with rentable opportunities and low on quality prospective and sitting tenants, building owners who do not pursue energy management policies will not be able to pass on the cost of energy inefficiency

7. To research or study the current situation, this initial study or "energy audit" includes _____.

   a. collection of the energy bills for at least 12 months and collation of consumption data

   b. analysis of trends

   c. on-site Survey of-equipment; capacity; condition, wear, leaks, etc; time-scheduling and other automatic controls; metering, and levels of service (temperature, lighting, etc.)

   d. all of above

Ⅱ. Language Ability Drill (语言能力练习)

(Ⅰ) Vocabulary Exercise

1.1 The suffix —y can be added to nouns to form adjectives, with the meaning "full of, having, containing, covered with, or inclined to(想要)", e.g.

fun	+—y	→ funny: full of fun
cloud	+—y	→ cloudy: having clouds
salt	+—y	→ salty: containing salt
dust	+—y	→ dusty: covered with dust
sleep	+—y	→ sleepy: inclined to sleep

Now form adjectives by adding —y to the nouns listed below and then use them in the following sentences:

noise   health   dirt   smell   storm
sun   smoke   rain   mud (泥浆)

1. The children looked wonderfully _____ with their bright eyes and rosy cheeks.

2. "Don't touch the biscuits (饼干) with your _____ hands," cried Mrs. Johnson to

her son Tom. "Go and wash them!"

3. You can hear the _____ motorcycle from a distance.
4. "Big Jim" and his friends began to smoke after lunch and soon made the room _____.
5. It is too _____ to sail today.
6. I hope it will be _____ tomorrow. We have had too many _____ days.
7. When you walk on _____ ground, you get mud on your shoes.
8. Take the _____ fish out of the refrigerator!

1.2 Compound adjectives can be formed by combining adverbs with past participles. Study the following compound adjectives formed in this way and then use them in the given sentences.

much-handled   much-used   ill-advised(不明智的)   well-known
well-informed   well-paid   well-travelled   poorly-dressed

1. To give up such a chance would be an _____ decision.
2. Though he has a _____ job and a good family, he still feels that his life is somewhat empty.
3. This _____ phrase has lost its former freshness.
4. The news comes from a _____ source.
5. Depend upon it, that _____ gentleman isn't poor at all.
6. Mr. Black is a _____ man. At 35 he has been to most of the countries in Europe and America.
7. He took out a _____ note-book from his pocket and wrote down my telephone number in it.
8. The restaurant is _____ for its roast duck (烤鸭).

1.3 In the English language, quite a few verbs may be converted (转化) into nouns and nouns into verbs. Hence many a word can be used both as a noun and as a verb, e. g.

Queen Elizabeth II knighted Chichester after he had sailed round the world single-handed. (n. -->v)

The old man had a bad fall and broke a rib (肋骨). (v. -->n.)

Now choose one of the words listed below to complete each of the following sentences:

root   retreat   mask   approach   board   dream   notice

1. The edible(可以食用的) part of this plant is its _____.
2. Did you _____ her pale face at the party last night? I suppose she was not quite herself at the time.
3. When the enemy began to lose heavily, their commander ordered a _____.
4. The whistle is blowing. Let's _____ the train now.
5. Tom hid ills hatred for his master under the _____ of loyalty (忠诚).
6. After months of fighting, the enemy troops began to _____.

7. Winter is _____. Have you any plan for the forthcoming (即将到来的) vacation?
8. There was a hand-written _____ on the bulletin board(布告栏).
9. Every culture is _____ in tradition(传统).
10. I always, feel sick as soon as I am on _____ a ship.
11. The silly girl spends all her time _____ of becoming a movie-star.
12. Sunset announces the _____ of night.
13. His smile could not very well _____ his anger.
14. _____ do come true sometimes.

(Ⅱ) Cloze

I once thought I would be a perfect parent. It took 1 sixteen years to learn 2 I could not be. I know that I made 3 mistakes. If I raised my 4 again, I would not make those 5 . Maybe I would make 6 ones, but I would do a better job.

I would try to understand my 7 towards my children. I often did what my own 8 would have done. I 9 their ways of raising children control me. For example, I had my teenage 10 David come home early. He hated this rule. He said no reason 11 it. As a girl, I had to be 12 early. I wanted my son to do 13 . Today I would think more about 14 I wanted things done in a certain way.

My father was sick when I was 15 . My sister, my brother, and 16 were quiet at 17 . We did not yell in anger. We did not shout for 18 . I wanted my children to be quiet too. I never 19 to ask "why?" 20 was hard for me to let my children show anger. I stopped my children when 21 started to get angry. Now I would tell my 22 . "It is all 23 to show love. It is all right to show 24 . Your feelings are good. I love you 25 what you feel."

1. A. more	B. me	C. in	D. my
2. A. this	B. what	C. since	D. that
3. A. some	B. few	C. no	D. any
4. A. hand	B. questions	C. demand	D. children
5. A. answers	B. says	C. mistakes	D. friends
6. A. old	B. new	C. some	D. little
7. A. questions	B. love	C. actions	D. mistakes
8. A. children	B. belief	C. parents	D. strength
9. A. love	B. open	C. let	D. go
10. A. son	B. mister	C. young	D. friend
11. A. at	B. for	C. by	D. of
12. A. natured	B. loved	C. home	D. quick
13. A. the same	B. a lot	C. well	D. at once
14. A. what	B. which	C. why	D. whom
15. A. taught	B. told	C. young	D. naughty
16. A. we	B. he	C. I	D. me

17. A. all times	B. no time	C. some time	D. the time
18. A. joy	B. anger	C. all	D. games
19. A. believed	B. worried	C. realized	D. stopped
20. A. It	B. I	C. There	D. Sometimes
21. A. parents	B. suddenly	C. had	D. they
22. A. parent	B. children	C. neighbour	D. brother
23. A. in all	B. men	C. agreed	D. right
24. A. love	B. anger	C. yourselves	D. around
25. A. no longer	B. no more	C. no wonder	D. no matter

(Ⅲ) **Complete the following sentences, using the words in brackets:**

1. The people of the United States were greatly shocked at the news of the Japanese attack on Pearl Harbor(珍珠港).

   The news of the Japanese attack on Pearl Harbor .... (stun)

2. The wild animals started to run when the hunters came closer.

   The wild animals started to run .... (approach n.)

3. The film on TV held such a great attraction for me that I forgot to do my homework.

   I was .... (caught up in)

4. Although the Second World War ended more than fifty years ago, it remains a bitter memory for many people.

   Although the Second World War ended more than fifty years ago, many people still .... (painfully)

5. Her face was no longer wearing a cheerful smile when she heard the badnews.

   The cheerful smile .... (vanish)

6. Although America's divorce rate is high, most Americans want to have a happy marriage.

   In spite of .... (dream of)

Part 2. Dialogue

Maintenance Service
（维修服务）

Ⅰ. **Typical Sentences**（经典短句）

(Ⅰ) **Daily Conversations**（日常用语）

  To Echo

  （随声附和）

  1. Well...

    嘿！/这个……

  2. Let me see...

    我想想看……

3. Is that so?
   是吗？
4. I'm sorry to hear that.
   我很抱歉。
5. That's too bad.
   那太糟了。
6. Congratulations.
   祝贺您。
7. Yes, indeed.
   果真是这样。
8. Not exactly.
   不一定。
9. It depends...
   这依靠……
10. Yes, I can imagine.
    我可以想像得出了。

(Ⅱ) **Professional Conversation**（专业会话）

维修服务语言：
接到住户电话：
How are you! Maintenance Department, What can I do for you?
您好！维修部，请问有什么要求？
Your address, please? Phone number?
请告诉我您的地址和电话号码。
We'll send someone to your house as soon as possible.
我们立刻派人到您家。
Any other demand?
您还有什么要求？
接待住户来访：
Hello, What can I do for you?
您好！请问有什么事？
Would you explain more exactly?
您可以详细解释一下吗？
I assure you, the repairman will arrive in no time.
我向您保证，修理工马上就到。
Now we are short of personnel, can we fix another time.
我们暂缺人手，是否另约时间。
You can carry it to the repair department and get it repaired.
您可以把它拿到修理部去让人修理一下。

237

Ⅱ. Conversation Passages

(Ⅰ) Passage 1.

A: How are you! Maintenance Department, What can I do for you?
您好！维修部,请问有什么要求？

B: The air conditioner in my house doesn't work properly.
我家的空调工作不太正常。

A: Would you explain more exactly?
您可以详细解释一下吗？

B: At first, it sounds strange. Now it doesn't work at all.
一开始声音不太对。现在根本就不工作了。

A: I see. Your address, please? Phone number?
我知道了。请告诉我您的地址和电话号码。

B: I live in the Building 3, gate 1, 4th floor, room 1, my telephone number is 24321567.
您住在3号楼1门401室,我家电话是24321567。

A: We'll send someone to your house as soon as possible.
我们立刻派人到您家。

B: Thank you very much.
谢谢你。

A: You are welcome!
不用谢。

(Ⅱ) Passage 2.

A: Good afternoon, sir. Did you call for air conditioner reparation?
下午好,先生。是您打电话报修空调吗？

B: Yes, it's me. It doesn't work at all.
是我。它一直都不工作。

A: Oh, where is it?
您的空调在哪了？

B: It's right there in the bedroom.
在卧室里。

A: Can you describe the problem?
您能重复一遍现象吗？

B: Yes. This morning, when I turned it on. I found the sound of the machine is strange. Then after 5 minutes, it doesn't work at all.
好的,今天早上当我开机时,就发现声音不对了。后来又过了5分钟的样子,就根本不工作了。

A: I see. Can you bring me a chair so that I can reach it?
我知道了,您可以给我一把椅子吗？

B: Ok, I'll get it, wait a minute.

好的,我去拿。请稍等。

A: Thank you.

谢谢。

B: Here it is.

给您。

A: Oh, I'm afraid the engine broke down.

恐怕是电机烧了。

B: So can you fix it right here?

您能在这修好它吗?

A: Oh, sorry. I can't. I must carry it to the repair department and get it repaired, because I do not have the tools here.

噢,对不起。我必须把它拿到修理部去修理一下。因为我在这没有工具。

B: I see. So how long do you think it will cost?

我明白了,那您看这需要多久才能修好呢?

A: About 4 hours, I think. Anyway, I will try my best.

大概4个小时吧。我会尽力的。

B: Thank you.

谢谢你。

A: You are welcome.

不用谢。

III. Exercises for Dialogue

(Ⅰ) **Fill in the following blanks by considering Chinese.** (按照中文完成以下填空)

A: I'm afraid _____.

恐怕是电机烧了。

B: So can you fix it right here?

您能在这修好它吗?

A: Oh, sorry. I can't. I must _____, because _____ here.

噢,对不起。我必须把它拿到修理部去修理一下。因为我在这没有工具。

B: I see. So how long do you think it will cost?

我明白了,那您看这需要多久才能修好呢?

A: About 4 hours, I think. Anyway, _____.

大概4个小时吧。我会尽力的。

B: Thank you.

谢谢你。

A: _____.

不用谢。

(Ⅱ) **Make a conversation with your partner about finding a parking place.** (there should be at least 3 turn-taking in the dialogue)

IV. **Spoken Language Drill** (fill in the blanks according to the Chinese translation)

Dialogue 1.

A: Which train do I take to Philadelphia?
   去费城乘哪趟车?
B: _____ 4 at 9:30.
   9点半,4轨道的车。
A: How long does it take?
   火车要开多久?
B: It's _____ in at noon.
   正午到达。
A: What's the _____ fare?
   来回票价多少?
B: It's $25.00 one way or $45.00 for a weekend excursion.
   单程票价25元,周末旅行来回票价45元。

Dialogue 2.

A: What _____ does the train for Boston leaves?
   去波士顿的火车几点开?
B: 9:25 on Track 12.
   9点25分,12轨道。
A: When does it _____?
   什么时候到那儿?
B: It should be there at 11:45, but it may be a little late.
   应该是11点45分到那里,但也可能稍晚一点。
A: How much is a one-way ticket?
   单程车票多少钱一张?
B: It's $32.00 coach and $50.00 club car.
   二等车厢票价32元,头等车厢票价50元。

Dialogue 3.

A: What time's the _____ train to Washington?
   下一趟去华盛顿的车几点开?
B: That's 9:26 on Track 16.
   9点26分,16轨道。
A: When does it get there?
   什么时候到那里?
B: It's _____ to arrive at 11:50.
   按照列车时刻表是11点50分到。
A: How much is it?
   多少钱?

B: It's $30.00 _____ or $55.00 round trip.

单程票价 30 元,来回票价 55 元。

Dialogue 4.

A: What track does the Metroliner _____ from?

"华一纽特快"从第几轨道开出?

B: That's track 1 at 9∶45.

1 轨道,9 点 45 分开。

A: What time does it get in?

什么时候到达那里?

B: It gets in around 11∶45.

大约 11 点 45 分到。

A: What's the _____?

车费多少?

B: Coach is $32.00.

二等票价 32 元。

Part 3. Supplementary Reading:

Don't Sweat the Small Stuff

Surprisingly, the smallest grievances are often the ones that interfere most with marital happiness the minor hassles and frustrations, unreturned phone calls, messes, disagreements, responsibilities. You'll find that if you can let go of the distractions of the small stuff, you'll discover new ways to nurture and love one another. Here are six of our own favorite strategies to become better friends with your spouse:

1. Throw away the score card. It's tempting to keep track of all your contributions and sacrifices in a relationship. But when you constantly remind yourself of your own hard work, you begin to feel angry with your partner. You feel taken advantage of and burned out, and loving feelings diminish. In turn, your partner senses your resentment and becomes defensive. Both parties dig in and start adding up their own contributions score cards are flying!

When you catch yourself doing this, stop. Try to bring yourself back to a loving feeling. Think not of what your partner isn't doing, think instead of what he is doing. You may soon discover that your frustration is not reality but simply a habit that has crept into your thinking.

Each time you dismiss your "this isn't fair" thinking, you'll be contributing to the good will of your relationship.

2. Take charge of your own happiness. The concept seems rather obvious, but how many of us do take full responsibility for our own happiness? How often do we say to ourselves, "Why can't my wife be different?" or "It makes me so mad when my husband acts

that way"? The implication is that: "If only he were different, I'd be happy. He has to change. Not me, no way. It's him!"

If you believe the answer to your unhappiness lies in someone else's hands, you're in for trouble. Even if your partner accommodates you with occasional changes, eventually you'll be let down. You'll be left with that helpless and dependent "It's her fault" feeling.

Were not saying that your partner doesn't play a role in your happiness. But ultimately, you alone are responsible for making yourself happy. When your life isn't working, you need to make changes or see things differently. You may have to make difficult choices, have painful or uncomfortable discussions or compromise in some way.

By recognizing your own power to make yourself happy, you take a great deal of pressure off your partner: "It's okay for you to be human. You can make mistakes. You don't have to worry that I'll freak out every time you disappoint me." You open the door to a relationship based on honesty, responsibility and wisdom.

3. Recognize your quirks. It's funny, but you can love someone deeply and still get annoyed by the simple act of sharing the same space. That day to day, wash the toothpaste down the sink, close the toilet seat stuff can drive you crazy. But if the same things are bothering you constantly, it helps to ask, "Whose quirk is this, anyway?"

Here's one scenario: Husband David is obsessively neat and organized. One night, wife Pamela leaves a piece of lettuce in the sink after doing the dishes. Irritated, David stands at the kitchen sink and yells, "Pamela, are you going to get over here and finish cleaning up your mess in the kitchen?"

Now, whose quirk is this, anyway? Obviously his.

If David were able to see that he is the one with the quirk, he would be able to laugh at himself and stop putting such high expectations on his wife. On the other hand, if Pamela were able to understand David's quirk and see it as his problem, she would be able to brush it off without taking it too personally.

4. Learn to accept apologies. Sadly, many people find it difficult to apologize. One reason might be that when we do apologize, it's accepted in a less than graceful manner.

While sitting in a coffee shop, we overheard a woman tearfully tell her husband that she was sorry that her work had been so consuming. We gathered that this was taking a toll on the family and their relationship. But rather than hug her, hold her hand or even reassure his wife, the husband gave her a disapproving look that seemed to make her heart sink. It appeared that he was trying to make her feel even more guilty than she already felt.

Most of us would probably not be as ungraceful as this man, but we might push our partner away in more subtle ways. We might, for instance, mutter under our breath, sigh, make a condescending comment such as "It's about time" or in some other way minimize the apology. This kind of response can bring about bitterness and resentment.

An apology gives couples an excellent opportunity to deepen their love and commitment. It's an ideal time to make a genuine effort to listen deeply and respectfully, to feel gratitude that your partner is willing to apologize. Further, when you accept an apology, it also makes it far more likely that your partner will do the same for you when it's your turn to apologize. So the next time your spouse offers an apology, soften your edges and open your heart.

5. Don't pencil them in. It's easy to get overwhelmed with all the responsibilities of life, to fall short of time and find ourselves scrambling. As the saying goes, "Something has to give." Unfortunately, it's often our loved ones who get pushed to the back of the line.

It's important to become aware of how easily this tendency can sneak into your relationship, and to make a regular effort to spend more time alone together. Whatever your hectic schedule, it's possible to make adjustments, set boundaries and limits, and learn to say no to requests that are interfering with your loving connection.

6. Do it yourself. One way we create ill feelings in our relationships is by demanding that our partner never slip up. We say things like "You forgot to do the dishes" or "You put the towels in the wrong bathroom," as if our partner is a robot needing reprogramming. In reality, your spouse is simply a person, just like you, who innocently forgot, or was tired or preoccupied.

A less abrasive, more loving way to deal with your partner's slip ups is to simply do the task yourself not with resentment or regret, but quietly, selflessly and lovingly. If the dishes in the sink are bothering you, wash them. If your partner neglected to pay a bill, go ahead and pay it yourself instead of reminding him how forgetful he can be.

Some may protest, "But if I took that lenient approach, my partner would never do another dish or pay another bill." On the contrary, if you can avoid lecturing, snapping, yelling or otherwise reacting, you may be amazed at how helpful your partner will become. And without those negative little distractions, you'll have more energy to focus on the truly important aspects of your relationship good communication, spiritual growth, sharing, laughing and loving.

参考译文：

莫为小事烦恼

令人不解的是，一些极小的委屈常常会成为最能妨碍夫妻间幸福的因素——诸如一些微不足道的争执和失意、几个未回的电话、胡乱摆放物品，以及意见上的某些分歧和家庭的责任等。你会发现，如果你能不去在意让你分心的这些小事，你将会找到夫妻间相互体谅和爱慕的新的方式。这里有六条我们特别喜爱的策略，它们会使你成为你伴侣的好朋友。

1. 扔掉那些记录卡。记录下你为家庭所做的贡献和牺牲是挺吸引人的。但在你不断地让自己想起你所付出的辛劳时，你就会转而生你伴侣的气。你感到自己上当了，精疲力竭了，于是爱的情感逐渐消逝。反过来，你的伴侣察觉到你的愤懑便也开始为自己辩白。于是双方都使劲找自己的贡献,并不断地加码,——记录书满天飞舞!

当你发觉自己正在做这种事情时,请赶快停止。努力把自己带回到爱的情感中来。不要想你的伴侣没在做什么,而是想他正在做什么。你也许很快会发现你的失意并不真实,它只是潜入你思维中的一种习惯。

每一次你丢掉"这不公平"的想法,都将有助于维持你们关系的良好愿望。

2. 快乐由自己负责。这种想法似乎是相当明显的,但我们中有多少人确实做到了对我们自己的快乐完全负责呢?我们会时常对自己说,"为什么我的妻子不能不那样?"或者"我的丈夫那样做简直把我气坏了"其潜台词就是:"假如他不那样做,我会很高兴。他必须得改变,而不是我,没门儿。就得是他!"

如果你相信使你不快乐的原因在别人手上,你准会自寻烦恼。即使你的伴侣偶尔会为你做些改变,最终你仍会感到失望。你会带着无助和"那是她的错"的依赖思绪过下去。

我们并不是说你的伴侣对于你的快乐不起作用。但最终还得是你个人对自己的快乐负责。当你的生活不对劲时,你需要做些改变或者换个方式看问题。你可能得做出艰难的选择,去进行痛苦的或令人不快的探讨或者以某种方式妥协一下。

认识到你拥有使自己快乐的能力,你就卸下了你伴侣肩上的一大部分压力:"你是个独立的人,这样做当然可以。你可以犯错误。你不必担心每次你令我失望时,我会反常的举动。"这样,基于忠诚、责任和智慧,你向伴侣敞开了胸怀。

3. 认识到你的怪癖。这听起来很可笑,但你可能深爱某人,但还是令对这个与你共同生活的人的琐细行为感到恼怒。那些日复一日的刷洗脸盆里的牙膏斑迹、放下马桶座的活儿会让你发疯。但如果这些相同的事情老是烦扰你,你就应该这样问问,"这究竟是谁有怪癖?"

有这样一幕剧:丈夫戴维是一个非常爱整洁和有条理的人。有一天晚上,妻子帕梅拉洗过碗后在洗涤槽中留下了一片莴苣,于是戴维站在厨房的水池子边大声吼叫,"帕梅拉,你打算将厨房的垃圾清理干净,完成这里的活儿吗?"

现在看看,究竟是谁有怪癖?显然是他。

如果戴维能认识到自己是一个有怪癖的人,他就会笑话自己,并且不会再对他的妻子寄予这么高的期望。另一方面,假如帕梅拉能理解戴维的怪癖,并且把它看成是他的毛病,她也就能不带太多的情绪地把脏物洗掉。

4. 学会接受道歉。令人悲哀的是,许多人发现道歉很困难。其中的一个原因或许就是当我们道歉时,对方总是以一种不够友善的方式接受。

有一次我们坐在一个咖啡厅里,无意中听到一名妇女正流着泪对她的丈夫说,她的工作总是那么地劳神费力,这使她很歉疚。我们推测这给他们的家庭和彼此的关系敲响了警钟。然而她的丈夫没有去拥抱她或握她的手,甚至没有对妻子说让她消除顾虑,而是不满地看了她一眼,这使得她的心沉了下去。这样丈夫似乎要让他的妻子愧上加愧。

我们中的大多数人或许不像这个男子那样没有风度,但是我们可能会以更微妙的方式排斥我们的伴侣。比如我们可能会低声抱怨、叹气、或屈尊般地感慨道"该是时候了",或者用其他方法来弱化道歉。这种反应一样会引起伤感和愤懑。

道歉会带给夫妻一个加深爱情和彼此相依的好机会。这是一个真正努力去深切而尊重地倾听、感知伴侣道歉态度的理想时机。并且,你接受了道歉,就会使你伴侣更有可能在你道歉时也同样地接受你。因此,下一回你的伴侣道歉时,你可一定得温和一些,并且向他

(她)敞开你的心扉。

5. 不要把他(她)们圈入其中。人们很容易变得身负生活的重任,时间不够用并发现自己在勉强应付。正如老话所讲,"有些事情必须得舍弃。"不幸的是,往往正是我们至爱的人被推至这条线后。

意识到这种势头是多么容易侵入破坏你们的关系,这很重要,经常努力创造更多的独处机会也同样重要。不管你的活动日程安排得多么紧张,它都可能变动,要为自己确定一个界限和尺度,要学会对干扰你们亲密联系的请求说"不"。

6. 自己动手。我们的夫妻关系中制造不良感受的一个办法就是使用命令,而我们的伴侣却从不吃这套。如我们说"你忘记洗碗了",或"你把毛巾放错了洗澡间",仿佛我们的伴侣是一个需要重新输入程序的机器人。事实上,你的伴侣就是一个普通的人,像你一样,只是一时忘记了,或者是太累了,或者是走了神。

一个摩擦较小且更显关爱的对待伴侣疏忽的办法,就是你自己去做这些事——不是心怀不满或遗憾,而是平静、无私而又充满关爱的去做。如果伴侣忘了洗水槽里的碗,槽里的那些碗盘烦扰了你,那就去洗洗它们。如果你的伴侣由于疏忽忘了付账单,那你就走上前去把账付了,而不要去说他有多么健忘。

有些人可能会抗议,"但是如果我采取了那种宽容的作法,我的伴侣就永远不会再洗碗碟或再去付账了。"事实上恰恰相反,如果你能不去遣责、厉声怒斥、大吼大叫或做出其他什么样的激烈反应,你也许会惊奇地发现你的伴侣会变得多么能干。并且,没有了那些性质消极且又令人分心的小事,你就能把更多的精力集中到夫妻关系真正重要的方面——良好的交流、情感的增加、分享生活、爱和欢笑。

Exercises for the reading:

1. What interferes most with marital happiness?
   A. The minor hassles and frustrations.
   B. Unreturned phone calls.
   C. Messes.
   D. All of the above

2. Which is not the strategy to become better friends with your spouse?
   A. Take charge of your own happiness.
   B. Recognize your quirks.
   C. Learn to accept apologies.
   D. Keep track of all your contributions and sacrifices in a relationship.

3. If you are not happy with your spouse, what should you say to yourself?
   A. "It makes me so mad when my husband acts that way."
   B. "He has to change. Not me, no way. It's him!"
   C. "It's okay for him to be human. He can make mistakes."
   D. "It's all her fault."

4. What will make your spouse become more helpful and careful?
   A. If your partner neglected to pay a bill, go ahead and pay it yourself.
   B. Snap to your partner, "You forgot to do the dishes."

C. "You put the towels in the wrong bathroom."

D. Think your partner as a robot needing reprogramming.

5. Why do many people find it difficult to apologize?

A. Because they feel shameful to apologize.

B. Because it is no use to do it.

C. Because when they do apologize, it's accepted in a less than graceful manner.

D. We don't know.

Part 4. Practical Writing

演讲致辞

演讲致辞开始一般都要以 Ladies and gentlemen 称呼听众。结束时候一般要以 Thank you 致谢。下面是一些各种致辞的开头举例:

1) 欢迎辞 It is my special pleasure to welcome our new staff member, Mr. John Water, who has come here from the United States.

2) 欢迎辞 It is really a great honor and pleasure for me to attend and speak at the opening ceremony of 1995 Summer Chinese Program for the Canadians. On behalf of Anhui University, I extend my warm welcome to all Canadian friends who...

3) 欢迎辞 On behalf of the Organizing Committee of the 1975 Beijing International Swimming Meet, I extend my warm welcome to all of you to this opening ceremony.

4) 开幕辞 Allow me now to call the meeting to order. First, I welcome you all on behalf of the Executive Committee of the Congress on the Peaceful Use of Atomic Energy.

5) 开幕辞 Welcome everybody. Merry Christmas to you all! Thank you for coming tonight to celebrate this happy and joyous occasion.

6) 开幕辞 Happy New Year, everybody. I am very happy to see all of you here to celebrate the arrival of the new year.

7) 祝酒辞 I'd like to propose a toast to Mr. Black on his seventieth birthday.

8) 欢送辞 We are very sad to say good-bye to Mr. Brown.

9) 欢送辞 We enjoyed every minute that we worked with you.

10) 祝贺辞 I am truly happy to speak for all of us in congratulating Mr. Brown, the winner of the contest.

11) 祝贺辞 We are all thrilled that you won in such a famous contest.

12) 祝福语 I wish you the best of luck in the new year.

13) 祝福语 I hope you will have a very enjoyable stay.

14) 祝福语 I take great pleasure in bidding you all a hearty welcome.

15) 答谢辞 Words cannot express how grateful I am to you all. I am truly honored by the kindness and attention you have shown me today.

16) 答谢辞 I wish, first of all, to thank my host and hostess for inviting me to this Christmas dinner.

期 末 测 试

Part 1. 专业练习(总共四题,满分150分)

一、Translate the following sentences into English.(共10小题,每小题3分,满分30分)

1. 物业经理和保洁工作承包商之间进行良好的、诚实的合作,对于获得高质量的服务是非常必要的。
2. 物业经理可以在任何时间以书面通知的方式,在合同允许的范围内调整大楼的保洁区域。
3. 预防性维护的质量越高,定期设备维修的可能性就越低。
4. 没有投标文件,服务承包人很容易篡改服务程序以降低投标价格。
5. 制冷需要24小时而不是瞬间的控制方式。
6. 挑选符合要求的最适合的、最便宜的、使用最方便的燃料,同时要考虑成本和供应收益的未来的发展趋势。
7. 表面上相似的东西之间效率可能不同,价格肯定不是最好的指南。
8. 一旦人员的疏散问题都解决妥当之后,还是需要尽可能地保护好财产安全。
9. 在火情发生时对人的生命威胁最大的就是建筑物中不断上升的烟和热气。
10. 检查设备的磨损件、易损件,对任何明显的不正常运行或对正常设计性能形成的偏差进行补偿。

二、Fill in the following blanks with considering Chinese.(共5小题,每小题10分,满分50分)

1. C: Sir! Sir! _____! (我已经站这儿等了差不多二十分钟啦!)
   S: I'm sorry, sir. _____? (我能帮您做点什么?)
   C: Well, _____. (我等得不耐烦了。)
   S: I'm terribly sorry, sir. _____ (我们今天人手不够。)

2. C: It is still too much. _____? (就不能多降点吗?)
   S: Sorry, but this is the best price. _____. (你买不到比这儿更便宜的了。)
   C: Are you sure?
   S: Yes, _____.

3. C: Can I specify a date?
   S: Yes, _____. (但最早可能是25号。)
   C: OK. _____? (顺便问一下,这是免费的吗?)
   S: Yes, service is not extra.

4. A: Good evening, sir. _____? (请问您要去哪?)

B: Yes, I think it is 1-1-301.

A: Pardon?

B: It's _____. (1号楼1门301房间)

A: That it is. I see.

B: _____? (我能把车停在小区里吗?)

A: Yes, of course, you can. But please park it in the area for guests.

B: Thank you.

A: _____. (不客气)

5. A: Good evening, Mr. Wang. Oh, is this your son?

B: Yes. _____! (喊,"叔叔!")

C: Good evening, uncle.

A: _____! _____? (多可爱呀! 你叫什么名字?)

C: My name is Wang Hua.

A: _____? (和你爸爸在外面玩得开心吗?)

C: Yes, I did. And my father bought the color chalk for me.

A: How beautiful they are! _____? (你要用它们干什么呀?)

C: I want to paint the wall with the green one, then draw little flowers on it.

A: That must be a lovely picture. _____. (可是好孩子从来都不在墙上或地上画画的。)

C: Really?

A: And _____. (好孩子从不随地吐痰,将垃圾丢到垃圾桶里,而不是随手扔。)

C: But where do they draw with chalk?

A: Oh, they will do it on the blackboard. _____. (我这就有一块小黑板。给你吧。)

C: Thank you, uncle.
（谢谢,叔叔。）

B: Thank you.
（谢谢你。）

A: _____. Bye-bye, little Wang Hua. _____. (记得要爱护公共卫生呀。)

B: I will. Thank you. Bye-bye.

三、Choose the best answer（选择最佳答案）(共10小题,每小题3分,满分30分)

1. Have you heard that Joan failed again? She ought to _____ harder.

   A. have worked

   B. have been working

   C. working

   D. be worked

248

2. Preparations are being made for the Olympic Games _____ in Beijing in 2008.
   A. held   B. holding   C. to be held   D. to hold
3. It's clear that _____ little money he earns can hardly support _____ family as large as his.
   A. the;a   B. a;the   C. 不填;a   D. 不填;the
4. It seems to me that no reason _____ you gave us for your mistake is sound.
   A. what   B. why   C. which   D. that
5. —Shall we repair the roof tomorrow?
   —_____.
   A. Yes,we do   B. No, not yet
   C. It depends on the weather   D. Unless it is fine
6. We had a discussion _____ the lecture about creative education was over.
   A. soon   B. immediately   C. quickly   D. rapidly
7. The falling of the new building _____ its soft base.
   A. resulted in   B. suffered from
   C. led to   D. lay in
8. All Yang Yang wanted to do when she got her first gold medal was _____ thanks to her coach and teammates.
   A. say   B. said   C. saying   D. about to say
9. The Greens live in a house _____ tall trees all around.
   A. of   B. for   C. with   D. by
10. In France dogs can go _____ their owners can because people there love pets very much.
    A. no matter where   B. anywhere
    C. somewhere   D. nowhere

四、Read the following passages and choose the best answer to complete each of the statements that follow.（共 15 小题；每小题 2 分，满分 30 分）

(一)

THE CLEANING PROCESS

As a Property Manager, it is part of your overall responsibilities to arrange and co-ordinate the cleaning of all common areas and the outer facade of a building. You may also be called upon to arrange cleaning for and on behalf of the tenants in the building. The purpose of this session is to examine some of the key issues associated with cleaning contracts. In particular, better understanding your client's needs, the tendering process, common cleaning contract clauses and problems associated with a cleaning contract and its implementation.

The procedures followed in setting up a cleaning contract for either tenanted space or common areas are very similar, and can be summarised as:

Compilation of a Building Cleaning Survey
Setting up Cleaning Specifications

249

Invitation to Tenders Based on Cleaning Specifications
Analysis of Tenders and Award of the Contract
Recovery of Cleaning Costs

UNDERSTANDING THE CLIENT'S REQUIREMENTS

It is essential to meet the building representative/owner at an initial meeting, to attempt to establish a rapport and discuss the building layout, design, various tenant's locations, and the actual areas to be cleaned. The record of that meeting should include a description of the materials used in constructing/fitting-out the building/areas to be cleaned (e.g. glass, brick, wood, carpet, tiles, vinyl, concrete, plaster) and whether the external facade of the building is also to be cleaned. Refer to Appendix A for an example of this type of report, which could also be used in conjunction with a plan of the building.

Particular note must be taken at this meeting to record on a plan of the building, details such as the tenancy areas and the net lettable areas, as opposed to the common areas; the number of floors and the carparking spaces, and the exact area and location of the different uses of the building e.g. a retail shop on the ground floor, a medical suite on the second level, a computer room, etc. Accurate recording of the building information should also include the location and size of the tea rooms, toilets, lifts, foyers, plaza and plantrooms. The amount of traffic or usage and the type of material to be cleaned is also of major consideration when determining cleaning specifications.

Cleaning the building to an acceptable standard goes a long way to ensuring that the tenants' expectations are met and generally that the building operates efficiently. This also maximises the lifespan of the building's fittings and inclusions, such as carpet, which can deteriorate quickly without proper cleaning. It also minimises the possibility of the building owner being sued under common law for not complying with Occupational Health and Safety issues and for claims of negligence arising under the umbrella of "sick building syndrome".

THE CLEANING SPECIFICATIONS

The specification for the cleaning contract comprise a document detailing the areas to be cleaned, the standard of cleaning required and the frequency of the cleaning, i.e. on a daily, weekly, monthly, quarterly, 6-monthly or annual basis. The specifications are explicit instructions listing in detail the cleaning jobs to be performed in each area. It is recommended that a Property Manager prepare a draft list of every conceivable cleaning job and then tailor this list to achieve a desired match for the cleaning required for the particular building in question.

An example to highlight the amount of detail required to be specified in cleaning a tearoom is:

mop floors clean
clean and wipe stainless sinks and drains
clean all cabinet tops

empty and clean tea leaf containers

remove dust and marks from outside faces of cupboards, refrigerators, walls

perhaps even collect and clean all crockery

The specification should separately list periodical cleaning tasks, such as shampooing the carpet, on an "as required" or "as directed" basis. This achieves several objectives:

1. Listing this item as a periodical, allows tender documents submitted by tendering contractors to be analysed and compared on an equivalent basis, as usually only the routine cleaning job will be listed. Thus analysis of the tenders will highlight if one tender is charging too much for a particular task.

2. The contractor, in order to earn more money, generally will recommend that a periodical item such as shampooing the carpet be done, which means the Property Manager will not have to remind himself that the job needs to be done.

3. By listing the periodical items separately, the onus tends to fall to the cleaning contractor to advise the Property Manager when a job needs doing. The Property Manager can then determine whether the contractor's assessment is correct, and instruct the contractor to arrange the task. The Property Manager can then inspect the job.

In cases where the periodical items were paid for as part of the normal monthly cleaning charges, the cleaner could have arranged the periodical items to be performed without input or control from the Building Manager. The Manager may have to take the cleaner's word that the work had been done.

In order to avoid any confusion, a covering letter should be forwarded with the specification documents. This letter, often referred to as "Information to Tenderers", should expand on the information contained in the specification and set out clearly whether the contract is to be fixed for a set period or alternatively whether the contract is on a rise and fall contract. Other information that may need to be considered includes, any security procedures for the building and staff, and a contact name and number for the building owner.

An example of a typical Commonwealth Government specification is included as Appendix C.

PREPARATION OF TENDER DOCUMENTS
The Documents

1. Instructions to Tenderers & Conditions of Contract

This document should include the following information to the tenderers:

   a. Areas to be cleaned throughout the building including the net lettable areas of tenancies.

   b. Conditions of the contract e.g. termination, rise and fall or fixed price, performance, building hours and times cleaning can be carried out, insurances required etc.

2. Specification

The specification spells out the cleaning standard you require and contains the frequency of which specific tasks are to be carried out.

3. Labour Analysis & Cost Analysis Schedules

The labour analysis schedule provides you with a breakdown of hours the contractor proposes to take in carrying out the various daily duties including supervision.

The cost analysis schedules provide you with the data you need to analyse the tenders.

Tender List

It is advisable to call for tenders from 5 or 6 reputable cleaning contract firms who have proven experience in carrying out similar sized contracts and have a good track record in the industry.

It is a good idea to seek references and recommendations from a selection of their other clients.

Before calling for the tenders, you should provide a tender list to the building owner for prior approval as the owner may require you to include or indeed exclude a specific contractor previously known to him or her.

1. It is part of a Property Manager overall responsibilities to arrange and co-ordinate the cleaning of _____.
   a. all common areas
   b. the outer facade of a building
   c. of the tenants in the building
   d. all of above

2. Which of the following statements about "the purpose of this cleaning session" is not true _____?
   a. To examine some of the key issues associated with cleaning contracts.
   b. Better understanding your client's needs, the tendering process.
   c. Setting up a cleaning contract for either tenanted space or common areas are very similar.
   d. Better understanding common cleaning contract clauses and problems associated with a cleaning. contract and its implementation.

3. Which of the following statements about "cleaning the building to an acceptable standard" is not true?
   a. meet the building representative/owner at an initial meeting, to attempt to establish a rapport and discuss the building layout, design, various tenant's locations, and the actual areas to be cleaned.
   b. goes a long way to ensuring that the tenants' expectations are met and generally that the building operates efficiently.
   c. maximises the lifespan of the building's fittings and inclusions, such as carpet, which can deteriorate quickly without proper cleaning.
   d. minimises the possibility of the building owner being sued under common law for not complying with Occupational Health and Safety issues and for claims of negligence arising under the umbrella of "sick building syndrome".

4. The Specification for the cleaning contract comprise a document detailing _____ i. e. on a daily, weekly, monthly, quarterly, 6-monthly or annual basis.
   a. the areas to be cleaned
   b. the standard of cleaning required
   c. the frequency of the cleaning
   d. all of above
5. "It is a good idea to seek references and recommendations from a selection of their other clients." In this sentence, "it" means _____.
   a. to call for tenders from 5 or 6 reputable cleaning contract firms who have proven experience in carrying out similar sized contracts and have a good track record in the industry
   b. to seek references and recommendations from a selection of their other clients
   c. to provide a tender list to the building owner for prior approval as the owner may require you to include or indeed exclude a specific contractor previously known to him or her
   d. to take in carrying out the various daily duties including supervision

(二)

LIFT MAINTENANCE AGREEMENTS

It is a requirement by the Department of Industrial Relations Occupational Health and Safety that lifts be regularly serviced and tested and that such work be carried out by suitably qualified and licensed personnel.

There are two standard types of contracts:

Comprehensive

Service and Inspection

Each contract has several points in common.

1. It is a simple binding contractual agreement between the owner of the building, or other organisation responsible for the maintenance of the lifts, for example a building tenant, and the chosen service company.
2. Includes periodic charges with a variations formula being the basis for rise and fall calculations.
3. Defines the start date and the length of the term of the contract.
4. Defines the owner-client's responsibility and that of the service company, along with any limitation of liability.
5. Includes conditions under which the contract may be terminated by either party.
6. Schedules details of the equipment covered and general scope of works.
7. The contract is then signed and witnessed by both parties. Two copies are made out, one for each party.

The services covered differ with each type of contract and service company. In each type, the responsibilities of the service company and the owner are clearly defined.

The most widely used contract is the "Comprehensive Agreement", which is offered on all new equipment of original manufacture and some older equipment. This can also be called an "All Care and All Responsibility" type agreement.

The other type of contract is a "Service and Inspection Agreement". This agreement is available for new equipment and older equipment, along with equipment manufactured by others. It could also be called an "All Care and No Responsibility" type agreement. All repairs must be approved by the building owner and paid for separately.

The agreements provide for routine servicing and testing and are the same for either contract type.

The main difference between the two relates to call-outs and replacement parts.

As its name implies, "Comprehensive" covers all call-outs and replacement parts (with the exceptions given later) for the term of the contact. This can be for from five to 20 years, by which time some major repairs, eg. re-roping, will be required, the cost of which is included in the regular quarterly charges.

The exceptions to the non-chargeable call-outs are those due to factors outside the contractor's control, eg. vandalism, misuse, "nuisance" calls, water damage, etc.

Service and Inspection Contracts have a limited range of call-outs included in the contract price.

These are generally?

1. Call-outs between the weekday hours of 7:30am and 3:30pm (normal day shift) and requiring adjustent or repair only, are not chargeable (subject to the same exceptions as in the Comprehensive Agreement).

2. Call-outs between those hours which require replacement parts are chargeable at ruling rates.

3. All call-outs outside those hours are also chargeable.

The Service and Inspection Contract incurs a lower quarterly price than a Comprehensive Contract. However, over the life of the contract, the Comprehensive will, in all probability, be cheaper than the Service and Inspection due to the latter's costs of call-outs and replacement parts. The longer the term, the greater overall savings.

This is also important for budgeting considerations. It can be reasonably assumed that the quarterly charges forthe Comprehensive Agreement will be the all-up charges for that budget period with the applied CPI increases. However, with the Service and Inspection Contract, allowances must be made for those call-out and replacement parts that will incur charges and these can vary greatly from year to year, especially if a lift motor should bum out.

Other variations may be negotiated to the Service and Inspection Agreement. They are an "All-Calls-Chargeable" Contract, which is used for small lift installations or those which receive little use.

It is cheaper than the Service and Inspection.

For those units which receive little or no use, a Caretaker Maintenance Agreement may be arranged, which requires service to the unit on a quarterly basis so that the unit remains in a registered condition. This is used predominantly in buildings which are closed for whatever reason, but which are normally expected to be reopened at some time in the future. It is normally necessary to spend some time re-tuning the unit prior to being put back into operation.

1. The most widely used contract is _____.
   a. "Comprehensive Agreement"
   b. "Service and Inspection Agreement"
   c. "All Care and No Responsibility"
   d. "All-Calls-Chargeable"

2. The exceptions to the non-chargeable call-outs are those due to factors _____.
   a. inside the contractor's control, eg. vandalism, misuse, "nuisance" calls, water damage, etc.
   b. outside the contractor's control, eg. vandalism, misuse, "nuisance" calls, water damage, etc.
   c. under contractor's control, eg. vandalism, misuse, "nuisance" calls, water damage, etc.
   d. with contractor's control, eg. vandalism, misuse, "nuisance" calls, water damage, etc.

3. Service and Inspection Contract incurs a _____ quarterly price than a Comprehensive Contract.
   a. cheaper
   b. lower
   c. higher
   d. more expensive

4. However, with _____, allowances must be ade for those call-out and replacement parts that will incur charges and these can vary greatly from ear to year, especially if a lift motor should bum out.
   a. Comprehensive Agreement
   b. the Service and Inspection Contract
   c. Caretaker Maintenance Agreement
   d. "All-Calls-Chargeable" Contract

5. It is normally _____ to spend some time re-tuning the unit prior to being put back into operation.
   a. Important
   b. reasonable
   c. used
   d. necessary

(三)
BASIC TYPES OF LIFTS
Every application in which lifts are being considered calls for the right choice of equipment. The following is a brief survey of equipment options.

Oil Hydraulic Lifts
For offices, hospitals and factories, normally have a travel limit of 15 metres. This lift has no counter? eight and Raise the load plus the weight of the car and hydraulic ram. Its energy needs, therefore, are higher than for a traction lift of equal duty. However, it will continue to be relevant for some hospitals and in industry where it can raise greater loads over short distances, although at relatively slow speeds.

Geared Traction Lifts
Are designed for low to medium height buildings and usually vary in speed from 0.5 to 2m/s, which is considered the upper limit for mechanical efficiency, hoisting machine wear factors and noise emission. Depending on the degree of levelling accuracy and smoothness of ride desired, the two speed AC drive for industrial and commercial use, or the more sophisticated variable voltage AC and DC drives with variable speed control for more critical applications could be considered.

Gearless Lifts
Are normally found in quality buildings over 12 floors where short waiting intervals and high handling capacity are desirable. Typical speeds are from 3 m/s to 7 m/s, or higher where the application may call for 40 or more floors. Gearless lifts are seldom installed as single unit and, typically, are found in banks of three or more, often in multi-bank configurations. They are mainly used for medium to high rise buildings, hospitals, prestigious projects and the like.

Escalators and Moving Pathways
Are used as inclined or horizontal transport and are important in the mass movement of people.

Whilst lifts serve both low level structures and skyscrapers, escalators and pathways have the special ability to meet sudden, heavy and continuous traffic demands in localised areas with little or no passenger congestion. Typical applications are shopping centres, airports, railway stations, sporting venues and similar large buildings.

1. Oil Hydraulic Lifts are used for _____.
   a. offices   b. hospitals
   c. factories   d. All of above
2. Normally Oil Hydraulic Lifts have a travel limit of _____ metres.
   a. 0.5 to 2   b. 12   c. 3 to 7   d. 15
3. Geared Traction Lifts are used for _____.
   a. low to medium height buildings
   b. offices, hospitals and factories

    c. quality buildings over 12 floors

    d. inclined or horizontal transport

4. Gearless lifts are seldom installed _____.

    a. as single unit

    b. in banks of three or more

    c. in multi-bank configurations

    d. medium to high rise buildings, hospitals, prestigious projects and the like

5. Escalators and Moving Pathways, typical applications are _____.

    a. shopping centres, airports

    b. railway stations, sportingvenues

    c. similar large buildings

    d. All of above

Part 2. 能力练习(总共四题,满分 120 分)

一、单项填空(共 15 小题,每小题 1 分,满分 15 分)

从 A、B、C、D 四个选项中,选出可以填入空白处的最佳选项,并在答题卡上将该项涂黑。

1. The workers here get paid by _____ day, most of whom can get 30 Yuan _____ day.

    A. The;a   B. 不填;a   C. a;a   D. The;the

2. —He seldom has lunch at school, _____?

   —_____.

    A. does he;No, he hasn't   B. does he;No, but he did

    C. has he;Yes, he has   D. hasn't he;Yes, he doesn't

3. —I failed again. I wish I _____ harder.

   —But you _____.

    A. had worked;hasn't   B. worked;don't

    C. had worked;didn't   D. worked;didn't

4. The students were given less time _____ was needed, so many of them failed in the exam.

    A. that   B. which   C. as   D. than

5. The theory he stuck to _____ true.

    A. prove   B. proving   C. proved   D. be proved

6. —He seems to be a good teacher.

   —_____. He has been a teacher for 20 years.

    A. So does he   B. So he does   C. So is he   D. So he is

7. It is said that Ms Blackery _____ a novel last year, but I don't know whether she has finished it.

    A. has written   B. wrote   C. had written   D. was writing

8. —Why did you come to see the play you didn't like?

—I shouldn't like _____ ,but my friend insisted . I like _____ .
   A. having come, to dance   B. to have come, dancing
   C. to come; to dance   D. coming; dancing

9. —Airport, please. I have to be there by 7 o'clock.
   —_____ , but I'll do my best.
   A. I can't promise   B. I can't do that
   C. No problem   D. OK

10. Be open-minded, but confident, _____ ?
    A. isn't it   B. aren't you
    C. will you   D. are you

11. The company has a free long-distance telephone number _____ customers may call with any questions they have about the products.
    A. when   B. so that   C. while   D. as

12. —You must be excited about going abroad for schooling.
    —_____ , but I am worrying about my poor English.
    A. I'm not sure   B. Certainly not
    C. Well, I ought to   D. not at all

13. Do you know the foreigner our English teacher _____ about English study in our school yesterday?
    A. has spoken   B. had spoken   C. has speak   D. had speak

14. The boy the teachers considered _____ failed in the exam, _____ surprised them very much.
    A. to be the best; which   B. as the best; that
    C. to have been studying well; it   D. being the best; which

15. —Shall we set off right now?
    —Sorry. I'm too busy to _____ for the moment.
    A. get through   B. get away   C. get off   D. get together

二、完形填空(共 20 小题,每小题 1.5 分,满分 30 分)

阅读下面短文,掌握其大意,然后从 36～50 各题所给的四个选项中选出一个最佳选项,并在答题卡上将该项涂黑。

As I was looking at (16) on the shelves in Mc Carley's Bookstore in Ashland, the shop owner, asked if I'd like (17) . I needed to start (18) for college, so I said yes. I worked after school and during summers for the lowest wages, and the job helped (19) my freshman year of college. I would work many other jobs: I made coffee in the Students Union during college, I was a hotel maid and (20) made maps for the Forest Service. But selling books was one of the most (21) .

One day a woman asked me for books on cancer. She seemed fearful. I showed her almost everything we had at that time (22) and fond other books we could order. She left the store less (23) . I've always remembered the (24) I felt in having helped her.

258

Years later, as a (25) in Los Angeles, I heard about a black child born (26) his fingers connected, web-like. His family could not (27) a corrective operation, and the boy lived in (28), hiding his hand in his pocket.

I (29) my boss to let me do the story. After my story was broadcast, a doctor and a nurse called, offering to perform the (30) for free. I visited the boy in the (31) room soon after the operation. The first thing he did was to hold up his (32) hand and say, "Thank you." I felt a sense of (33).

In the past, (34) I was at Mc Carley's Bookstore, I always sensed I was working for the customers, not the store. Today it's the (35). NBC News pays my salary, but I feel as if I work for the viewer, helping them make sense of the world.

16. A. advertisement	B. titles	C. articles	D. reports
17. A. a book	B. a job	C. some tea	D. any help
18. A. planning	B. saving	C. preparing	D. studying
19. A. pay for	B. fit for	C. run for	D. enter for
20. A. so	B. ever	C. even	D. still
21. A. boring	B. surprising	C. satisfying	D. disappointing
22. A. in need	B. in all	C. in order	D. in store
23. A. worried	B. satisfied	C. excited	D. puzzled
24. A. pride	B. failure	C. regret	D. wonder
25. A. doctor	B. store owner	C. bookseller	D. TV reporter
26. A. in	B. with	C. by	D. for
27. A. pay	B. offer	C. afford	D. spend
28. A. shame	B. honor	C. horror	D. danger
29. A. advised	B. forced	C. persuaded	D. permitted
30. A. action	B. program	C. treatment	D. operation
31. A. waiting	B. recovery	C. reading	D. operation
32. A. repaired	B. connected	C. injured	D. improved
33. A. pleasure	B. sadness	C. interest	D. disappointment
34. A. if	B. though	C. until	D. while
35. A. difference	B. same	C. possibility	D. request

三、阅读理解(共 20 小题,每小题 2 分,满分 40 分)

阅读下列短文,从每题所给的 A、B、C、D 四个选项中,选出最佳选项,并在答题卡上将该项涂黑。

(一)

A nurse and her elder uncle were waiting for a bus at a corner in downtown Chicago. Buses came by, but not the one they wanted. The woman finally half-entered one of the buses and asked the driver if the bus she wanted stopped at that corner.

The driver looked at her but made no answer, so she repeated the question. To her surprise, he then closed the door, on her arm, and drove off.

The woman, her arm stuck in the door, ran alongside the bus, shouting. Passengers said the driver stopped after almost a block only because they, too, were shouting.

When the driver finally did stop and open the door, the woman jumped on the bus to get his bus number. Then he took off again and went another couple of blocks before other shouting passengers persuaded him to stop and let the woman off.

After the driver's bosses at a tax-supported governmental company (CTA) heard of the incident, they looked into it and set his punishment: a five-day suspension(停职) without pay. That struck me as rather light.

But Bill Baxa, the company's public-relations man, said, "That's a pretty serions punishment."

Five days off work is a serious punishment for dragging a woman alongside a bus by her arm? Baxa said, "Any time you take money away from someone, it is a terrible punishment. The driver makes $14 an hour. Multiply(乘) that by 40 and you can see what he lost."

Yes, that comes to $560, a good sum. Bot we know that people in the private company are fired for far less serious mistakes every day. If the people who run bus company think that the loss of a week's pay is more than enough. I offer them a sporting suggestion: Give me a bus. Then have their wives stick their arms in the doorway of the bus, and I'll slam the door shut, start the bus quickly and take them for a fast one-block run.

And I'll pay $560 to anyone who is bold enough to try it. Any takers? Mr. Baxa? Anyone?

I didn't think so.

36. The nurse half-entered one of the buses because _____.
  A. the bus they wanted didn't stop there
  B. she wanted the driver to stop the bus
  C. she wanted to get some information from the driver
  D. she and her uncle couldn't wait any longer at the corner

37. How many blocks was the woman away from the corner where she waited when the bus driver finally let her off?
  A. Almost one block.
  B. Almost two blocks.
  C. Probably three blocks.
  D. Probably five or six blocks.

38. Why did the author offer a sporting suggestion?
  A. Because the CTA paid little attention to the incident.
  B. Because the bus driver had not been fired.
  C. Because he wanted to threaten the CTA people.
  D. Because he thought the punishment was unreasonably too light.

39. Which of the following is NOT true?

A. The company is a bus company supported by the government.

B. The writer and Mr. Baxa disagreed with each other on the bus company's decision.

C. The driver finally stopped the bus under the pressure of the passengers.

D. The writer asked the bus company to give him a bus if his suggestion was refused.

(二)

Whenever we are involved in (投入) a creative type of activity that is self-rewarding, a feeling overcomes (takes control of) us -a feeling that we can call "flow". When we are flowing, we lose all sense of time and awareness(意识) of what is happening around us; instead, we feel that everything is going just right.

A rock dancer describes his feeling of flow like this:"If I have enough space, I feel I can radiate an energy into the atmosphere. I can dance for walls. I dance for floors. I become one with the atmosphere." "You are in an extremely happy state to such a point that you don't exist," says a composer, describing how he feels when he "flows". Players of any sport throughout the world are familiar with the feeling of flow; they enjoy their activity very much, even though they can expect little reward like money. The same holds true for surgeons (外科医生), cave explorers and mountain climbers.

Flow provides a sort of physical sensation along with a changed state of being. One man put it this way:"Your body feels good and awake all over. Your energy is flowing". People who flow feel part of this energy; that is, they are so involved in what they are doing that they do not think of themselves as being separate from their activity. They are flowing along with their enjoyment.

Besides, they concentrate intensely(keep all their attention) on their activity. They do not try to concentrate harder, however, the concentration comes automatically(自动). A chess player compares this concentration to breathing. As they concentrate, these people feel immersed(专心致志) in the action, lost in the action. This sense of time is changed and they skip meals(don't eat) and sleep without noticing their loss. Sizes and spaces also seem changed; successful baseball players see and hit the ball so much better because it seems larger to them. They can even recognize the seams(线缝) on the ball approaching(coming near to) them at 165 kilometers per hour.

40. To experience the feeling of "flow", a person should _____.

    A. enjoy an activity   B. want rewards like money or other things

    C. feel that his or her body is alive   D. feel like a fish swimming in water

41. Many people who experience "flow" say it _____.

    A. causes a change in their lives

    B. makes them feel separate from their activities

    C. is a special state of mind and body

    D. helps them breathe well and do everything successfully

42. "Flow" causes people to _____.

    A. think deeply   B. forget things easily

C. sleep a lot   D. forget to eat and sleep

43. The word "put" in the sentence "One man put it this way." means _____.
    A. dealt with   B. showed
    C. explained   D. made out

(三)

When a consumer(消费者)finds that something he or she bought is faulty or in some other way does not live up to what the producer says for it, the first step is to present the warranty(保单), or any other records that might help, at the store of buying. In most cases, this action will produce results. However, if it does not, there are various means the consumer may use to gain satisfaction.

A simple and common method used by many consumers is to complain(投诉)directly to the store manager. In general, the "higher up" the consumer takes his or her complaint, the faster he or she can expect it to be settled. In such a case, it is usually settled in the consumer's favour, taking it as true that he or she had a just right.

Consumers should complain in person whenever possible, but if they cannot get to the place of buying, it is acceptable to phone or write the complaint in a letter.

Complaining is usually most effective when it is done politely but firmly, and especially when the consumer can show clearly what is wrong with what was bought in question. If this cannot be done, the consumer will succeed best by presenting specific information as to what is wrong, rather than by making general statements. For example, "The left speaker does not work at all and the sound coming out of the right one is unclear." is better than "This stereo(立体音响)does not work." The store manager may advise the consumer to write to the producer. If so, the consumer should do this, stating the complaint as politely and as firmly as possible. But if a polite complaint does not achieve the expected result, the consumer can go a step further. He or she can threaten(恐吓)to take the seller to court or report the seller to a public organization responsible for protecting consumers' rights.

44. When a consumer finds what he bought has a fault in it, he should first _____.
    A. complain personally to the manager
    B. show something provable in written from to the store
    C. threaten to take the matter to court
    D. write a firm letter of complaint to the store

45. The most effective complaint about what was bought can be made by _____.
    A. showing the fault of it to the producer
    B. saying firmly it is of poor quality
    C. asking politely to change it
    D. explaining exactly what is wrong with it

46. The passage tell us _____.
    A. how to make the complaint have a good effect

262

B. how to settle a consumer's complaint

C. how to avoid buying something wrong

D. how to deal with complaints from consumers

47. According to the passage, the last way a consumer has to use is _____.

   A. to write to the producer

   B. to quarrel with the manager

   C. to warn the seller that he or she will turn to the court or a consumers' organization for help

   D. to collect several fighters to threaten the seller

(四)

BERLIN-Germany will admit up to 20,000 foreign high-tech workers, under a plan announced on May 31. Chancellor(总理)Gerhard Schroeder sees this as a way to keep the country from falling behind in information technology.

The plan for these so-called "green cards", not unlike the US work permit system, came in answer to industry complaints that there were not enough qualified workers to fill positions.

Workers who come to Germany under the new rules, effective from August, will be given a five-year work permit after proving they have completed studies in a related field, or can promise to make at least 100,000 marks(US$ 48,000)in yearly salary.

Family members are also allowed to receive work permits. "There is strong competition in the rest of the world for these people," Schroeder said, mentioning not only the United States but also Britain and France. "Germany would be making a mistake if it didn't take part in this competition." He said employers have already offered 11,000 jobs through a "green card hot line" and some 4,700 applicants (people who ask for a position) have e-mailed information requests.

The Chancellor also said that the number of workers and the time limit of their stay may be extended, impossible under current German law.

Allowing the workers to stay longer means they could finally become citizens. Since the beginning of the year, foreigners who have lived in the country for eight years can ask to be naturalized(使加入国籍).

48. From the first paragraph we know that _____.

   A. Germany is a less-developed country

   B. Germany used to be a developed country

   C. Germany is short of high-tech workers

   D. Germany once lost interest in information technology

49. If a high-tech worker wants to work in Germany, he or she can enter Germany _____.

   A. in June   B. after July   C. before August   D. at any time

50. According to this passage workers from foreign countries usually ask for jobs

263

by _____.

    A. telephone   B. letter   C. internet   D. telegram

51. To be naturalized as a German, according to this passage, seems _____.

    A. difficult   B. easy   C. impossible   D. popular

(五)

    On July 16, 1960, Jane Goodall, a 26-year-old former secretary from England, began to study the behaviour of chimpanzees in the wild. Until that time, scientists had mostly observed and studied chimpanzees in laboratories and zoos. Few scientists had gone to study chimpanzees in the remote areas of Africa where the chimps live. When scientists had studied the chimpanzees in the wild, they hadn't spent long periods of time observing them Jane Goodall planned to watch chimpanzees in Africa over a ten-year period and see exactly how they behaved. She was not a professional scientist when she started out. Her book, In the Shadow of Man, tells how she began her project and what she discovered.

    As Goodall said in 1973, "I had no qualifications at all. I was just somebody with a love of animals." Her love of animals drew her to Africa, where she met Dr Louis S. B. Leakey. Leakey was a world-famous scientist who was studying how prehistoric people lived. Since chimpanzees are humans' closest living relatives, Leakey thought prehistoric people might have lived in the same ways that chimpanzees live today. Leakey told Goodall that studying chimpanzees might give clues about the way that early people lived.

    Leakey asked Goodall to study the chimpanzees on the shores of Lake Tanganyike in Africa. The chimpanzees were very shy and the country was very difficult to travel through. Goodall took on the difficult job of finding and watching the chimpanzees.

52. It is clear from the text that Jane Goodall decided to study chimpanzees _____.

    A. because she was working in a laboratory

    B. when she was doing research for a book

    C. because of her scientific work in England

    D. after she met Dr Leakey in Africa

53. According to the text, Dr Leakey was a scientist who _____.

    A. worked at Lake Tanganyika

    B. studied how prehistoric people lived

    C. researched the behaviour of animals in zoos

    D. taught people to identify different species of chimpanzees

54. Dr Leakey thought that studying chimpanzees would help his work because chimpanzees _____.

    A. are easy to locate in the wild

    B. are closely related to humans

    C. enjoy interaction(相互作用)with humans

    D. have predictable behaviour patterns

55. According to the information, finding chimpanzees in Africa would be a difficult task

for Jane because _____.

A. the country was rugged and the animals were timid(easily frightened)
B. the chimpanzees may not remain in the area for ten years
C. Jane would have to identify areas where prehistoric people had lived
D. Dr Leakey was not aware of the conditions in which the chimpanzees lived

四、写作(共两题,满分35分)

(一) 短文改错(共10小题,每小题1分,满分10分)

此题要求改正所给短文中的错误。对标有题号的每一行作出判断;

如无错误,在该行右边横线上画个勾(√);如有错误(每行只有一个错误),则按下列情况改正:

此行多一个词:把多余的词用斜线(\)划掉,在该行右边横线上写出该词,并也用斜线划掉。

此行缺一个词:在缺词处加一个漏字符号(∧),在该行右边横线上写出该加的词。

此行错一个词:在错的词下划一横线,在该行右边横线上写出改正后的词。

注意:原行没有错的不要改。

A newspaper is a medium(媒介)that tell the new of the day	56._____
and the other things. There are good newspapers and worse	57._____
newpapers. You can know more and more interested	58._____
in it even if you read a good newspaper each day	59._____
A good newspaper should have well-train and	60._____
reliable people worked for it. One of the important people	61._____
in the newspaper staff (工作人员)is the reporter. It's the	62._____
reporter job to be sure that the facts are checked	63._____
after they are printed. A newspaper may also give some	64._____
comments on the news , that can help you work out how	65._____
the news may affect you	

(二) 书面表达(25分)

根据下面所示内容,用英语写一篇100词左右的短文,简述乘飞机或火车旅行的利弊及你的观点。短文应包括图表所提示的全部内容,标题与文章的第一句已经给出,不计入总词数。

交通工具	飞机	火车
价格	900元	250元
施行时间	2小时	58小时
优点	省时、舒适、便于休息	便宜、可以观光
缺点	昂贵	耗时、拥挤、不利休息

以从青岛到广州为例。

Train Travel and Air Travel

Air travel had two advantages over train travel...

附录一 本书练习答案 Keys

Unit 1.

Part1. Text

Ⅰ. Keys to the exercises of the Text

(Ⅰ) Decide whether the following sentences are True or False according to the content of the text.

T T F F T F T F T T

(Ⅱ) Connect the word of column A to the explanation that is similar to it in column B with a bar

| e | h | i | d | a | j | b | g | c | f |

(Ⅲ) 1d 2d 3a 4c 5b 6a 7b 8b 9c 10d

(Ⅳ) Translate the following Chinese into English

1. In simple term, property means what one owns.
2. Property management has long been an underrated function in the real estate industry.
3. The task calls for training, good judgement, and a variety of technical skills.
4. Good property management is the major controllable influence on residual cash flow.
5. Some investors have the feeling that real estate manages itself.
6. Property management is the process of overseeing the operation and maintenance of real property to achieve the objectives of the property owner.
7. That is a highly challenging task.
8. Traditionally, however, the emphasis in the real estate industry has been on the so-called permanent elements of the investment.
9. Both rent rates and operating expenses are largely shaped by market forces.
10. His contribution was management expertise.

(Ⅴ) Extra Reading

1. b 2. c 3. a 4. d 5. d

Ⅱ. Language Ability Drill

(Ⅰ) Vocabulary Exercise

1. careful cared careless care carefully carelessness carelessly careful

2. addition   additional   add   additional
3. use   useless   use   useful   used   use
4. meaning   meaningful   means   means
5. comfortably   comfort   comfortable   comfort   comfortable
6. probably   probability   probable   probably

(Ⅱ) Cloze

1. A. 根据下文中 throughout the test,可断定此处答案。
2. C. 根据常识,应为批阅卷纸,四个选项中,只有 mark 符合搭配。
3. C. 根据上下文语境可以确定"十二个男生犯了完完全全相同的错误"。
4. B. 本空所在句子的动词为一般现在时,表示真理性内容或一般状况。"考试中的什么不算真正新鲜?"作弊。
5. A. 根据下文中 Mrs. O'Neill 的一系列做法,可以推出此处为否定。
6. C. 根据下文介绍以及常理,学生做错事,应挨骂。
7. A. either 一词可以提示此处应为否定。
8. D. 根据上下文意思。确定欧内尔小姐既没有问问题,也没有责怪我们。
9. A. 根据开篇 Thomas Macaulay 的名言可确定。
10. D. 四个选项都是及物动词,但意义不同。repeat 为"重说",get 为"得到",put 为"放置",copy 为"抄写"。此处为罚抄,D 项最合适。
11. B. 根据语境,应为"我不知道其他 11 个男孩。"
12. A. 后文讲的作者自己的感受。
13. C. chance 表示"机会",incident"事变",lesson"教训",memory"记忆"。根据全文可知这是一次教训。
14. D. 根据语境,应为"自从我首次拜读麦考利那句话后,至少已有三十余年了。"be introduced to 为"初次与…相识"之意。
15. B. even 为"甚至",still 为"仍然",always 为"一直",almost 为"几乎"。与上文中 thirty years 的时间相转折。
16. A. 根据句意应为"方法"。
17. B. 与下句中的"all"相对应。
18. C. 国家参战或部队战斗应属重大决定。
19. D. call for 意为"要求"与 demand 近意,用于此处语气太强,不合适。call up 意为"打电话",不符题意。call on sb. to do"让某人做某事"近意于 ask sb. to do 语气正合适。
20. A. 与下文中的 should the extra change received… 并列。
21. B. 前后具有选择关系。
22. A. 根据文意,多找的零钱才会让我们犹豫不决。
23. D. 根据上下文语境,应为"该忘掉还是该还回去?"
24. B. 根据下文 But you have to live yourself,可确定。
25. C. 根据文意,作者此处提出建议"倘若你以你所尊重的人的标准来约束你自己,那会更好"。

(Ⅲ) **Fulfill sentences according to the words given in the bracket**(按照括号中的中文完成句子)：

1. so that I could read it when I was free.
2. so that she could receive it in the afternoon.
3. so that everybody could hear you.
4. and some eggs as well.
5. and plays as well.
6. and America as well.
7. and swims and skates as well.
8. give them a reply as soon as you can.
9. Read over this book as quickly as you can.
10. write home as often as he could.

Part 2. Dialogue

Ⅲ. **Exercises for Dialogue in text**

Fill in the following blanks while observing the conversational manner
（按照日常会话习惯完成以下填空）

1. How are you!
2. Can I help you?
3. Thank you (very much).
4. You are welcome.

Ⅳ. **Spoken Language Drill** (fill in the blanks according to the Chinese translation)

Dialogue 1. & Dialogue 2.
get   miss   long   straight   five-minute
Dialogue 3. & dialogue 4.
wonder   a little   blocks   right   takes

Part 3. Supplementary Reading
Passage A
1. D   2. C   3. D   4. C   5. C

Unit 2.

Part1. Text

Ⅰ. **keys to the exercises of the Text**

(Ⅰ) **Decide whether the following sentences are True or False according to the content of the text.**
F F T F T T F T T F

(Ⅱ) **Connect the word of column A to the explanation which is similar to it in column B with a bar**

| g | d | a | f | h | i | j | e | b | c |

(Ⅲ) 1a 2b 3c 4a 5c 6b 7b 8c 9b 10d

(Ⅳ) **Translate the following Chinese into English**

1. This paucity of information has a number of implications, all of them negative.

2. Much greater attention is now being paid to building and maintenance issues.

3. For a maintenance plan to be truly effective, it should or must prevent a failure.

4. Building owners and managers are also now required to provide a minimum standard of maintenance with respect to the control of microorganisms.

5. Service Records play a vital role in preventive maintenance.

6. Many buildings are now reaching an age when the owners need to decide whether to refurbish or rebuild.

7. More attention is being paid to preventative maintenance in an attempt to defer the high costs of replacement.

8. Unfortunately this results in a wide range of costs.

9. Maintenance service schedules need to be provided for each item of equipment.

10. Automatic control systems are the most important single item in any building air-conditioning system.

(Ⅴ) **Extra Reading**

1. d 2. b 3. a 4. c 5. d

Ⅱ. **Language Ability Drill**

(Ⅰ) **Vocabulary Exercise**

1. experience inexperience experiencing inexperienced experienced experienced
2. doubtful doubt doubted undoubtedly doubtfully undoubtedly
3. unfortunate Fortunately fortune Misfortune unfortunately fortunate

(Ⅱ) **Cloze:**

1. D. 根据下文中 Here's a fellow who just walks into a bank. 可确定。

2. D. search for 表示"寻找"; hold up 表示"阻滞"; take over 表示"接管"; break into 表示"破门而入;闯入",此处最恰当。

3. A. 根据上下的 break into 可知劫匪走进银行。

4. C. help oneself to sth. 表示"未经允许随意取用",此处意为"窃取"。

5. B. 下文 So much money to pay back 已说明开办加油站搞到资金的难处。

6. D. 根据语境,应为他开办加油站所需的资金。

7. C. 此处 papers 意为"文件"。sign papers 表示"签署文件"。

8. A. last 表示"持续",常与一段时间连用。如,That war lasted for four years. continue表示"延续",也可指中断后的"继续"。从句末的时间状语 twenty minutes later,可以确定此空表示中断后继续播送的新闻,故选 A。

9. D. 从下文中 pushed out the driver,可以推出应为 stopped 表示"拦截"。

10. D. send out 表示"发放出去";find out 表示"查明,弄清";leave out 表示"留出,遗漏";push out 表示"推开,攮走"。此处只有 D 项最符合。

11. C. head for 表示"朝…方向前进"最符合此处的语境。

12. D. voice 表示人的说话声,根据 of the announcer,D 项最合适。

13. A. Look out for 是固定搭配,表示"小心;注意……"。

14. B. pick up"中途搭乘"之意,根据语境应为不要让陌生人搭车之意。

15. C. gas stations 是为人提供服务的地方,do service to 是固定词组,表示"为…提供服务",用于对加油站的告诫最恰当。

16. A. 根据语境,托德站起来,只是设法看了看寒冷的黑夜。

17. B. 根据上文介绍的情况,我们知道 Todd 在此开加油站,对此应很了解。learn 表示"听说",此处不合适。

18. A. Just then 意为"就在那时",符合故事情节发展的时间顺序。

19. C. 下文中 When the tank was full 提示,这辆小汽车到加油站是为加油。

20. B. 下文紧接着给出车牌号 LJR1939,所以 number 最符题意。

21. A. 下文中提到 Todd asked while making up his mind for sure,不难断定此处应为 make a decision. 做出决定。

22. D. 根据"Yes,sir?",可确定 ask。

23. B. cover up 是"盖住";fill up"加满";check up"检查;核对";tie up"捆,绑"。根据上文的 a car pulled in for gas. 可确定司机的回答应为加油。

24. C. 根据常识,来加油站与 Todd 打交道的应为 driver。

25. B. 这是警察经常说的一句话。and 连接两个相继发生的动作。

(Ⅲ) Fulfill sentences according to the words given in the bracket(按照括号中的中文完成句子):

1. couldn't help thinking
2. he woke up
3. dissuade him from
4. set out to improve
5. had previously met
6. be by far the most

Part 2. Dialogue

Ⅲ. Exercises for Dialogue in text

Fill in the following blanks while observing the conversational manner(按照日常会话习惯完成以下填空)

1. That's all right.
2. May I have your name, please?
3. My name
4. Thank you.
5. Of course

6. That's very kind of you.

Ⅳ. **Spoken Language Drill** (fill in the blanks according to the Chinese translation)

Dialogue 1. & Dialogue 2.
really while honor early delicious
Dialogue 3. & dialogue 4.
farewell same coming more pleasant

Part 3. Supplementary Reading
1. d 2. d 3. a 4. c 5. b

Unit 3.

Part1. Text

Ⅰ. **Keys to the exercises of the Text**

(Ⅰ) Decide whether the following sentences are True or False according to the content of the text.
T T F F T T F T F

(Ⅱ) Connect the word of column A to the explanation which is similar to it in column B with a bar

| b | a | e | d | c | g | f | j | i | h |

(Ⅲ) 1a 2a 3a 4b 5d 6b 7c 8c 9c 10c

(Ⅳ) Translate the following Chinese into English

1. The performance of the building services is a key factor in the building occupants' assessment of their environment.

2. These service systems are generally not automatically adaptable to changing tenants' requirements.

3. Historically, the maintenance of building services systems has been the responsibility of contracting organizations.

4. The building owner enters a contract with an air-conditioning maintenance contractor.

5. A further important area that requires scrutiny and close management is the tenancy fitout modifications to buildings.

6. It must be continually maintained at an appropriate level if satisfactory performance is to be achieved throughout the life of the building.

7. The building owner is generally obliged to engage the installation contractor for the ongoing maintenance of the lifts.

8. In some instances the maintenance agreement is a comprehensive contract.

9. In the past there has been a tendency for tenants to alter their fitout layouts without reference to the Building Manager.

10. The Building Manager is dependent on a combination of his or her own knowl-

edge, in-house expertise, and/or external consultants.

(Ⅴ) Extra Reading

1d　2c　3d　4d　5b

Ⅱ. Language Ability Drill

(Ⅰ) Vocabulary Exercise

1. shortens　widened　sharpen　broadens　quicken　darkened
2.1 excitement　excited　excited　excitedly　excites　exciting
2.2 disappointment　disappointing　disappointed　disappointed　disappointing
2.3 patiently　patience　patient　patience
2.4 reluctant　reluctance　reluctantly　reluctant
2.5 efficiency　efficient　efficiently　efficient

(Ⅱ) Cloze

1. D. 由下文中 In her eyes he couldn't do anything wrong. 以及母亲对儿子无微不至的照顾可以看出 Ella Fant 非常爱自己惟一的儿子 John。

2. B. in one's eyes 或 in the eyes of sb. 是固定的介词短语,表示"在某人的心目中"或"在某人看来。"

3. A. 从上文中 She loved John very much. 以及下文中她观看儿子行军的态度,足以判断出她坚信儿子不会做错事。

4. C. in bed 为固定词组,意为"卧床"。

5. B. 四个选项的动词中,只有 B 项和 to 构成不定式短语,作后置定语修饰 the papers 与上下文语境相符,read the papers 是"读报纸"的意思。

6. A. 四个选项中的形容词均可用于"too...to..."句型,表示"太……以至不能……",但通过下文的 in fact he had tried a few jobs. 可确定为 A。

7. D. 上句谈论的话题是 work,而与 work 有相同意义的可数名词为 job,此处最恰当。

8. C. 四个选项中的动词都是及物动词,都可以带宾语,符合此处的语法。但是根据下文,可以看出 John 一直在做错事,所以应选"C. break",意指他工作失误,打碎玻璃。

9. C.根据下文他的遭遇 on his second day a passenger stole his bag with fares collected,断定这里指他当上了公共汽车售票员。

10. A. day 与 on 相搭配,表示特定的某一天,故为最佳选择。

11. B. 上文叙述 John 开始时玻璃清洁工的工作就没做好。做汽车售票员时,所收的车费又被偷了。再联系这里由于工作失职而丢掉邮递员的工作,这一件接一件不幸事情的发生,应由 even(甚至于)来加强语气。

12. C. 根据上句结果可判定用 because 引导原因状语从句来解释原因。

13. D. 由上文一连串的失败的遭遇可以推出表否定意义的形容词 no。

14. D. 四个选项都可以接不定式。但仍根据 John 的许多次失败,以至于 It seemed that there was no suitable work for him 可以想到他最后决定参军。

15. A. 根据下文 that she told the news to all her neighbours,可以判断 Mrs. Fant 对儿子参军之事的兴奋心情。

16. C. incident 表示"事件,尤指事变";change 表示"改变";matter 常指"一件小事"在此处都不合适;news 意为"消息",应为最佳选项。

17. B. 此处也是考查词语辨析能力。范特太太说:我的约翰要去当兵了,我说他将是过去从未有过的最优秀的士兵。在四个选项 yet,ever,never 和 just 中,只有副词 ever 具有"at any time in the past"(在过去任何时候)的意思。

18. C. 先行词为 the great day 表示时间,四个选项中只有关系副词 when 可以引导修饰时间的定语从句。

19. A. 根据文中 Mrs Fant 对邻居说的话"He is going to be the best soldier there ever was, I can tell you."可以清楚看出她的自豪心情,故填 proud。

20. B. 感到自豪的母亲那天早早就进城了,为的是确保在人群中找到一个好位置。

21. D. 根据日常生活常识,我们应该得知刚刚入伍,走在队列中的约翰旁边是他的"战友",而不会是"他的领导"(A 项)、"军官"(B 项),更不可能是"他的母亲"(C 项)。

22. A. "can't help doing"是固定词组,表示"不禁;忍不住……"

23. B. 通过下文中 Ella Fant 高声呼喊的"……Isn't he the best!"可以体会出她愉快的心情。

24. A. 下文中提到 They're all out of step except my John! 主语给出信息词 They,此处应用其宾格 them。

25. D. 四个选项均可与 out of 搭配。out of sight 表示"看不见",out of order 表示"发生故障",out of mind 表示"精神不正常",out of step 表示"步调不一致",由上文中 the one who couldn't keep pace with the other 可确定 D。

(Ⅱ) Fulfill sentences according to the words given in the bracket.

1. can endure
2. at the occasion of
3. to pick it up
4. aren't sure of
5. was disappointed
6. Discontent

Part2. Dialogue

Ⅲ. Exercises for Dialogue in text

Fill in the following blanks while observing the conversational manner(按照日常会话习惯完成以下填空)

1. tell
2. going
3. Congratulations on your marriage!
4. By the way

Ⅳ. **Spoken Language Drill**(fill in the blanks according to the Chinese translation)

Dialogue 1. & Dialogue 2.

mind　　exactly　　possible　　chance　　Until

Dialogue 3. & dialogue 4.

wondering　think　over　lend　holidays

Part 3. Supplementary Reading

　　1. c　2. c　3. b　4. d　5. d

Unit 4.

Part1. Text

I. Keys to the exercises of the Text

(I) Decide whether the following sentences are True or False according to the content of the text.

F T F F F T T F

(II) Connect the word of column A to the explanation which is similar to it in column B with a bar

| j | i | e | g | c | f | d | h | b | a |

(III) 1b　2d　3b　4a　5c　6b　7d　8b　9b　10c

(IV) Translate the following Chinese into English

1. It is meant that the users of those keys may only be given access to the building during designated hours.

2. Security is a unique subject, which applies both to the asset and the building users.

3. This selective keying system allows you to authorize only certain people in the building between certain hours, and into certain areas.

4. Key cutting can only be undertaken with the authorization of the Building Ownership or the Building Manager, and generally only at specialist or nominated facilities.

5. Tenants using the building during both normal office hours, and after hours, require the knowledge that both they, their property and their own business are safe.

6. Today, for a whole variety of reasons, tenants can and are being targeted for bomb threats, bribery, larceny, computer associated crimes.

7. The purpose of alarms is to detect unauthorized access or movement in, or through a particular area.

8. This is usually a design component, which needs to be reviewed by the Property Manager at the time of construction of the building with the building's architect.

9. Also corridors, service bays, lanes, plant rooms, fire corridors etc. all need special consideration.

10. The tendency today is away from internal night watchman services towards the services of an external security patrol company.

(V) Extra Reading

　　1. a　2. c　3. b　4. d　5. b

Ⅱ. Language Ability Drill

(Ⅰ) Vocabulary Exercise

1. honestly   dishonest   honesty   honest   honest
2. childish   childishly   child   childhood   childhood
3. activities   act   active   act   actively   Action   activity
4. emotional   unemotional   emotion   Emotionally   emotional
5. acceptable   acceptably   accept   acceptance   accept
6. distraction   distracted   distracts   distracting   distractions

(Ⅱ) Cloze:

1. D. 四个选项很难一开始就确定,暂放一放,当读到下文"I mean we are assistant bell ringers for the church"可以选定 D。

2. C. 根据下文中"nonstop"和"protest"推出应为不停摇铃表示抗议,而摇铃习惯搭配为 ring the bell。

3. B. 根据下文中"They make it difficult to sleep at night"推出应为词组 day and night 表示"日日夜夜"。

4. B. 上文提到 protest,那一定是使"人睡难"。

5. A. 固定词组 do damage to 表示"对……造成破坏"。

6. C. historical interest 表示历史古迹。

7. A. 在下文中学生建议建新道,显现此处应为假设条件,"如果这些噪声大的卡车必须在道上运行的话,为什么不在城填周围建一条新路呢?"

8. D. 从上下文中,我们可以看出大卡车造成的噪声污染给居民带来很大痛苦,他们抗议大卡车在镇子里通行,所以路应是围绕着镇子而不能穿过(through)。

9. C.

10. B. 学生们仍在说镇子不适合拥挤的交通。因为它也不比大村庄大多少。

11. C. 上文已介绍 Jean Lacey 是 a biology student。下文中介绍用了 also,情况如下。

12. D. 上文已交待出她们在敲钟而且"People of Berlington are being disturbed by the sound of bells."那么他们显然是在制造噪声。

13. C.

14. A. stand 在此意为"忍受、承受(to be forced to accept an unpleasant or difficult situation)"

15. B.

16. B.

17. A. 文中的"they come in for meetings and that, and the Town Hall is soundproof."是解题关键。市政厅应是政府官员所在处。他们不住在这儿,而只是来开会。因此,也就不会注意到这噪声。

18. D. event 指"重大事件"如,the events of 1999 九九年的大事;loss 是"损失"如,The Great Britain suffered great loss in the second world war. 英国在二战中遭受巨大损失;action 是"行为行动",如 take action 采取行动;problem 表示"问题",指失业,罢工,游行,抗议

275

等一些社会问题。

19. Hardly 表示"几乎不", unwillingly 表示"不愿意", mostly 表示"大部分", usually 表示"通常"。此处意思应该是"她认为公众大部分站在他们一边(支持他们),即使过去不是如此,很快也会是"。

20. A. 根据最后一句得知"我"是采访此事的人。

21. B.

22. D. 警察若到来,也应是要阻止他们,那么正常心理应为害怕。

23. A. 根据下句解释 I mean we are assistant bell-ringers for the church 可确定 proper bell-ringers. 专门敲钟的人。

24. D. point"理由"搭配为 There's no point in doing sth. 表示"没有做某事的理由"。cause"原因",主要表示事件的起因,如 What's the cause of the fire? 火灾的起因是什么? need"必要",搭配应为 There's no need to do sth. 没必要做某事。law 是"法律,法规"正是答案,"没有法律禁止练习。"

25. A. 根据上文语境,"I"为采访者,采访结束后,离开教堂。

(Ⅲ) Fulfill sentences according to the words given in the bracket(按照括号中的中文完成句子):

1. come up with some ideas
2. are prohibited from
3. to communicate with one another
4. to bring together people
5. in its birth rate
6. because of

Part 2. Dialogue

Ⅲ. Exercises for Dialogue in text:

Fill in the following blanks while observing the conversational manner(按照日常会话习惯完成以下填空)

1. This is   speaking   I help you
2. May I speak to
3. Hold on
4. May I leave a message?
5. I can do for you
6. I think that's all   for your help
7. You're welcome

Ⅳ. **Spoken Language Drill** (fill in the blanks according to the Chinese translation)

Dialogue 1. & Dialogue 2.
appointment afraid possibly openings convenient

Dialogue 3. & dialogue 4.
speak   hold on   out   message   of course

Part 3. Supplementary Reading
1. c 2. a 3. c 4. c 5. b

Unit 5.

Part 1. Text

Ⅰ. Keys to the exercises of the text

(Ⅰ) Decide whether the following sentences are True or False according to the content of the text.
1. T 2. F 3. F 4. F 5. T 6. F

(Ⅱ) Connect the word of column A to the explanation which is similar to it in column B with a bar

2.1
1c 2i 3f 4b 5a 6e 7d 8j 9g 10h

2.2
1. 你认为怎么合适就怎么办吧。proper
2. 军民关系像鱼水。relationship
3. 这是党政工作人员的重大职责。responsibilities
4. 你领会他说话的含义吗？imply
5. 那是一件穿破了的上衣。worn
6. 他提醒了我,否则我就会把这事给忘了。otherwise
7. 他们正在替换已不适用的设备。unserviceable
8. 那是一个明显的错误。evident
9. 他这样说是没有理由的。warrant
10. 滴水穿石。Wore
11. 在今后两到三周内我将很忙。course

2.3
1b 2b 3a 4b 5a 6b 7c 8c 9d 10d 11a 12d

(Ⅲ) Translate the following Chinese into English

1. Comprehensive contract maintenance provides ongoing maintenance.

2. Inspect the equipment for worm, burnt, broken and compensate for any evident irregular running or deviation from normal design characteristics.

3. In respect of lifts, renew all wire ropes when necessary and equalize the tension on all hoisting ropes.

4. Periodically examine all safety devices and governors and carry out tests as required by relevant statutes, regulation sand requirements.

5. Stock such spare parts and materials as are reasonably necessary for performing preventative maintenance.

6. Upon notification of any such emergency breakdown by the owner, the equipment will be serviced as soon as practicable.

7. The attending contractor's representative may reserve the right to charge the owner.

8. At the request of the owner and at reasonable notice, the specialist contractor will perform the additional services.

9. Perform any of the works listed outside normal working hours.

10. Contractor received the additional costs incurred in performing such work.

(Ⅳ) Extra Reading

1b 2d 3a 4c 5d.

Ⅱ. Language Ability Drill

(Ⅰ) Vocabulary Exercise

1. snow-white 2. lifelong 3. color-blind 4. world-wide 5. carefree 6. knee-deep 7. duty-free 8. seasick

(Ⅱ) Cloze

1. B. 上文说到：从事医学研究的科学家有了一个有趣的发现，下文必然阐述："他们能够……"be able to 在这里表示"能力"。

2. A. inside us 指的是"我们的体内"。

3. D. rise 同 fall 是一对反义词，在此表示体能的上升与下降。

4. C. making 在此意为"使……"，作伴随状语，进一步说明上面的意思，即"生物钟控制我们体能的升降，使我们一天与另一天有所不同"。本题最大干扰项为 D，但 change 填入后句型结构不通(change 后不接形容词作宾补)。

5. D. "生物钟"是一种假说，一种构想。本题最大干扰项是 B。idea 与 opinion 虽属同义词，但两者之间还有区别：idea 是动态名词，多表示对某件事的计划、判断、理解、建议及其实现可能性的评测，即"主意、思想、构想、想法"之意；opinion 是状态名词，表示对某件事、某个人的看法或舆论，即"意见、看法、见解"之意。

6. C. 从下文所述内容及我们生活中的体验来证实，"生物钟"这一假说的提出并不令人奇怪。

7. B. 此处为被动语态，表示"大多数生物的生活由 24 小时的循环来控制着"。

8. B. 正是因为疲劳所以才睡觉。and 在此连接两个形容词表示因果。A 项 dull 意为"迟钝的、呆的"(＝showing slowness in thinking, understanding and action)，dreamy 意为"活在梦中的、顶呱呱的"，peaceful 意为"平静的、安宁的"，均不切题。

9. C. 表示白天我们变得生机勃勃，充满活力。

10. A. disturb 意为"打乱、扰乱"，shorten 意为"变短"，reset 意为"重放、重拨"，显然 A 项切题。

11. D. feelings 指"知觉、感觉"(即 consciousness of something felt)；sense 指"辨别力、观念、意识"(即 power to understand and make judgments about sth)，多作单数用。此处用 feelings 切题。

12. D. 从 to working 可判断此空该填 used，be used to doing sth 表示"习惯于……"。

13. C. lack 表示"缺少、缺乏"，lack of sleep 表示"睡眠不足"。

14. A. perform 不仅指"演出"，也可作"执行、履行"(＝to do, to carry out)解。此处表示在"工作中干得不好"。

278

15. B. as well as 意为"不但……而且"。全句意思是：we also have other cycles as well as the daily cycle of sleeping and（waking）。except（除……之外），rather than（而不是），with（随着……），均语意不通。

16. D. sleeping and waking 互为反义。

17. C. last 表示"时间持续的长短"（＝to measure in length of time），在此表示还有一些循环比之"白天工作、夜晚睡觉"这种循环持续时间更长。本题最大干扰项为 B：remain。该词含义是"仍然、依旧"（to continue；to be in an unchanged state），用于此句显然不通。

18. A. agree，believe，realize 都可接 that 从句，此处用 agree 表示与科学家们所提的关于"生物钟"的想法有同感（agree：to say yes to an idea，与文意相符）。

19. D. others 与 some days 相呼应。

20. A. just 用作副词表示强调。此题 B 项为最大干扰项。虽然 just 与 only 都可表示强调，但含义有所不同。only 基本含义为"惟一的"，用作副词表示强调，仍与其基本义有关，且一般不用于否定句。just 基本意思是"公正、合理"，作副词用来表示强调，具有"正好、恰恰、不偏不倚"等含义。

(Ⅲ) Fulfill Sentences according to the words given in the bracket（按照括号中的中文完成句子）：

1. could have bought a coat
2. couldn't have succeeded in the experiment within such a short period of time
3. could have made
4. could have lent you
5. could have helped her

Part 2. Dialogue

Ⅲ. Exercises for Dialogue in text：

Fill in the following blanks while observing the conversational manner（按照日常会话习惯完成以下填空）

1. Do you have a car parking card   exchange your driving license
2. in the grass or the sidewalk
3. Your parking area is No. 9

Ⅳ. Spoken Language Drill（fill in the blanks according to the Chinese translation）

Dialogue 1. ＆ Dialogue 2.
clearing   last   hope   Beautiful   stay
Dialogue 3. ＆ dialogue 4.
sunny   better   later   improvement   over

Part 3. Supplementary Reading
1. c   2. a   3. d   4. c   5. a

期 中 测 试

Part 1. 专业练习

一、

1. Both rent rates and operating expenses are largely shaped by market forces.

2. Property management is the process of overseeing the operation and maintenance of real property to achieve the objectives of the property owner.

3. More attention is being paid to preventative maintenance in an attempt to defer the high costs of replacement.

4. Automatic control systems are the most important single item in any building air-conditioning system.

5. In the past there has been a tendency for tenants to alter their fitout layouts without reference to the Building Manager.

6. It must be continually maintained at an appropriate level if satisfactory performance is to be achieved throughout the life of the building.

7. The purpose of alarms is to detect unauthorized access or movement in, or through a particular area.

8. Also corridors, service bays, lanes, plant rooms, fire corridors etc. all need special consideration.

9. Upon notification of any such emergency breakdown by the owner, the equipment will be serviced as soon as practicable.

10. Inspect the equipment for worm, burnt, broken and compensate for any evident irregular running or deviation from normal design characteristics.

二、

(一)

1. to, to
2. Fine, and you   I am fine
3. Have
4. sorry
5. kind
6. have
7. Would
8. My pleasure
9. With pleasure.
10. on
11. In
12. This is   Of course.
13. What
14. to for
15. excuse me

(二)

1. may I speak to Mr. Wang, please

Who's that

it's you.

It doesn't matter

has told me

And I have manage that for you.

Thank you very much.

I will be here waiting for you.

You're welcome.

2. What kind of card

Would you please just let me drive in

En，OK. I see

With pleasure.

3. Can you do me a favor?

What's your problem?

More specific?

Good idea.

With pleasure.

三、1. b   2. d   3. a   4. d   5. d   6. d   7. b   8. a   9. d   10. d

四、

（一）1. c   2. d   3. a   4. a   5. d

（二）1. c   2. d   3. b   4. d   5. a

Part 2. 能力练习

一、(每小题1分，共15分)

1～10 CBDBC DACDA   11～15 ACDBC

二、(每小题1.5分，共30分)

16～25 ACDBA CDCDA   26～35 CDACA BBCBA

三、(每小题2分，共40分)

36～45 BACDB BCAAC   46～55 BABCC BDADC

四、短文改错

（一）(每小题1分，共10分)

British public libraries linked by computers. If your nearest	1. are
Library in London doesn't have the book you want to borrow,	2. √
a librarian will go on-line to see whether some of the other	3. any
nearby libraries have. If no library has the book in store, the	4. it
librarian will search for further, connecting libraries in other	5. √
city like Manchester . If a copy of the book is located, an	6. cities
arrangement will be made for it to be sent your library, and	7. to
in a day and two, you will be able to check it out. It is also	8. or
possibly for keen readers to borrow books from university	9. possible

281

and college libraries, even if we are not students.　　　　10. they

(二)

One possible version:

May I have your attention, please? I have an announcement to make. The Student Union is going to hold a party on Saturday evening, August 15, to welcome our friends from the United States. The party will be held in the roof garden of the Main Building. It will begin at 7:30 P.m. There will be music, dancing, singing, games and exchange of gifts. Will everybody please bring along a small gift for this purpose. Remember to wrap it up, sign your name and write a few words of good wishes.

Don't forget: 7:30, Saturday evening, roof garden, Main Building. There's sure to be a lot of fun. Everybody is welcome.

Unit 6.

Part1. Text

I. Keys to the exercises of the text

(I) Decide whether the following sentences are True or False according to the content of the text.

1. T　2. F　3. T　4. T　5. F　6. F　7. F　8. T　9. F　10. T

(II) Connect the word of column A to the explanation which is similar to it in column B with a bar

2.1　1. e　2. h　3. a　4. g　5. i　6. j　7. d　8. c　9. b　10. l　11. f　12. k

2.2

1. 他只是表面上保持中立。facade
2. 椰子是热带特有的。particular
3. 我们对历史人物应该有一个正确的评价。assessment
4. 在这件事上我们没有挑选的余地。alternative
5. 资本来到世间,从头到脚,每个毛孔都滴着血和肮脏的东西。Capital
6. 他们使敌人陷入被动。passive
7. 那是海滩反射的强光。reflective
8. 从统计数字角度看来,维生素缺乏和疾病之间存在一定关系。significant
9. 请允许我把布朗先生介绍给你。Present
10. 这部小说确实是一部出色的作品。performance
11. 他在前排的一个座位上坐定下来。Install
12. 有利条件超过不利条件。Outweigh

2.3

1. b　2. c　3. a　4. c　5. a　6. b　7. b　8. a　9. a　10. a

(III) Translate the following Chinese into English

1. Property owners are increasingly seeking ways to minimize the total owning cost of air-condition-ing systems.

2. Air-conditioning designers are becoming more heavily involved in the assessment of

the energy implications of alternative building facades.

3. Capital is more commonly invested in double glazing, external shading and reflective glazing.

4. Although reflective glazing docs present a useful thermal facade solution, the problems of reflection of heat to neighbours, possible disruption due to glare and night time internal light reflection, must be considered.

5. Engineers are now considering a building system as a totally interactive energy equation.

6. It can substantially reduce the cost of producing cooling for buildings by reducing electrical demand.

7. The cooling is produced in a controlled fashion over 24 hours rather than by an instantaneous demand.

8. Costs for electrical demand can be reduced by up to 50% using this design technique.

9. Increasing energy costs will continue the trend towards designs that produce more efficient systems in buildings into the future.

10. Most recent designs have enabled the incorporation of ice storage.

(Ⅳ) Extra Reading

1. c 2. a 3. b 4. d 5. a

Ⅱ. Language Ability Drill

(Ⅰ) Vocabulary Exercise

1. management 2. managed 3. inspected 4. inspection 5. consulted
6. consultation 7. bore 8. Bored 9. assembled 10. assembling

(Ⅱ) Cloze

1. A. 题目中提到学校,下文谈到学生可以不必在教室上课,空格后又有 in rows 提示,故此空填 desks 恰当。

2. C. 既然是学校,按照常理,学生需要 go to class,但在 free school 里,no one had to go to class,这正是令作者无法相信之处。

3. B. 前面的 Ahtouth 和下面的 no"lights out"表明"我们不必按时睡觉",故填 nobody 适合。

4. D. 从上段看,freeschool 的学生很少受约束,而"几乎所有的学生都主动去上课",作者对此自然感到惊奇了。

5. A. 几乎所有学生都上课与很少有人熬夜是并列关系,故用 and 连接。

6. C. Only 引出一些新生 stayed up or missed class,与前面群体学生相对照。

7. B. 从下文 this never lasted long 可判定此处该填 at first(起初)。

8. A. freedom 由 free 而来。正是 freedom(from school)即 free school 使之成为习惯。

9. D. 一般说来,上学的都是孩子,但老师却不将他们看做孩子,与孩子相对的只有 grown-ups(成年人)。

10. C. 下文"sit down","stand up","speak out"均是动作,play 不仅有"玩",还有"做"

的意思,在此表示学生们不必做起立、坐下一类的动作。

11. D. hear from:收到……来信,feel like:想要,think about:考虑,know of:知道。作者身在学校,尚不知道有不努力的学生,故此处用 know of 恰当。

12. B. 文中最后一句"between the free school and the regular school"可说明。

13. C. 春秋季节,植物学不上课,正好说明其教学方式与一般学校大不相同。

14. A. 菜园和花园只有和 planted 搭配。planted two gardens 意思是"种植了两个园子"。

15. B. 根据上文的 spring 和 fall 及下文的 winter,可断定答案为 then。

16. D. 从种植园学到的东西肯定比从书本上学到的东西特殊。

17. C. 学生在数学课上建造的储藏室绝不会是大房子,此处用 of course 加强语气。

18. B. had a great time=had a good time,对于孩子们来说,设计、绘图、测量肯定是很好玩的。

19. D. 在四个选项中,只有 figure out(计算出)与数学有关。

20. A. 此句及前后几个句子都在谈论数学,故断定应选 math。

21. C. 文中说,"我"未选上数学课,因为难以忍受测量啊、设计啊、计算啊什么的,何况我会基本数字运算,这就够了。

22. A. 文章最后一段是对全文的总结,将 free school 与 regular school 进行比较,此段开头用 on the whole(总的说来),给人以整体印象。

23. B. 从下文看,作者认为,自己与同龄人一样能读会写,因此在 free school 学习是比较好的一位。下文 I can think better 已经点明。

24. C. difference between...and...为常见的固定搭配。

25. D. 上文交代:"I can think better(我较善于思考)",因而得出结论:free school 与 regular school 的最大不同之处或许就在"思考"的多少上。

(Ⅲ) Fulfill sentences according to the words given in the bracket(按照括号中的中文完成句子):

1. are the basis for any good relationship
2. keep their bedrooms neat
3. was held up by a thick fog over the airport
4. two major earthquakes in its history, one ...
5. the professor was often absent-minded in his personal life.
6. an employee's being tired

Part 2. Dialogue

Ⅲ. Exercises for Dialogue in text

Fill in the following blanks while observing the conversational manner(按照日常会话习惯完成以下填空)

1. But the taxi is forbidden to enter the community
2. would you please tell me which resident you are going to visit?
3. floor and room he lives in?
4. would you please fill in this form of record for visitors

Ⅳ. **Spoken Language Drill** (fill in the blanks according to the Chinese translation)
Dialogue 1. & Dialogue 2.
 fits   terrific   lucky   goes   with
Dialogue 3. & dialogue 4.
 perfectly   amazing   look   matches   sale

Part 3. Supplementary Reading
 1. d   2. b   3. c   4. c   5. d

Unit 7.

Part 1. Text

Ⅰ. Keys to the exercises of the text

(Ⅰ) Decide whether the following sentences are True or False according to the content of the text.
 1. F   2. T   3. F   4. T   5. T

(Ⅱ) Connect the word of column A to the explanation which is similar to it in column B with a bar
2.1 1. e 2. a 3. i 4. f 5. b 6. j 7. c 8. d 9. g 10. h 11. n 12. r 13. q 14. s 15. t 16. k 17. u 18. p 19. l 20. m 21. o

2.2
1. 社会主义革命和社会主义建设必须有党的领导。essential
2. 这是无足轻重的。consequence
3. 你知道那本杂志的创刊号吗？initial
4. 民兵大力帮助边防军搜索敌人。assist
5. 得到谁的许可？authority
6. 采取防鼠措施。preventive
7. 道路的养护是重要的。Maintenance
8. 我不知道他们有什么理由拒绝我们进去。warranty
9. 你必须检查外出的行李。inspect
10. 他介绍我入的党。Recommended
11. 已征集到一百万人的签名。secured
12. 整顿工作风是必要的。Rectify
13. 别把全部注意力集中在一两个问题上而不顾其他问题。Exclusion
14. 郊外有一小时一班的火车。Hourly
15. 火车正以每小时80千米的速度前进。Rate
16. 毫无疑问 doubt
17. 站稳！footing
18. 这些结果已经过仔细核对和比较。Compared
19. 我们收到的稿件超过我们所能发表的数量。Submissions
20. 物质的运动总是表现为一定的形式。assumes
21. 他的丰富经验不可小看。discounted

22. 在操作机器时，我们必须谨慎。caution

2.3

1. a   2. c   3. b   4. a   5. d   6. c   7. c   8. b   9. a   10. d

(Ⅲ) Translate the following Chinese into English

1. During this period the consulting engineer generally sees copies of maintenance reports and ensures that maintenance is performed properly.

2. Preparing detailed maintenance specifications, putting them to tender and recommending the appropriate service contractor.

3. Mechanical services maintenance is usually performed by a mechanical services contractor.

4. Annual preventive maintenance costs for office buildings administered by experienced consulting engineering firms are usually in the range of $1.20 to $3.50/m air-conditioned space.

5. Breakdown maintenance is additional to this and varies considerably with the age and condition of the plant.

(Ⅳ) Extra Reading

1. c   2. d   3. d   4. a   5. c

Ⅱ. Language Ability Drill

(Ⅰ) Vocabulary Exercise

1. sampler beginner liar shoppers beggars actor sailors translators

2.

2.1   evidence Evidently evident evident

2.2   kind kindly Kindness kindly

2.3   eagerly eager eagerness eager

2.4   sincere sincerely sincerity sincere

2.5   occasional occasionally occasion occasionally

(Ⅱ) Cloze

1. D. "我拎着一个大箱子爬上三楼"，自然感到很累，同时又感到寂寞。

2. C. 从下文 and fell 可知父亲一脚踩空了，miss 在此含有 fail to do sth. 之意。

3. A. roll down：滚下，pass down：传下，drop down：掉下，turn down：拒绝，把……开小。上文交代：父亲踩滑了脚，摔了一跤，手中的箱子该是滚下楼梯。

4. C. 父亲脸一红，麻烦就要来了，暗示：父亲脸一红，就要发火。

5. B. 既然麻烦要来，就要小心。

6. D. 四个动词都可接动词不定式作宾补。但上文表明：父亲一旦脸红，就要发火，怎样使他卸下负担不致朝我嚷叫呢？unloading the car 此处用作引申义，表示"发泄"。下文 Get him into a chair 亦是对此题的暗示。

7. B. screaming at me and making a scene in front of the other girls 意为"当着其他女孩子的面冲着我嚷叫和发火"；make a scene 意为：吵闹、争吵，介词 without 用于其前表示

否定。

8. D. 因为这是新学期的开始,不是一年的开始,一年已经过去了一部分,接着又度过的是一年的其余部分。

9. A. 父亲拎着箱子爬楼,又摔了跤,走起路来很费劲。

10. C. 父亲情绪不好,又摔了跤,使我"觉得她的大学生活有了一不好的开端"。Get off to a good/bad start:有良好(不好)的开端。

11. B. 从下文可知:"I"已经知道自己的房间号码是316,但尚未找到自己的房间,故急于想找到房间。search(搜索),enter(进入),book(订)均不切题。

12. D. then again:"还有,另外"。上文作者在想:"给他弄一张椅子坐下,让他平静下来。"but 转折后,接着用 then again 表示:"但是还有就是,不知道316房间有没有椅子?" once more 表示"再来一次",不合题意。

13. B. or 与上句表示"二者之一";"316房间有没有椅子,或者是间空房?"下文 the room wasn't empty at all 亦是对此题的暗示。

14. A. 从上楼到找到房间经历了一个过程,"终于"找到了房间。

15. C. Push the door open 表示"推开门"。

16. D. 父亲仍在埋怨伤了膝盖,火气未消。

17. A. 房间是找到了,但有无椅子让父亲坐下而使父亲平静下来呢?我准备着最坏的情况。此题若选 B,则 the chair 表示特指,"我"期待的并非特指某个椅子,而是泛指,故判定 B 错。

18. C. 房间的情况恰恰与我 expecting 的相反,故使我感到"惊讶"。

19. A. 住在同一间房子里的该是 roommate。

20. B. 因为在这说话,故将音乐声关小。

21. A. 下文 "And of course, you're Mr. Faber." 暗示 Amy 此时在打量着我的父亲。

22. C. 从上文"Greeting me with a nod, she said in a soft voice.",可知 Amy 与她的新室友和其父亲初次见面时十分客气、友好,此处用 smiling 恰到好处。

23. C. 第一段中 his face turned red 表明我的父亲一直在生气,Amy 的友好接待使我父亲的怒气平息下来,故他的脸 turned less red。

24. 答案?then. 表示"当时"(=at that time)、"那时",与上文有关联;soon 表示时间短暂;later 表示需要往后推迟一段时间,与作者口气不合。

25. B. 下文 would be a success 表明我此时因遇上一个好朋友,信心十足,心情极佳。

(Ⅲ) **Fulfill sentences according to the words given in the bracket**(按照括号中的中文完成句子):

1. He looks as if he is putting on weight.
2. It feels as if it is made of cotton.
3. Their accent sounds as if they do.
4. They look as if they do.
5. It smells as if it is fresh.
6. They taste as if homemade.
7. He looks as if he is hungry.

8. It sounds as if African.

Part 2. Dialogue

Ⅲ. **Exercises for Dialogue in text**

Fill in the following blanks while observing the conversational manner（按照日常会话习惯完成以下填空）

1. pets should be fasten with belt when walk outside room
2. walking dogs is forbidden in or around the Kids' Garden no pissing or shiting for pets on the path
3. Thank you for your cooperation with our work

Ⅳ. **Spoken Language Drill**（fill in the blanks according to the Chinese translation）

Dialogue 1. & Dialogue 2.
like   something   really   can't   choice
Dialogue 3. & dialogue 4.
decide   studying   sad   bad   passed

Part 3. Supplementary Reading
1. c   2. c

Unit 8.

Part 1. Text

Ⅰ. **Keys to the exercises of the text**

(Ⅰ) Decide whether the following sentences are True or False according to the content of the text.
1. F   2. T   3. F   4. F   5. T   6. T   7. F   8. F   9. T   10. F

(Ⅱ) Connect the word of column A to the explanation which is similar to it in column B with a bar
2.1   1. d   2. e   3. f   4. b   5. a   6. c
2.2
1. 除非牵涉到两个物体,否则就不会有力存在。involved
2. 那是中国商品检验局。Inspection
3. 合同规定用钢窗。specifies
4. 这是生产过程简图。outline
5. 他努力工作。diligent
6. 这是燃眉之急的问题。issue
2.3
1. b   2. a   3. c   4. b   5. d   6. a   7. c   8. a   9. b   10. c

(Ⅲ) Translate the following Chinese into English
1. It is essential to develop a professional relationship between the Property Manager

288

and the cleaning contractor.

2. Inspections should be carried out as early as possible in the morning, ideally before the tenants have commenced work.

3. Good and honest communication between the Property Manager and the cleaning contractor is essential in obtaining a quality service which is ongoing.

4. The contractor will execute/perform the specified cleaning tasks to the reasonable satisfaction of the Property Manager/Building Owner.

5. If the contractor docs not remedy the default within 7 days from the date of notice, the contract may be cancelled.

6. Have the work performed or redone by others in respect of the default

7. The Property Manager may at any time by notice in writing, vary the portions of the building to be cleaned under the contract.

8. The contractor must effect and keep the appropriate Occupational Health and Safety insurance.

9. Direct the contractor to rectify or satisfactorily carry out work within specified time and withhold any payment until work is satisfactorily carried out.

10. If the work is not carried out to the satisfaction of the Property Manager, the remedies may be available.

(Ⅳ) Extra Reading

1. a　2. c　3. b　4. d　5. c

Ⅱ. Language Ability Drill

(Ⅰ) Vocabulary Exercise

1. manly　cowardly　brotherly　fatherly　scholarly　beastly

2.

2.1　implication　implying　implied　implication

2.2　surprised　surprising　Surprisingly　surprised　surprising　surprise

2.3　response　responded　irresponsible　responsible　responsibility　responsible

2.4　incorrect　correcting　correct　correctness　correctly　correcting

2.5　smoothly　smoothing　smooth　smoothness　smoothed

2.6　dead　deadly　deadly　died　death　dead

(Ⅱ) Cloze:

1. C　从这四个词的意思上来区分,case 是"事例,案例"的意思,reason 表原因,factor 意为"因素",situation 的意思是"形势,状况",文中句子的意思是"上述条件是使英国成为工业革命中心的重要因素"。故选 C. factor。

2. A　根据上下句的意思,应选一个表转折的连词,只有 A. but 符合题意。

3. A　else 意为"其他,别的",如:What else can I say? 别的我还能说些什么呢？extra 意为"额外的,外加的",如:an extra loaf of bread 多加的一条面包,而这句话要表达的是"也需要其他条件",而不是"额外条件",排除 C. extra。near 和 similar 意思相差较远,故选 A。

4. D 根据下句的解释,应选"有创造性的",creative 符合题意。generating(产生的、生产的)、motivating(有动机的)和 effective(有效的)意思上不贴切。

5. B sources 意为"来源,根源",如 sources of power 意为"能源",符合题意。origin 的意思是"起因,由来"。如:the origin of a river 河流的源头;base 是"基础"的意思;discovery 是"发现"的意思。

6. B 根据句子的意思,应选 create"创造,发明"这个词。

7. A come from 的意思是"出自,来自",与后面 background 搭配,意为"出于……背景"。stem from 意为"起源于",如:Her interest in books stems from her childhood. 她对书本的兴趣是从童年开始的。B、C 项的意思不对。

8. C more...than... 是固定搭配,意为"与其说……不如……"。本句的意思是,"与其说是科学家,不如说是发明家"。

9. C pure 的意思是"纯粹的,单纯的",genuine 的意思是"真正的",practical 的意思是"实际的",clever 的意思是"聪明的",句子的意思是"一个单纯的科学家主要致力于精确的科学研究。"

10. D accurately 的意思是"精确的",符合题意。Happily(愉快的)、occasionally(时而的,偶然的)和 reluctantly(勉强的)均不合题意。

11. D so that 是固定搭配,表目的。

12. C 这句话的意思是"一个发明家或热衷于应用科学的人通常试图创造有使用价值的东西。"

13. B 这句话的意思是"通过运用科学理论",use 意为"使用,运用",故选 B。

14. A theories of science 的意思是"科学的理论"。

15. D 根据句子的意思,"他为了明确的结果而工作"。specific 的意思是"明确的";specialized 的意思是"专门的";sole 的意思是"独有的,单一的";single 的意思是"单独的,一个人"。

16. C 根据题意,one of many other objectives"许多其他东西中的一种"。all,全部;few,几乎没有;those,那些;均不合题意。

17. B develop (使)发展。如:to develop a business,发展业务。另一个意思是"研制、开发",用在这里恰当。如:Many new products have been developed to meet the needs of the people. 开发了许多新产品以满足人们的需要。propose 建议。如:I propose resting for half an hour. 我提议休息半个小时。supply 提供、供应。如:The government supplies free books to schools. 政府为学校免费提供图书。offer 提供、出价。如:Will you offer the guests some coffee. 你能给客人准备些咖啡吗?

18. A 本题要求选用的是与 no 意义相近的不定代词,在四个选项中,只有 A little 的意思是"几乎没有",后接不可数名词,符合题意。

19. B 本题要求填入的是一个连词,用来连接一个表示与过去事实相反的虚拟条件句。本句的意思是说:"如果没有科学家早年打下的基础,那些在科学上接受过很少或没有接受过教育的人就不可能有所发明创造"。if 的意思是"如果,假使",通常用在虚拟条件句中。

20. D 本题要求填入的副词用来修饰一个过去完成时的谓语动词,即表示过去某个时间以前发生的动作,因而只能用 D. before。如:He would not have achieved so much in the research if he had not studied chemistry years before. 如果他早年没学过化学的话,他在这项研究中就不可能取得这么大的成绩。ago 只与一般过去时连用,表示从现在角度看过去的某一时间。如:He studied chemistry many years ago. 他好多年前学过化学。

(Ⅲ) Fulfill sentences according to the words given in the bracket(按照括号中的中文完成句子):

1. have taken the place of gas ring in many household in this city.
2. was taken as a disgrace to a family but it has become more acceptable now.
3. walking towards him made the thief feel very nervous.
4. were shocked by the way to law was broken.
5. he was extremely eager to get started.
6. not interrupt her.

Part 2. Dialogue

Ⅲ. Exercises for dialogue in text

Fill in the following blanks while observing the conversational manner(按照日常会话习惯完成以下填空)

1. this is ChenMing from Property Management department speaking
2. We're going to give the notice by this noon
3. Anything else I can do for you
4. We will send someone to collect them

Ⅳ. Spoken Language Drill (fill in the blanks according to the Chinese translation)

Dialogue 1. & Dialogue 2.
goodbye   good   Remember   say   flying
Dialogue 3. & dialogue 4.
try   Take care   calling   touch   everything

Part 3. Supplementary Reading
1. c   2. d   3. d   4. c   5. c

Unit 9.

Part1. Text

Ⅰ. Keys to the exercises of the text

(Ⅰ) Decide whether the following sentences are True or False according to the content of the text.

1. F 2. T 3. F 4. F 5. T 6. F 7. F 8. T 9. F 10. T

(Ⅱ) Connect the word of column A to the explanation which is similar to it in column B with a bar

2.1   1. d   2. h   3. f   4. b   5. g   6. i   7. a   8. c   9. e   10. j

291

2.2
1. 随机应变。circumstances
2. 把伤病员从战斗地域撤走。Evacuate
3. 他首先采取的步骤是进行彻底调查。Procedure
4. 占这位子的人是李红。Occupant
5. 他是一所商业学校的学生。commercial
6. 这所房子朝南。aspect
7. 这是到达（或进入）大楼的通路。access
8. 试验结果使我们很满意。satisfied
9. 你必须遵守图书馆的规则。comply
10. 这是燃眉之急的问题。issue

2.3
1. c 2. a 3. c 4. b 5. b 6. c 7. b 8. d 9. b 10. c

(Ⅲ) Translate the following Chinese into English

1. When placed in the position, it may be difficult to make the decision to evacuate a major property.

2. Although once the people factor in the equation has been satisfied, the asset needs to be protected as best as possible

3. Extinguisher placement, sprinkler installation, stairwell pressurization devices, smoke spill fans and fire rated doors which are controlled by regulations and which need to be maintained correctly in order to preserve their operational ability in the event of an emergency.

4. In most cases research indicates that the victims were overcome within an estimated two to five minutes of the discovery of the fire and were in fact overcome by the volume of smoke and other toxic hot gases rising from the area of the fire.

5. It is essential that emergency procedures are in place.

6. It may well be considered the Property Manager's responsibility to put in place procedures to enable the quick and safe evacuation of premises in the event of an emergency arising.

7. However, it is worth remembering that the authorities indicate that the action taken in the first five minutes after the incident may have a very serious bearing on the ability to prevent or reduce injury and loss of life.

8. Buildings whether be retail, commercial or industrial all have aspects of occupancy and public access which need to be considered at all times.

9. The greatest hazard to human life in files is the smoke and hot gases that rise through a building.

10. It is invaluable to any strategy for the minimization of injury and death from this situation.

(Ⅳ) Extra Reading

1. b 2. d 3. c 4. b 5. c

Ⅱ. Language Ability Drill

(Ⅰ) Vocabulary Exercise

1.

1.1 heart   heart   mind   mind   mind   mind   heart

1.2 find out   find   find out   found   find out   found out

2.

2.1 The committee's findings will be published in the Daily News.

2.2 At the beginning, he gave all his earnings to his mother.

2.3 It took all his savings to buy the house.

2.4 Darwin's writings on evolution produced a tremendous impact on the development of biology.

2.5 Comrade Mao's teachings about the united front is still of great significance today.

(Ⅱ) Cloze

1~10 DACBA,DBCCB   11~20 ADDAC,BBCDA

Fulfill Sentences according to the words given in the bracket(按照括号中的中文完成句子):

1. unable to understand the simplest instructions.

2. differ greatly even among teachers of the same subject.

3. are smaller in terms of population compared to China cities.

4. has the ability to learn and use language.

5. people of different cultures is very complex but not impossible.

6. hardly recall the place where we had agreed to meet.

Part 2. Dialogue

Ⅲ. Exercises for Dialogue in text:

Fill in the following blanks while observing the conversational manner（按照日常会话习惯完成以下填空）

1. script on the wall or on the floor

2. don't spit everywhere, throw the garbage into the dustbin instead of throwing the them everywhere

3. I have a small one, and I can give it to you.

Ⅳ. **Spoken Language Drill** (fill in the blanks according to the Chinese translation)

Dialogue 1. & Dialogue 2.

trouble   plenty   back   have to   promise

293

Dialogue 3. & dialogue 4.
catch   stuck   jam   appointment   change

Unit 10.

Part 1. Text

I. Keys to the exercises of the text

(I) Decide whether the following sentences are True or False according to the content of the text.

1. F   2. T   3. F   4. T   5. T   6. F   7. F   8. T   9. F   10. T

(II) Connect the word of column A to the explanation which is similar to it in column B with a bar

2.1   1. h   2. l   3. i   4. j   5. b   6. g   7. k   8. d   9. e   10. c   11. a   12. f   13. p   14. n   15. m   16. o   17. t   18. q   19. r   20. s

2.2

1. 工厂的安全设备有了很大的改进。improvement
2. 他住在有小厨房和卫生设备的小套公寓房间。efficiency
3. 我们一直认为世界人民的革命斗争就是我们自己的斗争。identified
4. 我想以茶代咖啡。substitution
5. 这是一个开罐头用的器具。appliance
6. 将收支列成细目单。Schedule
7. 他已经改变了对我的看法。revised
8. 节约等于增加收入。Saving
9. 认真对待自己的职责。mindful
10. 每天送信三次。deliveries
11. 这是最近一期(十一月号)的《中国建设》。issue
12. 疾病一直纠缠着他,直到他去世。pursued
13. 我是不会上当的。imposed
14. 这个词具有多种意义。syndrome
15. 我们的词典是打算给学生用的。intended
16. 七月到九月生产达到了高峰。peaked
17. 这样做毫无意义。point
18. 振作起来。comfort
19. 他做出这个决定太匆忙了些。previous
20. 提防危险! Beware

2.3

1. c   2. c   3. b   4. a   5. b   6. a   7. a   8. c   9. d   10. c   11. b   12. c   13. d   14. a   15. d   16. a   17. b

(III) Translate the following Chinese into English

1. Improvements in efficiency may involve identifying and evaluating ways to reduce

energy consumption, while maintaining or even improving services.

2. Of course, the energy manager should be mindful of the most important "part" of any building: the PEOPLE who occupy it.

3. Fuels vary in price, according to factors such as supply and demand, cost of conversion or delivery, and government regulations.

4. Pursue the correct sizing of equipment for the intended duty.

5. Many buildings use the same equipment for comfort heating and hot water, so a large boiler must operate all year just to provide hot water for hand washing.

6. Pick the most appropriate, cheapest, convenient fuel for the purpose, with an eye to future trends in cost and supply issues.

7. Efficiencies vary between apparently similar models, and price is certainly not the best guide.

8. Providing a small, separate, heater for hot water would overcome this problem.

9. Changes to routines may reduce operating costs.

10. While this approach may be lucrative for "tariff analysts", it can be VERY expensive in the long run depending upon the energy used.

(Ⅳ) Extra Reading

1. d 2. b 3. a 4. c 5. c 6. d 7. d

Ⅱ. Language Ability Drill

(Ⅰ) Vocabulary Exercise

1. healthy dirty noisy smoky stormy sunny rainy muddy smelly

2. ill-advised well-paid much-used well-informed poorly-dressed well-traveled much handled well-known

3. root notice retreat board mask retreat approaching notice rooted board dreaming approach mask dreams

(Ⅱ) Cloze

1. B 2. D 3. A 4. D 5. C 6. B 7. C 8. C 9. C 10. A 11. B 12. C 13. A 14. C 15. C 16. C 17. A 18. A 19. D 20. A 21. D 22. B 23. D 24. B 25. D

(Ⅲ) Fulfill sentences according to the words given in the bracket(按照括号中的中文完成句子):

1. greatly stunned the people of U.S.

2. at the approach of the hunters.

3. so caught up in the film on TV that I forgot to do my homework.

4. remembered it painfully.

5. vanished from her face when she heard the bad news.

6. high divorce rate in America, most Americans dream of a happy marriage.

Part 2. Dialogue

Ⅲ. Exercises for dialogue in text

Fill in the following blanks while observing the conversational manner（按照日常会话习惯完成以下填空）

    1. the engine broke down
    2. carry it to the repair department and get it repaired, because I do not have the tools
    3. I will try my best.
    4. You are welcome

Ⅳ. Spoken Language Drill（fill in the blanks according to the Chinese translation）

Dialogue 1. & Dialogue 2.
Track　due　round-trip　time　arrive
Dialogue 3. & dialogue 4.
next　scheduled　one way　leave　fare

Part 3. Supplementary Reading
    1. d　2. d　3. c　4. a　5. c

期　末　测　试

Part 1. 专业练习

一、

1. Good and honest communication between the Property Manager and the cleaning contractor is essential in obtaining a quality service which is ongoing.

2. The Property Manager may at any time by notice in writing, vary the portions of the building to be cleaned under the contract.

3. The higher the quality of preventative maintenance, the less likelihood of regular equipment breakdowns.

4. Without a tender document, it becomes too easy for the service contractor to manipulate a service program so as to lower the tendered price.

5. The cooling is produced in a controlled fashion over 24 hours rather than by an instantaneous demand.

6. Pick the most appropriate, cheapest, convenient fuel for the purpose, with an eye to future trends in cost and supply issues.

7. Efficiencies vary between apparently similar models, and price is certainly not the best guide.

8. Although once the people factor in the equation has been satisfied, the asset needs to be protected as best as possible

9. The greatest hazard to human life in files is the smoke and hot gases that rise through a building.

10. Inspect the equipment for worm, burnt, broken and compensate for any evident irregular running or deviation from normal design characteristics.

二、
1. I have been standing here for almost twenty minutes
   What can I do for you
   I'm not used to being kept waiting
   We are short-handed today.
2. Can't you make it any cheaper than that
   You can't get it any cheaper than here.
   I'm sure.
3. but the earliest date possible is the 25th.
   By the way, is it free of charge
4. Would you please tell me which resident you are going to visit?
   Building 1, Gate 1, 3th Floor and Room 1.
   Can I park my car inside the community.
   With pleasure.
5. Call "uncle"!
   What a lovely boy!   What's your name
   Did you have a good time when going out with your father
   What are you going to do with them?
   But good kids will never do that on the wall or on the floor.
   good kids don't spit everywhere, throw the garbage into the dustbin instead of throwing the them everywhere.
   I have a small one, and I can give it to you.
   You are welcome.   Remember: keep the place clean.

三、1. A   2. C   3. A   4. D   5. C   6. B   7. D   8. A   9. C   10. B

四、
(一)
1. d   2. c   3. a   4. d   5. b
(二)
1. a   2. b   3. b   4. b   5. d
(三)
1. d   2. d   3. a   4. a   5. d

Part 2. 能力练习
1~5   ABCDC   6~10   DDBAC
11~15 BCDAB   16~20   BBBAC   21~25   CDAAD
26~30 BCACD   31~35   BAADB   36~40   CCDDA
41~45 CDCBD   46~50   ACCBC   51~55   ADBBA
56. tell-tells   57. worse-bad   58. 第二个 more 前加 be
59. 去掉 even   60. well-train-well-trained
61. worked-working 或 work   62. √   63. reporter-reporter's

64. after-before   65. that-which

书面表达参考答案：

Train Travel and Air Travel

　　Air travel has two advantages over train travel. First, it can save much time. We can fly form Qingdao to Guangzhou just in two hours, hut by train we have to spend 58 hours or more. Second, air traveling is more comfortable because the plane flies so smoothly that we can rest well during the trip, while the train is crowded sometimes and passengers have to sit a long time, which makes them tired. But train travel also has its own advantages. For example, traveling by train costs only 250 yuan while traveling by air will take us 900 yuan. Besides this, through the train's window, we can enjoy the view of many big cities, such as Jinan, Zheng Zhou, Wuhan, Changsha, etc. So I think different people like different ways of travelling.

附录二 物业管理从事人员日常用语

Unit One 员工日常用语

一、问候语：你好！——How are you!（回答为：Fine,thank you!）Hi! Hello!

早晨好！下午好！晚上好！——Good morning! Good afternoon! Good evening!

路上辛苦了。——Did you have a tiring trip?

你回来了。—— You are back.

二、欢迎语：欢迎！——Welcome!

欢迎光临！——Welcome to our ...!

欢迎指导！——Welcome to guide!

欢迎您来我们住宅小区。—— Welcome to our residential estate(area)!

欢迎您入住本楼。—— Welcome you to move in this building!

三、致歉语：对不起！——Sorry!

打扰您了。—— Sorry to bother you.

失礼了。——Excuse me!

请原谅！——Beg your pardon!

请谅解！——Please forgive me!

"请接受我的道歉。""没关系。"——"Please accept my apologizes". ——"That's OK".

我必须为给您带来的不便而道歉。——I apologize for inconveniencing you. 或 Please forgive me for having inconvenienced you.

"非常抱歉给您添麻烦。——I'm sorry to trouble you like this."

对不起，失陪一下。——May I be excused(for a second)? 或 Will you excuse me?

我很抱歉让您久等，不过请再等一会儿好吗？——I'm sorry to keep you waiting, but will you please wait a few more minutes?

对不起，我没懂你的意思。——Sorry, I don't see what you meant.

非常抱歉延迟了。——We are very sorry for the delay.

很抱歉不能为您效劳。——We are sorry we couldn't help you.

原谅我来晚了。——Excuse me for being late.

您好，抱歉打断您的谈话，能给我一点儿时间吗？——Hello, sorry to interrupt you. Could you spare me a few minutes?

四、致谢语：谢谢！——Thank you!（应答为：That's all right. 或 My pleasure.）

多谢关照！——Thanks for your caring!

多谢指正！——Thanks for pointing out our mistakes!
非常感谢您的好意。——Thank you very much for your kindness.
谢谢,您真是太好了。——Thank you. That's very kind of you.
非常荣幸,先生(女士)。——My pleasure, sir(mum).
谢谢您的夸奖。——It's very kind of you to say so.
您真帮了我的大忙。——You are very helpful.

五、见面语：请进！—— Come in, please!
请坐！——Sit down, please!
请用茶！——Have some tea, please.

六、祈请语：请稍等一下。——Please wait a moment.
请稍候。——-Just a moment, please.
请留步！——I can see my set out!
请问贵姓？——May I have your name, please?
您先请。——After you.
请再次光临。——Please come again.
请您填一下这张表,好吗？——Would you please fill out this form?
请这边走。—— This way, please.

七、祝贺语：一路平安！——Have a safe trip.
祝你好运并祝旅途愉快！——Wish you good luck and a pleasant journey!
祝一切顺利,心想事成！——All the best!
祝你如愿！——Good luck to you!
祝你健康。——I wish you health!
祝你生意兴隆！——Hope you have a successful business.
祝你生日快乐。——Happy birthday!
祝你们全家好。——All the best with your family.
新年快乐！——Happy new year!
愿事事顺利！——I hope everything goes well.
祝你们幸福！——May you both be very happy!
祝你长寿幸福！——Wish you a good health.
多保重！——Take care!
祝你周末愉快！——Have a good weekend!
希望你早日康复！——I wish you could recover soon.
请允许我表达我最衷心(热烈)的祝贺！——Allow me to express my warmest congratulations!
祝贺你们喜结良缘！—— Congratulations on your marriage!
祝贺您晋升了！——Congratulations on your promotion.
听说你获得了成功,这真是好极了！——It's great to hear about your success.

听说你找到份好工作,这好极了! ——It was great to hear you've got a good job.

八、辞别语:再见! ——See you! Goodbye!

下周见! —— See you next week!

晚安! ——Good night!

保持联系! ——Keep in touch!

九、应答语:好的,没问题。——Sure. No worries.

当然可以。——Of course.

没关系。——It doesn't matter.

请你帮个忙,行吗? ——非常乐意。——Can you do me a favour? ——My pleasure.

你愿意给我讲讲住宅小区的事吗? ——没问题。——Do you mind telling me something about a residential estate? ——Of course not.

谢谢你的帮助。——这是我应该做的。——Thank you for your help. ——With pleasure.

Unit Two 办公室接待来电、来访用语

一、接到电话:

"您好!"——Hello.( )物业( )室(部、处),"请问您有什么事? ——What can I do for you?""我今天上午买了些电器,但是门卫却不准我运进来。——I bought some electrical appliances this morning, but the superintendents don't allow them in."问明事由后,迅速判断解决问题的方法、时间;重要事项作好记载;请示有关领导。回答:"我们将在( )时间内为您解决( )"——We'll solve it in (24 hours). 如遇有解决不了或难以答复的问题,或请示领导后再回答,或做耐心解释。再问:"请问还有什么事?"——Anything else I can do for you? 如果没有,说:"谢谢,再见。"——Thank you. Goodbye.

打电话时说,"请找李先生。——May I speak to Mr. Li, please?"

接电话时说,"请问您哪里? ——May I ask who's calling?"

二、接待来访:

1. 先生/女士,有人接待您吗? ——Have you been helped, sir/ mum?

"您好!请坐!请用茶!请问您有什么事?"——Hello. Please sit down. Have some tea, please. " What can I do for you?"事情是关于我今天买的电视机和微波炉的事。门卫说我不能就这样运进来。——It is about a new TV set, a microwave cooker I bought. The guards at the door said I can't get them into this building. 很抱歉,您得先办理一些手续,不过门卫也是在履行他们的职责。——I'm sorry, but you need to handle some procedures. But the superintendents are doing their duties. 问明事由后,迅速判断解决问题的方法、时间;重要事项作好记载;请示有关领导。回答:"我们将在( )时间内为您解决。"——We'll solve it in (24 hours). 如遇有解决不了或难以答复的问题,或请示领导后再回答,或做耐心解释。再问:"请问还有什么事?"——" Anything else I can do for you?" 如果没有,说:"欢迎再来,您慢走,再见。"——You are welcome to come again. Take care. Goodbye.

2. 如果来访者要求见经理,而经理很忙,就说:"Sorry. I'm afraid the manager is fully engaged.——很抱歉,恐怕经理的日程已经安排满了。"请稍等,让我帮您查一下。——Just a moment, please. Let me check on that for you. 再说:"你看我们能不能把见面的时间换到明天?——I wonder if we could change the time of the meeting to tomorrow."或"明天下午怎么样?——那就明天下午见吧。——好的。——What about tomorrow afternoon?——Then I'll see you in the afternoon.——OK."或者说:"恐怕他会很忙。您能不能换个时间?——I'm afraid he's fully engaged. Could you make it another time?"再说,"您觉得哪一天合适?——What day would suit you? 您要指定日期吗?——Would you like to specify a date?""你什么时候方便?——这周末可以。——When will it be convenient for you?——This weekend would be OK with me."

3. 如果你的解释令来访者不满意,可进一步解释说,"那不是我要说的意思。——That's not exactly what I meant. 换句话说……——Let me put it another way... 对不起,让我再解释一下……——Sorry, let me explain... 让我再说一下……——Let me try that again... 我知道的不多,不过……——I don't know a lot about it, but... 这是个难题,不过……——That's a difficult question, but... 我可能错了,不过……。——I may be wrong, but... 那可能是对的,不过我觉得……——That may be true, but in my opinion... 一般而言,我同意您的看法,不过……——Generally speaking, I agree with you, but... 我对这个不熟,不过我想…——I'm not very familiar with this subject, but I think... 我认为我们找不到更好的办法了。——I don't think we can find a better way." 我不敢肯定,我去问问经理,请稍等。——I'm not sure, I'll ask my boss. Wait a moment, please. 我去叫经理来,请你当面与他讲。——I'll get the manager, you can speak with him.

4. 经理不在,而来访者非要见经理,可以说,经理每星期都会不事先通知而到办公室来几次。The manager drops in unannounced at the office several times a week. "您要在这等或者待会儿再过来?——Would you like to wait or come back later? 我们明天给您答复,可以吗?——May we give you the answer tomorrow?"

5. 如果来访者想选房,你给他一些建议,可说:您的预算在多少的价格范围之内?——What (kind of) price range do you have in mind? 您定了什么大致价钱吗?——What price range did you set? 您打算付多少钱?——How much would you like to pay? 您预算的最高价是多少?——What's the maximum price you have in mind? 我们有许多式样供您选择。——We have many patterns for you to choose. 特价中。——They are on sale. 我们向您提供优惠价格。这可能是您惟一的机会。——We are making a special offer to you. And this could be your only chance. 今天是最后一天我们以这么低价格出售。——Today is the last day we sale them at this low price. 抱歉,这是我们的最低价,不能再低了。——Sorry, this is our lowest price. We can't go any lower. 女士,您觉得怎么样?——How do you like it, mum? 您想要订购吗?——Would you like to order it? 您是不是现在就订购呢?——Would you like to go ahead and place an order? 今天订购的话有折扣。——You receive a discount by ordering today. 我可以记下您的电话号码吗?——May I have your telephone number? 它设计很好,看起来舒服,结构也合理。——It's well-designed, it looks pleasing and has a reasonable structure. 老顾客的反应证明它质量超群。——The re-

sponse of the old customers has proved that it has a superior quality.

我们的品质值得您所花的每一分钱。——Our quality is worth every penny. 对我们来说最重要的是质量。——What's most important to us is their quality. 我们从2月16日至3月3日实行大减价。——We are having a sale from Feb. the 16th to Mar the 3rd. 岁末酬宾季节从今起30天时间。——The year-end gift season is 30 days from today. 廉价销售只有几天时间,不会太久。——They are bargain-priced only in a couple of days. It couldn't be much longer. 你觉得这里的一切怎么样?——How do you find things over here? 如果我能帮什么忙的话,请尽管说。——If I can be any help, please let me know.

6. 来访者选好房后要讨价还价,你可说:这差不多是成本价了。——It's almost the cost price. 这价格够便宜了。——The price is moderate enough. 我们的价格不能再降了。——We can't cut our prices any more. 抱歉,这是我们能够出的最低价了。——I'm sorry, but this is as low as we can go on the price.

Unit Three 维修服务语言

一、接到住户电话,说:"您好!维修部,请问有什么要求?" " How are you! Maintainance Department, What can I do for you?" "……工作不太正常。——It doesn't work properly." 请告诉我您的地址?电话号码?——Your address, please? Phone number? 询问清楚需要维修的内容及地点,判断是否有能力、有人手及时维修。如有能力、有人手,说:"我们立刻派人到您家。——We'll send someone to your house as soon as possible." 如缺能力、缺人手,说:"我们暂缺人手,是否另约时间" "Now we are short of personnel, can we arrange another time?" 或"对不起,我们暂不提供此项服务。" " excuse me, we do not provide this service at present." 再向住户确认一次维修内容、时间、地点之后,再问"您还有什么要求?" "Any other demand?" 最后说:"再见!"——Goodbye.

二、接待住户来访,说:"您好!请问有什么事?——Hello, What can I do for you?" "我家浴室的一个水龙头漏水,弄得地板整天又湿又脏,把整座房子都搞得一团糟。——One faucet in the bathroom of my house is leaking, making the floor very wet and dirty all day. It makes the whole house a mess, too. 你可以想像有多麻烦。——You can imagine all the trouble." 询问清楚需要维修的内容及地点,"我感到非常抱歉。——I do apologize." "您可以详细解释一下吗?——Would you explain more exactly?" 判断是否有能力、有人手及时维修。如有能力、有人手,说:我们立刻派人到您家。——We'll immediately arrange for somebody to your house. "你最好现在就派人。这真是糟糕透了。——You had better do it right now. It is really awful. 我向您保证,修理工马上就到。——I assure you, the repairman will arrive in no time. 如缺能力、缺人手,说:"我们暂缺人手,是否另约时间" "Now we are short of personnel, can we fix another time"或"您把它拿到修理部去让人修理一下。——You can carry it to the repair department and get it repaired."或"对不起,我们暂不提供此项服务。" " excuse me, we do not provide this service at present." 再向住户确认一次维修内容、时间、地点之后,再问"请问您还有其他要求吗?——"Any other demand?"最后说:"您走好!" "Get along well!"

三、如上门维修,说:"您好!我是维修部的,请问是否您家的……需维修?" "How are you! I am the personnel of Maintainance Department, please ask if your house... need to

303

be maintained?"检查维修项目情况,若为有偿服务,应向业主(住户)声明收费标准,与业主(住户)意见一致后进行维修,完成后清场,征询意见。说:"请您验收,签意见!"。"Please check before acceptance, and sign the opinion!"谢谢,再见!""Thanks and goodbye!"

四、如果维修项目较多,可说:"我们要逐项检查。"——"We'll go through it for you."我们今天人手不够。——We are short-handed today. 我想想……可能要三四天。——Let me see... I think it takes three or four days.

五、如果维修中涉及改制方案或选用新型材料时说,这是目前最流行的。——This is the most popular now. 它十分适合您。——It looks good on you. 它相当流行。——It is quite in fashion. 您想要新潮的吗?——Do you want anything that is up-to-date. 我觉得这种颜色和它是很好的搭配,你觉得怎么样?——I think this type of colour is a good match for it. How are you doing? 这比原来那个贵100元,您看行吗?——It's 100 yuan more than the original, is it all right? 您不会有任何损失,而只会赢得一个崭新的面貌。难道您认为不值得吗?——You have absolutely nothing to lose. And an entirely new world to gain. Don't you think it's worthy of it?

六、维修结束后,嘱咐业主说,在操作或调节本机前,请仔细阅读这些说明。——Before operating or adjusting this product, please read these instructions completely. 请保管好此说明书。——Please save this manual. 这台机器有三年保修期。——This machine has a three years' guarantee. 这只表保用两年。——This watch is guaranteed for two years. 它只有六个月免费保用期。——It has only 6 months guarantee free of charge. 您一定要按说明书来操作。——You must operate it according to the manual. 这是中英文对照的说明书。——This is an Chinese-English bilingual instruction. 对于顾客本人使用不当造成损坏的商品,我们概不退换。——We don't exchange any items that is improperly used or damaged by the customer himself.

七、判断维修内容时可说,有些零件弄坏了。——Some parts have been badly damaged. 情况既然是这样,那修理就相当复杂了。——That being the case, the repair would be rather complex. 查看之前我不能肯定。——I can't say before I check on it.

八、判断清维修内容后可说,在您通知的24小时之内,我们会派人维修您的机器。——We'll service your machinery within 24 hours after your call. 我们的修理人员可以上您那儿。——Our repairman can come to you. 明天以前我们会派人过去。——We'll have someone there by tomorrow. 我想得收费用,因为保证期已过。——I think there will be a charge because the warranty has expired. 还修得好吗?——修得好,不过要花一些时间。——Is it still repairable?——Yes. But it will take some time to repair it. 我想两天内会修好。——I think it will be ready in two days. 修好时我们会电话通知您。——We'll call you when it's ready. 但我们实在没办法,一般都要这么久的。——But there's nothing we can do about it. This is how long it usually takes. 您是在华荣公寓7幢501房间吗?——Are you in Huarong Flats, Building 7, Room 501? 我将尽全力完成那项任务——I will finish that to the full extent of my ability. 我一会儿就去。——I will be with you in a second. 请问您的大名(地址,电话号码)?——May I have your name(address, telephone number), please?

Unit Four 保安员日常用语

一、当来访客人进入值班室时,起身询问:

请问先生(女士),有什么事? ——Please ask the Sir(Mum), what's your trouble?

您找谁? ——Who are you looking for?

早安,先生。能为您效劳吗? ——Good morning, Sir. May I help you?

晚上好,李先生。我能帮助您吗? ——Good evening, Mr. Li. Can I be of any assistance?

女士,午安。我能为您做些什么吗? ——Good afternoon, mum. What can I do for you?

有什么事情我可以为您效劳吗? ——Is there anything I can do for you?

要我效劳吗? ——Have you been waited on?

请慢慢看。(请随意参观)。——Please take your time. (Go right ahead.)

请便。——Please take your time.

请随意。——As you please.

二、接待业主报案时:

先生(女士),别急,慢慢讲。—— Sir(Madam), take it easy, speak slowly.

请您出示证件。—— Please show your certificate.

谢谢合作。—— Thanks for corporation.

请再说一遍好吗? ——Pardon (me)? 或 Beg your pardon?

抱歉,我不了解您的意思。——I'm sorry, I didn't understand you.

麻烦您再说一遍(您的问题),好吗? ——Would you mind repeating your question, please?

可否请您讲慢一点? ——Would you please speak more slowly?

恐怕我没办法用英语解释。——I'm afraid I can't explain it in English.

抱歉,您说什么? ——Excuse me. What did you say?

对不起,您说'grocery'是什么意思? ——Excuse me. What do you mean by 'grocery'?

是这样吗? ——-Is that so?

我明白了。——I see.

请您再说一次好吗? ——Would you please say it again?

你懂我的意思吗? ——Do you follow me?

三、在巡逻中,处理突发事件时:

请问先生(女士),发生什么事? ——Please ask Sir(Madam), what happened?

对不起,请到值班室协助我们调查。——Excuse me, please go to duty room to help us to investigate.

What's up? ——什么事? 怎么啦?

Try to find out what's up。——查查发生了什么事?

I wish you could manage the time to come and talk to us. ——我希望你能安排出时间来跟我们谈谈。

实在太谢谢您的帮助了。——不客气。要是有什么其他的事要我为你做,你就告诉我。——我会的,那好,再次感谢您。——Thank you very much indeed. ——That's all right. But let me know if there's anything else I can do for you.——I certainly will。Well, thank you again.

我来帮你拿行李好吗？——Can I help you with your luggage?

I'll do it right away.——我马上就做这件事。

打扰一下,有件事你得帮我一下。——有什么问题吗,太太？——我的房间里没有纸了。——哦,对不起,我马上给你拿。——Excuse me, there's something you could help me with.——What seems to be the problem, ma'am?——There in't any paper in my room.——Oh, I'm sorry. I'll get it right away.

您一直走,会看到一个指示牌,然后左转,就在您的正前方——If you go straight down, you will see a sign. At the sign turn to the left. It is right ahead of you. 一直走到尽头。——Keep going until you come to the end。

小心那条狗,它有时咬人。——Be careful of the dog. It sometimes bites people.

当心！——Be careful!

小心！——Watch it!

别碰它。——Let it alone!

四、发现业主家中有异常情况时：

请问,您有什么需要帮忙？—— Please ask, may I help you?

对不起,打扰了。—— Excuse me.

我看到冒烟就知道出事了。——I knew something was up when I saw the smoke.

Unit Five 车辆管理服务用语

一、车辆进入管理区时：

请先生用驾驶证换取车位牌。——Please exchange your driving license to car parking card.

对不起,久等了！——Sorry for making you wait for me so long!

二、发现车辆违章停放时：

先生,对不起,请您按位泊车。—— Sir, excuse me, please park your car in the proper position.

请不要停在人行道。——Please don't park the sidewalk.

请不要停在绿化地。——Please don't park in the grass.

三、发现车辆未关好门时：

先生请关好车门,窗。——Sir, please shut the door and window of your car.

请锁好车。—— Lock your car.

四、检查可疑车辆时：

请问,先生贵姓？住哪栋哪座？属何单位？——Please what's your surname? Which building do you live in? which company do you work in?

请出示证件。—— Please show your certificate.

五、解释司机或业主疑问时：

对不起,我们按规定办事,请谅解！——Excuse me, we handle affairs according to regulations, please understand me!

Unit Six 清洁员用语

一、纠正不文明行为时：

对不起，请爱护公共卫生！—— Excuse me, please keep the place clean!

请不要随地吐痰！—— Please don't spit everywhere!

请不要随手扔垃圾！—— Please do not throw the garbage everywhere!

请扔到垃圾桶内！—— Please throw the garbage into the dustbin!

小朋友，听话，不要乱涂、乱画。—— Kid, obedient, behave yourself, don't doodle. (No scripts.)

先生，请不要吸烟，请将烟熄灭！—— Sir, please don't smoke, please put out the cigarettes!

请您别在这里吸烟好吗？——Would you please refrain from smoking here? 或 Would you mind not smoking here?

抱歉，请您到吸烟室去抽，好吗？——Excuse me. Would you mind smoking in the lounge?

请您把伞放在门外好吗？——Would you please leave your umbrella out of the door?

二、不文明行为改正后：

多谢合作！—— Thanks for cooperation!

对不起，谢谢！—— Excuse me, thanks!

当正在进行清洁的工作或实施卫生检查时，对过往行人说："先生（女士），请让一下，谢谢！" "Sir(mum), excuse me, thanks!"

当有人对影响清洁的行为不改正，反而刁难时，应耐心解释，说："请别生气，请支持我们的工作，请谅解！" "please do not get angry, please support our work, and please understand me!"

Unit Seven 绿化工作服务用语

施工场地，请绕道行！—— Construction field, please take other ways!

请爱护树木！—— Please take good care of trees!

请不要在草地上玩耍！—— Please do not play on the lawn!

对不起，请不要在此堆放物品，请马上搬走。—— Excuse me, please do not heap articles here, and please move out right away.

附录三 物业管理常用的信函、文本与合同（中文参考）

物业管理中必须让业主随时了解物业的各种情况和管理公司开展的各项管理工作。比如某一些重要工程（水箱清洗、电梯维修、电线线路改造等）影响业户生活，应及时通知业户。再比如住户已超期未缴管理费，要提醒其及时缴费以避免罚款等，这些沟通工作有的是公告性的，要张贴在公告栏上，有些是对个别住户的，则要通过信函通知。

此外，物业公司有时还需对业户的一些查询、投诉作解释性质的回复，这些都需要从事物业管理工作的人员具有良好的书写信函的能力和公关意识。一封简洁明了、书写规范、有礼貌的信函送达业户手中，既节省了许多时间和精力，又对管理工作的顺利开展起到非常大的作用，所以能写一封合乎标准的信函是物业管理人员的必备素质之一。不少物业管理公司在实践中，总结出一批合乎实际需要的标准信件样本，现举例如下：

通知业户办理装修工程申请手续的信函

尊敬的业户：

欢迎您成为（物业名称）之住户。根据您与物业管理公司签订之契约，您必须呈交该房屋的装修图及装修计划，由物业管理公司批核。

为符合要求，请住户参阅契约第＿＿＿＿项，有关副本已交住户。

有些装修工程如制冷、机电、消防设备更改及水管等安装工程，必须交由本公司指定的专业工程公司施工。为使上述工程公司了解业主之要求，在其施工期间，须由代表业主之工程师负责监管。现随函附上有关专业工程公司及其负责人之资料，详情请见附件＿＿＿＿。

如装修工程由住户自己落实装修公司，本公司建议住户应指派一工程负责人，以便进行装修工程事宜之联络。请住户的装修商直接与本公司指定的专业工程公司联络，以便在施工前，将有关装修图细则及规划交于业主批核。在提交图纸的同时，住户应将同意的装修工程报价单同时递交。有关图纸的审批通常需要一周时间。

随函附上申请装修程序指南一份（见附件＿＿＿＿），以供参阅。

假如住户未能找到合适的装修公司，本公司乐意推荐若干装修公司供住户选择。有关公司的名称及电话已随函附上（见附件＿＿＿＿），请直接与对方进行联系。

如有任何疑问，可直接与本人联络（电话：＿＿＿＿）。

如本人不在，请与＿＿＿＿同志联络，乐意为住户服务。

此致

贵住户

＿＿＿＿＿＿启

＿＿＿＿＿＿代办

日期：年　月　日

1. 住户进行装修注意事项。
2. 住户进行的装修工程必须达到最好的专业水平,以保证质量。
3. 住户必须申请一切有关公共服务机构的许可证及负责有关费用。
4. 住户及其承办商必须负责每天将有关装修工程所产生的废料及垃圾搬离大厦。如果没有及时清理,或随便乱堆,物业公司有权安排清理此类废物并向住户追讨有关清理费,同时按照公司有关规定进行处罚。住户必须负责指示其承办商经常采取安全措施,以防止因其装修工程而引致大厦或其他住户的装修受损。住户必须确保其承办商所进行的装修工程不会造成任何危险。
5. 住户的装修工程必须与前业主或其承办商,或其他住户的工程配合及确保其装修工程将不会干扰或延误大厦内的任何其他工程。

违章通知单

违章通知单

经查实,您(单位)从事_____行为,违反_____规定,现正式通知您:

1. 请立即停止上述行为;
2. 限期_____天恢复或_____处理好;
3. 赔偿经济损失_____元(人民币);
4. 没收_____；
5. _____限于_____天内到_____接受处理,逾期加倍处罚,并按规定强制执行。

若有疑问或异议,请于　　年　　月　　日前到_____查询或复议。

_____管理处
年　　月　　日

增加管理费通知

增加管理费通知(附有关文件)

尊敬的业户:

本住宅小区(大厦)的管理费自_____年_____月_____日调整以来,通货膨胀及管理成本不断增加。基于以上原因,根据××文件第××条,本住宅小区(大厦)的管理费自_____(日期)起需再作调整。

在以往_____个月来,住宅小区(大厦)开支不断上升,而经未来一年的收支预算后,决定住宅小区(大厦)的管理费由现时每平方米_____元调整至每平方米_____元,各单元住房新收费标准如下:

住户户型	管理费
两房一厅	每月_____元
两房二厅	每月_____元
三房一厅	每月_____元
三房二厅	每月_____元
四房一厅	每月_____元

20_____年度及本年度的预算表及经审核的_____年度结算表已张贴于管理处

的告示板上,以供参考。住户如对有关账目有任何疑问,可与管理人员或公司经理联系。附上××文件供参考。

此致
贵业户

_____公司
年　月　日

催缴管理费通知书(第一次催缴)(样本)
催缴管理费通知书

尊敬的_____先生/女士:

本公司谨提醒阁下,贵户应缴的物业管理费共计人民币_____元,至今未交到本公司。

若阁下已缴付上述款项,请毋须理会本通知书。

此致
贵住户(_____幢_____单元_____号)

_____公司
年　月　日

催缴管理费通知书(第二次催款)(样本)
通　知　书

尊敬的_____先生/女士:

本公司于_____年_____月_____日致住户信中所提及_____月份之_____费共计人民币_____元,迄今您这户仍未付清。直到目前为止包括本月份费用之和应缴付款人民币_____元。

假如本公司(日期)前仍未收到您这户金额(人民币)_____元之付款,公司将在无法选择的情况下将此案转交律师诉至法院,并采取一切适当行动追讨上述欠款而毋须作另行通知。

为避免对住户造成难堪,本公司希望在迫不得已进行下一步行动之前,住户能尽力缴清上述欠款。

此致
贵住户(_____幢_____单元_____号)

_____公司
年　月　日

(注:此为最后通牒,确定缴款期限,如住户/租户仍不支付欠款,此案将诉至法院代为追讨)。
通知住户暂停某项服务的信函
暂停电力及饮用水供应

尊敬的住户:

现接到供电部门的通知,由于需要对_____(地点)的主要电力系统进行检修,小区内_____幢至_____幢楼宇的电力供应,将于_____至_____(时间)暂停。而小区内的供水系统在上述期间也因此暂停供应。

本公司对上述工程可能引致的不方便,深表歉意。

此致
各住户

                _____公司
                 年 月 日

通知住户暂停电梯服务的信函

暂停电梯服务

尊敬的住户：

  由于进行电梯修理工程的检查，电梯服务将于_____至_____（时间）暂时停止。如住户有特殊事情感到不便，望告知物业管理公司，本公司将尽力排忧解难。

  本公司对上述工程可能引致的不方便，深表歉意。

  此致
各住户

                _____公司
                 年 月 日

通知住户在进行外墙维修、清洁期间保安安排的信函

外墙维修

尊敬的住户：

  本公司委托的专业维修清洁公司将于_____至_____（日期）在_____（地点）进行外墙维修、清洁工程。

  在施工期间，本公司除在上述地点做出适当的保安安排之外，更希望阁下能配合进行相应的防御措施，将窗户妥为关闭。

  若阁下有任何疑问，请打电话_____与物业管理公司联系。多谢合作。

  此致
各住户

                _____公司
                 年 月 日

意外事故报告

  某些意外事件如盗窃、抢劫、打架、伤亡、水管爆裂、水淹、火警、电力中断或其他天灾人祸等等，往往造成人身或财产的损失，值班人员如遇到此类事件应立刻报告上级来处理，但作为第一目击者，亦可帮助管理公司及其上级人员解决问题，因第一手资料是相当重要的，所以务必要填写意外事故报告书。

意外事故报告书（样本）

  协助单位：_____

  意外性质：盗窃□ 打架□ 火警□ 抢劫□
           受伤/死亡□ 电力中断□

  受伤人数_____贵重物品摘要_____失窃/抢劫

  大约损失_____

  意外事故详细情况：_____
      _____

当事人姓名_____楼层_____电话_____
管理处行动_____

```
        当局行动：
      公安局□  市政局□  消防局□
         电力公司□  其他□
    负责同志姓名_____职务_____
      其他_____抵达时间_____
```

现时状况及采取行动：_____
意外发现报告人 报告联络中心（非办公时间）
时间/日期_____
姓名_____
职位_____单位_____

事件/议报人	中心负责人批示	
	申报公共保险： 是 否	
日 期		日 期
	附件：录音/录像 当局报告	
	信件 其他	

提醒住户防止某些事故（自然灾害）的通告（样本）
以防台风措施通告为例介绍

防台风措施的通告

尊敬的住户：

近来很多住户都关注在恶劣天气下（如遇到台风侵袭时），雨水渗入屋内的问题。基于以往的经验，本公司提醒各住户，目前一般楼宇所安装门窗，在台风侵袭期间一般不能完全防止雨水渗入。以下几项建议措施，可能对住户有所帮助：

1. 在台风侵袭期间，强风可能会将玻璃窗吹毁，故室内人员都应尽量远离有玻璃窗的地方，尤其是正对风向位置，并应以胶布贴于玻璃上，防止玻璃破裂后四处飞溅。

2. 住户应确保所有窗户及门锁紧闭，并在台风期间经常检视其情况，因强风随时有可能将上述设施破坏以致脱落。

3. 所有花盆、植物、家具等应移离露天露台，并检查所有的排水管道是否阻塞，提前排除阻塞。

4. 若没有防风板、防风卷闸等设施，住户应自行安装和拆卸。住宅小区（大厦）管理人员因在台风期间需负责公共地区的公共设施的防风措施，故不能协助个别住户在其屋内进行防风工作。

此外，住户须注意有关贵单位之台风保险事宜，有关索赔详情，可与投保的保险公司联络。

此致

贵住户

_____物业公司
年　月　日

关于业户回访和投诉处理表(附业户来访、投诉登记表)(样本)

回 访 记 录 表

部门：　　　　　　　　　　　　　　　　　　　　　　　　　　年　月　日

栋号房号		回访人		回访形式	
回访事由					
回访记录	记录人：　　业主(住户)签名：　　年　月　日				
主任意见	签名：　　年　月　日				

来 访 登 记 表

登记部门：　　　　　　　　　　班：

序号	时间	来访形式	来访人			来访事由	记录人	处理情况
			姓名	联系电话	地址或单位			

注：如属投诉将内容填到《投诉登记表》上，来访形式按来人、电话、函件、传真、转达内容填写。

投 诉 登 记 表

登记部门：

序号	投诉时间(日时)	来访人			投诉内容	处理表号码	处理情况
		姓名	联系电话	地址或单位			

注：接待人将内容登记在《投诉处理表》上并通知责任人取表进行处理，处理完成后，验证人在此表上填上完成时间并签名。

投诉处理表

单位：		班组：		No：	
投诉人		联系电话		地址	
投诉时间：年 月 日 时 分 内容： 记录人：年 月 日				投诉类型 Ⅰ□ Ⅱ□ Ⅲ□	
调查情况、结果： 属有效投诉□ 无效投诉□ 调查人： 年 月 日					
处理意见 责任人： 年 月 日					
回访验证(上门/电话/信函)： 业主(住户)签名： 验证人： 年 月 日					

业户意见征询表

业户(住户)意见征询表

小区(大厦)名称：年 月 日

业主姓名：		栋号房号：			联系电话：
序号	服务项目	总体评价			不满意原因或管理意见与建议
		满意	较满意	不满意	
1					
2					
3					
4					
5					
6					
7					
8					
9					
10					
11					
说明	1. 请您在总体评价的项栏内打"√"； 2. 房管服务即为管理处日常的来访接待、安排维修服务、办理入住和装修管理、投诉处理等； 3. 请于 年 月 日前,将此表返回				

附录四 本书生词表 Word List

access	['ækses]	n.	通路，访问，入门
		vt.	存取，接近
activity	[æk'tiviti]	n.	活动性，能动性，敏捷，活跃；活动
aggravation	[ægrə'veiʃən]	n.	恼火，恶化
agreement	[ə'gri:mənt]	n.	协定，协议；同意，一致
alarm	[ə'lɑ:m]	n.	警报，惊慌，警告器
		vt.	恐吓，警告
allocate	['æləukeit]	vt.	分派，分配
allowance	[ə'lauəns]	n.	补助，津贴，供给量；允许；考虑
alternative	[ɔ:l'tə:nətiv]	n.	二中择一，可供选择的办法，事物
		a.	选择性的，二中择一的
alternatively	[ɔ:l'tə:nətivli]	ad.	做为选择，二者择一地
amend	[ə'mend]	v.	改善，修正，修订，更改
apparent	[ə'pærənt]	a.	显然的，外观上的
apparently	[ə'pærəntli]	ad.	明显地，显而易见地；表面上地，貌似地，外观上地
appliance	[ə'plaiəns]	n.	应用，适用；用具，装置；器械
apprehension	[æpri'henʃən]	n.	理解，领悟；担心，忧虑
appropriate	[ə'prəupriit]	a.	适当的
approximately	[əprɒksɪ'mətlɪ]	ad.	近似地，大约
aspect	['æspekt]	n.	（建筑物等的）方向，方位
assess	[ə'ses]	vt.	对（人物、工作等）进行估价，评价
assessment	[ə'sesmənt]	n.	（为征税对财产所作的）估价，被估定的金额
asset	['æset]	n.	（单项）财产；宝贵的人（或物）
assist	[ə'sist]	v.	援助，帮助
assist	[ə'sist]	vt.	援助，帮助
assist		vi.	援助，帮助
assist		n.	援助，帮助
assistance	[ə'sistəns]	n.	帮助；援助
assume	[ə'sju:m]	vt.	承担；设想；采取
attendance	[ə'tendəns]	n.	参加，出席；出席率；护理，照料
authoritative	[ɔ:'θɒritətiv]	a.	官方的，当局的；有权威的，可相信的
authority	[ɔ:'θɒriti]	n.	[复]当局，官方

315

单词	音标	词性	释义
award	[ə'wɔːd]	n.	决断；判决；奖品
beware	[bi'wɛə]	vt.	(用于祈使句,或与 must, should 等连用)谨防,当心
body	['bɔdi]	n.	团体,机关；主体,正文
boiler	['bɔilə]	n.	锅炉,热水贮槽；煮器
booster	['buːstə]	n.	＜美俚＞热心的拥护者,后推的人,支持者,后援者,调压器
breakdown	['breikdaun]	n.	(机械等的)损坏；故障；倒塌
bribery	['braibəri]	n.	行贿,受贿,贿赂
calendar	['kælində]	vt.	把……列入表中；(为文件等)作排列,分类和索引
capital	['kæpitl]	n.	资本,资方
		a.	资本的；基本的,首要的,重要的；致死的；第一流的
capitalization	[kəpitəlai'zeiʃən]	n.	资本化,股本,资本总额,大写
caution	['kɔːʃən]	n.	小心,谨慎；警告；与众不同的人或物
challenging	['tʃælindʒiŋ]	a.	引起挑战性兴趣的,挑逗的
characteristic	[ˌkæriktə'ristik]	a.	特有的,表示特性的,典型的
		n.	特性,特征
charge	[tʃɑːdʒ]	n.	费用；靠人赡养的人；主管；充电
chiller	['tʃilə]	n.	冷却装置
circumstance	['səːkəmstəns]	n.	(通常用复数)与某事件或某人有关的情况、事实等；环境；情势
clause	[klɔːz]	n.	条款,项目,从句
comfort	['kʌmfət]	n.	舒适,安逸；安慰；使生活舒适的事物；盖被
commence	[kə'mens]	v.	开始；得……学位
commercial	[kə'məːʃəl]	a.	商业的,商业上的；商务的；商品化的
comparable	['kɔmpərəbl]	a.	可比较的,比得上的
compare	[kəm'pɛə]	vt.	比较,对照；比喻
		n.	比较
compensate	['kɔmpenseit]	vt.	补偿,赔偿,酬报；(机)补整,补偿
competent	['kɔmpitənt]	a.	胜任的,有能力的；应该做的；适当的；权限内的
complaint	[kəm'pleint]	n.	诉苦,抱怨,牢骚,委屈,疾病
complement	['kɔmplimənt]	n.	补足物
		vt.	补充,补足
compliance	[kəm'plaIəns]	n.	依从,顺从
comply	[kəm'plai]	vi.	照做
component	[kəm'pəunənt]	n.	成分
		a.	组成的,构成的

词	音标	词性	释义
comprehensive	[kɔmpri'hensiv]	a.	内容广泛的,综合的,承包的
conductive	[kən'dʌktiv]	a.	传导性的,传导上的
confine	[kən'fain]	n.	(常用复)境界,边缘,区域,范围
consequence	['kɔnsikwəns]	n.	结果,后果
consumption	[kən'sʌmpʃən]	n.	消费(量),消耗
continuity	[kɔnti'njuiti]	n.	连锁,连续;节目说明
contract	['kɔntrækt]	n.	契约,合同
contractor	[kən'træktə]	n.	承包人,承包商,包工头,订约人;收缩物
contribution	[ˌkɔntri'bju:ʃən]	n.	捐献,贡献,投稿
conversion	[kən'və:ʃən]	n.	变换,转化;更换
corridor	['kɔridɔ:]	n.	走廊
costly	['kɔstli]	a.	昂贵的,代价高的;价值高的,豪华的
council	['kaunsil]	n.	政务会;理事会;委员会;地方自治会;地方议会
critically	['kritikəli]	ad.	评论性地;对……感到不满地;关键性地;应急所必须地
damper	['dæmpə]	n.	起抑制作用的因素,节气闸,断音装置
dawn	[dɔ:n]	n.	黎明,拂晓,破晓
		vi.	破晓,开始出现,变得(为人所)明白
deduct	[di'dʌkt]	vt.	扣除,减去,折扣;推论
default	[di'fɔ:lt]	n.	不履行,拖欠
		v.	缺乏;错误
deficiency	[di'fiʃənsi]	n.	缺乏,不足
define	[di'fain]	vt.	定义,详细说明
deliberately	[di'libəritli]	ad.	审慎地,故意地;蓄意地
delivery	[di'livəri]	n.	交付,交货;投递,传送;发出;释放
demonstrate	['demənstreit]	vt.	示范,证明,论证
		vi.	示威
depression	[di'preʃən]	n.	沮丧,消沉,低气压,低压
deteriorate	[di'tiəriəreit]	vt.	使恶化
		vi.	降低;变坏;衰退;损坏
deterioration	[diˌtiəriə'reiʃən]	n.	变坏,退化,堕落
deviation	[divi'eiʃən]	n.	偏差
diesel	[di:zəl]	n.	内燃机,柴油机
		a.	柴油发电机的
diligence	['dilidʒəns]	n.	勤奋
diligent	['dilidʒənt]	a.	勤劳的,勤奋的,努力的,刻苦的
discipline	['disiplin]	n.	纪律,学科
		v.	训练
discount	['diskaunt]	vt.	打折;贴现;对……持怀疑态度;看轻

英文	音标	词性	释义
dispute	[dis'pju:t]	n.	争论,辩论;争执,争端
disruption	[dis'rʌpʃən]	n.	分裂,瓦解;破坏
distribution	[ˌdistri'bju:ʃən]	n.	分配;销售;分布;分配装置,分配系统;区分,分类
duty	['dju:ti]	n.	(机器在给定条件下所做的)功,能率,负载,工作状态;责任,义务
dynamic	[dai'næmik]	a.	动力的,动力学的,动态的
economically	[ˌi:kə'nɔmikəli]	ad.	节约地;节俭地;在经济学上
effectiveness	[i'fektivnis]	n.	有效,生效;有力;实在,实际
efficiency	[i'fiʃənsi]	n.	效率,功效,效能,实力
elimination	[iˌlimi'neiʃən]	n.	排除,消除,消灭
encounter	[in'kauntə]	v.	遭遇,碰见,打击,冲突
engagement	[in'geidʒmənt]	n.	约定,契约;衔接;交战,接近
enhance	[in'ha:ns]	vt.	提高,增强
		vi.	提高
equalize	['i:kwəlaiz]	v.	调整
equation	[i'kweiʃən]	n.	均衡,平均;(个别或综合的)因素
escalate	['eskəleit]	vi.	逐步升高,逐步增强
		vt.	使逐步上升
	['eskəleitə]	n.	(建)自动楼梯
essential	[i'senʃəl]	a.	必要的,必不可少的
evacuate	[i'vækju'eit]	vt.	疏散
evacuation	[i'vækju'eiʃən]	n.	撤离,疏散
evaluate	[i'væljueit]	vt.	评价,估……的价
evident	['evidənt]	a.	明显的
excessive	[ik'sesiv]	a.	过多的;过分的;极度的
exclude	[iks'klu:d]	v.	拒绝,隔绝,排除
exclusion	[iks'klu:ʒən]	n.	被排除在外的事物;排斥
expectation	[ˌekspek'teiʃən]	n.	期待,预料,指望,展望,[数]期望(值)
expenditure	[iks'penditʃə]	n.	支出,花费
expense	[ik'spens]	n.	费用,代价,损失,开支,费钱之物
expertise	[ˌekspə'ti:z]	n.	专家的意见,专门技术
expire	[iks'paiə]	v.	期满,终止,呼气,断气,届满
expiry	[iks'paiəri]	n.	(期限、协定等的)满期,终止
extension	[iks'tenʃən]	n.	延伸,广度;扩展;附加;大学公开演讲
extensive	[iks'tensiv]	a.	彻底的,粗放的,延伸的,扩大的,大范围的
external	[eks'tə:nl]	a.	外部的;客观的;外用的;表面的;外国的
extinguisher	[iks'tiŋgwiʃə]	n.	熄灭者,消灭者;熄灯器,灭火器
facade	[fə'sa:d]	n.	(房屋的)正面,立面;表面,外观,(掩饰真相的)

			门面
facility	[fəˈsiliti]	n.	容易，简易，灵巧，熟练，便利，敏捷，设备，工具
factor	[ˈfæktə]	n.	因素，要素，因数，代理人
fan	[fæn]	n.	扇子，风扇，鼓风机
fashion	[ˈfæʃən]	n.	方式；风尚
feasibility	[ˌfiːzəˈbIləti]	n.	可行性，可能性
federal	[ˈfedərəl]	a.	联邦的，联合的；联邦制的
flexibility	[ˌfleksəˈbiliti]	n.	弹性，适应性，机动性，挠性
flow	[fləu]	n.	流程，流动，(河水)泛滥，洋溢
		vi.	流动，涌流，川流不息，飘扬
		vt.	溢过，淹没
footing	[ˈfutiŋ]	n.	立足点；地位，基础；关系；总额
foreclosures	[fɔːˈkləuʒə(r)]	n.	丧失抵押品赎回权，排斥
fundamental	[ˌfʌndəˈmentl]	a.	基础的，基本的
		n.	基本原则，基本原理
glazing	[ˈgleiziŋ]	n.	窗用玻璃；(总称)玻璃窗；玻璃装配工作；磨光
governor	[ˈgʌvənə]	n.	调速器
hazardous	[ˈhæzədəs]	a.	危险的，冒险的
hoist	[hɔist]	v.	提高，提升
hourly	[ˈauəli]	a.	每小时的，每小时一次的；时时刻刻的
hydraulic	[haiˈdrɔːlik]	a.	水力的，水压的
hydraulics	[haiˈdrɔːliks]	n.	水力学
identification	[aiˌdentifiˈkeiʃən]	n.	辨认，鉴定，证明，视为同一
identify	[aiˈdentifai]	vt.	认为……一致；识别，鉴定
illumination	[iˌljuːmiˈneiʃən]	n.	照明，照明度；解释；灯饰
implication	[ˌimpliˈkeiʃən]	n.	含有……的意思；牵连；影响
imply	[imˈplai]	vt.	含有……的意思，暗指，暗示，意指
impose	[imˈpouz]	vi.	施影响；利用；欺骗
		vt.	征税；把……强加
improvement	[imˈpruːvmənt]	n.	改进，改良，增进；改进措施
inclusion	[inˈkluːʒən]	n.	包含，包括；内含物
incorporate	[inˈkɔːpəreit]	a.	合并的，结社的，一体化的
		vt.	合并，使组成公司，具体表现
incorporate		vi.	合并，混合，组成公司
incorporation	[inˌkɔːpəˈreiʃən]	n.	结合，合并，社团，公司；混合
indicate	[ˈindikeit]	vt.	指出，显示，象征，预示，需要，简要地说明
initial	[iˈniʃəl]	a.	最初的，词首的，初始的
		n.	词首大写字母

英文	音标	词性	释义
initial	[i'niʃəl]	a.	最初的,开始的
inspect	[in'spekt]	vt.	检查,审查
inspection	[in'spekʃn]	n.	检查,调查,验收;监督
install	[in'stɔ:l]	vt.	任命,安装,安置
installation	[ˌinstə'leiʃən]	n.	安装,设置,安置;装置,设备;(军事)设施
insulation	[ˌinsju'leiʃən]	n.	隔离,孤立,绝缘,绝热
insurance	[in'ʃuərəns]	n.	安全保障;保险单;保险费;保险业
integrity	[in'tegriti]	n.	正直,诚实,完整,完全,完整性
intend	[in'tend]	vt.	打算使……成为;意思是;想要
intended	[in'tendid]	a.	打算中的,预期的;故意的,有意的
intensify	[in'tensifai]	vt.	加强,加剧
interactive	[ˌintər'æktiv]	a.	相互作用的,相互影响的
interfere	[ˌintə'fiə]	vi.	干涉,干预,妨碍,打扰
interference	[ˌintə'fiərəns]	n.	冲突,干涉
intervention	[ˌintə'venʃən]	n.	介入,干涉
investment	[in'vestmənt]	n.	投资,可获利的东西
involve	[in'vɔlv]	vt.	免不了,需要;包含;遍及;占用
issue	['isju:]	n.	结果,结局;问题,争端,争论点;(土地,地产等)的收益;流出,放出;出口;结果,结局;发行;问题,争端
lane	[lein]	n.	小路,巷,里弄,狭窄的通道,航线
larceny	['la:sni]	n.	盗窃罪
layout	['leiˌaut]		规划,设计,(书刊等)编排,版面,配线,企划,设计图案
		n.	(工厂等的)布局图,版面设计
leakage	['li:kidʒ]	n.	渗漏物
ledge	[ledʒ]	n.	(自墙壁突出的)壁架;架状突出物
legislative	['ledʒislətiv]	a.	立法的
		n.	立法机关
lighting	['laitiŋ]	n.	照明,照明设备;点火,发火;(画面的)明暗分布
likelihood	['alikihud]	n.	可能(性);可能发生的事物;可能成功的迹象
localize	['ləukəlaiz]	vt.	集中,使限制于局部
lucrative	['lju:krətiv]	a.	有利的,生利的,赚钱的;值得作为目标的
maintain	[men'tein]	vt.	维持,保持,继续;维修,保养
maintenance	['meintinəns]	n.	维护,保持,生活费用,抚养
maintenance	['meintinəns]	n.	维护,保持,生活费用,抚养
malfunction	['mæl'fʌŋkʃən]	vi.	失灵,发生故障,机能失常
		n.	失灵,故障
management	['mænidʒmənt]	n.	经营,管理,处理,操纵,驾驶,手段

单词	音标	词性	释义
mandatory	['mændətəri]	a.	命令的，强制的，托管的
manipulate	[mə'nipjuleit]	vt.	篡改，伪造账目等；熟练的地使用；摆布；操作器
mindful	['maindful]	a.	留心的，注意的，记住的，不望的
minimization	[ˌminimai'zeiʃən]	n.	极度轻视，把……估计得最低
minimize	['minimaiz]	vt.	使减到最少，使缩到最小
minimum	['miniməm]	a.	最小的，最低的
		n.	最小值，最小化
modification	[ˌmɔdifi'keiʃən]	n.	更改，修改，修正
modified	['mɔdifaid]	a.	改良的，改进的，修正的
monitor	['mɔnitə]	v.	控制，管理；探索；报警；调节
negligence	['neglidʒəns]	n.	忽视，疏忽；粗心大意
negotiate	[ni'gəuʃieit]	v.	（与某人）商议，谈判，磋商，买卖，让渡（支票、债券等），通过，越过
nominate	['nɔmineit]	vt.	提名，推荐，任命，命名
notification	[ˌnəutifi'keiʃən]	n.	通知，通报；布告；通知单
nuisance	['njusns]	n.	麻烦的事；讨厌的事；多余的事
occupancy	['ɔkjupənsi]	n.	占有，占用，居住；占有期间；建筑物的被占用部分；占有率
occupant	['ɔkjupənst]	n.	占有人，占有者；居住者
occupational	[ˌɔkju'peiʃnl]	a.	职业的，与职业有关的
ongoing	['ɔngəuiŋ]	a.	正在进行的，前进的
ongoing		n.	进行，行动，事物
optimize	['ɔptimaiz]	vt.	使最优化
optimum	['ɔptiməm]	n.	最适宜
		a.	最适宜的
option	['ɔpʃən]	n.	选择，选择权；选择自由；（供）选择的事物；在规定时间内要求履行合同的特权；被保险人对赔款方式的选择权
originate	[ə'ridʒineit]	n.	起源，开始出现
otherwise	['ʌðəwaiz]	ad.	另外，别样；在其他方面；要不然，否则
outline	['autlain]	vt.	概述，画轮廓
outweigh	[aut'wei]	vt.	在重量上超过；在价值上超过
oversee	['əuvə'si:]	v.	俯瞰，监视，检查，视察
oversight	['əuvəsait]	n.	勘漏，失察，疏忽，失败，小心照顾
owner	['əunə]	n.	所有人，物主
paramount	['pærəmaunt]	a.	极为重要的
particular	[pə'tikjulə]	n.	细节，详细
		a.	特殊的，特别的，独特的，详细的，精确的，挑剔的

英文	音标	词性	释义
passive	[ˈpæsiv]	a.	被动的,受动的,消极的;无利息的
paucity	[ˈpɔːsiti]	n.	极小量
peak	[piːk]	a.	最高的,高峰的
penalty	[ˈpenlti]	n.	惩罚,罚款;困难,不利后果
performance	[pəˈfɔːməns]	n.	履行,执行,完成;成绩;演出;性能,效能,效率;生产力(率)
perimeter	[pəˈrimitə]	n.	周边,周长;(兵营或工事外的)环形防线
periodic	[ˌpiəriˈɔdik]	a.	周期的,定期的,循环的;一定时间的
periodically	[ˌpiəriˈɔdikəli]	ad.	定期地,周期地
permanent	[ˈpəːmənənt]	a.	永久的,持久的
personnel	[ˌpəːsəˈnel]	n.	人员,职员
petroleum	[piˈtrəuljəm]	n.	石油
placement	[ˈpleismənt]	n.	放置,布置;(人员的)安排,安插;(足球等的)定位踢
point	[pɔint]	n.	意义,目的,用途;论点;地点;特征
power plant			发电站,发电厂;(机动车辆等的)动力设备
premise	[ˈpremis]	n.	房屋(及其附属建筑、基地等)
present	[ˈpreznt]	vt.	介绍,引见;提出,呈递;出示,上演
pressurization	[ˌpreʃəraiˈzeiʃən]	n.	压力输送;挤压;气密,密封;增压,加压
preventative	[priˈventətiv]	a.	预防性的
preventive	[priˈventiv]	a.	预防的,防止的
previous	[ˈpriːvjəs]	a.	以前的;过早的
procedure	[prəˈsiːdʒə]	n.	过程,步骤;程序;礼节
process	[prəˈses]	n.	过程,作用,方法,程序,步骤,进行,推移
		vt.	加工,处理
production	[prəˈdʌkʃən]	n.	生产;制作;演出;提供
productivity	[ˌprɔdʌkˈtiviti]	n.	生产率;生产能力;丰饶,多产
professional	[prəˈfeʃnl]	n.	自由职业者,专业人员,职业运动员,职业艺人
		a.	业务的,专业的,职业的
profile	[ˈprəufail]	n.	剖面,侧面,外形,轮廓
proper	[ˈprɔpə]	a.	正当的,规矩的;出色的,极好的
property	[ˈprɔpəti]	n.	财产,所有物,所有权,性质,特性,(小)道具
provision	[prəˈviʒən]	n.	供应,(一批)供应品,预备,防备,规定
pump	[pʌmp]	vt.	用抽机抽液体,用打气筒打气;盘问,追问;倾注;使疲惫;使劲地握手(pumping 抽水,泵送)
pursue	[pəˈsjuː]	vt.	追赶,追击;追随,跟随;追求,寻求;进行,从事
		vi.	追赶;继续进行
radiant	[ˈreidjənt]	a.	放射的,辐射的;发出辐射热的;喜悦的;光辉灿烂的

英文	音标	词性	释义
rate	[reit]	n.	价格;比率;速率;等级;房地产税率
		vt.	调整快慢差率;对……估价,对……评定
reassess	[ˌriːəˈses]	vt.	对……再估价,再鉴定,再征收
reciprocal	[riˈsiprəkəl]	a.	相互的
recommend	[ˌrekəˈmend]	vt.	推荐,介绍;劝告,建议
rectify	[ˈrektifai]	vt.	改正,纠正,整顿;清除
redundancy	[riˈdʌndnsi]	n.	多余,剩余度;过多,重复
reflective	[riˈflektiv]	a.	反射的,反映的,思考的,沉思的
regulation	[ˌregjuˈleiʃən]	n.	规则,规章,法规
relationship	[riˈleiʃənʃip]	n.	关系,联系;家属关系,亲属关系
relevant	[ˈrelivənt]	a.	有关的,贴切的,中肯的,恰当的;成比例的,相应的
remedy	[ˈremidi]	n.	补救;改善;纠正
		vt.	治疗;赔偿
renegotiate	[ˌriːniˈɡəuʃiːˌeit]	vt.	重新谈判
renewal	[riˈnjuəl]	n.	更新,恢复;修补;重做;续订
replacement	[riˈpleismənt]	n.	归还,复位,交换,代替者,补充兵员,置换,移位
representative	[ˌrepriˈzentətiv]	n.	典型;代表,代理人,继承人;众议院议员
reputable	[ˈrepjutəbl]	a.	规范的,声誉好的,可尊敬的
reserve	[riˈzəːv]	vt.	储备,保留;推迟;预定
residential	[ˌreziˈdenʃəl]	a.	住宅的,与居住有关的
respect	[risˈpekt]	n.	关于
responsibility	[risˌpɔnsəˈbiliti]	n.	责任,责任心;职责,任务
retail	[ˈriːteil]	a.	零售的;零售商品的
reticulation	[ritikjuˈlei(ə)n]	n.	网状物
revise	[riˈvaiz]	vt.	修订,校订;修改;对……
routine	[ruːˈtiːn]	n.	例行公事,常规,日常事务,程序
		a.	日常的
satisfy	[ˈsætisfai]	vt.	符合,达到(要求,标准,规定等);满足,使满足,使满意
saving	[ˈseiviŋ]	n.	节约;挽救;(复)储蓄(金);存款
schedule	[ˈskedʒul]	vt.	将……列表,将……列入计划表;安排
scope	[skəup]	n.	范围,余地,机会,眼界;导弹的射程;目的,意图
secure	[siˈkjuə]	vt.	使安全,保卫;保证;关紧;招致
security	[siˈkjuəriti]	n.	安全
selective	[siˈlektiv]	a.	选择的,选择性的
sensing	[ˈsensiŋ]	n.	测向,偏航显示
significance	[sigˈnifikəns]	n.	意义,意味;重要性,重大

significant	[sig'nifkənt]	a.	有意义的,意义(或意味)深长的;表明……的;重要的,值得注意的;有效的;非偶然的
size	[saiz]	vt.	依一定的尺寸制造
		n.	规模,尺寸
sizing	['saiziŋ]	n.	填料,上胶,上浆
solar	['səulə]	a.	太阳的,日光的,利用太阳光的
solely	[soul]	ad.	单独地,惟一地
sophistication	[səˌfisti'keiʃən]	n.	强词夺理,诡辩,混合
specialist	['speʃəlist]	n.	专家;专业人员
specification	[ˌspesifi'keiʃən]	n.	(载有约定条件等的)说明书;列入说明书的一个项目
specify	['spesifai]	vt.	确定,规定;详细说明
spill	[spil]	vi.	溢出,溅出;充满;泄密
		n.	溢出,溅出;溢出量,溢出的东西
sprinkler	['spriŋklə]	n.	洒水器,洒水车,喷水设备,洒水灭火系统(屋内的管道系统,通常在火灾时因温度激增而自动洒水或喷出其他灭火液)
stairwell	['stɛəwel]	n.	(建)楼梯井
statute	['stætju:t]	n.	法令,章程
statutory	['stætjut(ə)ri]	a.	法令的,法定的
stock	[stɔk]	vt.	储备,备有;给(商店)办货
storage	['stɔ:ridʒ]	n.	保管;库存量;仓库
strategy	['strætidʒi]	n.	战略,战略学;策略,计谋
structural	['strʌktʃərəl]	a.	构造的;结构的
subcontractor	['sʌbkən'træktə]	n.	转包人,分包者;转包工作的承包者
submission	[səb'miʃən]	n.	提出,提交;谦逊;服从
subsequently	['sʌbsikwəntli]	ad.	其后,其次,接着
substantially	[səb'stænʃ(ə)li]	ad.	充分地
substitution	[ˌsʌbsti'tju:ʃən]	n.	代替,替换
superannuation	[sju:pərænjueiʃən]	n.	退休,废弃,淘汰
supervise	['sju:pəvaiz]	vi.	监督,管理
supervision	['sju:pə'viʒən]	n.	监督,管理
syndrome	['sindrəum]	n.	同时存在的事物
systematically	[ˌsisti'mætikəli]	ad.	有系统地,成体系地,有秩序地,有规则地,有组织地;分类(上)地,分类学地
tamper	['tæmpə]	vi.	干预,玩弄,贿赂,损害,削弱,篡改
		vt.	篡改
		n.	捣棒,夯,填塞者
tariff	['tærif]	n.	关税(率);收费表,价目表

tear	[tɛə]	v.	撕裂
tenant	['tenənt]	n.	租户,房客;不动产占有人;居住者
		v.	出租
tender	[tendə]	vi.	投标
tension	['tenʃən]	n.	(物)张力,拉力,牵力;(蒸汽等的)膨胀力,压力
terminate	['tə:mineit]	v.	终止,满期;接在端头上
thermal	['θə:məl]	a.	热的,由热造成的;温泉的
		n.	上升暖气流
thermostatic	[,θə:məs'tætik]	a.	恒温的;(灭火设备等)根据温度自动启动的
throughout	[θru(:)'aut]	ad.	到处;始终;彻头彻尾
timer	['aimə]	n.	定时器,自动按时操作装置;跑表,计时员
toxic	['tɔksik]	a.	有毒的,有毒性的
unauthorized	[ʌn'ɔ:θəraizd]	a.	未被授权的,未经认可的
underrate	[,ʌndə'reit]	vt.	低估,看轻
undoubtedly	[ʌn'dautidli]	ad.	毋庸置疑地,的确地
unserviceable	[,ʌn'sə:visəbl]	a.	不能使用的,不适用的,无用的;不耐用的
utility	[ju:'tiliti]	n.	实用,效用;有用的东西;公用事业
		a.	实用的;有多种用途的
valuation	[vælju'eiʃən]	n.	估价,评价,计算
viable	['vaiəbl]	a.	可行的;生存的
		n.	生存性;生活力
victim	['viktim]	n.	受害者,牺牲者,受骗者
view	[vju:]	vt.	看,检查,估计
warrant	['wɔrənt]	v.	保证
warranty	['wɔrənti]	n.	保证(书),担保(书);保单
wear	[wɛə]	v.	磨损
withhold	[wið'hould]	vt.	抑制,扣留;拒绝给予
worn	[wɔ:n]	a.	耗尽的,变得衰弱的

附录五 不规则动词

1. 按规律分类
A. 三种形式及读音皆同者：

cost	[kɔst]	cost	[kɔst]	cost	[kɔst]	花费
cut	[kʌt]	cut	[kʌt]	cut	[kʌt]	切割
hit	[hit]	hit	[hit]	hit	[hit]	击中
hurt	[hə:t]	hurt	[hə:t]	hurt	[hə:t]	损伤
let	[let]	let	[let]	let	[let]	让
put	[put]	put	[put]	put	[put]	放置
set	[set]	set	[set]	set	[set]	放置
shut	[ʃʌt]	shut	[ʃʌt]	shut	[ʃʌt]	关
spread	[spred]	spread	[spred]	spread	[spred]	展开

B. 两种形式相同者：

(1) 元音发生音变：
a. i[ai]→ou[au]

find	[faind]	found	[faund]	found	[faund]	找到

b. i[i] →u[ʌ]

dig	[dig]	dug	[dʌg]	dug	[dʌg]	挖
stick	[stik]	stuck	[stʌk]	stuck	[stʌk]	刺入

c. ee/ea[i:] →e[e]

feed	[fi:d]	fed	[fed]	fed	[fed]	喂养
meet	[mi:t]	met	[met]	met	[met]	遇见
speed	[spi:d]	sped	[sped]	sped	[sped]	速进
lead	[li:d]	led	[led]	led	[led]	领导

d. 其他

hang	[hæŋ]	hung	[hʌŋ]	hung	[hʌŋ]	悬挂
stand	[stænd]	stood	[stud]	stood	[stud]	站立
shine	[ʃain]	shone	[ʃɔn]	shone	[ʃɔn]	照耀
sit	[sit]	sat	[sæt]	sat	[sæt]	坐
strike	[straik]	struck	[strʌk]	struck	[strʌk]	打击
hold	[həuld]	held	[held]	held	[held]	握住
fight	[fait]	fought	[fɔ:t]	fought	[fɔ:t]	战斗
light	[lait]	lit	[lit]	lit	[lit]	点火
read	[ri:d]	read	[red]	read	[red]	读

shoot	[ʃu:t]	shot	[ʃɔt]	shot	[ʃɔt]	射击
win	[win]	won	[wʌn]	won	[wʌn]	得胜

(2) 辅音发生音变
a. d[d]→t[t]

bend	[bend]	bent	[bent]	bent	[bent]	折弯
lend	[lend]	lent	[lent]	lent	[lent]	借出
send	[send]	sent	[sent]	sent	[sent]	寄送
spend	[spend]	spent	[spent]	spent	[spent]	花费
build	[bild]	built	[bilt]	built	[bilt]	建设

b. ll[l]→lt[lt]

smell	[smel]	smelt	[smelt]	smelt	[smelt]	嗅闻
spell	[spel]	spelt	[spelt]	spelt	[spelt]	拼写

c. →t[t]

burn	[bə:n]	burnt	[bə:nt]	burnt	[bə:nt]	燃烧
learn	[lə:n]	learnt	[lə:nt]	learnt	[lə:nt]	学习

d. 其他

lay	[lei]	laid	[leid]	laid	[leid]	放下
pay	[pei]	paid	[peid]	paid	[peid]	支付
have	[həv]	had	[hæd]	had	[hæd]	有
make	[meik]	made	[meid]	made	[meid]	做

(3) 元音、辅音皆发生变化者
a. ea[i:]→ea[e];/ →t[t]

deal	[di:l]	dealt	[delt]	dealt	[delt]	分发
dream	[dri:n]	dreamt	[dremt]	dreamt	[dremt]	做梦
lean	[li:n]	leant	[lent]	leant	[lent]	倾斜
mean	[mi:n]	meant	[ment]	meant	[ment]	意指

b. ee[i:]→e[e];/ →t[t]

feel	[fi:l]	felt	[felt]	felt	[felt]	感觉
keep	[ki:p]	kept	[kept]	kept	[kept]	保持
sleep	[sli:p]	slept	[slept]	slept	[slept]	睡觉
sweep	[swi:p]	swept	[swept]	swept	[swept]	打扫
weep	[wi:p]	wept	[wept]	wept	[wept]	哭泣

c. ell[el]→old[əuld]

sell	[sel]	sold	[səuld]	sold	[səuld]	卖
tell	[tel]	told	[təuld]	told	[təuld]	告诉

d. atch[ætʃ]→aught/ought[ɔ:t]

catch	[kætʃ]	caught	[kɔ:t]	caught	[kɔ:t]	抓着
teach	[ti:tʃ]	taught	[tɔ:t]	taught	[tɔ:t]	教
bring	[briŋ]	brought	[brɔ:t]	brought	[brɔ:t]	带来

think	[θiŋk]	thought	[θɔ:t]	thought	[θɔ:t]	想	
buy	[bai]	bought	[bɔ:t]	bought	[bɔ:t]	买	

e. 其他

leave	[li:v]	left	[left]	left	[left]	离开	
lose	[lu:z]	lost	[lɔst]	lost	[lɔst]	丢失	
flee	[fli:]	fled	[fled]	fled	[fled]	逃走	
hear	[hiə]	heard	[hə:d]	heard	[hə:d]	听见	
say	[sei]	said	[sed]	said	[sed]	说	

(4) 原形和过去式或过去分词相同者

a. 原形和过去式相同者

beat	[bi:t]	beat	[bi:t]	beaten	[bi:tn]	打	

b. 原形和过去分词相同者

run	[rʌn]	ran	[ræn]	run	[rʌn]	跑	
come	[kʌm]	came	[keim]	come	[kʌm]	来	
become	[bi'kʌm]	become	[bi'keim]	become	[bi'kʌm]	变成	

c. 三种形式皆不相同者

① 元音发生音变者：

i[i] → a[æ] → u[ʌ]

begin	[bi'gin]	began	[bi'gæn]	begun	[bi'gʌn]	开始	
drink	[driŋk]	drank	[dræŋk]	drunk	[drʌŋk]	喝	
ring	[riŋ]	rang	[ræŋ]	rung	[rʌŋ]	按铃	
sing	[siŋ]	sang	[sæŋ]	sung	[sʌŋ]	唱歌	
sink	[siŋk]	sank	[sæŋk]	sunk	[sʌŋk]	下沉	
spring	[spriŋ]	sprang	[spræŋ]	sprung	[sprʌŋ]	跳跃	
swim	[swim]	swam	[swæm]	swum	[swʌm]	游泳	

② 元音发生音变，过去分词加 N 者：

a. a[ei] → oo[u] → a[ei]

shake	[ʃeik]	shook	[ʃuk]	shaken	['ʃeikn]	摇	
take	[teik]	took	[tuk]	taken	['teikn]	拿	

b. i[ai] → o[u] → i[i]

drive	[draiv]	drove	[drəuv]	driven	['drivn]	驾驶	
ride	[raid]	rode	[rəud]	ridden	['ridn]	乘骑	
rise	[raiz]	rose	[rəuz]	risen	['rizn]	上升	
write	[rait]	wrote	[rəut]	written	['ritn]	写	

c. ow [əu] → ew [u:] → ow [əu]

blow	[bləu]	blew	[blu:]	blown	[bləun]	吹	
grow	[grəu]	grew	[gru:]	grown	[grəun]	生长	
know	[nəu]	knew	[nju:]	known	[nəun]	知道	
throw	[θrəu]	threw	[θru:]	thrown	[θrəun]	扔	

d. → o[əu] → o[əu]

speak	[spi:k]	spoke	[spəuk]	spoken	['spəukən]	讲
steal	[sti:l]	stole	[stəul]	stolen	['stəulən]	偷
break	[breik]	broke	[brəuk]	broken	['brəukən]	打破
freeze	[fri:z]	froze	[frəuz]	frozen	['frəuzn]	结冰
choose	[tʃu:z]	chose	[tʃəuz]	chosen	['tʃəuzn]	挑选
wake	[weik]	woke	[wəuk]	woken	['wəukən]	唤醒

e. ear[ɛə] → ore[əə/ɔ:/] → or [ɔ:]

bear	[bɛə]	bore	[bɔə/bɔ:]	born(e)	[bɔ:n]	负担
tear	[tɛə]	tore	[tɔə/tɔ:]	torn	[tɔ:n]	撕扯
wear	[wɛə]	wore	[wɔə/wɔ:]	worn	[wɔ:n]	穿

f. 其他

forget	[fəget]	forgot	[fəgɔt]	forgotten	[fəgɔtn]	忘记
get	[get]	got	[gɔt]	got/gotten	[gɔt(n)]	得到
give	[giv]	gave	[geiv]	given	[givn]	给
draw	[drɔ:]	drew	[dju:]	drawn	[drɔ:n]	拖拉
hide	[haid]	hid	[hid]	hidden	['hidn]	藏
see	[si:]	saw	[sɔ:]	seen	[si:n]	看见
fall	[fɔ:l]	fell	[fel]	fallen	['fɔ:lən]	落下
eat	[i:t]	ate	[eit]	eaten	['i:tn]	吃
fly	[flai]	flew	[flu:]	flown	[fləun]	飞
lie	[lai]	lay	[lei]	lain	[lein]	躺下
do	[du:]	did	[did]	done	[dʌn]	做
go	[gəu]	went	[went]	gone	[gɔn]	走
be	[bi:]	was	[wɔz]/were [wə:]	been	[bi:n]	是

③ 过去式规则,过去分词加 n 者:

sew	[səu]	sewed	[səud]	sewn	[səun]	缝纫
show	[ʃəu]	showed	[ʃəud]	shown	[ʃəun]	展示
sow	[səu]	sowed	[səud]	sown	[səun]	播种
prove	[pru:v]	proved	[pru:vd]	proven	[pru:vn]	证明

④ 过去式发生音变,过去分词规则:

dive	[daiv]	dove	[dəuv]	dived	[daivd]	潜水

2. 按字母顺序排列

be	[bi:]	was	[wɔz]	been	[bi:n]	是
bear	[bɛə]	bore	[bɔə/bɔ:]	born(e)	[bɔ:n]	负担
beat	[bi:t]	beat	[bi:t]	beaten	[bi:tn]	打
become	[bikʌm]	became	[bikeim]	become	[bikʌm]	变成
begin	[be'gin]	began	[be'gæn]	begun	[begʌn]	开始
bend	[bend]	bent	[bent]	bent	[bent]	折弯

blow	[bləu]	blew	[blu:]	blown	[bləun]	吹
break	[breik]	broke	[brəuk]	broken	['brəukən]	打破
bring	[briŋ]	brought	[brɔ:t]	brought	[brɔ:t]	带来
build	[bild]	built	[bilt]	built	[bilt]	建设
burn	[bə:n]	burnt	[bə:nt]	burnt	[bə:nt]	燃烧
buy	[bai]	bought	[bɔ:t]	bought	[bɔ:t]	买
catch	[kætʃ]	caught	[kɔ:t]	caught	[kɔ:t]	抓着
choose	[tʃu:z]	chose	[tʃəuz]	chosen	['tʃəuzn]	挑选
cost	[kɔst]	cost	[kɔst]	cost	[kɔst]	花费
come	[kʌm]	came	[keim]	come	[kʌm]	来
cut	[kʌt]	cut	[kʌt]	cut	[kʌt]	切割
deal	[di:l]	dealt	[delt]	dealt	[delt]	分发
dig	[dig]	dug	[dʌg]	dug	[dʌg]	挖
dive	[daiv]	dove	[dəuv]	dived	[daivd]	潜水
do	[du:]	did	[did]	done	[dʌn]	做
draw	[drɔ:]	drew	[dru:]	drawn	[drɔ:n]	拖拉
dream	[dri:m]	dreamt	[dremt]	dreamt	[dremt]	做梦
drink	[driŋk]	drank	[dræŋk]	drink	[drʌŋk]	喝
drive	[draiv]	drove	[drəuv]	driven	[drivn]	驾驶
eat	[i:t]	ate	[eit]	eaten	['i:tn]	吃
fall	[fɔ:l]	fell	[fel]	fallen	[fɔ:lən]	落下
feed	[fi:d]	fed	[fed]	fed	[fed]	喂养
feel	[fi:l]	felt	[felt]	felt	[felt]	感觉
fight	[fait]	fought	[fɔ:t]	fought	[fɔ:t]	战斗
find	[faind]	found	[faund]	found	[faund]	找到
flee	[fli:]	fled	[fled]	fled	[fled]	逃走
fly	[flai]	flew	[flu:]	flown	[fləun]	飞
forget	[fə'get]	forgot	[fə'gɔt]	forgotten	[fəgɔtn]	忘记
freeze	[fri:z]	froze	[frəuz]	frozen	[frəuzn]	结冰
get	[get]	got	[gɔt]	got/gotten	[gɔt(t)]	得到
give	[giv]	gave	[geiv]	given	[givn]	给
go	[gəu]	went	[went]	gone	[gɔn]	走
grow	[grəu]	grew	[gru:]	grown	[grəun]	生长
hang	[hæŋ]	hung	[hʌŋ]	hung	[hʌŋ]	悬挂
have	[hæv]	had	[hæd]	had	[hæd]	有
hear	[hiə]	heard	[hə:d]	heard	[hə:d]	听见
hide	[haid]	hid	[hid]	hidden	['hidn]	藏
hit	[hit]	hit	[hit]	hit	[hit]	击中
hold	[həuld]	held	[held]	held	[held]	握住

hurt	[hə:t]	hurt	[hə:t]	hurt	[hə:t]		损伤
keep	[ki:p]	kept	[kept]	kept	[kept]		保持
know	[nəu]	knew	[nju:]	known	[nəun]		知道
lay	[lei]	laid	[leid]	laid	[leid]		放下
lead	[li:d]	led	[led]	led	[led]		领导
lean	[li:n]	leant	[lent]	leant	[lent]		倾斜
learn	[lə:n]	learnt	[lə:nt]	learnt	[lə:nt]		学习
leave	[li:v]	left	[left]	left	[left]		离开
lend	[lend]	lent	[lent]	lent	[lent]		借出
let	[let]	let	[let]	let	[let]		让
lie	[lai]	lay	[lei]	lain	[lein]		躺下
light	[lait]	lit	[lit]	lit	[lit]		点火
lose	[lu:z]	lost	[lɔst]	lost	[lɔst]		丢失
make	[meik]	made	[meid]	made	[meid]		做
mean	[mi:n]	meant	[ment]	meant	[ment]		意旨
meet	[mi:t]	met	[met]	met	[met]		遇见
pay	[pei]	paid	[peid]	paid	[peid]		支付
prove	[pru:v]	proved	[pru:vd]	proven	['pru:vn]		证明
put	[put]	put	[put]	put	[put]		放置
ride	[raid]	rode	[rəud]	ridden	['ridn]		乘骑
ring	[riŋ]	rang	[ræŋ]	rung	[rʌŋ]		按铃
rise	[raiz]	rose	[rəuz]	risen	['rizn]		上升
run	[rʌn]	ran	[ræn]	run	[rʌn]		跑
say	[sei]	said	[sed]	said	[sed]		说
see	[si:]	saw	[sɔ:]	seen	[si:n]		看见
sell	[sel]	sold	[səuld]	sold	[səuld]		卖
send	[send]	sent	[sent]	sent	[sent]		寄送
set	[set]	set	[set]	set	[set]		放置
sew	[səu]	sewed	[səud]	sewn	[səun]		缝纫
shake	[ʃeik]	shook	[ʃuk]	shaken	['ʃeikn]		摇
shine	[ʃain]	shone	[ʃɔn]	shone	[ʃɔn]		照耀
show	[ʃəu]	showed	[ʃəud]	shown	[ʃəun]		展示
shut	[ʃʌt]	shut	[ʃʌt]	shut	[ʃʌt]		关
sing	[siŋ]	sang	[sæŋ]	sung	[sʌŋ]		唱歌
sink	[siŋk]	sank	[sæŋk]	sunk	[sʌŋk]		下沉
sit	[sit]	sat	[sæt]	sat	[sæt]		做
sleep	[sli:p]	slept	[slept]	slept	[slept]		睡觉
smell	[smel]	smelt	[smelt]	smelt	[smelt]		嗅
sow	[səu]	sowed	[səud]	sown	[səun]		播种

speak	[spi:k]	spoke	[spəuk]	spoken	['spəukən]	讲	
speed	[spi:d]	sped	[sped]	sped	[sped]	速进	
spell	[spel]	spelt	[spelt]	spelt	[spelt]	拼写	
spend	[spend]	spent	[spent]	spent	[spent]	花费	
spread	[spred]	spread	[spred]	spread	[spred]	展示	
spring	[spriŋ]	sprang	[spræŋ]	sprung	[sprʌŋ]	跳跃	
stand	[stænd]	stood	[stud]	stood	[stud]	站立	
steal	[sti:l]	stole	[stəul]	stolen	[stəulən]	偷	
stick	[stik]	stuck	[stʌk]	stuck	[stʌk]	刺入	
strike	[straik]	struck	[strʌk]	struck	[strʌk]	打击	
sweep	[swi:p]	swept	[swept]	swept	[swept]	打扫	
swim	[swim]	swam	[swæm]	swum	[swʌm]	游泳	
take	[teik]	took	[tuk]	taken	['teikn]	拿	
teach	[ti:ʃ]	taught	[tɔ:t]	taught	[tɔ:t]	教	
tear	[tɛə]	tore	[tɔ:]	torn	[tɔ:n]	撕扯	
tell	[tel]	told	[təuld]	told	[təuld]	告诉	
think	[θiŋk]	thought	[θɔ:t]	thought	[θɔ:t]	想	
throw	[θrəu]	threw	[θru:]	thrown	[θrəun]	扔	
weep	[wi:p]	wept	[wept]	wept	[wept]	哭泣	
wake	[weik]	woke	[wəuk]	woken	['wəukən]	唤醒	
wear	[wɛə]	wore	[wɔə/wɔ:]	worn	[wɔ:n]	穿	
win	[win]	won	[wʌn]	won	[wʌn]	得胜	
write	[rait]	wrote	[rəut]	written	[ritn]	写	

参 考 文 献

1 《新英汉词典》编写组编. 新英汉词典. 上海:上海译文出版社,1981
2 唐玉华编著. 物业管理英语. 第1版. 广州:中山大学出版社,1998